AF656994

A SHORT HISTORY OF ENGLISH LITERATURE

VOLUME – I

GEORGE SAINTSBURY

Foreword by
MOHIT K. RAY

ATLANTIC
PUBLISHERS & DISTRIBUTORS (P) LTD

Published by

ATLANTIC

PUBLISHERS & DISTRIBUTORS (P) LTD

7/22, Ansari Road, Darya Ganj, New Delhi-110002
Phones : +91-11-40775252, 40775214, 23273880, 23275880
Fax : +91-11-23285873
Web : www.atlanticbooks.com
E-mail : orders@atlanticbooks.com

Branch Office: Chennai
Phones : +91-44-48531784, 28291383
E-mail : chennai@atlanticbooks.com

Copyright © Atlantic Publishers and Distributors (P) Ltd., 2005, 2020

All rights reserved. No part of this publication may be reproduced, stored in a retrieval system, transmitted or utilized in any form or by any means, electronic, mechanical, photocopying, recording or otherwise, without the prior permission of the copyright owner. Application for such permission should be addressed to the publisher.

Disclaimer

- The author and the publisher have taken every effort to the maximum of their skill, expertise and knowledge to provide correct material in the book. Even then if some mistakes persist in the content of the book, the publisher does not take responsibility for the same. The publisher shall have no liability to any person or entity with respect to any loss or damage caused, or alleged to have been caused directly or indirectly, by the information contained in this book.
- The author has fully tried to follow the copyright law. However, if any work is found to be similar, it is unintentional and the same should not be used as defamatory or to file legal suit against the author.
- If the readers find any mistakes, we shall be grateful to them for pointing out those to us so that these can be corrected in the next edition.
- All disputes are subject to the jurisdiction of Delhi courts only.

Printed & bound in India by Atlantic Print Services

FOREWORD

IT is a pleasure to place in the hands of our readers a reprint of George Saintsbury's *A Short History of English Literature,* an invaluable, pioneering book on the History of English Literature. The book is particularly remarkable as one of the earliest specimens of fine literary historiography. Any literary historian has to serve two gods: History and Criticism. A historian is guided only by historical principles while a literary critic is governed by critical principles alone. But a literary historian has to bear in mind both the critical principles and the historical principles while writing the history of literature of a nation. A successful historian combines, as Saintsbury remarkably does, the historical and the critical principles into a harmonious whole. Saintsbury was a prolific writer, and according to any moderate estimate his works would easily run into more than hundred volumes. In sweep and depth, in perceptivity and lucidity Saintsbury is almost incomparable. In his original preface Saintsbury clearly stated his purpose; "The object of this book ... is to give, from the literary point of view only and from direct reading of the literature itself, as full, as well supplied, and as conveniently arranged a storehouse of facts as the writer could provide."

Saintsbury has an aristocratic disdain for the simplistic overview of a vast arena. He looks upon the history of literature as a continuous process marked by several stages of its development. In order to indicate the transition from one stage to another Saintsbury provides what he calls inter-chapters. A reading of Saintsbury's *History* is a pleasant aesthetic experience where the reader is gently led through the ups and down of the British History of English Literature. It marks, in the main, the general consensus of critical opinion of the period and as the reader goes on he is bound to be impressed by Saintsbury's occasional appeals from criticism to history and his insistence on the literary achievements of the makers of the English Literature.

It is sometimes said that the history of a national literature must take into account the whole history of the nation in order to place it in a proper perspective. But that is only an idealistic position which can never be realised in practice. To try to grasp everything would only blur the vision and put literature out of focus. Saintsbury all along keeps a tight hold on the development of English Literature starting with the preliminaries of English Literature and ending with the late Victorian period. What Saintsbury says in his "Conclusion" only shows his insight and practical wisdom: "All those who possess or claim the right to be guides in the journey will not agree with this particular road-book; there must be differences on small points, and there may be differences, not unwarranted even on some great ones. But, as it has been less object to air crotchets than to write with what has been called a 'reasoned orthodoxy' ... such differences may perhaps be made matter of agreement, of compromise, at least of suspended discussion."

Since nobody can cross his own shadow a critic is bound by the *Zeitgeist* or the spirit of the age in which he lives. With the benefit of hind sight we can always quarrel with some of the evaluations of Saintsbury. But we can never undervalue him because of his conspicuous sincerity tempered by profound scholarship.

A word must be said about Saintsbury's style which is always lucid and precise. The book is written in such a fashion that even the common reader who is not specialist in English Literature will find this book a pleasant reading. George Sampson had once remarked: "We have conquered space and lost spaciousness. But there is a remedy. The mind can expatiate in history and broaden its range over a wild field of human achievements. For this remedial liberation of the spirit the history of literature offers rich and ample scope." And when this historical tour is undertaken under the able guidance of George Saintsbury the experience is as rewarding as it is fascinating.

Dr K.R. Gupta, Chairman, Atlantic Publishers and Distributors, New Delhi deserves our special thanks for making this invaluable book available to the students of English Literature.

While the students of English Literature will find this book extremely useful. Any reader interested in English Literature will also find it extremely interesting.

Mohit K. Ray

PREFACE

THE object of this book, which was undertaken more than four years ago, is to give, from the literary point of view only, and from direct reading of the literature itself, as full, as well supplied, and as conveniently arranged a storehouse of facts as the writer could provide. The substitution of bird's-eye views and sweeping generalisations for positive knowledge has been very sedulously avoided; but it is hoped that the system of Inter-chapters will provide a sufficient chain of historical summary as to general points, such as, for instance, the nature and progress of English prosody and the periods of prose style. No part of the book has been delivered as lectures; and the sections of it concerning the Elizabethan period and the Nineteenth Century are not replicas of previous work on those subjects.

None but a charlatan will pretend that he has himself written, and none but a very unreasonable person will expect any one else to write, a history of the kind free from blunders. The sincerest thanks are owed to Mr. W.P. Ker, Fellow of All Souls and Quain Professor of English Literature in University College, London, and to Mr. G. Gregory Smith, Lecturer in English in the University of Edinburgh, for their great kindness in reading the proofs of the book, and for their most valuable suggestions. But the author is wholly responsible, not merely for all the errors of fact that may have escaped their scrutiny, but for all the critical opinions put forward in the volume. Nor has his object been to make these opinions prominent, but rather to supply something approaching that solid platform, or at least framework, of critical learning without which all critical opinion is worthless, and upon which such opinion can be more easily built or hung afterwards. Reading of the books themselves is the only justification precedent in such a case on the part of the writer; and his only object should be to provoke and facilitate reading of the books themselves on the part of his readers.[1]

Edinburgh, 29th *July* 1898.

1. *Note to Eighth Edition*—In all the preceding reprints of this book the text has been read through, oversights corrected, and small additions made, the latter with especial reference to new works or editions. This process has been repeated with great care in the present issue. I had at one time thought of endeavouring, by means of an Appendix, or of end-notes to the chapters of the last Book, to include the most distinguished men of letters who have died since the beginning of the twentieth century, as I have actually done in my *Nineteenth Century Literature.* But such additions would themselves have been of necessity incomplete; they would have had a patchy and ill-composed appearance; and I think all experts will agree that it would be difficult, if not impossible, to write them in a key exactly corresponding to that of a survey originally made as it were "horizontally"—at any rate consecutively and at once—of the literature of some fifteen centuries past. I have therefore confined myself to additions and corrections in the original text. Those who want more will find it, very fully in some cases, in the book above named, and in my Histories of *Prosody* and of *Prose Rhythm.* G.S.

CONTENTS

BOOK - III

CHAUCER AND HIS CONTEMPORARIES

BOOK - IV

THE FIFTEENTH CENTURY

BOOK - V

ELIZABETHAN LITERATURE TO THE DEATH OF SPENSER

VOLUME 2

BOOK - VII

CAROLINE LITERATURE

BOOK - VIII

THE AUGUSTAN AGES

BOOK - IX

MIDDLE AND LATER EIGHTEENTH-CENTURY LITERATURE

BOOK - X

THE TRIUMPH OF ROMANCE

BOOK - XI

VICTORIAN LITERATURE

Book I

The Preliminaries of English Literature

1

THE EARLIEST ANGLO-SAXON POETRY

Widsith—Beowulf—Waldhere and the *Fight at Finnsburg—Deor.*

THE oldest document which has a possibly authentic claim to be English Literature,[1] if but English Literature in the making and far off completion, is the poem commonly called *Widsith*, from its opening word, which some take to be a proper name.[2] Others simply see in it the designation of a "far-travelled" singer, who here recounts his journeyings in 143 lines of no great literary beauty, and only interesting as sketching the gainful and varied life of a minstrel

Widsith.

1. Fuller English treatments of this matter will be found in Mr. Stopford Brooke's *History of Early English Literature*; in Mr. H. Morley's *English Writers*, vols. i and ii; in Professor Earle's *Anglo-Saxon Literature;* and in the translation of Ten Brink's *English Literature*, vol. i. The texts discussed in this chapter form the first five numbers of Grein-Wül(c)ker's *Bibliothek der angelsächsischen Poesie*, vol. i, pp. 1-277, which gives two texts of *Beowulf.* This latter has been frequently edited and translated; Professor Earle's *Deeds of Beowulf* is a good translation without text.
2. Some high authorities, looking upon *Widsith* as a "made-up" thing, hold it to be later, and would assign the priority to the *Finnsburg* fragment or others. No opinion one way or the other is expressed here; indeed, the writer holds that the evidence is insufficient for adopting any. But it may be convenient to make the point an occasion *in limine* for a respectful request to readers not to take absence of mention of theories of this kind, or statements in the text apparently antagonistic to them, as proof of ignorance on the writer's part. This book attempts to be a history, not of the latest or any opinions about literature, but of that literature itself. The practically endless questions of authenticity, integrity, date, and so forth, must be, as a rule, left to special study.

in the Dark Ages, were it not for the proper names which bestrew the piece. Not a few of these occur, or seem to occur, in other early verse, and have the interest of the "parallel passage." But there are, or seem to be, those of persons well known to history—Eormanric or Hermanric,[3] King of the Goths; Ætla or Attila, the Scourge of God and the King of the Huns; and, lastly, a certain Ælfwine, whom some think identical with Alboin or Albovine, King of the Lombards, the husband, the insulter, and the victim of Rosmunda. It is, of course, obvious at once that though it is not impossible for the same man to have been contemporary with Hermanric, who died in 375, and Attila, who died in 453, no contemporary of either could have seen the days of Alboin, who felt his wife's revenge in 572. Therefore either Ælfwine must be somebody else or the poem is doubtful. Into such discussions this book will never enter, unless there is the strongest reason of a purely literary character for them, and there is none such here. It is sufficient to say that *if* Eormanric is the Hermanric known to history, and *if* "Widsith" saw his day, this document dates within the confines of the fourth century, at a time when no other modern language can show proofs of having had even a rudimentary existence.

The MS., the famous Exeter Book[4] of *gehwilcum þingum* ("things of sorts"), which Bishop Leofric gave to his Cathedral some 700 years later than Hermanric's day, and which still remains there, could, of course, not be expected to give us the original form of the "word-hoard," of which in his first line[5] the Far-Traveller declares the unlocking. Yet it shows us a language very remote indeed from English in appearance (though this same word "word-hoard," which appears with the omission of a single letter, shows the remoteness to be more apparent than real), but also different from Continental Old-Saxon, and from Icelandic, its nearest relations, neighbours, and contemporaries.

3. See Gibbon, *Decline and Fall*, chap. xxvi.

4. Ed. Thorpe (London, 1842); in course of re-editing for the Early English Text Society by I. Gollancz (vol. i, London, 1895), in both cases with translations. Its contents will be noted later.

5. *Widsith matholade*: *word-hord onleac* = "Widsith spoke, (he) unlocked (his) word-board."

This language—a point more important to literature—is arranged, or can be arranged, in lines of not strictly regular length, and obeying no law of rhythm that apparently resembles those of any modern or classical prosody, except that there is a sort of far-off echo of trochaic cadence, and that the lines approach the ordinary octosyllable or diameter more than any other form. There is no rhyme, for though it is by no means uncommon for two or more adjacent lines to end in the same syllable, this syllable is one on which the voice would lay no stress. Neither is there assonance or vowel-rhyme, the preliminary to rhyme itself in most of the Romance tongues. But there is a very curious, though, in *Widsith,* elusive and irregular, system of *alliteration,* by which certain words, often, though far from always, two in the earlier half of the line and one in the later, begin either with the same consonant or with a vowel. And it is further usually arranged that the stress, accent, length, or whatever word be preferred, shall fall on these alliterated syllables whether it falls on others or not.[6] As for the purely literary characteristics, the nature of the piece, which, as has been said, is little more than a catalogue of names, gives very small scope. Imaginative critics have, however, discovered in it that specially English delight in roving which has distinguished many of our race—as well as, for instance, such hardly English persons as Ulysses and Sindbad.

Beowulf.

There are names in *Widsith*—Heorot, Hrothgar, and others—which connect the poem, so far as they go, with one of much greater extent, interest, and merit, though, if the furthest age which each can reasonably claim be assigned, decidedly younger. This is the famous *Beowulf,* according to some the first on the beadroll of substantive and noteworthy poems in English, using that word in the most elastic sense, and according to all who have given themselves the trouble (now minimised by scholarly assistance, if the help

6. This account of prosody is based in the first place on *Widsith,* and is not intended as controversial against those who, with Dr. Sievers, insist on the exact character of the Anglo-Saxon scheme such as it was. It acquired, no doubt, a good deal of such exactness in time; though any one who will reflect on the consequences of the fact that the texts exist almost invariably in single MSS., will be slow to accept any but wide conclusions.

of the scholars be taken and their snares resisted) to acquaint themselves with it, a saga of undoubted age, originality, and interest. Adopting the same system which we adopted in the case of *Widsith,* that of selecting the earliest dated name that can be reasonably identified with one mentioned in the poem, *Beowulf,* so far as subject goes, would be as old as the second decade of the sixth century, 520 or a little earlier, when a certain fairly historical Chochilaicus, raided the Frisian coast, according to Gregory of Tours. This Chochilaicus is plausibly conjectured to be the Hygelac of the poem. But beyond this it will not be safe to go, for scholarly conjecture, or perhaps it were better to say conjectural scholarship, has for the better part of a century let itself loose over the date, scene, meaning, and composition of the piece. Whether it was brought from Jutland by the Saxon invaders and Anglicised or was composed in England itself; whether the scenery is that of the east or the west coasts of the North Sea; whether it is an entire poem or a congeries of ballads; whether it is a literal history embellished poetically, a deliberate romance, or a myth—all these questions have been asked with the pains, answered with the confidence, and the answers all poohpoohed with the disdain usual, if not invariable, in such cases. We shall only say here that the date, admittedly uncertain, is somewhat unimportant; that the question "History, fiction, or myth?" is not of the kind here dealt with; and that while some have been hardy enough to pronounce with confidence that the scenery must be Northumbrian and no other,[7] the present writer would undertake to find twenty coast districts in England, and feels certain that there are twenty times twenty and more also out of it, which would perfectly fit.

To the student of literature who can be content to pretermit the unnecessary, *Beowulf* presents itself in a manner which may be summarised as follows: It is a poem, in rather less than

7. For is there not a Bowlby Cliff close to Staithes in Yorkshire? and is it not the tallest on the English and Scottish mainland? and does not Bowlby = Bow-wowlby = Beowulf by? and did not Caedmon live at Whitby, a few miles off? Indeed, for a commentatorial sorites the logic is rather unusually perfect.

3200 lines, which must of necessity be very old, and which, for reasons to be mentioned presently, is in its original form very likely as old as, or older than, all but the first invasion of Britain by the Saxons. The history of its unique MS.,[8] though too long to be given in detail here, adds to its interest. This is part of one (Vitellius A. xv) of those famous treasures of Sir Robert Cotton's which form almost the most precious part of the British Museum Library, and one of those which were only saved so as by fire in 1731. It is not known where it came from, and though it was catalogued by Humphrey Wanley a quarter of a century before the fire, he unfortunately mistook its subject, and the interest which then still prevailed as to Anglo-Saxon literature (though it afterwards waned for the greater part of the century) was not immediately directed to it. Its supposed connection with Denmark, in Wanley's description, attracted the learned Icelander Thorkelin to it, and, after vicissitudes, his version appeared in 1815, since which it has been constantly re-edited and translated. Meanwhile the MS. had been going from worse to worse ever since the fire, and the superstructure of commentatorial editing has been constantly adding more and more superfluous matter. One of the few, if not facts, yet opinions which seem worth holding fast, is that in its present form the MS. is probably not older than the tenth century, and that the poem had by that time undergone divers changes in shape and dialect. Another fact of the first literary value is that the chief incidents of its first part reproduce themselves in the most curious way in one of the five great Icelandic sagas, that of *Grettir the Strong*.[9]

As for its subject, there is, as is very usual in poems of its class, a sort of genealogical prologue wherein there is a confusion of Beowulfs. The proper action does not begin for a hundred lines or so, when we hear of the happiness of Hrothgar, a king whose court is at Heorot, and its marring by a monster named Grendel who enters the hall by night and slaughters the thanes. This continues for twelve years, till Beowulf, our Beowulf, a thane of King Hygelac's, who dwells over the sea, hears of

8. Which also contains *Judith*; *see* next chapter.

9. Englished by Morris and Magnusson, London, 1869.

the nuisance and determines to end it. He journeys towards Heorot, and, after some demurs by the coastguard thereof, arrives and is hospitably received by Hrothgar and his queen, though there is some jealousy among the nobility. The adventure is committed to Beowulf, and Grendel does not fail to come at night. Indeed, he has seized one warrior before Beowulf grips him. Then begins the first and not one of the worst of the fights of English poetry—which has good fights. The monster is not vulnerable by steel, so that Beowulf's men cannot help him; but the chief tears off the fiend's arm, shoulder and all, and he flies to die in the mere where his den is, making it boil with his blood. There is much triumph, feasting, singing, gift-giving, and the like.

But after all something renews the attacks on Heorot, and an atheling of high blood is carried off. Beowulf is not in the hall, having been guested elsewhere, but he soon hears from the King that his adventure is not done, and determines to finish it in the mere itself. He dives fearlessly in, and on reaching the bottom is caught by a water-hag, Grendel's mother, who has killed the atheling. The fight is fiercer than that with her son; the hero's earthly weapons are useless against the hag, and he is actually beaten by her in wrestling and for a moment at her mercy. But his byrnie (mail-shirt) is better as a defence than his sword in offence, and hard by him, on the cave floor where the fight takes place, he sees a mighty falchion within reach. He gains it, draws it, and cuts the hag's head off, doing the same afterwards to the dead body of Grendel, which he finds near by; but the blood of the fiends is so venomous that the sword itself, though it had strength to slay, melts in the poison.

Meanwhile Beowulf's men above on the bank have given him up for lost, and Hrothgar's men have gone away. But his own comrades remain, welcome him as he swims up triumphantly with Grendel's head, and escort him in triumph to court with the head and the hilt of the sword. The most interesting part of the poem is over, but only just half its length is exhausted. Proper ceremonies at Heorot follow, and a long report of Beowulf to Hygelac. This king falls in battle (perhaps, as said above, historically), and Beowulf succeeds him, to be plagued in his turn not by a water fiend, but by a land dragon, whose hoard has been rifled, and who in revenge lays waste the country, burning all houses, even the palace, with his fiery breath. Beowulf determines to meet him single-handed and does so, all his men but one flying in terror. He slays the dragon, but is mortally injured by the teeth and fire-jets of the enemy. The poem finishes with laments, condemnation of the cowardly fliers, and the rummaging of the dragon's hoard.

The vehicle of it is a line of the same kind (with minor variations) as that described under *Widsith,* but the different nature of the subject (and, no doubt, also the greater genius of the author, and the wider scope afforded) raises it much above that composition as poetry. As is the case with all the pieces in this section, it has been rather wildly and unreservedly praised, and has been made to bear all sorts of meanings and messages which the unilluminated may fail to discover. But it is a good verse-saga, spirited in incident, not destitute of character, and showing, though an early and rudimentary, yet a by no means clumsy or puerile system of poetic phrase, composition, and thought. The fights are good fights; Beowulf, though, as we should expect, something of a boaster, is a gentleman and a tall man of his hands. Hunferth, Hrothgar's jealous courtier and "orator," is, after his fashion, a gentleman too—it is he who lends Beowulf a sword for the second encounter; the appearance of Hrothgar's queen is gracious; the pictures of the sea and the mere (its waters over-shrouded by trees with writhen roots), and the spear-stalks in the hall, ash-staved and grey-steel-tipped, are not to be despised.

This is the verdict of the strictest criticism of intrinsic merit, putting the historic estimate aside altogether. And if, as we are surely entitled to do in a history, we do *not* put the historic estimate aside,—if we take into consideration the fact, which is all but a certain fact, that *Beowulf* is the very oldest poem of any size and scope in any modern language, that it has no known predecessors,[10] and has the whole literature of romance

10. There are, of course, those who say that it had many. But if so, these many "have the defect of being lost," and perhaps it may be said also

for successors,—then without attributing to it merits which it cannot claim, or muddling it up with myths which simply minish its interest, we shall see that it is a very venerable document indeed, well worth the envy of the nations to whom it does not belong. Even if it were no older than its MS., *Beowulf* would be the senior of the *Chanson de Roland* by nearly a century, the senior of the *Poema del Cid* by two, the senior of the *Nibelungen Lied* by two or three. In reality it is possibly the elder of the eldest of these by half a millennium. Some of those who love England least have been fain to admit that we have the best poetry in Europe: it is thanks mainly to *Beowulf* that our poetry can claim the oldest lineage and poetical coat-armour from the very first.

Waldhere and the *Fight at Finnsburg.*

The other remains which certainly or probably belong to the same class chronologically with *Widsith* and *Beowulf* are of much shorter length, and, with one exception, of less interest. The fragment (about sixty lines) called *Waldhere* ("Walter") would seem to belong to an old, if not oldest, edition, so to speak, of that cycle of Burgundian sagas of which the *Nibelungen Lied* presents us with a later handling, though this particular fragment has nothing to do with that poem. So, too, the *Fight at Finnsburg* (fifty lines), another fragment, has for its main, if not its sole, English interest, besides the language, the fact that the subject is mentioned in *Beowulf* as the theme of song, though, of course, not necessarily of *this* song. But the third, the fifth of the whole group as usually arranged, has greater attractions. This is the so-called *Complaint of Deor,* which in the first place is, though a short, a complete piece; in the second, has not merely unity as a composition, but individual spirit and interest as a poem; and in the third, shows us an immense advance in poetical form.

Deor.

Deor is a minstrel who has fallen out of favour with his lord, his supplanter being a certain Heorrenda, skilled in song. The fifty-two verses of the poem are individually like those already noticed, but they are arranged in a different fashion, being divided into stanzas of irregular length by a refrain—

that of not being known ever to have existed. The text speaks only of known and existing work of epical form.

Thaes ofereode : thisses swa maeg.
That was got over : so may this be.

The instances which he alleges to confirm himself in his *hoc olim meminisse juvabit,* the trials of Wayland the great smith, the betrayal of Beadohild, with other woes of Geat, of Theodoric, of Hermanric, have some attraction of curiosity, and the general tone of pluck facing luck is manly and interesting. But the advance in form is the real charm of the poem. If *Deor* is really very old, its author had attained, though only in a rough and rudimentary fashion, to some of those secrets of lyrical poetry which were as a rule hidden from Anglo-Saxon bards even of a much later day. He had grasped the *stanza,* the great machine for impressing form upon the almost formless void;[11] and he had grasped the *refrain,* which is not only a mighty set-off to poetry in itself, but has the inestimable property of naturally suggesting rhyme, the greatest and most precious of all poetical accidents. When the ear has once caught the charm of repeated sound in this way, the brain almost inevitably suggests the multiplication of it without damage to sense, by repeating not the whole line, but part of the line only. We have not in *Deor* reached really exquisite poetry, but we are safely on the way towards it. We have the passionate interpretation of things felt and seen; we have the couching of that interpretation in rhythmical utterances subjected to and equipped with arrangements and ornaments beyond those of the mere integral line; and we have the confinement of the utterance within a reasonable length. When you have these things in poetry, you have not yet everything, but you are on the way to have it.

The reserved point, in reference to this batch of poems, which has been more than once mentioned above is this that in no one of them is there the slightest evidence, apart from their existence in more or less antique forms of Anglo-Saxon, of any connection with England. The supposed indications of scenery are, as has been said above, and must be very seriously repeated, the shadow of a shade, the dream of a dream; no one

11. There is a theory that the stanza came first; but here again all the other examples are lost, and none are known to have existed.

who has had any share of training in the appreciation of evidence will attach the slightest importance to them. There are passages in *Widsith,* in *Beowulf,* in *Deor* which seem to argue a knowledge of Christianity; but all of these may be interpolations, and none of them is decisive to a balanced judgment. And such historical or quasi-historical references (the more important noted above) as we do find seem to carry us back to periods about the fourth and fifth centuries; while there is nothing in any of them, except the quite indecisive Alboin identification, which suggests a date later than 520, and nothing, even this, that goes later than 600.

Therefore it has seemed to no bad wits not impossible, or even improbable, that this group may represent the documents, certainly not "fifty volumes long," or at least the traditions, which the Anglo-Saxon-Jutes carried with them as "cabin-furniture" in their invasion of the Greater England, and may actually be the workings up of such documents, or at least such traditions, not so very much later. We cannot prove this, and we should very carefully abstain from the large generalisations from supposed characteristics in these poems which have sometimes been made as to the English spirit. Indeed, we should rather say that ascertained or imagined characteristics of the English spirit are in these exercitations carried back to the poems, and discovered there after having been carried. But we cannot disprove either the antiquity or the relationship, and it would be a great pity if we could.

2

CAEDMON, CYNEWULF, AND THOSE ABOUT THEM

Anglo-Saxon poetry mostly sacred—MSS.—Caedmon and Cynewulf—The Scriptural poems—Caedmon—*Judith*—The *Christ*—The Lives of Saints—Other sacred poems—Secular poems—The *Ruin*—The *Wanderer* and *Seafarer*.

IT would seem likely that the whole of the work mentioned in the last chapter, though it may have been here and there rehandled in a Christian sense, is heathen in origin. But the bulk of Anglo-Saxon poetry,[1] a bulk which is not itself very large, is entirely Christian in tone, and is definitely religious in subject. Probably not a twentieth part of the *Corpus Poeticum* in oldest English, putting *Beowulf* aside, has for subject anything but paraphrases of the Bible and Lives of Saints, which in their turn are paraphrased or translated from Latin originals. Although the texts are handled in some cases with sufficient freedom, it is undeniable that this fact communicates to Anglo-Saxon poetry not merely a certain monotony, but also a very distinct want of first-hand interest—a want which extends over its whole period, and to prose as well as to verse.

Anglo-Saxon poetry mostly sacred.

Yet it would have been extremely surprising if anything else had been the case. In the first place, it is always necessary to remember—especially in face of the extravagant eulogies of which it has been the subject, as a revulsion from the equally

1. Most of the texts referred to in this chapter will be found in Grein-Wül(c)ker or the Exeter Book, or both; where to find the others will be noted.

extravagant, and because more simply ignorant much more discreditable, contempt which it had undergone before—that this literature is, after all, the literature of a childhood, the lispings of a people. No vernacular writings other than their own can have been before these ancestors of ours, for none existed. Although, after the welter of the Saxon Conquests had a little subsided, culture of no such beggarly kind was to be found in England, it was necessarily, if not confined to, yet centred in the clergy and the monasteries. More classical knowledge, not merely in Latin but in Greek, undoubtedly survived during the darkest of the Dark Ages than the scialism of the eighteenth century used to allow; but there is also no doubt that the tide—the incalculable, inexplicable tide of knowledge and thought—receded steadily all over Europe from the fifth century to the tenth. In the first years (which in such an age are the first centuries) of conversion to a new faith religious zeal thinks no subject but religion worthy of attention, and in the contented reaction therefrom professional guardians of religion think nothing but religious matter worthy of preservation. It is more wonderful that we have any profane poetry at all—not for the present to mention prose—from this time, than that we have so little.

The verse, profane in small proportion, sacred in large, which dates from the period succeeding the comparative settlement of the Saxon realms, and which, though almost the whole, if not the whole, of it is West Saxon in its present form, seems by pretty common consent to have been originally composed in Northumbria, survives to us for the most part in

MSS.

four unique MSS. Of these three are the aforesaid Cottonian, which, besides giving us *Beowulf,* contains an incomplete poem on *Judith;* the so-called Junian Manuscript, now at Oxford, which contains the poems attributed to Caedmon, four in number, three of which are paraphrases of the books of Genesis, Exodus, and Daniel, while the fourth is a composite piece to which the title of *Christ and Satan* has been given; and the Exeter Book, containing, besides *Widsith* and *Deor,* a poem or poems on *Christ,* others on *Azariah* (one of the Three Children), *St. Guthlac,* and *St. Juliana,* a large collection of verse-riddles, and not a few smaller poems, sacred and profane, the complete list being given in a note.[2] The fourth, called the Vercelli Book, from its rather unexpected place of discovery sixty years ago, gives among Homilies a variant of one of the poems (the *Address of the Soul to the Body*) in the Exeter Book, two very interesting Lives of Saints (St. Andrew and St. Helena), the *Dream of the Rood,* which is at least of the highest interest as a puzzle, a short poem on the *Fates of the Apostles,* and a fragment on *Human Falsehood.*

Some notice of the more remarkable contents and characteristics of these poems will be given presently. As to their authorship, which has been much discussed, we practically know nothing whatever about it in any case. But the Venerable Bede, in a charmingly told and commonly known story, has related how a certain Caedmon, who towards the end of the seventh century was a servant of the monastery of Whitby, under the great abbess Hilda, having had to leave festive meetings owing to his inability to use and accompany with song the harp which was handed round, was miraculously inspired to write sacred poetry. And the contents of the Junian MS. were, from the first attention paid to it in Milton's days, identified with this, while much later the discovery on the Ruthwell Cross, some miles from Dumfries, of the words "Caedmon made me," forming part of a Runic inscription (the rest of which coincided pretty closely with part of the *Dream of the Rood* above mentioned), was for a time thought to confirm the idea. Again, examiners of the poetry of the Exeter and Vercelli Books found in some of them Runic charades or acrostics which compose the name "Cynewulf"; and out of these dead runes a great poet who wrote not merely the poems in which they appear, but others, has been resolutely manufactured and equipped with a life, sentiments, and experiences extracted by critical

Caedmon and Cynewulf.

2. First come a score of pieces arranged by the Germans and Mr. Gollancz, as *Christ;* then *Guthlac, Azarias, The Poenix, Juliana, The Wanderer, The Endowments of Men, A Father's Instruction, The Seafarer, A Monitory Poem, Widsith* ("The Scôp"), *The Fortunes of Men, Gnomic Verses, Wonders of Creation, The Rhyming Poem, The Panther, The Whale, The Soul to the Body, Deor, Riddles* (in three batches), *The Exile's Complaint, A Fragment* (sometimes interpreted differently), *The Ruin,* and a few minor pieces.

imagination from the poems in question. Further, the work formerly attributed to Caedmon has been taken to pieces with the usual industry and dexterity of the Separatists, and a considerable portion of it heaped upon Cynewulf with the corresponding industry and dexterity of the Agglomerators; the *Dream of the Rood* has been confidently assigned to the new favourite; and the poems in general have been divided into A's and B's, credited or debited with interpolations, dated, redated, and undated. In particular, much stress has been laid on the recent discovery of corresponding Old-Saxon fragments of a *Genesis* version in the Vatican.

But with these things we do not busy ourselves. The testimony of so trustworthy a historian as Bede establishes the existence of a Whitby poet named Caedmon, who, miraculously or otherwise, displayed sudden and unexpected faculties for song, and composed poems on the Creation and several other Biblical subjects before the end of the seventh century. The Ruthwell Cross[3] and a reliquary preserved at Brussels show phrases and passages taken, or very slightly altered, from the *Dream of the Rood*. From the well-ascertained historical facts of the superiority of Northern to Southern culture, and of the complete, or almost complete destruction of both, but especially the former, by the Danish fury at the end of the eighth century and later, it is reasonable to conclude that these poems were written in Northumbria, and before 800. But of the exact date and the exact authorship of no one of them can anything be said to be certainly known; and if the rune-charade of Cynewulf is correctly deciphered, this signature cannot be accepted as going more than a very little way to establish even the most shadowy personality. As for their autobiographic character, it will be time to take this seriously when it is shown that the

3. This extremely interesting monument is now well cared for and enshrined conveniently for inspection in an apse built for it in Ruthwell Parish Church. It was ordered for destruction in the evil days of the seventeenth century (1642), but only broken into three pieces and left in the churchyard, where it remained till 1802. It was then set up in the manse garden, and in 1887 put in its present place. There is a facsimile of the cross (which is nearly 18 feet high, and may date from the end of the seventh century) in the Museum of Science and Art, Edinburgh.

author of *Maud,* who, it may be pointed out, certainly did visit Brittany like its hero, also shot his beloved's brother in a duel, and passed some time in a madhouse afterwards.

We are therefore left with the poems themselves, and they will afford us quite sufficiently interesting study. In the all-important point of prosodic form they resemble those mentioned in the last chapter, except that in some at least the alliteration is still more precisely managed; while in others, especially in the poems first attributed to Caedmon, the line is almost indefinitely extended at times by the admission of unaccented syllables, so that it becomes more impossible than ever to adjust the whole to any rhythmical swing tunable to modern ears. Even the comparatively rudimentary metrical nisus of *Deor* does not seem to have agitated any of these singers, and if it were not for the accented and alliterative syllables, the whole would bear the appearance of embryonic rhythmed prose, for which it was actually taken until the scheme of Anglo-Saxon prosody was discovered.

Of their subjects, and of the extent to which they display such non-metrical properties of poetry as phrase, arrangement, and poetic spirit, there is naturally more to be said. In regard to subject, they may be divided into three groups—the directly sacred poems with a fringe of allegorical verse, in which the fantastic zoology of the Dark and Middle Ages is adjusted not unhappily to religious use; a very small but very precious body of poetry without a purpose, or with only a subordinate one; and a miscellaneous collection of riddles, charms, gnomic verses, and "oddments" of different kinds. The last group is chiefly, if not wholly, interesting to the philologist and the student of manners and civilisation, though some of the riddles have not a little poetical merit; the others are of wider appeal.[4]

The sacred poems may again be subdivided into three classes—paraphrases from the Scriptures or poems directly

4. Anglo-Saxon poetry in translation is best represented by a very close rendering, stave for stave, with the words kept as far as possible and their order likewise. Straightforward modern prose may come next; any modern English verse form last, the resemblances and the differences of language and rhythm alike making it dangerously misrepresentative.

based on them, Lives of Saints, and miscellaneous devotional work.

The Scriptural poems. Caedmon.

Of the first subdivision, the chief interest, if not the chief merit, belongs to the Caedmonian *Genesis* and *Exodus,* especially to the passages in the former which respectively bring to mind the Bede story, and the supposed indebtedness of Milton in *Paradise Lost* to the eldest of his poetical forefathers, with whose work he might actually have been acquainted through his friend Junius the editor. With regard to the first point, no actual English equivalent of Bede's Latin abstract or paraphrase (he warns us that ft is only this) occurs in Caedmon; but there is in one MS. of the History a very old and possibly original Northumbrian version, transliterated into West Saxon in King Alfred's English Bede. Neither of these agrees in wording with the opening of the so-called *Genesis A,* but the meaning is sufficiently near to suggest different wordings of the same original draft. As for the Miltonic parallels, some of which are extraordinarily close, they come chiefly but not wholly from the other part, or *Genesis B* where the paraphrase is drawing on apocryphal or mediaeval legend (and himself) for a description of the sufferings of the Fallen Angels. Both parts of *Genesis* and *Exodus* have, when the subject gives opportunities, bursts of poetry by no means contemptible, and by no means wholly due to the original; and the first named is a poem very considerable in bulk. It runs, taking it as a whole, to nearly 3000 lines, of which not a few are of enormous length. *Exodus* (the best part of which is naturally the crossing of the Red Sea) has not quite 600. Of the others, *Daniel* has seldom been praised; *Christ and Satan,* which includes a fine description of that very favourite subject, the *Harrowing of Hell* (interesting as possibly the first to compare with Langland's, certainly the best in any like poetic dress), is much better.

Judith.

About *Judith* doctors differ much, and its authorship is sheer guess. We have only the end of it, but that, giving in some 350 lines the slaughter of Holofernes and the triumph of the Jews, is the most interesting part of a story which has generally inspired both pen and pencil well, and which certainly does not fail to do so here.

The Cynewulfian poem, or group of poems, which opens the Exeter Book, and which it is for the present the fashion to call *Christ,* certainly contains fine passages, the finest being inspired by that fruitful parent of mediaeval poetry the adoration of the Cross. In Mr. Gollancz's arrangement it has nearly 1700 lines.

The Christ.

Of the four important Lives of Saints—*Andreas, Elene, Guthlac, Juliana*—all ascribed by some to Cynewulf, the palm may lie between the first and the third. *Andreas* is a legend of St. Andrew, telling how he was miraculously inspired and miraculously helped to cross the sea in order to release St. Matthew from prison in "Mermedonia"; how he succeeded, and how he punished the violence of the heathen to himself. The stormy voyage, always a favourite subject with Anglo-Saxon bards, and the rage of the elements on the doomed heathen city, are fine passages. *St. Guthlac* has perhaps fewer lines of the "show" variety; but the description of Guthlac's conflict in his loneliness with the powers of evil, and that of his death, are curiously fascinating, and worth comparing with *St. Simeon Stylites. Elene* (the English saint St. Helena, mother of Constantine and finder of the Cross) has admirers; *Juliana* fewer, owing to a long and rather tedious wrangle between the saint and a fiend who is sent to tempt her. Hut the recurrence of the name "Juliana" as a hemistich by itself, and in apposition rather than as direct object or subject, has almost a refrain effect, and soothes the ear marvellously. Indeed, though only occurring now and then, and on no system, it produces an effect not unlike that of the similar word "Oriana" in Tennyson's poem. The short *Fates of the Apostles* has little merit, but, as it is signed, some have wished to tack it on to the unsigned *Andreas*—a process slightly suggestive of what is said to be occasionally practised on violins.

The Lives of Saints.

In so far as positive poetic beauty goes, the third subdivision, small as it is in bulk, has no reason to fear comparison with either of the others. The *Dream of the Rood* has, like *Genesis,* the adventitious interest of its connection with the Ruthwell Cross inscription, but could do without it. The *Rood* itself speaks, and speaks to the purpose. The *Address of the Soul to the Body,* existing in two parts,[5] the speakers being respectively a cursed soul and a blessed one, is the earliest of a long line;[6] and the speech of the reprobate has that peculiar grimness which is one of the most unquestionable gifts of Anglo-Saxon verse. The *Phoenix,* the *Panther,* and the *Whale,* adaptations of Latin verse or prose in the allegorical "bestiary" kind, are all fine, and the first has a famous and really exquisite passage, one of the few in this poetry to which the word can be applied, describing, after Lactantius, the beauties of paradise. "The Phoenix" itself, of course, is Christ; as is the "Panther," the sweet-breathed, lonely, harmless beast; while the "Whale" (based upon the well-known Greek-Eastern story of sailors landing on the whale's back) is the Devil or Hell. These, as well as a mere fragment believed to be part of a similar poem on the *Partridge,* evidently came from some earlier Greek or Latin *Physiologus* or collection of zoological allegories; of the *Phoenix,* the original, by or attributed to Lactantius, is, is has been said, known. It is quite a long poem of nearly 700 lines; the others are much shorter.

Other sacred poems.

The small group of secular poems above referred to is of much greater interest, not at all because of any general or necessary superiority of profane to secular poetry—a point upon which two such great and dissimilar critics as Dr. Johnson and Mr. Matthew Arnold seem to have been led wrong by different but equally fatal fallacies—but because, the poems being in all probability original instead of pretty certainly translated or paraphrased, we can see much better what the real strength of the poets was. The *Ruin,* the *Wanderer,* the *Seafarer,* the (so-called) *Wife's Complaint,* the (so-called) *Husband's Message,* make a very small bundle of verse. Even in the Grein-Wül(c)ker edition, with editorial apparatus, corrected versions of text, and the

Secular poems.

5. The first occurs in the Exeter and in the Vercelli Books; the second only in the latter.

6. See the interesting collection in the Appendix of T. Wright's *Poems of Walter Mapes* (Camden Society, 1841).

like, they do not fill thirty pages; yet, for these thirty, one could cheerfully resign almost all but the few just-named passages of the sacred books (with perhaps a riddle or two) of the poetry mentioned in this chapter. For they are real documents; it is excessively unlikely that they had any originals in another language, and if they had, we at least do not possess these originals. Even "common form" was not, so far as we know, furnished to them by any predecessors, as it inevitably was to homilists and hagiographers, practitioners of sacred allegory, and paraphrasers of the Scriptures. Here, and perhaps here only, Anglo-Saxon poetry shows what it could do with a commonplace—the best subjects of poetry are all commonplaces—but without a common form; and it comes out of the test with no small credit.

The *Ruin.*

The best of the five is in my judgment beyond all question the *Ruin.* Indeed, I do not know any other Anglo-Saxon poem which in conception, composition, and expression so nearly deserves the name of a masterpiece. As we have it, it is in a state which strangely corresponds to its title and subject—a broken mass of some five-and-thirty lines, which the painful ingenuity of editors has got into about five-and-forty, rather more regular in some parts, but much wounded in others. Conjecture thinks that it may have been originally intended for the wreck, after Saxon devastation, of no less a Roman colony than Bath; there is, at least, nothing contrary to reason in accepting it as relating to one or other of the many stately creations of the first invaders which were reduced to ruin by the second. The corruption of the text makes a certain rendering practically impossible. But nothing can obscure the genuineness of its poetry, or (as it seems to me) its enormous superiority to the possibly contemporary Welsh lament over the destruction of Uriconium with which Mr. Stopford Brooke rather unfavourably compares it. The Welsh piece shows a further advance in poetical form, more *clichés* ready for use, more tricks of trade and manners of behaviour. The English shows actual poetry. Perhaps the deepest and noblest of all emotions, not merely personal and sensual, the feeling for the things that are long enough ago, finds expression, and worthy expression, as the poet looks on the masonry shattered by fate, the crumbling mortar gemmed with hoar-frost, as he imagines the once stately heights reduced to ruinous heaps, the warriors, high of heart and bloody of hand (for though Shakespeare never knew the *Ruin,* we may borrow his phrase), who sat there long ago, the hot baths (this is the ground for the identification with Bath) boiling in their lake-like cistern, the busy market-place silent, the merry mead-halls overwhelmed by the fiat of Destiny. He could *see,* this poet of the *Ruin,* and he could tell what he saw. We shall hardly come to any one like him for seven hundred years in England.

The majority of critics, I believe, assign higher rank to the *Wanderer* and the *Seafarer.* The *Wanderer* also contains a passage of merit about a ruin, but is chiefly a study of "Weird" (Fate or Destiny), and the way in which a man is "hurled from change to change unceasingly, his soul's wings never and furled"—as the most Saxon of nineteenth-century English poets has it—his comradeships incessantly broken, and only the Weird constant in its inconstancy. The idea of the poem is undoubtedly fine, and its lines give fair scope; but that poetic imagery which is so great a part of poetry seems to me not so well managed as in the *Ruin.* The *Seafarer,* longer still, and perhaps composite, is a much more difficult poem, as may be guessed from the fact that the critics are not agreed whether it is a monological reflection upon its subject or a dialogue between an old sailor and a young sailor, or only colourably occupied with seafaring at all, its real purport being an allegory of human life. It may be observed that this last interpretation, which seems to me much the most probable, is only to be avoided by the device, at once easy and violent, of supposing the close of the poem to be a Christian forgery, or at least addition. The chief literary merit of the piece is to be found in the earlier part, where the description of a wintry storm at sea, attributed by some to the old sailor, has much of the merit already noted in Anglo-Saxon handlings of this subject.

The *Wanderer* and *Seafarer.*

The remaining pair, the so-called *Wife's Complaint* and *Husband's* or *Lover's Message,* have a more personal note than the others. The first appears[7] to some to be the utterance, real or dramatic, of a woman who has been falsely accused and banished from her husband's presence. The second is an agreeable piece, in which, with a pleasant seventeenth-century touch, the wooden tablet bearing the lines of the message is made (like the "book" addressed by later singers) itself to carry the tale to the beloved (or at least addressed) one. Neither is long, but both have an unpretentious and sincere feeling, if not exactly passion, and both stand interestingly at the head of a class of similar poems, in which English has since been richer than all other languages put together. They date too from a period long antecedent to that of either troubadour or minnesinger.

The arrest of Anglo-Saxon poetry by the Danish fury seems to have been very nearly total. The verse, other than mere sacred paraphrases, which we have of a later date than Alfred is but scanty even in total bulk, and only four pieces of it can be said to have much literary attraction, though, curiously enough, two of these are much better known than any of the older and better work. These are the short poem inserted in the *Chronicle* (*vide infra*), on the triumph of Athelstan at Brunanburgh over the Scots and Danes, and the very late, gloomy, but fine *Grave Poem* familiar to almost every Englishman who cares for poetry, with its beginning, "For thee was a house built."[8] In this latter the idea and the grim, direct, uncompromising delivery of it are the chief merits. The Brunanburgh poem, though a spirited war-song, perhaps attracted more attention by its setting of the stock Anglo-Saxon reference to the raven, eagle, and wolf, "that grey beast the wolf of the weald," as spoilers of the dead, than would have

7. It ought perhaps to be said that the usual interpretations of these pieces are more than half guesswork. There is really nothing in what Thorpe more prudently calls *The Exile's Complaint* to identify the speaker as a wife, nor anything in the other piece (his as prudently named *Fragment*) to point to a husband or even lover.

8. Text in Guest, *English Rhythms,* 2nd ed., p. 369, or in Thorpe's *Analecta,* ed. 1868, p. 153. Longfellow translated it not long, I think, after Conybeare first made it known. It is thought to be as late as the twelfth century, and shows signs of *metrical* influence in its rhythm.

been the case if the earlier examples from *Beowulf* and the Finnsburg poem downwards had been known.

Of the two remaining pieces, one has the attraction of subject, the other that of form. The *Battle of Maldon* or the *Death of Byrhtnoth* has a less happy subject (a defeat not a victory) than the Brunanburgh piece, but it is more genuine, contemporary, and fresh. The production known as the *Rhyming Poem,* or *Conybeare's Rhyming Poem,* is found in the Exeter Book. This, though far inferior in intrinsic and poetical interest, has great historical importance. It is probably a Biblical paraphrase, like so many others, and as it is in the Exeter Book, it must be as old at least as the tenth century, or the very earliest eleventh. Now, not merely at that time, but much later, Anglo-Saxon was rebel to rhyme;[9] even two hundred years after, in Layamon, the appearances of that instrument are but occasional and very rudimentary. In the *Rhyming Poem,* however, though there is still alliteration, and the general structure of the lines is not very different from the staple of Anglo-Saxon verse, they are arranged in couplets, or sometimes even larger groups, not merely tipped with end rhymes, but endowed with leonine or middle rhymes as well. Sometimes the rhyme is not much more than assonance, but oftener it is full rhyme, and not seldom it adopts the kind which later English poetry discourages, though it is allowed in other languages, the actual repetition of the same complete words or group of letters, *onwrah, onwrah, hiwum, hiwum,* etc. Once there is a batch of seven lines with the same rhyme—*ade,* varied a little by *ide* and *ede*—in the middle and at the end of each; in another place one of five lines similarly equipped with words in *iteth;* and sometimes the couplet shrinks to a single line with leonine adjustment. Of course this is inartistic and overdone : the poet is thinking so much of his new toy of rhyme that he has not much time to think of his poetry. But he is ahead of his fellows

9. There were, however, other outbreaks, or rather *in*breaks of it. See especially the remarkable verse-fragment in the *Chronicle* (A. 1036, edited in Grein-Wül(c)ker, i, 384-85), describing Godwin's outrages on the "guiltless etheling" Alfred and his men.

by two centuries if not by three, and that is something and much.[10]

10. This *tour de force,* which is only partially intelligible, and in which there is good reason to suppose the invention of words for the purpose, has been thought to be imitated from Icelandic. A few things of little literary interest—paraphrases of the Psalms, a dialogue of *Solomon and Saturnus,* a piece on Doomsday, etc.—complete the tale of Anglo-Saxon poetry.

3

ANGLO-SAXON PROSE

The works of King Alfred—The *Boethius*—The *Orosius*—The *Bede*—The *Pastoral Care*—The *Anglo-Saxon Chronicle*—Elfric—Wulfstan.

THE prose division of Anglo-Saxon literature is of less literary interest than the verse; but it is more abundant in quantity, and it is not separated from the later developments of the language by any such sharp gulf as that which cuts off the prosody and rhythm of Anglo-Saxon from the prosody and rhythm of English. We may, indeed, observe in it that curious, yet, when considered, very far from unintelligible combination of earliness and immaturity, rapid development up to a certain point and inability to go beyond that point, which meets us in the poetry; but there is not the bar to any further development which existed in that case.

In all languages poetry as literature comes before prose, the immortal jest of Molière owing its piquancy to exactly this, that though prose is more obviously natural to man in conversation, he never, till after considerable experience, seems to understand that it is fit to be made a medium of recorded thought or formal writing. But it would appear that it was, in Anglo-Saxon, pretty early. Professor Earle speaks[1] of "obscure but well-evidenced remains of the fifth and sixth centuries," but as so enthusiastic an authority does not himself dwell much on these, or on the laws of Ina attributed to the seventh, we may afford to pass them over. It is in the eighth century that Mr. Earle claims something like literary competency for the

1. *English Prose*, London, 1890, p. 370.

earliest English prose, and the examples which he chooses are a deed of remission of port dues by King Ethelbald of Mercia, and the somewhat famous passage of the *Saxon Chronicle* relating the death of King Cynewulf *(not* the poet), the first of these dating a little before and the second a little after the very middle of the eighth century itself. With the later passage, too, Mr. Sweet begins the prose specimens in his *Anglo-Saxon Reader,*[2] and it seems to be generally allowed the position of the earliest distinctly spirited piece of prose literary composition in the language.

To such spirit, or, in other words, to the motive power of *style,* laws, title-deeds, and similar documents can, in the very nature of the case, seldom lay claim. It would, in fact, be decidedly out of place in them, and the bare enumerations, specifications, common forms of legal and other speech, etc., which they contain could be of little illustrative use, even if they were not, as in most cases they may be suspected to be, pretty closely copied from Latin originals. But the story of the attack made by the atheling Cyneheard on the King Cynewulf, when the latter had imprudently left most of his guard behind while visiting a lady-love, gives better opportunities. The incident is told at no great length, and without much personal characterisation, except in the notable answer of the thanes to Cyneheard's offers of bribes and arguments from kinship, that "no kinsman was dearer to them than their lord, and they never would follow his bane." Except that the piece seems contemporary, one would imagine a rough prose "unrhyming" of some ballad or romance. But if we are to consider the thing as prose merely, it may give us some pause to find that of the two authorities above cited, Mr. Sweet, though giving it the high distinction of being "by far the oldest historical prose in any Teutonic language," thinks the style "of the rudest character...abrupt, disconnected, obscure, and full of anacolutha," while Professor Earle discerns, and thinks that every one must discern, the evidence of "a literary tradition already of mature standing," and "a syntax not more rugged than that of Thucydides." Thucydides has, of course, a sort of traditional repute for crabbed syntax, so that the eulogy is, after all, not unqualified.

2. Oxford, 7th ed., 1894.

By the next century (the ninth), however, there is no doubt about the plentiful production and the at least relative accomplishment of Anglo-Saxon prose. Of the three writers of it who alone may be said to have a personal reputation, King Alfred, Elfric, and Archbishop Wulfstan, the first belongs to this century, the last third of which was covered by his glorious and beneficent reign. The *Saxon Chronicle,* in its continuous and fairly accomplished shape, may be a little older than Alfred himself, though it is thought to have taken final form under him. The King and the *Chronicle* will at any rate well deserve separate and independent notice.

The works of King Alfred.

Alfred's works are, with the exception of some original insertions, wholly translation—indeed, as we have seen with the verse, so we shall see with the prose, and to an even larger extent, that the merit of originality in matter is about the last that Anglo-Saxon as a literature can claim. But in the special circumstances this makes far more for the King's honour than for his dishonour. His literary work was inspired not by any desire of fame, nor by any need of satisfying a peremptory personal craving to write, but wholly and solely by the wish to benefit his people, to do something that might help England out of the slough of barbarism into which she had been plunged by the Danish ravages and the efforts necessary to check them. To this end it would have been not merely presumptuous, but, in the circumstances and at the time, positively silly to have attempted original composition, when there was plenty of good Latin work lying ready to hand. From this Alfred selected a book in what may be called general practical science, the *History and Geography* of Orosius; one in domestic history, the unrivalled *Ecclesiastical History* of Bede; the most popular ethical and philosophical treatise of the Dark Ages, the *Consolation* of Boethius; and an ecclesiastical book, the *Cura Pastoralis* of Pope Gregory. The first of these is not precisely a work of genius or one of much authority, but it was a popular manual of its day; the second and third could hardly have been bettered for the purpose, inasmuch as they were the work of two men who represented the best character and ablest intellect of the age immediately preceding, and whose thought, style, and tone were in complete harmony with the spirit of the actual age; the fourth was a respectable book, well suited for the purpose, and having some special claim on the attention of Englishmen.

The most interesting of the four,[3] in so far as actual matter goes, is the *Orosius,* because of the additions which Alfred made from information supplied to himself; but the most interesting as literature is unquestionably the *Boethius*. There are many greater books in the literature of the world than the *De Consolatione;* but there are few that have had a more interesting literary history, and still fewer that seem to have, with such strange prescience, gauged the literary and philosophical requirements not merely of their own time but of times that were to follow for almost a millennium. One of the first documents in English prose is this translation of King Alfred's; probably the very first document in the earliest development of the Romance tongues, Provençal, is the verse-paraphrase which gives us the majestic if slightly monotonous harmony of the *langue d'oc* a century or two after Alfred. When Anglo-Saxon and the Middle language have at length given place to complete English, the most accomplished piece of prose that the all-accomplished muse of Chaucer admits among his greater verse is again a translation of Boethius; and yet another translation, this time partial, is attributed to Queen Elizabeth, at the very time when the far-off heralding of Alfred, the director promises of Chaucer, were about to be fulfilled.

The *Boethius.*

As "the last of the Romans" is not now in every one's hands, it may not be superfluous or impertinent to say that Anicius Manlius Severinus Boethius, as his barbarically assorted travesty of the old Roman nomenclature went, was born somewhere about the beginning of the last quarter of the fifth century. He is said to have studied under Proclus at Athens, which is possible, but barely possible, if the death of Proclus be taken at the ordinary date of 485. He attained distinction at Rome, and having been consul in 510, attracted the notice of

3. The *Boethius* and the *Orosius* are easily obtainable in Anglo-Saxon (old-printed) and English, in Bohn's "Antiquarian Library." The E.E.T.S. has given critical editions of the *Orosius* and the *Bede* and the *Pastoral Care.* A version of St. Augustine's *Soliloquies* is probably also Alfred's.

Theodoric the Ostrogoth, and was for some time in favour with him. But being accused of fomenting or conniving at an Italian conspiracy against Gothic rule, he was imprisoned at Ticinum, and brutally put to death (clubbed, it is said) in or about 524-525. The *De Consolatione Philosophiae* is supposed to have been written in prison. It was not his only contribution to mediaeval knowledge, for he exercised an immense influence on scholastic logic by his commentaries on Aristotle and Porphyry and Cicero; but it was perhaps his most popular and non-technical. It consists of a medley of dialogue between Wisdom and the author, interspersed with metrical insertions. Two versions of Alfred's translation exist, in one of which the metrical portions are rendered into prose, while in the other they are versified. Although there is difference of opinion on the subject, there does not seem to be any insuperable difficulty in admitting both forms as authentic, though very likely the King had help from others. If the "metres" in their Anglo-Saxon form are really his, they are of the greatest interest to the literary historian, because they show that at this time Anglo-Saxon was proof against the temptations of rhyme, classical metre, and the like, to which in its enfeebled Early Middle English or "Semi-Saxon" stage it afterwards succumbed. The translation is by no means slavishly executed; indeed, the reproach of want of originality against Anglo-Saxon generally is largely mitigated by the fact that the translations are much more paraphrases with interpolations *ad lib.* than simply faithful versions. It is quite possible that deficient scholarship may to some extent account for this freedom, but it would be as uncritical as it would be illiberal to take this as the sole, even as the chief, reason. Alfred's moral purpose in the *Boethius,* like his scientific and practical purpose in the *Orosius,* induced him and authorised him not merely to rearrange, but to add gloss and comment here and there. It is a pity that, in the edition of the *Boethius* most accessible, a rhymed and sophisticated Englishing by the late Mr. Martin Tupper takes the place of the rendering into rhythmical prose which alone can give any proper equivalent for Anglo-Saxon verse in modern English.

The *Orosius,* it has been said, has, or rather would have, nothing like the intrinsic interest of the *Boethius,* were it not for the insertions, which in the *Boethius* itself have chiefly the interest of curiosity. Paulus Orosius was a Spanish priest, who was a disciple of St. Augustine's in the second decade of the fifth century, an antagonist of Pelagius, and a friend of St. Jerome. He wrote, as befitted an Anti-Pelagian, a book about free-will, and other matters; but his name has been chiefly preserved by the work which Alfred translated, the *Historia adversus Paganos,* one of the numerous summaries of universal history which the decline of classical times and the Dark Ages saw, but differentiated by a special intention to refute the Pagan argument that the decline and fall of the Roman Empire were due to the neglect of the ancient deities. It is, for the most part, a mere compilation from previous compilations, and in no part a work of any literary merit; but like all books of the kind, not hopelessly incompetent, it has the advantage of keeping the general course of history before the reader. It would, however, be folly to suppose that Alfred had any philosophical consideration of this kind in view when he chose the book. It was an orthodox and popular manual, it gave opportunities for insertions of a kind specially interesting to himself and specially useful to his people, and he took it and altered it accordingly, displaying, as in the *Boethius,* no great reverence towards the text, but in the nature of the case making somewhat smaller alterations in arrangement, and rather fewer additions of reflection and suggestion, though in parts a good deal more reduction to the character of an epitome.

The *Orosius.*

The interesting parts, to us, are the insertions in the earlier chapters on the geography of Northern Europe, beginning "Othere told his Lord King Alfred," and "Wulfstan said," these being cither known, or reasonably taken to be, reports of voyages either distinctly made under the King's commission, or at any rate indicating his desire for the best and latest direct information. Othere tells of a voyage to Lapland and the White Sea; Wulfstan of an exploration of the Baltic, and especially of the Esthonians, the folk about the mouth of the Vistula. It should be observed that both the *Boethius* and the *Orosius* are abundantly furnished with vernacular "contents" to facilitate their reading and understanding by the people.

Alfred's translation of Bede's History has yet again a different kind of interest; and to us it is especially welcome because it brings the Venerable one within the compass of a history of English literature. Invaluable as Bede in his Latin dress is to the historian proper, he would have been dearer to the literary historian if he had lived a little later, so that he might have been tempted to write in the vernacular. That he could have done so there can be no doubt, for he was, as the famous and charming description of his death by his reader Cuthbert says, "learned in our poetry," and on his deathbed summed up the situation—the vanity of all knowledge but such as will guide a man's soul right at the last—in a memorable stave of five Anglo-Saxon verses. But in his day—he was born in 673, entered the monastery of Wearmouth at seven years old, was soon transferred to that of Jarrow, and lived his whole life there, dying in 735—it was more important to digest learning, both sacred and profane, in Latin for popular consumption, and this Bede did. Even as it is, the interesting story of Caedmon referred to above may be said to be the beginning of English literary history, and here Alfred's translation (or another's if it was not his) is particularly important, because, while Bede's account is in Latin, it has preserved to us what may possibly be the very words of Caedmon's actual inspiration.

The *Bede.*

At any rate, the translation of Bede shows us that Alfred was not so anxious merely to instruct his people in general and foreign learning that he wished to divert their attention from "things of England"; and it is impossible not to take it in conjunction with the great enterprise of the *Saxon Chronicle,* of which, as an aspirant to learning once remarked in an examination (probably taking the *Chronicle* for a daily paper), "Alfred was editor."

The fourth book has, at the present day, the least interest for us in itself. Gregory's *Regula* or *Cura Pastoralis,* as far as its intrinsic claims are concerned, must be studied in the original; and, moreover, Alfred, either out of respect or otherwise, has here translated much more exactly than in the other cases. But fortunately he prefixed an original introduction, and this introduction

The *Pastoral Care.*

contains a constantly quoted and extremely important account of the state to which polite learning in England, in the middle of the ninth century, had been reduced by the Danish invasions. “There was a time,” quoth Alfred, “when people came to this island for instruction, now we must get it from abroad if we want it.” “There were,” adds the King, “very few on this side Humber who could so much as translate the Church Service or an ordinary Latin letter into English [for “Englisc” has taken its place once for all as the general name of the tongue], and not many on the other side” (there being still apparently remnants of the old Northumbrian culture). There was not, he ends, with a gentle and more than pardonable boast, one such south of Thames, when he himself took the kingdom. It has been well pointed out that though this decay of culture may have been lamentable in itself, yet it was fortunate in a way for English, inasmuch as it stimulated translation, and so gave practice in the vernacular, instead of tempting men, as Bede had been tempted, simply to abstract and compile in Latin itself, and, even when they wrote original work, to write it in Latin. The translations may not be of first-rate literary importance, but they are at any rate better than the Latin summaries; and precious as the *Historia Ecclesiastica* is, it would have been ten times more precious had it been in English, if only because the actual original text of Caedmon could then have been given.

Other works of Alfred are spoken of—especially a Commonplace-book or book of Table-talk—which should have been interesting; but they have not survived. The so-called *Proverbs of Alfred,* in Middle English, to which we shall come in due time, have value, and may to some extent represent work of the King’s, but they can hardly be accepted even as a direct modernised version thereof. It is, however, at least possible that the *Chronicle* itself in part represents his work, as it certainly represents his influence, and it is in any case by far the most important monument of Anglo-Saxon prose, carrying us, with at least only partially broken sweep, in contemporary vernacular history from the middle of the eighth century to the middle of the twelfth, preserving amid drier annals some exceedingly interesting fragments of composition of the more

The *Anglo-Saxon Chronicle.*

original kind, both in prose and verse, manifesting an ability to manage the subject which was only much later shown in other vernacular languages, and bridging for us, with a thin but distinct streak of union, the gulf between the decadence or ruin of Anglo-Saxon even before the Conquest and the rise of English proper more than a century subsequent to it.

Like other works of the kind, and indeed necessarily, the *Chronicle*[4] was the work of monkish labour—one of those things by which the lazy monks, the drones of the Dark Ages, earned the polite and intelligent contempt of the philosophers of the eighteenth century. And it followed from this that it should not present a single text, or even sequence of texts, but should exist in more versions than one, as the work was carried on at different centres. The first of these centres was, as might have been expected, Winchester, for the historical use of English prose had not been discovered in the palmy days of Northumbrian literature, and Winchester was by far the most important place in Wessex, when the balance of power had been definitely shifted thither. The Winchester *Chronicle* is vigorous and full for the days of Alfred himself and Edward the Elder, but becomes rather meagre for the second and third quarters of the tenth century. It makes up for this, however, by inserting verse, the most important piece by far being the already-referred-to poem celebrating the battle of Brunanburgh. By the end of the century the tradition of chronicling seems to have died out in the Hampshire capital, and to have shifted to the metropolitan city of Canterbury, to Worcester (the main bulwark of England against the South Welsh border, and far from Danish reach), and to the rich and important abbey of Abingdon. The Winchester series extended a little beyond the Conquest, but the latest batch of English chronicle comes not from here but from Peterborough, in the neighbourhood of which the national, as opposed to the Norman, spirit was always strong. One of the very best known passages of the whole—the constantly quoted description of the sufferings of the country under Stephen's robber-barons and in their castles—

4. The *Chronicle* was printed as early as 1643, and has been repeatedly reprinted, re-edited, and translated since.

comes from this last batch, and indeed represents the final utterance of English historical writing for the time. It was stifled by the brilliant, but in the history of English literature irrelevant and interpolated, outbursts of Latin chronicle-writing which the middle of the twelfth century saw, and which only gave place later to the verse of Robert of Gloucester, and later still to the now fully English prose of Trevisa.

It would be more than a little unreasonable to expect that such a conglomerate, or batch of conglomerates, as the *Saxon Chronicle* should present any uniform literary features. The variations of hour and man make that quite impossible. At first, and indeed at intervals throughout, we get the barest annals, sometimes mere obituaries or calendars of translations, consecrations, coronations, and the like, only interrupted occasionally by less jejune accounts of the founding of a monastery, of such events as the assassination of Cynewulf at his leman's house, etc., where accident, personal interest, the chance possession of a poem or a deed, filled the writer's pen. Then, again, the wars of Ethelred and Alfred and Edward against the Danes inspire something like a regular history. The Peterborough part, as might be expected from its later date, has, in so far as we possess it, still more of this irregularity.

The two remaining known and distinctive writers of Anglo-Saxon prose come under the disqualification which attaches from the purely literary point of view to religious writers, in all cases but those of a very few periods and a few individuals outside them—the disqualification not at all that they are religious, but that they are second-hand. But the first of them, Elfric, is undoubtedly the greatest prose writer in the language. The influence and example of King Alfred, if it had not founded English prose, had at least given a great impetus to the founding of it, and this impetus was followed up throughout the tenth century, which has even, by some enthusiasts, been hailed as one of the great prose periods of the whole English language in its widest sense. Essential importance is assigned to the work and teaching of Ethelwold, Bishop of Winchester, a pupil of Dunstan, in the middle part of the century, who is thought to have had a wide influence,

Elfric.

in connection with his fostering of the Benedictine rule. The first proof of this is the collection of Anglo-Saxon sermons called *Blickling Homilies;*[5] while the greatest and most lasting is the work of Elfric, which in parts spreads beyond merely ecclesiastical or theological limits. Elfric,[6] who was a pupil of Ethelwold, as Ethelwold had been of Dunstan, began to write in the last decade of the tenth century, and first executed a large set (some eighty) of Catholic Homilies, which he followed up later with a series of homiletic Lives of the Saints in an alliterative rhythm, distinct from prose, but not quite reaching the limits even of Anglo-Saxon verse. His other writings were numerous, and include an interesting little set of books for the instruction of Englishmen in Latin—a grammar, a glossary, and an agreeable, interlined, Latin-English colloquy, which is the earliest example of the Hamiltonian-Ollendorfian method as applied to English. Elfric, of whose life not much is known, though he became abbot of Ensham near Oxford, and whose death-year is uncertain, is accused by some of having been rather too fond of alliteration even in his undoubtedly prose work, which includes translations of parts of the Bible. But his style is distinctly clear, flowing, and vigorous, and though only the enthusiasm above referred to could possibly see in it a medium suited for general literary exercises, it probably carried Anglo-Saxon as far in that direction as the immature character of the language itself permitted.

Elfric's life considerably overlapped that of the third writer referred to, Wulfstan, Archbishop of York, at whose Wulfstan. consecration in 1014 Elfric himself wrote one of his tractate-sermons by command. Wulfstan, who was for many years Archbishop of York, and during part of the time Bishop of Worcester also,[7] has left over fifty

5. Ed. Morris, E.E.T.S., 1874, *sq.* Not later than 971, probably earlier.

6. To be distinguished from an archbishop of the same name with whom he was long confused, and from his own pupil, Elfric Bata, who re-edited the *Colloquy.* An Elfric Society was formed more than fifty years ago to publish him; and its work has been resumed by the E.E.T.S. There is a pretty full selection in Thorpe's *Analecta.*

7. Distinguish again from the much later Bishop Wulfstan under the Conqueror.

homilies,[8] and a letter to the English people, or those of the province of York, which has interest. It is, however, quite impossible to grant the title of "fine prose," which Professor Earle postulates, either to his or to Elfric's, much more to the passage from another, to which the Professor especially refers, a figurative description of the Lord's Prayer:[9] "And his thought is more springing and swifter than twelve thousand holy ghosts, though each and every ghost have sundrily twelve feather-coats, and every several feather-coat have twelve winds, and every several wind twelve victoriousnesses sundrily." The conceit is vigorous and pleasing, and the compounding power of the language, which it has left to its heir, is observable in *sigefaestniss,* "victoriousness." But the arrangement and construction are of the very simplest kind, clauses of the same model being merely agglomerated. In Wulfstan we find more attempt at periodic prose than here; but the periods are inartistically arranged, and that fault which was later to mar so much seventeenth-century prose, the inability to resist the temptation of adding and piling up epexegetic clauses, already appears.[10]

---

8. Ed. A. Napier, 1883.
9. *Op. cit.* p. 382. The piece is from a prose form of the *Solomon and Saturn* dialogue.
10. The list of A.S. prose is, of course, by no means exhausted in the examples given. There are laws, "leechdoms," short tales, Biblical translations, etc. The most interesting are, for their connection with later and romantic literature, the story of Apollonius of Tyre (the original of *Pericles*), ed. Thorpe, 1834; a version of the episode of Alexander and Dindimus, and the wonders of Ind, from the great legend history of Alexander (ed. Cockayne in his *Narratiunculae*); and for its matter, Bishop Werfrith's translation (with a Preface by King Alfred) of the *Dialogues* of St. Gregory. This, which contains some quaint and characteristic things, was long inedited, but has at last appeared (ed. Hecht, Leipzig, 1900) as the fifth volume of Grein-Wül[c]ker's *Bibliothek der angel-sächsischen Prosa.*

4

THE DECADENCE OF ANGLO-SAXON

IT was long, and very naturally, a popular opinion that the Norman Conquest sufficiently accounted for, and directly caused, the practical disappearance of Anglo-Saxon literature. But the revived study of that literature itself, though it may in some cases have produced rather an exaggerated estimate of its intrinsic interest and merits, helped, and was helped by, the previous study of political historians to correct this delusion. Just as it was seen that the Norman Conquest, mighty as were its effects, was no absolute political cataclysm sweeping away the first England and replacing it with something else, to the same extent and in the same manner as those in which the Saxon Conquest had swept away Roman Britain, so it was discerned that the Conquest only helped and turned to good a process in language which had been independently begun, which was going on rapidly, and which, but for the Conquest itself, might have had more disastrous results.

In other words, it has now for some time been recognised that Anglo-Saxon, as a literary language, was, if not slowly dying, at any rate slowly passing into some other form, long before William landed at Pevensey. It is impossible to mistake the significance of the facts that it had produced at that date no poetry that can be called great, and little of any kind for some two hundred and fifty years; that its prose, though vigorously started under the highest auspices, and though brought to some measure of relative perfection by men like Elfric and Wulfstan, was itself failing, and had never, except in the form of generally meagre chronicle, produced any original non-sacred literature. There must have been something wrong, some want, some coldness in the literary constitution, to account for this. A language by weakness, by accident, by ill luck may never produce literature at all. But if it produces things like the *Ruin* and the *Phoenix,* like the best parts of the poems attributed to Caedmon, and those thought to be signed by Cynewulf, and then does nothing more—if it practically limits its prose energies to homilies and paraphrases and strictly business jottings, then undoubtedly it wants a change.

In the second place, it is admitted that the language itself was showing signs of a complete "break of voice," of an important biological alteration. Its inflections were getting loosened and weakened, whether from inherent old age or from the attraction and competition of the rival inflections of French and Latin must be matter of conjecture. But it appears that a similar change was taking place in its Continental kin. That its warring dialects had very much to do with this may be doubted. The West Saxon had after the downfall of Northumbria taken a distinct lead; and it does not seem that at any time the dialectic variations constituted an insuperable bar between Englishman and Englishman. But they must have helped a little, though they no doubt did less than the constant and age-long effect of the practically bilingual education of every man who aimed at learning in Latin as well as in English, and than, latterly, the establishment of French as a second, if not a first, court language in the Confessor's palace. The fact, however, seems to be beyond dispute, and the inevitable literary consequence of the fact still more so. You cannot write literature in a language which is not sure of itself, which is crumbling day by day. To which we may add that the signs of senescence and degradation are as evident in prosody as in the other parts of grammar proper. We have, as has been said, very little late Anglo-Saxon poetry, and the dates of what we have are extremely uncertain. But we can be nearly sure that in all of it strict alliteration was breaking down, rhyme was breaking in, and that for a time the contemptuous term absurdly applied to the true English prosody which emerged later, that of a "jumble," might have been applied without much injustice. Our ancestors at this time had lost grasp of their own rhythm and not learned metre; just as they were getting to mumble Anglo-Saxon, and had not learned to speak English. The old order was changing in every way, but it was some time before the new could get into regular form.

This is the rational and sufficient, the only rational and sufficient, explanation of the whole matter, that the time had come for Anglo-Saxon to die, that it died, and that it would have had to die if Harold had been as victorious at Senlac as at Stamford Bridge, though probably the result would have been less fortunate for England, as it would pretty certainly have been quite infinitely less fortunate for France. For it must never be forgotten—though it would be hardly an exaggeration to say that it has seldom been remembered—that France had little or no literature to give England, and that what she had (a *chanson de geste* or two, and some verse saint-lives rather less formless than England's own) were things of little importance and less influence. It is an amiable but entirely unhistorical imagination to suggest that French literature was brought to England by the Conquest. There was little or none to bring; and what arose later would have been equally brought by the increasing popularity of the French language and its vigour in face of Anglo-Saxon decay. Nay more, some of the greatest things in Old French were written under English influence, in districts which, though not English in soil, were under English rule, on subjects which were supplied by England from Teutonic as well as from Celtic stores. It is not insignificant that in the oldest French literature, the *Chansons,* "Normans" are spoken of with as much dislike, and sometimes in the same terms, as the perfidious Englishman of a later date has enjoyed. It is of even more significance that, although the original texts of the great Arthurian legend were, no doubt, all written in the French language, they are written on a "British matter," and partly by Englishmen. We had lost the key of our word-hoard : we had indeed never possessed any, had simply been fumbling for one, in regard to the largest and richest part of it. Latin and French, Latin even more than French, helped us at last to forge the proper keys of language, of style, and, best of all, of prosody. But they did not put the treasure there, they only helped us to find it and use it.

INTERCHAPTER 1

TO the short, but it is hoped not absolutely insufficient, account of Anglo-Saxon literature contained in the foregoing Book, there will now, according to the system explained in the preface, be subjoined a general summary of its accomplishments and character, disengaged from the previously necessary survey of individual facts.

We have seen that in its comparatively scanty bulk, and under the disadvantages of a political history not indeed short in time but very unsettled, and but scantily equipped and supplied by civilisation, Anglo-Saxon succeeded in producing work both in prose and verse which has not only intrinsic merit and interest, which has not only the additional historic claim of being the ancestor of one of the greatest literatures of the world, but which has the further attraction, also historic, but surely not negligible, of being for its time unique, or having only Icelandic for a doubtful competitor. Icelandic itself was probably some two centuries behind Anglo-Saxon in the use of vernacular prose.

But it is exceedingly important to take stock of the exact literary value of the accomplishments of this language both in themselves and in relation to its great descendant. One thing that Anglo-Saxon did is fortunately beyond all dispute. It "unlocked the word-hoard"—a word-hoard still very much in the rough, and with some disadvantages which will be considered more specially below. Like some metals, it needed blending with others before it became thoroughly useful. But in native strength, in backbone, in the power of standing rough usage and being the better for it, it had perhaps no superiors, and it possessed certain valuable, or rather invaluable, qualities. In particular, it had that gift which some languages almost wholly lack, of forming compounds freely. Caedmon's famous *heolster-sceado, holster-shadow,* "cover or sheath of darkness," gives at the second opening of the literature a measure of its capacities in this way, and they can hardly be exaggerated. A language that cannot combine thus, or can do it only with difficulty, is a poor thin thing, the worst stuff possible for poetry, and fit only for decent, perhaps elegant, but uninspired and uninspiring prose.

In prose itself, however, Anglo-Saxon did not do very much, and it could hardly be expected to do very much. It had not the subjects; its writers had not the demand; and if by any chance any man had both subject and demand, there was the fatal mistress Latin tempting him away from the homely English wife. For almost every man of letters was an ecclesiastic, and almost every man of letters, ecclesiastic or not, looked to the public not merely of his own burg or realm, but of Latin Christendom, which had its own universal tongue. Moreover the fully-inflected condition of Anglo-Saxon has to be taken account of, and its dialects, and above all the extreme insecurity and instability of political and social conditions at the time. War and ruin may sometimes—they do not by any means always—repay in song what they have exacted in suffering; but prose as a rule requires prosperity, business, leisure for its cultivation. However this may be, it is certain that, as literature, the achievement of Anglo-Saxon in prose is very much less than its achievement in verse, though there may be a less abrupt separation between this achievement and what follows in the same medium.

In poetry it did more, and there are few points of more importance for the general study and comprehension of English literature as a whole than a comprehension of the general poetical equipment and accomplishment of Anglo-Saxon. And as estimates of these points have too often varied between the extremes of passionate and partisan appreciation on the one hand, and complete ignoring or unfair, perhaps sometimes ill-informed, depreciation on the other, such a general view has not been very easy to obtain. Yet there is no real difficulty in taking it.

Anglo-Saxon poetry, then, as we see it in the sufficient if not very plentiful remains of its best period before the end of the eighth century, displays merits of what we may call poetical intention considerably surpassing those shown by most literatures in their early stages, and at least equal to those which some literatures have shown at stages far more advanced. It has passion—not so much in the conventional and limited sense of the passion of love, with which it deals very little, as in the general sense of subjective intensity—of evidence in song that the poet has felt, seen, thought, or at least wondered, with a deep and genuine movement. And much of this action of thought and feeling is directed to natural objects, in a fashion again very rare in most literatures, and almost entirely absent from some. Yet again, though the resources of form, of art at the poet's command are undeniably scanty and rude, yet, such as they are, they are used with care and skill. In other words, and this, is no mean praise, the Anglo-Saxon poet at best, and that pretty frequently, has no mean portion of the poetic spirit, and has a just reverence for what he knows of the poetic art. In the first respect the author of *Beowulf is* at least not less richly and variously endowed than even the author of the *Chanson de Roland;* in the second, the author of the *Phoenix* is very far ahead of the author of the *Poema del Cid.*

But valuable, or rather invaluable, as are these equipments, every Anglo-Saxon poet from first to last during the Anglo-Saxon period proper suffers from two drawbacks which hamper him cruelly—monotony of subject and clumsiness of form. In both respects his limitations are hardly even in the smallest degree a reproach to him. When we remember that, so far as is known, absolutely no great literature except Greek has ever been produced without other pattern literatures before it; when we remember what was the comparative civilisation of England up to the eighth century after Christ, and of Greece in the fifth and fourth centuries before Christ; when we remember further that Anglo-Saxon culture never had so much as a single century of quiet development on the great scale under favourable political and social conditions, and that hardly any profane patterns were before any but a very few writers, we shall certainly not feel inclined to indulge an ignorant and conceited contempt of the limitations of subject to religion in the main, and out of religion to a little legend, a little contemporary war-song, some rudimentary science, and the thinnest surplus of other matters. Take any poet from Chaucer to Tennyson and strip him only of what he owes in subject—putting other debts, and they are large, out of sight—to his predecessors, and a terrible reduction would have to be made. Caedmon, if Caedmon it was; Cynewulf, if Cynewulf there was; and all the anonyms, had practically no predecessors to oblige them, except the Bible, a few hymn- and homily-writers, the Fathers, and a small, a very small, part of the profane classics which had not gone utterly out of fashion or of reach.

Of what, under this immense, this to us simply incalculable, disadvantage they accomplished much must have perished, while what has perished *may* have largely exceeded what we have, not merely in bulk but in variety. On this head at least there is no fault to find, but rather infinite credit due to our ancestors, that while no other—Icelandic, perhaps, excepted—of the modern European languages had yet found its tongue at all, or had found it only to let the results disappear, they did what they did.

Nor is there exactly any "fault to find" with the defects of art and means which also beset them, but in this respect somewhat harsher language must be used. In the first place, putting enthusiasts aside, I do not think that any one can call Anglo-Saxon, in familiar phrase, a "pretty" language. Though not without a grave undertone of music in it now and then, it has a distinct uncouthness. Its inflections give it monotony without music; the rough consonant terminations give the word-structure an air rather of a dry-stone wall unwrought by hand than of cunning masonry. Afterwards, when this roughness was blended with softer forms and matter, it was to give the most perfect poetic medium—more perfect even than Greek—that has ever existed; at this time the destined completion had not been reached, and the language, full of forms in one way, was still formless; crammed with possibilities, was still void, chaotic, rudimentary.

That it chose the prosody most suited to it is no doubt true. Every language has, and must inevitably have, the prosody that it deserves, the prosody of which it is capable, whence is clear the folly of those who desperately attempt to force it into prosodic forms other than those into which it naturally goes. And that Old English prosody has limitations and shortcomings, probably inseparable from Old English vocabulary, there is little if any doubt. But there is no doubt at all that the limitations and the shortcomings are of the most serious character. With some of the objections made to the Anglo-Saxon *Ars poetica* we need by no means concur. The common complaint that there are no similes may be called almost silly. In the first place, there *are* similes; and in the second place, if there were none, why should there be any? The only possible answer that suggests itself turns upon such a childish argument or no argument as this, "Homer is a great early poet; Homer is rich in similes; therefore early poets who have no similes are not great." Moreover, simile or no simile, Anglo-Saxon poetry, like its cousin Icelandic, is admittedly rich in metaphor, which is only simile in the making. When a poet has once, called the sea the "swan's path," and thought the "breast-hoard," he has shown himself perfectly competent to write a simile in twenty lines—a simile like that at the end of the *Scholar Gipsy* itself—if he chose to do it. So too we shall not, if we are wise, shake our heads because it is rather long before we come to epanaphora or antithesis in Anglo-Saxon poetry. The absence or the slow coming of epanaphora and antithesis is no doubt very disheartening, but, as Deor himself has it, this also may we overgo.

The real faults of Anglo-Saxon poetry from the formal point of view lie in, and indeed are inseparable from, its staple of accented alliterative verse, it may be discretionary, it may be quite carefully and cunningly arranged as to syllables, but divided by a hard and fast section or middle pause. That fine effects in certain limited kinds may be and have been got out of this arrangement need not be denied; that it was a great advance on mere systemless chaos is of course undeniable. It lent itself with ease to that parallelism which is the most natural note of half-civilised poetry. The accents gave something of a "stand-by," something of a backbone, to save the rhythm from becoming merely prosaic. The alliteration supplied a musical charm which has never died out of English poetry, and therefore never can die out of it. The sections helped the parallelism, acted as stays to the prentice poet, and assisted the accent and the alliteration to give something like a real poetic form, as opposed to the form of prose. For a certain meditative kind of poetry, like that of the *Ruin* and the great *Phoenix* passage, the whole scheme is well fitted, and it does not do badly for romantic narrative, whether in its earliest form, as in *Beowulf,* or in its latest and almost last, as in Layamon. Nay more, it seems by no means absurd to find in it, as I believe some even of its specialist students are beginning to do, the germs not indeed of later English poetical rhythm, but of that wonderful English prose rhythm which, aimed at half-blindly from the fourteenth to the sixteenth centuries, found, whether consciously or not, in the seventeenth, but never deliberately practised, much less deliberately analysed, till within the last hundred years, has given something almost as much a pure hybrid between poetry and prose in form as drama is a hybrid between them in spirit.

But the defects of its qualities are many and great. When the normal scheme, with few unaccented syllables, is kept, it is excessively apt to become dull, monotonous, sing-song. When, in the poet's need for a longer line and greater variety, it receives the Caedmonian extension, it becomes perilously suggestive, of the "patter" which has been consecrated in more modern times to burlesque and grotesque. The excessive and regular alliteration not only becomes wearisome to the ear, but also, and inevitably, occasions the selection of words not because they are the right words, but merely because they begin with the right letter. And the sectional pause is the worst of all. It will always remain the most astonishing thing in that extraordinary monument of learned and ingenious paralogism, Dr. Guest's *English Rhythms,* that he should have failed to perceive that the beginning of great English poetry is synonymous with the abolition of the compulsory middle pause, and should even have endeavoured to convict Shakespeare and Milton of *lèse-poésie* because they do not obey it. That the middle pause is wanted in very long lines may be freely granted; in short ones and those of moderate length it cannot without disadvantage be more than a rule which admits the freest and most frequent exception.

It is probably due to these faults and disabilities, rather than to any want of genius, that the Anglo-Saxon poets did not do more than they did, and it is again and again to be repeated that it is surprising how much they did. But their poetry, indeed their whole literature, is a rudimentary literature, a literature *in statu pupillari,* and one which has not passed any but the lower stages even of pupilship. Even if the most elaborate theories of its prosody be admitted, the case will not be altered: for a certain etiquette of detail is consistent with a very early novitiate. It can manage simple prose very well, but it cannot achieve anything that requires style in the proper sense, though it can manage bombast. In the poetry we have been briefly reviewing we find some noble passages, especially of a serious and reflective cast, a few more showing the joy of battle well, still fewer, but some, evincing accurate observation and the power of putting it into words. But the class of poetical effects attained, and to all appearance attainable, is exceedingly limited, and excludes altogether those of the lighter kind. There is practically no lyric—a want which would of itself and at once relegate any poetry to a position below, and far below, the highest. In short, we have here a juvenile effort, as we may call it, of immense interest, but doomed in itself to failure, because the person or people making it has not come to its full strength, has not entered into possession of its full property, and is using clumsy methods and tools on a scanty material, instead of employing the results of the experience of the past in method on the gathered treasures of the past in stuff.

Book II

The Making of English Literature

1

THE TRANSITION

The sleep of English—Awakening influences—Latin—French influence—Geoffrey of Monmouth—Latin prosody in the early Middle Ages—The Hymns—Alliteration and rhyme—Rhythm and metre—French prosody—Syllabic equivalence in English—Helped by Anglo-Saxon—Law of pause in English.

TO say that English literature[1] dives underground some time before the Conquest, and does not emerge again till about the year 1200, would be an exaggeration; but it would only be an exaggeration of the truth. As a matter of fact, we have nothing certainly dating from any part of this long period of a hundred and fifty years except the later passages of the Worcester and Peterborough *Chronicles,* the latest of which does not go beyond the year 1155, though just before this there are pages of merit, especially that famous one already referred to as to the sufferings of the English people under Stephen. It is probable that the *Grave Poem,* and perhaps some other fragments in verse, date from this time; it is tolerably certain that some of the Anglo-Saxon Homilies and Saints' Lives which we possess, either as more

The sleep of English.

1. There is unfortunately no adequate literary history of the Middle English period. vols. iii and iv and the earlier part of vol. v of the late Professor Morley's *English Writers* deal with it, but are chiefly occupied with a crowd of extraneous matters. Ten Brink (vol. i books ii and iii) is much better, but not all-sufficing. There is ample information in vol. ii of the Variorum *Warton* (London, 1871), but it is necessarily chaotic and indigestible. Luckily the texts themselves are now fairly, though not fully, accessible; unluckily they have too often been edited from the merely linguistic point of view.

or less original compositions or refashionings of older ones, date from it. But these things only touch the fringe of literature, and there are extremely few of them.[2] Yet during this long sleep, so scantily broken, a process was going on analogous to, but far more momentous and thorough than, the ordinary refreshment by the "season of all natures." We have said that the powers of English, not merely as a literature but as a language, were obviously failing even within the very restricted circle in which they had walked before the Conquest itself; it remains now to indicate as briefly as possible what the influences were which came to transform and refresh these powers, and how they went to work. The actual instruments were two, Latin and French; and their working was directed to three different points of attack—the alteration of the language as such; the suggestion of new subjects and forms of literature; and, above all, the construction of a new prosody.

The notice of literatures and literary works not English has been limited, according to the plan of this book, to the strictest necessities, and among these necessities the present occasion must be counted. We can, moreover, economise under the first head of the last division, for the mere linguistic side of the matter but faintly concerns us. It is sufficient there to say that the different inflections of French and Latin (as, it is thought, the different inflections of Danish had already done) helped the already displayed tendency of the language to shake off inflection almost if not altogether, though this was a work of time; and that the swelling of the vocabulary with Latin or Romance words, though inevitable, is not, as we shall see when we come to actual literature once more, very noticeable in the first place. The effect of the exhibition of new forms and subjects was much more momentous, and to understand it we

2. For instance, Mr. Morley ekes out the assumption that "no doubt" there was verse, with the well-known Canute Poem, *Merry sang the monks of Ely,* the verses attributed to Godric of Finchale, and *Sumer is icumen in.* But if the Canute Poem has any interest of authenticity it must be much older, and *Sumer is icumen in* is pretty certainly much younger, than 1050-1150. Godric (d. 1170) is more to the point. His verses are but the meagrest scraps, but they show *rhyme* and *metre.*

must try a "Pisgah-sight" of Latin and French literature as each then was.

Awakening influences. Latin.

In considering the effect on English of Latin, we must not assume, as used to be assumed, that classical Latin was out of the ken or knowledge of the early Middle Ages. It was not; and there were then Englishmen, such as Joseph of Exeter, who could write excellent hexameters on a fairly Virgilian or at least Claudianic model, though they might sometimes condescend to leonine or middle rhyme; while, as we need not go beyond Chaucer to show, large parts of the classical poets, especially Ovid, were distinctly familiar. Indeed, it may perhaps be said with safety that of all classical writers Ovid had most influence, though others had some. But the singular and still slightly puzzling thing in connection with this subject is that readers, even readers of considerable education and great ability, seem to have observed no critical proportion whatever in their relative estimate of authorities, either from the point of view of matter or from the point of view of form. They preferred in the "Tale of Troy," not merely to Homer, whom they knew but little, but to Virgil, whom they knew fairly, and to Ovid, whom they knew well, two beggarly abstracts assigned to a certain Dictys and a certain Dares, for which they had absolutely no external authority, and which bore internal marks of absolute worthlessness as literature, if not of absolute untrustworthiness as history. They swallowed, though they had abundance of fairly sober abstracts of history, if they had not all original authorities, huge farragos of mere fairy tales about Alexander. And, generally speaking, the actual classics exercised, naturally enough, much less direct influence upon them, especially in the point of form, than the writers of the decadence and the darkness from the fourth century downwards. And, as was yet more natural, they attached more importance still to the Services of the Church, to the devotional writings of ecclesiastics in verse and prose; while by degrees they began to elaborate for themselves an almost entirely new system of philosophy, which the natural clearness and precision of Latin enabled them to make admirably systematic and scientific in terminology, though the terms might be barbarous in form. With Anglo-Saxon failing, and no other vernacular except the distant and thoroughly isolated Icelandic come to full maturity, the practice of history-writing became for a long period entirely Latin, and the usage of that tongue in the schools further established it as the language not merely of philosophy but of general science.

French influence.

The spoken influence of French, or at least Anglo-Norman, was naturally even greater, for it was for centuries the only court language, the language of superior business, and to some extent at any rate the necessary vehicle of communication between the upper and lower classes, though not between the upper lower classes themselves. But its literary influence was very considerably less. What has been already said must be repeated, that at the time of the Conquest, and much more, therefore, at the time of the first influence of French at the court of Edward the Confessor, the foreigners had little, or practically no, literature to offer as an example to England. They had no prose; their great national epics were only beginning; it is improbable that they had any finished lyric in durable form; the romances proper were in the British division not yet written (they had pretty certainly to come from England itself), and in the case of the classical division were only beginning to be written. French drama was lisping or still inarticulate; the great French *genre* of the *fabliau* was hardly born. In short, French literature could exercise no influence, because it as yet was merely struggling for existence itself.

No doubt, when it once began it made gigantic strides, while it so happened that the parts of France where some of these kinds saw the light were directly under the rule of or closely connected with the Kings of England. Provençal led the way, though probably not by much, in formal lyric; and more than half the Provençal-speaking districts were sooner or later brought under English rule by the accession of the Angevins and the marriage of Henry II with Eleanor of Guienne. The British and Roman "matters" were-specially Norman in place of treatment, and from England itself came a book which, though in Latin, had such an enormous influence upon English literature that it must receive exceptional treatment here. This is the *Historia Britonum* of Geoffrey of Monmouth, which was probably written almost simultaneously with—at least within a decade or two of—the last gasp of pure original Anglo-Saxon in the *Annals* of Peterborough.

Geoffrey of Monmouth.

Not much is known of Geoffrey, who must, however, have either been one of the most superlatively lucky persons in literary history or an original genius of the greatest mark. He was certainly consecrated Bishop of St. Asaph in 1152, and must have died about two years later. His book is dedicated to Robert, Earl of Gloucester, who died in 1147, so that it cannot be later than that date, while some have put it back ten or fifteen years earlier. He himself claims (with almost transparent "make-believe" as it seems to some) to have had a British original brought to him out of Armorica by a certain Walter, Archdeacon of Oxford. But nothing has ever been seen or heard of such a book, and even "Walter, Archdeacon of Oxford," is difficult, if not impossible, to identify. Nor have any other materials for Geoffrey's *History* been traced, save that in the case of its most famous, though far from its largest episode, the story of King Arthur, certain germs, excessively meagre in substance and very uncertain in date, can be found in certain documents attributed to Gildas, a monk of the fifth century, and Nennius, an unknown person who may have written in the seventh, the eighth, or the ninth, if not later, together with a *Life* of Gildas, which is certainly not much, if any, earlier than Geoffrey.[3]

The debt which English literature owes to this curious book is not limited to the Arthurian part, for Geoffrey has given us the original story of *King Lear,* the most heartrending of English, or any, tragedies; the ending at least of *Comus,* the

3. Geoffrey himself, Gildas, and Nennius will be found conveniently translated in one volume of Bohn's "Antiquarian Library," entitled *Six Old English Chronicles.* I do not know any translation of the *Vita Gildae* (ed. Stevenson), and the Latin published half a century ago for the English Historical Society is not very accessible. The texts of Nennius vary a good deal.

most exquisite of English, or any, masques; and other things. But in magnitude, in interest, and as a literary *origin,* the Arthurian invention dwarfs all other things in the book. It should be observed that by no means the whole story of Arthur, as we familiarly know it from Sir Thomas Malory's greatest of all compilations, is in Geoffrey. He represents the treason of Vortigern to Britain as partly repaired by two brothers, Ambrosius and Uther. The latter, reigning alone, falls in love with Igraine, wife of Gorlois, Duke of Cornwall, gains her by the help of the enchanter Merlin, who has already played a great part in the story, and becomes the father of Arthur, who succeeds him, crushes opposition at home, marries a noble lady of Roman descent, Guanhumara (Guinevere), joins issue with and defeats the Romans on the Continent, is recalled by the treason of his nephew Mordred, whom Guanhumara has married, returns, defeats and finally slays the traitor, but is mortally wounded and gives up the crown, being carried to the Isle of Avilion to be healed of his wounds.

The Middle Ages, despite what we hear and talk about their defects of communication and the like, are famous for the almost unintelligible rapidity of their literary diffusion in some cases. But in none is this so remarkable as in the case of the Arthurian story, which, if not entirely invented on the meagre basis of Nennius by Geoffrey himself, can at most have some other basis of Welsh legends, chiefly about Merlin. We have seen that the book cannot have been written much earlier than 1130, and may not have been written till a few years before 1150. It appears that before the later date it was already turned into French verse by Geoffrey Gaimar, whose version is lost; and shortly after Geoffrey of Monmouth's own death by Wace of Jersey, whose version remains. Fresh legends or sheer invention furnished Wace with some important additions, and, as we shall see, he handed it on to the first English handler of the story, the poet Layamon. But the development of the whole into a real romance occupied pens in verse and prose during the later part, probably the third quarter, of the century, in a manner the exact account and distribution of which is still a mystery. The chief credit used to be assigned, and the present writer is still inclined to assign it, to Walter Map or Mapes, a native of the Welsh marches, and the author not merely of a very curious and interesting Latin miscellany called *De Nugis Curialium,* but, by possible attribution at least, of a still more interesting collection of student poems, satires on church dignitaries, etc., issued under the general *nom de guerre* of "Golias."[4] At much the same time, later or earlier, Chrestien de Troyes, a French poet, gave poetical versions of many parts of the legend. But the complete execution of this in verse or in prose belongs, in language at least, to French not to English literature, till it was magnificently vindicated for its native soil by Malory three centuries later. The probably earliest English version after Layamon will be found noticed in the next chapter but one, as that of Layamon will be found in the very next.

The opportunity of an example of unmatched pertinence has taken us a little way from the actual stream of English literature to illustrate the manner in which that literature drew its subjects from literatures other than English. This was all the more desirable because at this very time such new stocks of subject were simply pouring in from East and West and North and South alike. We must return to show how a change greater far than any mere introduction of subject—the introduction of the true and universal prosody of English instead of the cramped and parochial rhythm of Anglo-Saxon—came about, showing at the same time how the surviving virtue of that rhythm itself differentiates English metre, as it was to be, from that of other modern languages.

It appears probable, and the reasons which make it so have been already partly set forth, that it was Latin even more than French that effected this transmutation. It is therefore unnecessary for even the most sensitive patriot to be jealous of what has been rather absurdly called "the rhythm of the foreigner." Latin, to the Middle Ages, was not foreign in any

4. Both edited for the Camden Society by Thomas Wright, whose services to Middle English literature were inferior to those of no man dead or living, in his numerous editions of texts, and in his *Biographia Britannica Literaria* (2 vols. London—Anglo-Saxon Period, 1842; Anglo-Norman Period, 1846).

country, just as it was mother tongue in none. It was in Church and State alike the common speech, the common literary stock of Christendom; the very Italian himself, and still more the Goths and Franks who spoke the other Romance tongues, had hardly more part in it than the Anglo-Saxon. And the Latin prosody, as well as the Latin vocabulary, that affected English poetry once for all in the centuries between 1000 and 1400 A.D. was Latin enormously changed by influences which may have been themselves barbarian in origin. It is improbable that we shall ever exactly know the causes of the change which we first observe in Prudentius, and which becomes ever more noticeable. It may be that, as some will have it, the elaborate classical prosody of Latin was a mere interlude, that "the rhythm of the foreigner" was introduced from Greece, and for a time superimposed with crushing weight on a natural accentual prosody such as we see partly indicated in "Saturnian" fragments. But what is certain is that, from the end of the fourth century onward, there is observable a movement (whether of innovation or reaction is not here essential) which not only alters to the most material extent the quantity of syllables, but also, as a consequence or independently, conditions the structure of verse. And this change is seen more especially in the compositions which were certain to exert most effect upon the vernaculars, the Hymns of the Church. For not only were these sure to resound in millions of ears, the eyes corresponding to which were very unlikely to read written literature, secular or sacred, but the music by which they were accompanied was equally certain to familiarise the ear, and with the rhythm to impress it on the brain, and make it likely to be reproduced in vernacular composition, especially when the prosodic forms more specially belonging to that composition had gone almost entirely out of use.

Latin prosody in the early Middle Ages.

The Hymns.

Now, the characteristics of this kind of verse were chiefly two, and each of these was in direct and striking contrast with the corresponding characteristics of Anglo-Saxon. In the first place, though alliteration might by accident appear in them, its regular presence as a distinguishing poetic form, a regulator and mainspring of

Alliteration and rhyme.

rhythm, was entirely absent, and was replaced by rhyme[5] both middle and end, but especially the latter. And in the second place, the requirement of a certain number of "accented" syllables, not even itself insisted on with absolute rigidity, and accompanied by the vaguest and widest license of inserting syllables that were unaccented, was replaced by the system of definite-*metre*, composed of syllabic integers either identical or equivalent.

Rhythm and metre.

This influence had already exerted itself on the so-called Romance languages, and so in the case of the second foreign influence—French—Anglo-Saxon found itself confronted with an ally of Latin, or let us say with a pupil who had already passed his freshmanship. But French had received the Latin influence and instruction in its own way. One of those strange and infinitely interesting, though also infinitely mysterious, idiosyncrasies of language, which students of philology and phonetics too often neglect, had brought it about that French should be a language in which the distinction of syllabic value (call it "long" or "short," "accented" or "unaccented," "heavy" or "light," or by any opposition of words which may be preferred as least controversial) is, and seems always to have been, less marked than in almost any other. It followed from this that trisyllabic feet—that is to say, feet in which one syllable is intrinsically strong, long, heavy, or what not, enough to take two weaker, shorter, lighter ones on its back and preserve them distinct from others—were never prevalent in French, and for many centuries have been non-existent. And it followed from this again that "syllabic equivalence"—that is to say, the principle by which one strong, long, heavy syllable may be substituted for two weak, short, light ones, and *vice versa*—has in the regular prosody of France never had any place, while even in doggerel, in comic songs, and the like, syllables, if they are not

French prosody.

5. "Rhyme," not "rime." "Rime" in English means "hoar-frost," and we need not introduce an unnecessary ambiguity against the practice of all our greatest writers, save, perhaps, one. Nay, the suggested etymology of ῥυθμοί, if false, shows the instinctive recognition of the fact, first formulated by Mitford, that "rhyme is a time-beater," not a mere tinkling tag.

to count at full, have to be simply slurred or omitted, as may be seen in the printed works of the lighter French songsters.

Now there was, and from what has been said it will be seen that this also was natural, something of a reflex tendency in Latin non-classical verse to imitate this characteristic of the Romance tongues, which showed itself also in Provençal, in Italian, and to a less degree in Spanish. And undoubtedly the crucial question was whether English would follow it and them in this respect. For centuries, as we shall see, the question was undecided—nay, at the present day there are some persons of distinction who will have it that there is no syllabic equivalence in English, and who resort to slurring, to "extrametrical syllables," and to all manner of strange devices to twist out of this great, this cardinal, this supreme feature of our poetry. For it is this—the possibility, namely, of substituting almost anywhere, with due precautions, dactyl or tribrach or anapaest for iamb or trochee[6]—which, when the example of Spenser to some extent, and the inestimable license of the great dramatists far more, had given it an unquestioned right of place in literature, and when it had allied with itself the shaking off of the rigid caesura or pause, endowed English verse with that astonishing and unparalleled variety of music which puts it at the head of the poetry of the modern world.

Syllabic equivalence in English.

And we should be doing Anglo-Saxon a grave injustice if we did not recognise that one of its main poetical features undoubtedly helped to bring about this blessed result, and that was the old license of putting in unaccented syllables almost *ad libitum.* Indeed, some authorities would recognise a formal and regular equivalence in Anglo-Saxon itself. The sectional arrangement of Anglo-Saxon was less beneficial, and would, if maintained, as there was for some centuries a blind effort to retain it, have been very mischievous. But here too the dramatists, with Shakespeare at their head, came to the rescue, and, with

Helped by Anglo-Saxon.

6. Strictly speaking, of course only the tribrach corresponds to the trochee of iamb. But, as in Greek itself, dactyls and anapaests (though not, I think, cretics or amphibrachs) claim a place.

the aid of their mighty follower Milton, once for all established the following law:

In an English heroic line, as well as in any shorter one,[7] *the pause may fall* after the first or any subsequent syllable to the penultimate, *while there need not be any distinct pause at all.*

Law of pause in English.

But we must now see in detail what the actual history of Middle English literature was.

7. In the Alexandrine and longer lines a pause *is* necessary, somewhere about the middle, when they are used continuously, though not always in isolated applications like Spenser's. But it is a question whether these lines are not more or less disguised *distichs,* a fact of which the sixteenth-century practice of printing them in halves was a clumsy recognition.

2

FIRST MIDDLE ENGLISH PERIOD 1200-1250

Layamon's *Brut*—The *Ormulum*—Its spelling—Its metre—The *Ancren Riwle*—The *Moral Ode*—*Genesis and Exodus*—The *Bestiary*—The *Orison of our Lady*—Proverbs of *Alfred* and *Hendyng*—*The Owl and the Nightingale.*

THE dates of the books—not numerous, but, in some cases at least, both important and interesting—which compose the first growth of Middle English literature, or what used to be called "Semi-Saxon," are known with very little certainty. But a *circa* of reasonable probability can generally be attached to them, and there seems very little doubt that about the close of the twelfth and the beginning of the thirteenth centuries something like a distinct first-crop made its appearance. It is natural that the subjects of this new literature should, like those of the old, be at first mainly religious. But they soon ranged more widely, and, as it happens, the most important of all in bulk and in contents, if not also in actual literary quality, is secular.

Layamon's *Brut.*

This is the famous *Brut*[1] of Layamon, which we possess in two forms, one assigned by scholars to the earliest and the other to the latest years of the half-century which has been subsumed for this chapter. The differences between these two versions, though occasionally, as in the case of the name of the author's father,[2] a little puzzling, are of great value for linguistics,

1. Ed. Madden, 3 vols. London, 1847.
2. In the earlier text we have "Layamon the son of Leovenath," in the later "Laweman the son of Leuca."

and they are by no means unimportant for literary history proper, inasmuch as we perceive in the later version the distinct enlargement of the intrusion of rhyme, which is already noticeable in the earlier. But in mere contents the later version is, somewhat contrary to the wont of mediaeval times, shortened rather than watered out; and it is also in much worse condition, having suffered by that too famous fire in the Cottonian Library which plays in Early English literary history an actual and historical counterpart to Caleb Balderstone's thunderstorm in fiction. Fortunately for the student of letters, both are contained in one of the best, as in one of the handsomest, editions which have fallen to the lot of any Early English classic.[3]

Layamon, the son of Leovenath, of whom we know nothing save from his own words, appears to have been a priest at Arley or Ernley (a village near Bewdley, on the Severn), into whose hands Wace's translation of Geoffrey of Monmouth fell. He combined with it, as he tells us, Bede, historical works by "Albinus" and "Austin," which have not been identified, though the first may have been some lost Latin original of Bede's own,[4] and (but this he does not tell us) apparently either traditions of the Welsh marches, near which he lived, or some imaginations of his own. The result is a *Brut,* or British History, of great length,[5] displaying occasionally no small literary power, very interesting as the first English book on the great legendary history of England, and absolutely priceless as showing the inroads which the influences described in the last chapter were making upon the effete rules and weakened powers of Anglo-Saxon.

3. Sir Frederic Madden's *Layamon,* like Thorpe's *Caedmon* and *Exeter Book,* was published by the Society of Antiquaries, which unfortunately did not find encouragement to go further.
4. "Albinus" of Canterbury was one of Bede's authorities.
5. Text A contains over 32,000 lines or half-lines; Text B seems to have had about 24,000, of which more than the odd 4000 are lost or damaged. The older practice of printing Anglo-Saxon verse in half-lines is distinctly preferable here, because the change of rhythm and the inroad of rhyme are more clearly shown.

In mere vocabulary the change is by no means great. Authorities differ as to the number of French words used, but none sets it above an almost infinitesimal proportion.[6] Yet the forms of the language are unmistakably altering, and the forms of prosody are altering more unmistakably still. The general structure is still the unrhymed alliterative line of two short sections. But an absolutely perfect example of the older form—four accents, three alliterations, no rhyme whatever, and a rhythm often not marked at all according to any metrical system, and only vaguely trochaic when sensible—is the exception, an exception appearing at long intervals. Constantly the alliteration is broken down. Very frequently rhymes appear between the line-halves—rhymes of a simple and obvious kind, "brother" and "other," "king" and "thing," "night" and "light," etc., but for that very reason all the easier, all the more tempting, and all the more frequent in occurrence. Most important of all, the unmetrical or vaguely trochaic cadence tends steadily towards, and sometimes reaches, the full and exact octosyllabic couplet, rhymed and complete. When we come across such a couplet as:

> Tha answeraede Vortiger,
> Of elchen ufel he was war;

still more when we find that in the fifty years' interval between the two versions the terminations "Appollin" and "wel iwon" have been changed into "Appollin" and "of great win," the inference is unmistakable. Rhymed metre has challenged unrhymed rhythm, and is slowly driving it out.

As for the substance of Layamon, it may be regarded from two points of view: his additions to his predecessors, as far as we have these latter, and his handling of his subjects, original or added. The list of the former given by Sir Frederic Madden fills two large pages, and includes among its more important items the legend of Oriene (the name which Layamon gives to St. Ursula of the Eleven Thousand Virgins), a much fuller account of Rowena's appearance as Dalilah, the all-important

6. Madden allows about 50 in A, about 80 in B; Professor Skeat puts the total at 170.

additions to the Arthurian story that "elves" figured at the King's birth and took him to Avalon,[7] the foundation of the Round Table, and numerous details of Arthur's wars with rebels and invaders and Romans. From the latter point of view particular attention may be directed to the whole of the Rowena story, which Layamon works into a much completer romance-episode than any previous writer whose work has come to us,[8] and the whole of the Arthurian passages. These latter have not indeed received the immense addition to their interest which is given (possibly by Layamon's earlier contemporary and neighbour by birth, Walter Map) in the Anglo-French romances on the subject, but it is in itself a much greater advance upon Wace than Wace is upon Geoffrey, and it displays much more poetical capacity than the Jerseyman's. Indeed, when we give fair weight to the fact that Layamon was like an animal which is struggling out of its old shell or skin into a new one, and has not half completed the process, the poetical merit of his work deserves to be set far higher than it has usually been put. A "chronicler," as he is sometimes called, he is not, though he may have thought himself one. He is really the first writer of romance in English of whom we know.

The second great poetical work—or at least work in verse—of this time, the *Ormulum*,[9] is far inferior in interest of subject to the *Brut*, for it is simply one of the numerous and always more or less lame homiletic paraphrases of the Scriptures—in this case busied with the Gospels for each day. We have not the whole set, but a considerable part of it, extending to some 10,000 lines of fifteen syllables each, or double that number if the poem be divided into couplets of eight and seven. The author, of whom nothing is known except from this work, was one Orm or

The *Ormulum*.

7. Their queen is here "Argante," of course the same as the "Morgane" of the more usual stories and the "Urganda" of Peninsular revival *Amadis*.

8. It is luckily accessible to those who do not possess the whole in Morris and Skeat's *Specimens of Early English*, part i, p. 64. I could wish that (instead of the whole of *King Horn*, of which a fifth, or ten pages, would well suffice) much larger extracts from Layamon were given in this invaluable book. There is plenty to choose from.

9. Ed. White and Holt, 2 vols., Oxford, 1878.

Ormin, an Augustinian monk, probably resident somewhere in the east of England, or in Northern Mercia. He addresses a certain Walter, whom he terms three fold his brother—in the flesh, in faith, and in monastic order. Of actual poetical merit it is not too much to say that Orm has nothing, and it is at the same time not paradoxical to add that his work is much more valuable by reason of certain characteristics which it possesses than one of much greater poetical merit without these characteristics could have been to us.

The first of his peculiarities lies in his spelling. It would have been in any case probable that the jostling of English by French and Latin should have effected some confusion in English pronunciation, while this confusion would also be assisted by the variety of dialects still prevalent in "Semi-Saxon." At any rate Orm, who seems to have been a purist in the matter, and to have had a sensitive ear, was offended by this, and determined to adopt a plan which should at least prevent short vowels from being sounded long and *vice versa.* In order to do this he seized upon the principle—sound English to this day, and fatal to what is called American spelling—that *caeteris paribus,* and in the absence of special knowledge to the contrary, a vowel before two consonants will be pronounced short in English, a vowel before one consonant long. And regardless of the extraordinary effect produced to the eye—indeed this was of less consequence before the days of printing, and of least in the days when reading was not so much reading as recitation—he steadily doubled the consonant after every short vowel, even when there could, as in the case of the infinitive *brinngenn,* "to bring," be practically no danger. The effect in appearance is naturally hideous and grotesque; as a monument in literary, or at least linguistic, history the practice (the observance of which the author solemnly enjoins on any scribe who shall copy his work) is priceless.

Its spelling.

As valuable, and more strictly literary, is Orm's metrical arrangement. His prosody is distinguished from Old English by being neither accentual nor (at least regularly) alliterative, nor tolerant of extra-metrical syllables. It is distinguished from classical Latin by having no syllabic equivalence nor any trisyllabic feet. If its metre—a strict iambic form of tetrameter catalectic, or alternate dimeters acatalectic and catalectic—occurs anywhere in Latin hymns, it must be very rare, and Orm has no rhyme. The general opinion is that he adapted it from the hymns, in principle, whether from an actual example or not. Hut I suspect also the influence of French, where strict syllabic prosody had long been established.

Its metre.

Now nothing can be more reasonable as a matter of expectation, or more valuable as a matter of fact, than that in this period of groping and experiment, of endeavouring to suit the old bottle to the new wine, some one should have selected, as Orm apparently did, the method of hard-and-fast syllabic prosody, unhelped, uninfluenced even by rhyme. It is not a success; it is contrary to the genius of English, though strangely enough there are even now persons who cling to the idea. But there is no doubt that the attempt was one of the experiments which had to be made, if partially to fail, and that in the very failure it did good by curbing and restraining the English tendency to slipshod doggerel with rhyme to match.

Nor ought we to put the actual value of the *Ormulum* too low. It is stiff, monotonous, bolstered out here and clipped there to suit the hard-and-fast rhythm, occasionally of a most prosaic and provoking sing-song. But it ought to be remembered that sing-song was exactly what English wanted. It was the defect in cadence, the substitution of rhetorical for strictly poetical effect, which was the greatest shortcoming of Anglo-Saxon poetry. Here at least there was no such defect, though the verse not unnaturally tumbled into the opposite fault of too monotonous *ictus,* of an effect like that which has been whimsically transferred from the King of France in the rhyme to French verse, of marching up the hill and then marching down again with remorseless alternation. In morals to go into one extreme in order to cure the other is a dubious recipe; but in other matters it is the one most familiar, most generally applied, and perhaps most generally effective. That something better ought to come and would come than the half-alliterative, half-rhymed, half-rhythmical, half-metrical jumble of Layamon was clear; that it would be something also different from, and much better than, the stiff rhymeless cadence of Ormin was clear likewise. But this was the necessary tack in one direction as that was in the other, and between them, with other minor veerings to help, they brought the ship through the troublesome middle passage of the thirteenth and early fourteenth centuries safe into the open sea where Chaucer took command, and where she has sailed since, and may sail, we hope, for evermore.

The third capital work of the earliest period of Middle English is not like the *Brut* and the *Ormulum* in verse, but in prose, though it resembles the *Ormulum* in belonging to sacred not to profane literature. It is thus less important than either in the history of literary form, though as an example of pleasant, easy prose-writing it shows a considerable advance on any Anglo-Saxon prose that we possess, and its interest of subject, of tone, and temper is very considerable.

The *Ancren Riwle.*

This is the *Ancren Riwle*[10] or Rule of Anchoresses, written by an unknown person for the guidance of three ladies who had taken the vows, but belonged to no order, abiding in a free female hermitage at Tarrant Keynes in Dorsetshire. This book is partly a devotional manual, six of its eight books, or "deals," being devoted to what the author calls the Inner Rule—the cultivation of the soul by guarding against sin and practising piety. The first handles services and ceremonial matters; the last, the daily life of the recluses. The characteristic of these practical parts is a curiously wide and liberal spirit of charity, informed by good sense and human feeling. The hermitage of Tarrant Keynes was no Abbey of Theleme: its motto is *fais ce que dois* not *fais ce que voudras,*

10. Extracts of this appeared in Wright and Halliwell's *Reliquiae Antiquae* in 1841-43. It was completely published by the Rev. James Morton for the Camden Society in 1853. The authorship is quite uncertain : it has been assigned to two Bishops of Salisbury; Simon of Ghent, who died too late, 1313, to have written a book probably of the earliest years of the thirteenth century; and Richard Poore, who was certainly born and lived at Tarrant, and whose time (he died in 1237) suits well enough. But there is no evidence of his having written it. It was widely popular, and was translated both in prose and verse.

and the writer is perfectly well aware of what comes of the unlimited indulgence of sense and will. But he not only does not advise, he distinctly reprobates and forbids, excessive austerities, and is never weary of dwelling on the contrast between the Inner and Outer Rule, and the superior importance of the former. The strictly devotional parts are animated by a mysticism which is of the kindly order likewise, and the illustrations, parables, and the like are frequently of considerable literary interest, while the style shows at least possibilities of splendour as well as an actual command of ease.

The rhyming productions of this period are of less individual bulk, but in almost every case (except those of the Homilies and Lives of Saints) they possess literary as well as linguistic importance. One or two of these, if we could believe some authorities, preceded even Layamon and Orm by the greater part of a century. But this, as will be seen, is nearly inconceivable.

The *Moral Ode.*

The most important, perhaps, and according to the authorities just mentioned the oldest, is the somewhat celebrated *Poema Morale,* or Moral Ode, published early in the eighteenth century by Hickes.[11] This, which answers to its name, is a disquisition in verse on the rapid passing of life, on the fact that growth in years and in goods does not always, or often, mean growth in wisdom or in grace, on the importance of good works, the certainty of Judgment, and the like. It is, though necessarily dealing with commonplaces, good literature, and its metrical form is very remarkable; while the language, for all its age, is in parts so modern that scarcely anything more than the slightest alteration in spelling is necessary to make the first four lines intelligible:

> I am elder than I was in winter(s) and eke lorè;
> I wield more than I did : my wit ought to be morè;
> Well longè I have child ibeen in workè and eke in deedè;
> Though I be in winters old, too young am I in redè.

11. It has been several times reprinted, and will be found complete in two different texts (which are supposed to represent about the same difference, 1200 and 1250, as those of the *Brut*), in Morris and Skeat, *op. cit.*, i, 194 *sq.*

It will be seen that this form is different from anything hitherto noticed, and that it is identical, not only almost but altogether, with the most insignificant differences, with the swinging "fourteener" which was almost the staple verse of English literature at the end of the early and middle sixteenth century, and which has never gone out since.

Now Professor Ten Brink not only thinks that this metre is all but identical with Orm's, but believes that the poem may be as early as the reign of Henry I. The first position is, I think, a clear mistake. It is true that occasionally the lines of the *Ode* give us the full *Ormulum* fifteener with iambic cadence, while the feminine termination which distinguishes it is rigidly maintained. But as a rule, as the already given example will show, the first syllable is cut off, the cadence becomes trochaic, and what is more, there is a distinct tendency, if not to the definite insertion of trisyllabic equivalents, to a hop, a slur, a quaver, breaking the steady "thid-thud" of Walter's excellent brother. Nor is the rhyme a less important or a less disturbing addition. This, however, is one of those points which it may not be easy to make clear to a foreigner's ear—a fact which no doubt should render all foreigners chary of committing themselves on prosodies not their own. The other position is more arguable.

How is it possible, when we find after 1200 (the certainly earliest possible date of the *Brut*), even up to 1250 (that of the *Owl and Nightingale*, etc.), metrical as opposed to rhythmical scansion barely struggling in, that not long after 1100 a perfect metrical swing of the modern kind should have been attained by one poet, and should somehow or other have failed to appear in any other? Observe too, that the rhyme is not middle-rhyme, the earlier, but end-rhyme, the later kind; that the author keeps it up with ease, instead of using only the most obvious and recurrent rhymes, and lapsing continually, as Layamon, much later than 1100, did. Of the language I do not profess to speak as an expert in even a slight degree. But of the metrical form I will say boldly that it is rather astonishingly advanced even for the middle of the thirteenth century, which is the time most probably assigned to it. And it would be almost equally astonishing if the rhymed *Paternoster* which we also have, and which Ten Brink assigns to the later half of the twelfth century, were of that date, couched as it is in the regular octosyllabic couplets which again we only find struggling into existence in Layamon. There will be few occasions in the course of this history on which we can allow ourselves even as much discussion of controversial points as this. But the order of the change in prosody is too important to dispense with it wholly here.

As it so happens, however (and here, as in the case of Layamon, the possession is precious not merely for philological but for true literary reasons), we possess more versions than one of the *Poema Morale,* and the comparison of them establishes the unlikelihood of an early date for its more finished metrical form. The sober and even yet hardly disputed authority of the late Dr. Morris does not venture to put even the elder of these earlier than "before 1200," the later he dates more plumply as "1250." And even in the 1200 version we see that the proper metrical form is only struggling out of the shell, which it has not thoroughly chipped till later. In the earlier we find such a line as this—

> Elche time sal þe man of-þunche his misdade;

which becomes in the later—

> On hwuche tyme so euer the mon of-þinkeþ his mysdede—

an almost perfect fourteener such as might have been written (were it not for the *th* letter) in the early sixteenth, or for the matter of that in the late nineteenth, century. And generally it may be laid down with the utmost confidence that the procession from rhythm to metre is astonishingly regular, and perhaps affords as good a test of date as any other. Here and there, of course, individual study or genius will make a start in front; individual clumsiness or the unfavourable nature of surroundings will cause another to lag behind. But generally the procession is as regular is the growth of a tree; and it cannot be said to be in the least interrupted—it is at the most for a time paralleled and accompanied—by the curious alliterative revival which we shall have to notice in the fourteenth century.

A considerable part of the literature of this time is only literature by courtesy, Homilies and Lives of Saints, with rare exceptions, being merely refashionings of previous matter for present consumption. These are found both in prose and in verse, the latter gradually taking the form either of the rudimentary "fourteener" just noticed, or of the octosyllabic couplet, which, as we have seen, crops up even in Layamon. The so-called *Sawles Warde,*[12] a prose homily, has a certain interest because in one of those fits of agglomeration which have been and will be noticed, and which alternate with segregation in the philological ague, it has been sought to unite its authorship with that not merely of the *Ancren Riwle,* but of *Hali Meidenhad,*[13] the *Wooing of Our Lord,*[12] and the prose *Lives of* St. Margaret,[13] St. Juliana,[13] and St. Katharine. Identifications of this kind can at the best be conjectural, and are always exceedingly rash, but they may fairly be supposed to argue on the part of those who make them the apprehension of a certain literary unity in the styles as well as in the mere language of the different books. Even this is exposed to the objection that in matter which more than any other lends itself to the adoption of "common form," which is constantly based on similar Latin originals, and which must presumably have been written in schools of conventual practice, even a great similarity is probable without an identity of authorship being fairly to be inferred; while mere agreement in grammatical and dialectic forms is the very slenderest and most treacherous of clues.

Genesis and Exodus.

There is much more purely literary interest in a verse translation or paraphrase of the books of *Genesis and Exodus,*[14] which appears to have been executed about the middle of the thirteenth century, and which has great attraction not merely for its extremely

12. In full ed. Morris, *Old English Homilies* (E.E.T.S.); part of each given in Morris-Skeat, *Specimens,* vol. i.
13. Ed. Cockayne, E.E.T.S.
14. Ed. Morris, E.E.T.S.

sharp contrast of language and form with those of the Caedmonian paraphrases, but for the intrinsic character of the form itself. Here is a passage :

For sextene ger Joseph was old
Quane he was into Egipte sold;
He was Jacobes gunkeste sune,
Brictest of wasme and of witter wune;[15]
If he sag hise brethere misfaren,
His fader he it gan un-hillen and baren.

Now it must be evident here to the most careless reader who has any ear that we have stumbled upon one of the most famous of English measures, the great *Christabel* metre itself, or in other words, the iambic dimeter with wide license of trisyllabic substitution, catalexis, and metrical truncation so as to interpose trochaic chords. The enormous influence of this (through Scott's hearing part of *Christabel* before it was published) has long been a commonplace of literary history; and it has been also often pointed out, though less often, that it was only developed, not invented, by Coleridge, inasmuch as it occurs in Spenser's *The Oak and the Brere* (*Shep. Kal.* Feb.), and in other places, including even *Comus.* But not much attention has been called[16] to its occurrence practically full-fledged, though not with all its tricks of flight yet learnt, in the middle of the thirteenth century. And it cannot, I think, be necessary to point out how vain are efforts to make out an Anglo-Saxon ancestry for it. Except on the very rarest occasions, and then in the most distant and halting fashion, there is not even an accidental resemblance to it in any Anglo-Saxon verse from *Beowulf* to *Brunanburgh.* And there could not be, for it depends for its unmatched combination of freedom and harmony

---

15. "Brightest of form and of wise wont" (habits); *ger,* of course = "year"; *gunkeste* = "youngest"; *sag*—"saw"; *unhillen* = "un*hull*" = "discover." I have taken the text from the *Specimens* as more accessible, and also because some of the MS. asperities are softened, but the whole poem ought to be read to justify the above remarks.

16. In the E.E.T.S. edition the metre is noticed, briefly, by Professor Skeat. But no attention is drawn to it in the *Specimens,* and it has, I think, been generally ignored in literary histories.

on exactly the two effects which Anglo-Saxon poetry lacked—metrical, not rhythmical, cadence and final rhyme. Only the first could give the freedom without doggerel license; only the second could give "time beat"—the warning bell which prevents that license from being overstepped at the same time that it gives harmony to the verse.

The *Bestiary.*

A *Bestiary,*[17] of the same date or thereabouts—in itself one of the numerous mediaeval renderings of the fantastic mystical zoology which was so popular, and which has already met us far earlier in the *Whale* and *Panther* of the Exeter Book—possesses interest of the same kind though rather less. This interest lies in the fact that it oscillates between unrhymed accentuation and rhymed metre; for we shall almost invariably find (and it is surprising that poets like Campion and Milton centuries later failed to discern the fact) that rhyme and metre are in modern languages almost indissolubly bound together—English blank verse being mainly a "sport," though, as we shall see later, an extremely interesting and valuable sport. At one time in the *Bestiary* we find somewhat irregular and broken-down alliteration, not very dissimilar from the non-rhymed parts of Layamon. At another we come upon wandering and uncertainly octosyllabic couplets, fairly constant in their rhymes, but as "wobbling" in point of syllabic constitution as the nearly contemporary examples of the same metre that we find in Germany and Spain. Anon will come a series (evidently inspired by some hymn) of very respectable eights and sixes rhymed in quatrains, and a good deal better than Tate and Brady, but with the same tendency to sevens instead of sixes which we find in the unrhymed *Ormulum,* and which .may be accounted for by the still over-inflected state of the language. And yet again the unrhymed couplet of the *Ormulum* itself meets us to show the staggering state of the writer or writers. For even if—which would be rather improbable—the book were a composition from more hands than one, the absence of any prevailing metre would be equally noticeable and equally striking by

17. Ed. Wright, *Reliquiae Antiquae,* i, 208; ed. Morris, *Old English Miscellany,* p. 1. Some in *Specimens.*

contrast, especially with the almost tyrannous predominance of the regular octosyllable in all but strictly lyrical work in France at the same time. Most noteworthy of all perhaps is the fact that these quatrains or couplets are mixed, the writer sometimes, it would seem, being unable to hit upon rhyme, though he would if he could.

Nor does the same fruitful source of interest fail in an earlier production of the sacred kind—the so-called *Orison of our Lady,*[18] to which as early a date as 1210 is assigned. This is in couplets and very fairly rhymed, but the lines have not settled down into anything like even length. They range from the fourteeners and fifteeners of the *Ormulum* and the *Moral Ode* to—and this is where the importance of the poem comes in—examples of no less famous a form than the decasyllable itself.[19] It has always been matter of surprise that this famous form, the earliest staple of French, and in one way or another, as decasyllable or hendecasyllable, making its appearance early in the other Romance languages, should have been so late to appear in English. I do not mean that definite decasyllabic couplets can be found in the *Orison*—the writer's grip of his metre, or rather his conception of what he means to grip, is too loose for that. And indeed, though attempts of the kind are not uncommon in Hampole, it is extremely doubtful whether they are not merely accidental in all cases before Chaucer—the tendency either to the short octosyllable, the long line halved, or the composite fourteener being apparently irresistible. But that the decasyllable should appear at all (as it does later in Langland's alliteration) is the important thing. There is no simile or metaphor that suits these metrical appearances so well as the old one of the coral island, which first makes uncertain show just awash, with a few points, and in the course of ages establishes itself as a complete and continuous reef or atoll.

The *Orison of our Lady.*

18. Whole in Morris, *Old English Homilies,* i, 191; more than half in *Specimens.*

19. Cristes | milde | moder | seynte | Marie—
Al is | the heouen | e ful | of thin | e blisse.

The metrical uncertainty of the *Bestiary* and the *Orison* displays itself also in the curious *Proverbs of Alfred*,[20] to which, in their present form, no older date than the middle of the thirteenth century is assigned, but which must be far older in substance, and which may not quite fancifully be connected with the King's *Ephemeris* noticed above. They may be most conveniently taken in comparison with the somewhat later, but not much later, *Proverbs of Hendyng*,[21] attributed to a mythical person of that name, son of the equally mythical "Marcolf," who in scores of different forms holds colloquy with Solomon in mediaeval writings. The same familiar saws make their appearance in both with little variation—"A fool's bolt is soon shot," "Spare rod and spoil child," etc. This has of itself a genuine literary interest, because these products of the wisdom of many and the wit of one, thus passing through all English literature, act as tie-rods to maintain its continuity.[22] But the form has interest as well as the matter. The later or Hendyng proverbs are in regular six-lined stanzas of the so-called Romance form, rhymed *aabaab*. In those assigned to Alfred we have over again, but with a distinctly greater tendency toward the predominance of rhyme, the Layamon jumble of regular rhymed or even assonanced couplet, and of equally regular alliterated stave. Some of the sections, each introduced with a "Thus quoth Alfred," are rhymed throughout in couplets of a somewhat staggering dimeter; some show no rhyme at all; and in some it emerges and sinks again after much the same fashion as in the *Bestiary*. In fact, the moral to be drawn from all these poems, even singly but much more together, is that rhyme and metrical equivalence of verse, struggling still at the beginning of the thirteenth century, had by its middle got so distinctly the better that everybody turned to rhyme, that most

Proverbs of Alfred and Hendyng.

20. To be found, like the *Bestiary*, both in *Reliquiae Antiquiae*, i, 170, and in *An Old English Miscellany*, two texts (102, 103 *sq.*). Part again in *Specimens.*

21. *Rel. Antiq.*, i, 109. Extracts will be found in the *second* part of Morris and Skeat's *Specimens*, where the work is dated 1272-1307.

22. So, I may note in passing, the pet Elizabethan antithesis of "Wit" and "Will" appears at this time in a short piece given by Morris, *Old English Miscellany*, p. 192.

people tried to write pretty regular metrical verse, and that very fair success crowned both attempts. Such success was especially remarkable in the last poem of this period which will claim detailed notice, a poem which is at the same time one of the best.

The Owl and the Nightingale.

This is *The Owl and the Nightingale,*[23] a poem of some 2000 lines in fairly regular octosyllabic couplets, which is attributed to one Nicholas de Guildford, who lived at Portesham in Dorsetshire, and which cannot be much later than the middle of the thirteenth century. The form of it is the very common mediaeval one of the *débat,* as it is called in French—a metrical dispute between two persons or things, which may range from a mere exhibition of their several qualities, intended to instruct the reader and show the poet's learning, to a "flyting" of the kind popular mudi later in Scotland. The general scheme is, of course, a contest and conflict between "crabbed age and youth," between gravity and gaiety, but the Nightingale is the aggressor and the more violent in her language, while the poet seems rather to incline to the side of the Owl. Certainly the Nightingale indulges in the greater personality, and makes on the whole less ingenious use of her case. It is, for instance, a distinct hit of the Owl, when her rival has pleaded that she teaches priests to sing, and increases the joy of man, to retaliate that there are numerous countries where the Nightingale does not go at all, and that she had better make up for this by going and teaching the priests in Ireland and Scotland, in Galloway and Scandinavia, to do their duty. And the bird of Pallas has also a good "flyte" on the moral side (one which she could have justified abundantly from French and Provençal poetry) in her suggestion that the

23. I use Wright's ed. for the Percy Society, 1843. The poem (of which there are large pieces in the *Specimens*) was printed earlier (1838) for the Roxburghe Club by Stevenson, and later (1868) at Krefeld by Stratmann, the compiler of the completest M.E. Lexicon. Wright's ed. contains some interesting shorter poems, perhaps by the same author, and these with others (but not the *Owl*) reappear in an *Old English Miscellany.* The best of the latter is a *Love-Rune,* a (religious) Love Song, assigned to Thomas of Halys, and apparently versified from part of the *Ancren Riwle.*

principal effect of the Nightingale's song is to make women false to their husbands, and to get them into various sorts of trouble. This passage contains an allusion which seems to tie the poem down to the reign of Henry III.

On the whole, this is the best example of the octosyllabic couplet to be found before the fourteenth century. The poet (who, by the way, quotes "Alfred" repeatedly, and little else) occasionally commits the fault—specially unpleasing to modern English ears, but natural at his early date, and probably connected with the indifference of his French originals to identical rhymes—of making the same rhyme do for two successive couplets; but this does not occur often enough to interfere seriously with harmony. His variations from eights to sevens are not more than the genius of the language specially allows. His style is easy and his poetical imagery and apparatus generally, though comparatively simple, well at command, and by no means of a rude or rudimentary order. We cannot, of course, say that he may not have been directly indebted to a French original, for the theme is one which must almost certainly have tempted the tireless ingenuity of the troubadours and trouvères of the twelfth and thirteenth centuries in France and Provence. But we have no direct original, and in such a case it is only fair to credit Nicholas (or whoever he was) with independence. It should be observed that the name occurs in the poem as that of the referee selected by the birds and their audience-arbiter the Wren. He is very handsomely spoken of, and the bishops are reproached because he has only one "wonning"—and tithing, which has made some think that the author cannot have referred to himself. But this argument, which is a sound one at the date and in the circumstances of the *Shepherd's Calendar,* has not much weight in reference to a "finder" of the thirteenth century, at which date and in which class men were by no means wont to be troubled with excessive modesty. Moreover, there is a not impossible touch of humour in the passages relating to "Maister Nichole"—

> Through [whose] mouth and through [whose] hand
> It is the better into Scotland!

It should be remarked also, before concluding, that in this

poem, as in all others of the time, the language is by no means freely gallicised.

At no long time in front of this period romances must have begun to be written in English, and three of not the least interesting that we have, *Havelok, Horn,* and *Sir Tristrem,* are allowed even by jealous literary chronologists to be probably older than the year 1300. But the advantage of treating the Anglo-French romance together is so great and obvious, that it will be better to relegate these to a future chapter.[24]

24. The *fabliau* of *Dame Siriz* (Wright's *Anecdota Literaria,* 1844), *The Vox* [Fox] *and the Wolf (Reliquiae Antiquae,* ii, 272-78), an interesting and Early English version of *Reynard,* and others, might be added. The *Christabel* variation occurs in these also; but *Genesis and Exodus* appears to be much the earliest and most considerable example thereof.

3

SECOND MIDDLE ENGLISH PERIOD 1300-1360

Robert of Gloucester—Robert Manning—Lyrics—The *Ayenbite of Inwyt*—The Northern Psalter—Manning—William of Shoreham—The *Cursor Mundi*—Hampole—Adam Davy—Laurence Minot—*Cleanness* and *Patience*—*The Pearl.*

THE latter part of the thirteenth century is not a very fruitful period of English literature—so far at least as attributions that can be called in any way certain, or even probable, are concerned. We have glanced at possible romances. Of other work we have, dating from the extreme end of the thirteenth century and the earlier half of the fourteenth, a very considerable body of theological literature of the old kind, exhibiting characteristics frequently of linguistic and occasionally of literary interest; at least one named and known writer of such literature, Richard Rolle of Hampole, who, though his importance has, as usual, been exaggerated, is of some mark; at least one individual religious poem, the *Cursor Mundi,* which, though its authorship is unknown, is remarkable not merely for size; two most interesting and important new developments—the verse-history of more or less contemporary events, and the accomplished lyric in the new prosody; and (to mention only work of distinction) at the extreme close of the period, or a little beyond it, a group of companions of very remarkable poetical merit, which have been thought to be of common authorship, the *Pearl, Cleanness,* and *Patience,* to which some would add the very attractive alliterative romance of *Gawain and the Greene Knight.* This latter will be most conveniently dealt with later, the others had best be handled here. All four pieces were at any rate connected with a very curious literary phenomenon, the resurrection of alliterative verse, which had some good consequences, and but for Chaucer might have had many more bad ones.

The earliest of these works, or group of works, in point of time, and not the least interesting in literary history, if not of the first intrinsic literary merit, is the batch of verse-histories, of which Robert of Gloucester's is the oldest. This is dated about two years before the close of the thirteenth century, while Robert Manning, or Robert of Brunne, comes some thirty years later.

Robert of Gloucester.

Robert of Gloucester[1] is a very interesting person, and a much better poet than it has been the fashion to represent him, though his first object was not poetry, and though, had it been so, he was but ill equipped. It is not known when he was born, but he did not write, or finish writing, till quite the close of the thirteenth century, though he had personal remembrance of the civil wars in the latter part of Henry III's reign, and carried his own chronicle to the year 1272. He was not superior to the odd craze which induced most of the historians of this time to begin with the Siege of Troy, and he abstracts Geoffrey of Monmouth for a considerable part of his book with that docility which, though it may seem singular in the transferred sense of the word, was universal as far as almost all his contemporaries were concerned. With Anglo-Saxon history he deals slightly, and despite his ardent English patriotism—his book opens with a vigorous panegyric of England, the first of a series extending to the present day (from which an anthology *De Laudibus Angliae* might be made)—he deals very harshly with Harold Godwinson. From the Conquest onward he does his best to draw on French, Latin, and English sources alike, reinforcing them in the later years with personal recollections or reminiscences, as in the case of the Oxford town-and-gown row of 1263.

1. First printed by Hearne, with Manning, etc., in 1724. I use the 1810 reprint (4 vols.) of these.

Although, however, Robert is in many places agreeable to read for the story and for his spirited temper, yet the main interest in him for the literary historian is still connected with his form and vehicle. This is the long swinging verse, half-trochaic, half-anapaestic, which we have already watched in its development, as the new metrical prosody beat it out of the ancient alliterated and unmetrical stave, and which was to be ever improved and suppled from this date to that of Mr. Morris's *Sigurd the Volsung.* This line may be said to have two normal varieties, towards which it unconsciously directs itself. Of one of these, Robert's first line, hardly altered:

> Enge | land is a | right good | land, I | ween of all | lands the | best —

is a very fair average example, and the poet not unfrequently equals it. But he has also some inclination towards the other form, which in its perfection is simply the iambic fourteener so much spoken of in the last chapter—

> By her | he had | a daugh | ter sweet | the goo | dỳ queen | ỳ Maud |

But, as might be expected, he not merely oscillates between these two cadences, but frequently rolls or staggers into others—sometimes considerably less musical; while he is by no means free from the tendency to cut the line so short that with a slight change in pronunciation it would become neither more nor less than a decasyllable, as in—

> And took | him hos | tage good | at his | own will |

where no doubt the contemporary value of some words would disguise the length. Nor is this the only possibility which his uncertain movement develops, for again elsewhere we have approaches to the pure anapaestic tetrameter, also to become a favourite metre later—

> An house | of reli | gion of ca | nons ywis |

though in the same manner here the full syllabic value of "religion" would obscure for the time the cadence. The point has, however, been dwelt upon here because it is an interesting help towards the comprehension of the manner in which *all* the stock English metres resulted from the clash of the strict

French syllabic prosody, of the Latin syllabic equivalence, and of the Anglo-Saxon tolerance of extra-metrical, or rather extra-rhythmical syllables. That the French decasyllable itself helped the English analogue to emerge is perfectly true, but there is no need to regard the latter as a foreign importation.

The peculiarity of this metre (which, though its ancestor, is still not by any means the same as our hymn common measure, a strict iambic metre without trisyllabic liberties, and never shifting the foot to trochaic rhythm) is very closely reproduced in a large body of Lives of the Saints of about the same period, which accordingly good authorities have regarded as being also the work of Robert of Gloucester. Mr. W.H. Black, who edited one of them, that dealing with Becket, more than fifty years ago,[2] was very positive on the subject, and the latest authorities[3] seem to have no objection. The beautiful Celtic legend of *St. Brandan*[4] has also been edited from this collection, as well as others. It must, of course, be obvious that the adoption of the form for things so popular as Saints' Lives both testifies to its own popularity and would help to confirm and spread this. And it is perhaps not rash to add that there are points in it which would rather encourage the relapse on alliteration which we shall have to notice at the end of this chapter. In the first place, the extreme looseness of the verse—almost the most mobile of all English forms—tends that way; and in the second the great distance of the rhyme-safeguards from each other makes them more likely to be overpowered, if not overlooked.

From this same point of view the interest of Robert's forty years later successor, Robert Manning, is well sustained, though in other respects it falls short. This second Robert, whom we shall meet again in this chapter, was a Gilbertine canon, and derived his surname from

Robert Manning.

2. Percy Society, 1845.
3. Morris and Skeat (*Specimens*, ii, 1) reprint selections from the *Chronicle* and the *Life of St. Dunstan* as Robert's.
4. Ed. Wright, Percy Society, 1844. All, from Laud MS., E.E.T.S., ed. Horstmann, who has also given collections of Saints' Lives—*Alt-Englische Legenden*—Paderborn, 1875; Heilbronn, 1878 and 1881.

the place of his birth, Brunne or Bourn in Lincolnshire. The authorities are generous to him in the matter of life, supposing that it may have extended from about 1260 to about 1340, or even later; but this is mere guesswork. It seems that his history was not finished till 1338. Unlike Robert of Gloucester's, it was a translation, or rather, as all mediaeval translations are, an adaptation, of a single work, the chronicle written in French, but by an Englishman, Peter Langtoft, canon of Bridlington, with amplifications from Wace and other sources. Historically he has not much importance, nor can his work be said to equal the other Robert's in direct literary attraction.[5] But for the study of the history of English metre it is very valuable. Langtoft had written in the ordinary measure of the later *chansons de geste,* monorhymed *laisses* of twelve-syllabled lines, and Manning was clearly under the impression that he must get as near to this as he could. In his prefatory remarks he employs the regular octosyllabic couplet, the earliest of all our metres; but this would not have done for the body of the work. He accordingly, having none of his namesake's swing, contented himself with a very prosaic line, which at its best is the fourteener, at its worst an indefinite number of syllables which some might call a "verse of four accents" because of its rebelliousness to any more accomplished arrangement.

It was about rhyme, however, that Robert Manning seems to have been most careful and troubled. Sometimes he is content to let these shambling lines of his rhyme in couplets. But ever and anon his conscience seems to prick him, and he either adds middle rhyme or attempts the, in English almost hopeless, task of emulating the continued rhymes of his original. Of these he achieves sometimes as many as a score, but always with a result equally cacophonous and lame.

To those, however, who are not satisfied with merely formal interest, the next division to which we come will have far greater attraction, while to those who can appreciate both form and spirit it will have altogether exceptional charm. This

5. It ought to be said that important authorities, Sir Frederic Madden and Dr. Furnivall, have thought better of Manning's poetical power, but chiefly, I think, as shown in *Handlyng Synne.*

division consists of the first blossoming of English lyric properly so-called. The famous *Sumer is icumen in,* the Cuckoo-Song long ago printed by Sir John Hawkins, and made popular by Ellis in his *Specimens* for more than a century past, has generally had, as observed above, the credit assigned to it of being the actually oldest piece of the kind, and though such attributions are always rather temerarious, there is no need to disturb this particular one if the date is not carried back too far. The poem is in very short lines and of a simple and almost rude structure, besides being more noticeable for its fresh and genuine observation of nature than for any very poetical spirit. Rhyme is quite established in it, but it may easily be of the thirteenth century, and perhaps as early as its middle. It is not, however, till the close thereof that we get any considerable collection of lyrics of great merit on profane subjects.[6] This is the collection taken from the MS. known as 2253 Harl., preserved in the British Museum. Its prettiest piece, *Alison,* was also printed by Ellis, whose taste in these matters, though just a little touched with eighteenth-century Voltairianism, was excellent; but the whole collection did not appear till Thomas Wright, that benefactor of our literature, printed it for the Percy Society on 1st March 1842, a particularity of date which may be pardoned in consideration of the exceptional charm of the work and of its importance in English literary history. For though there must have been other poems of the kind written, and though we actually have a few, they have not been collected as they should have been into a *corpus,* and the total does not appear to be very large.

Lyrics.

It is obvious, though it is not the less important for its obviousness, that these poems, like all the lyrical work of Europe during the thirteenth century, were composed not in slavish imitation, but in generous yet none the less distinct following, of the troubadours of Provence and the trouvères of

6. The shorter poems mentioned in the last chapter (p. 60, note) must not be forgotten, but they are almost entirely sacred. At the same time, as the maiden asked the author of *A Love Rune* for an actual love-song, love-songs must have been written.

Northern France.[7] In the course probably of the twelfth century, certainly by its end, these poets had almost exhausted the possible combinations of lyric so far as strictly syllabic prosody went, and within the limitations of dissyllabic feet which the structure of both languages imposed. There are vestiges of trisyllabic arrangement in Northern French, but they disappear early. The English minstrel and the German minnesinger took these models and adapted them, but in each case gave more or less scope to the irrepressible craving of Teutonic lips and ears for the triple movement.

This Romance influence is plainly evidenced in the collection before us by the very fact of its being bilingual. Of the forty-two pieces printed by Wright, the three first and others later are in French. But the fourth, beginning

Middelerd for mon is made,

is in English, and at once introduces us to a complete and distinctly elaborate lyrical arrangement. There is still, as in almost all Middle English poetry—even in Chaucer himself—a great deal of alliteration, but it has no influence on the actual form. This consists of an eleven-line stanza, which proceeds as far as the octave in regular "eights," admitting catalexis, rhymed *abababab,* and completes itself with a six, eight, six *coda* or "bob" rhymed *cbc.* The next has ten-lined stanzas monorhymed in the octave, which consists of heavily alliterated "four-accent" doggerel tipped with a decasyllabic couplet differently rhymed, and approaching more closely to a regular decasyllable. This is not a good piece, but the next, the *Alison,* which is, or ought to be, as famous as *Sumer is icumen in,* is quite delightful—the first perfectly delightful thing in English poetry. The lovely intertwined music of its twelve-lined stanzas, composed of an eight and six quatrain, an eight triplet, a six, another eight triplet, and another six, rhymed *ababbbcdddc,* is not too good for the simple but fervid passion and the charming imagery of the piece. It is no exaggeration to say that the promise of Donne and Herrick, of Burns and Shelley, is in *Alison.*

7. The *direct* influence of Provence was probably very small. But it has been sometimes assumed on the strength of the marriage of Henry III.

A careful study of the various metres of these poems will show that, in spite of occasional lapses from strict metrical propriety, there was practically no secret of English prosody which was not at least ready to be unlocked for English poets. Even their greatest license, the shrinkage of the octosyllable to seven or even six, which is so freely allowed, had this of merit in it, that it served as an additional safeguard against the cast-iron syllabic uniformity of their Romance models, which would have fatally hampered the varied music of English. There is as yet less tendency to extend, and the influence of the same models as yet checks anapaestic movement. But even this appears, and it was certain to be encouraged by that beneficent process of regular dropping of inflections, and the final *è* in particular, which went on without cessation till the fifteenth century. When one man gave a word the value of three syllables and another that of two, it was practically impossible that an absolute mould like that of a Latin Alcaic, or a French scheme of any sort, should be adopted. Nor is the fact that in these poems we occasionally find polyglot French or Latin lines in alternation with English to be regarded as a matter of little consequence. For it cannot be too often repeated that what English wanted now was exactly that "madman to mix it" who, according to the proverb (of Spanish origin, I think), is required to make a good salad. The three tongues, with their different cadences, their different structure, their different prosodic ideals, could not be shaken up against each other too much in order to produce that matchless blend the English poetic language, with its unequalled combination of freedom and order, and its inexhaustible resources of varied melody.

The most noticeable metre, though not the best, that emerges from this pleasant welter of experiment is that romance sestet or *rime coućе* (its old French name), which, as we shall see in the next chapter, by degrees rivalled, and again by other degrees even outdid, the regular octosyllabic couplet as the favourite vehicle of narrative poetry. Its great drawback, the danger of a sing-song monotony, which Chaucer brought out in the memorable but rather unfair burlesque of *Sir Thopas,* appears at once. But English literature owes it a distinct debt.

If it is more exposed to this danger, it is less exposed to that of undistinguished fluency than the couplet, the "ungirt" character of which did much harm to French poetry and (till Chaucer showed how it might be strengthened and varied) to English. And it provided what was now specially wanted, a go-cart of fairly accomplished but not in the least difficult metrical stanza in which the growing language could practise itself. The earlier stages of no literature can be properly understood unless this function of exercise is apprehended. And such stages have the immense and untiring attraction of future, of promise, joined to that, more delicate but even more poignant, of antiquity and of the past.[8]

Although, as has been pointed out, the sacred division of this literature forms much the larger part in bulk, it is, for reasons already also indicated, of less literary importance than the profane. Linguistically, however, it helps very largely to build the bridge over what would be otherwise in most cases the unbridged gulf between the Anglo-Saxon of the eleventh century and the accomplished Middle English of the fourteenth; and in so far as it is in verse, it supplies many useful links and tell-tales in that surpassingly interesting examination of prosodic change which, as has been said, really constitutes, for literature, the chief attraction of this period in English.

The *Ayenbite of Inwyt.*

Of this attraction the prose part of this division of literature is necessarily divested, and its principal monument, the *Ayenbite of Inwyt*[9] of Dan Michel of Northgate (a translation from the same treatise, the *Somme des Vices et des Vertus* of a French monk named Laurence, which afterwards served as the stuff of Chaucer's *Parson's Tale),* is, with some sermons by the same author, of little or no interest as literature. Indeed it is almost the worst possible even of translations, executed with no intelligence,

8. Four of the best of these pieces, including *Alison* and the only less charming *Lenten is come with love to town,* will be found in Morris and Skeat's *Specimens.*

9. Ed. Morris, E.E.T.S. The eccentric-looking title only requires a minute's consideration to explain itself as the "again-biting" (= "re-morse," cf. Pecock's vocabulary in Book iv, *infra*) of inner wit (= conscience).

and simply beaten out, word for often mistaken word. Its quaint Kentish dialect, far more uncouth than that of much earlier work, and surprisingly so when we remember that it was probably written as late as the year (1340) of Chaucer's probable birth, constitutes an attraction for the philologist With its *z's* for *s's* and other peculiarities, it suggests the original of the kind of composite *patois,* now chiefly suggesting to us that of the extreme south-west, which we find in Shakespeare and in other literary English up to the present century. Nor is the contemporary Northern prose ascribed to Hampole or his disciples (of whom more *infra)* without a certain interest of curiosity, while it is distinctly less archaic and more literary than the *Ayenbite.* But in strictness there is no English prose that really deserves much attention from the literary point of view until the latter half of the fourteenth century. "Let the *Ancren Riwle* be saved alone by its flavour," as Saint-Evremond says of the snipe among brown meats.

With verse—still, as always in the Middle Ages, the maid-of-all-work of literature—the case is different. The verse Homilies and Lives of Saints steadily continue, and furnish us from time to time with fresh examples of the manner in which the ordinary versifier handled his tools. Of much greater interest is a certain Metrical Version of the Psalms[10] in Yorkshire or Northumbrian dialect, which is sometimes stated to be of the thirteenth century, but which the devotees of Hampole assign to their favourite, in which case it would be thirty or forty years younger at least. The present writer has no pretensions to decide on linguistic grounds, and is not of the Hampole fanatics. But the metrical arrangement of the Psalter certainly seems to favour rather the later than the earlier date, and in any case to argue a writer distinctly above the common in literary and poetical gifts. The metre is the octosyllable, seldom or never shortened to less than sevens, but often extended into that form which I have taken to be the probable original of the

The Northern Psalter.

10. First published by the Surtees Society in 1843; to be found in vol. ii, pp. 129-273, of Dr. Horstmann's great Hampolian Miscellany, London, 1896. Some examples in *Specimens.*

heroic couplet. The slight harshness (not going beyond an agreeable astringency) of the Northern dialect is compatible with, and here attains, a considerable dignity; the feeble fluency which is the curse of the octosyllabic couplet seldom or never appears; the expletives which are almost a greater curse not merely of the couplet but of stanza-writing at this time, and from which even Chaucer did not entirely free himself, are mainly absent; and the phrase and arrangement possess that grave stateliness which is so suitable to religious poetry, and which, except in the late sixteenth and early seventeenth centuries, it has too often lacked.

Manning.

There is not so much dignity, though there is rather more freedom and engagingness, in the *Handling Sin*[11] of Robert Manning, already mentioned as a historian. There is much significance for literary history in the fact that this, like Manning's secular work, was a translation from the French work of an English predecessor, in this case the *Manuel des Péchés* of William of Waddington. This work, containing, after homiletic fashion, stories of the pious *fabliau* kind, gave some practice in tale-telling, and is not unimportant among the ancestry of Chaucer. Contemporary with Manning, but in the South not the North, was another named writer of religious verse, William of Shoreham (the Kentish not the Sussex Shoreham), who lived and wrote in the first quarter of the fourteenth century at Leeds and Chart Sutton, in the district between Maidstone and Canterbury. Shoreham[12] dealt in verse with the Sacraments, the Seven Deadly Sins, the Ten Commandments, the service of Our Lady, and even the higher questions of theology, such as immortality and the existence of God. The curious thing—though it would not have seemed curious to anybody then—is the selection of lyric metres for such subjects. Thus, for instance, the *Poem on Baptism,* which is the most easily accessible of his works, being given in Morris and Skeat's *Selections,* is couched in a seven-line stanza, rhymed *xaxabxb,*

William of Shoreham.

11. Ed. Furnivall for the Roxburghe Club, 1862; for the E.E.T.S. 1901, *sq.*

12. Ed. Wright for the Percy Society, 1849.

in which *x* stands for unrhymed lines of *ad libitum* ending. And the unsuitableness of the form to modern eyes and ears is completed by the fact that while the first quatrain is of *Ormulum* eights and sevens, and the last couplet of the same, the fifth line is a "bob" or short catch of two or three syllables only. But there was nothing incongruous in this then to the reader or hearer, while the invincible patience of the mediaeval *scriptorium* made it no doubt easy enough to the writer.[13]

We have, as has been said, for this time a fair supply of verse homilies, usually in octosyllables; but by far the most interesting verse divinity of the period is contained in the huge poem or collection called the *Cursor Mundi.*[14]

The *Cursor Mundi.*

This enormous, but by no means tedious, production has been put at the service of every reader by the more than mediaeval diligence of the late Dr. Morris, in four parallel texts exhibiting different forms of dialect and substance, with appendices containing parts of others. The longest version just falls short of 30,000 lines, and the total in all forms cannot be much below five times this amount.

The poem, however, is of real interest and value. The author, who writes in octosyllabic couplets of considerable ease and spirit, begins by acknowledging the general desire for rhymes and romances of Alexander, of Troy, of Arthur, of Sir Isumbras and Sir Amadas, and of Charlemagne, most of which deal with earthly love. But earthly love fails, the love of Our Lady (in whose honour he writes his book) dies not. He intends to tell the whole of the Bible history—

Into Inglis tong to rede,
For the love of Inglis lede (people)—

and he does so.

But the way in which he does it is the true mediaeval divagation. Not merely does he dilate on such incidents as

13. The Athanasian Creed may be found paraphrased in sixains of eights and fours at p. 139 of Wright's edition.

14. Ed. Morris (E.E.T.S.), in seven parts.

please him with perfect freedom; not merely does he comment on them in the homiletic manner, letting the narrative stand-still, but in the arbitrary, uncritical, to us now inconceivable, but always charming, fashion of the time, he incorporates with the Scriptural narrative itself any fragments of hagiology, any traditional stories—sometimes of a more or less mundane character—and any, it may be, inventions of his own, that come into his head. The fall of the angels, the Creation, the loss of Paradise are expanded with rather less than the amplifications usual in these cases, until we come to that delightful legend, the Story of the Three Trees, which plays such an important part in the earlier stages of the Arthurian cycle. Afterwards, we pass few of the Biblical data without finding them enriched by fresh details, as that Lamech's daughter Noema was the first "webster," and that man became carnivorous after the Deluge only, because the earth had so much of the goodness washed out of it by the water that its fruit was not strong enough to support man, whose own constitution was likewise debilitated.

Among the pains least lost upon this interesting book, those spent upon the classification of its materials may perhaps be counted. Much seems to have been taken from the History of Petrus Comestor in the twelfth century, something from poems of Wace, who, as we have seen, was much in the hands of English writers, together with a good deal from Grostête's *Castle of Love,* the apocryphal Gospels of Matthew and Nicodemus, and the works of Isidore of Seville. The fact is that, at first or second hand, the books at the disposal of an ordinary mediaeval writer were pretty constant; and the frequent reappearance of the same or similar legends is not at all difficult to account for.

The important thing, however, in this as in all cases, is not the information which was at a writer's disposal, but the use he makes of it. The author of the *Cursor Mundi*—

The best book of all,
"The Course of the World" men do it call—

(as one enthusiastic copyist prefaces it)—knew very well indeed how to use his materials. Long as the book is, and familiar as is the main substance, if not the occasional settings-off, it can be read with ease and pleasure from beginning to end by any one who has time, and can be dipped into with satisfaction by those who have not. The Cotton version is perhaps, on the whole, the best to read, though there is not very much difference. The satisfaction comes from the easy but not at all slipshod way in which the writer manages his metre, the simple but by no means contemptible art with which he mixes and varies his materials, and the shrewd but kindly sense of his comments and observations. In speaking of the destruction of the Cities of the Plain—a subject generally exciting to mediaeval imagination—he cannot rise to the indignant passion of the later poem called *Cleanness* (*vide infra*), but he acquits himself very well, and never falls into the falsetto of moral indignation. The "Three Trees" story above referred to is told very effectively; and the Life of Christ, varied and heightened as it is by the additions from apocryphal story, makes a religious romance of high merit. He is proverbial without being over-sententious, good in description without descending to too much detail (an excellence rare in medieval times, perhaps not common in any); he has throughout his immense narrative a distinct sense of proportion. It is really a pity that we do not know his name, for if not exactly a great man or a genius, he must certainly have been a person of no ordinary ability.

Hampole.

Yet in the ignorance of the name of an author there is a certain consolation, inasmuch as he is less likely to be made the theme of uncritical criticism. This latter has been the lot of the one named author of importance who falls to be noticed in this chapter, Richard Rolle of Hampole, the author certainly of the *Stimulus Conscientiae* or *Prick of Conscience,* the author, more or less probably, of a considerable number of other works both in Latin and English, and the reputed author of many more still. Rolle is the first Middle English author of whom we have anything approaching to a full biographical account (we have even a portrait of him which may be authentic), and his history as told by himself is certainly not uninteresting. He must have been born about the meeting of the thirteenth and fourteenth centuries, at Thornton, in the North Riding of Yorkshire, not far from Pickering; his death is set by the author of his *Vita,* with more exactness, at 29th September 1349. It will have been observed from one or two scattered notices already, that the literary effacement of the North, which had been begun by the Danish fury in the ninth century, and had been renewed by the devastations of the Conqueror and the Scottish wars in the eleventh and twelfth, had shown signs of ceasing, and Richard Rolle seems to have had every advantage of education. His father, William, was a friend of Sir John Dalton, and may have been connected with the great family of Neville. At any rate Richard, after some home instruction, was sent to Oxford by Thomas Neville, Archdeacon of Durham. In the second decade of the fourteenth century there were no colleges but Merton, Balliol, Exeter, and University, nor does there seem to be any record of Rolle's connection with any of these. But the University itself was at the height of its vogue: halls and hostels were innumerable. Richard appears to have become fairly competent in the scholastic philosophy which was the chief study of the place, but, like other devotional mystics, to have mistrusted merely intellectual teaching, and is said to have left Oxford and returned to Yorkshire in his nineteenth year, determined to adopt the life of a hermit, *not* "unholy of works," as Langland was to put it a generation later. The way in which, still to borrow from his successor, he "shope him a shroud" was slightly grotesque, for he borrowed two of his sister's gowns, a grey and a white one, cut off the grey sleeves, then put on the white gown first and the grey over it, completed his uniform with one of his father's hoods (black, it may be presumed), and ran away. It is not surprising to hear that his injured sister thought him mad and cried out that he was so. He had known the young Daltons at Oxford, and this or some other reason induced him to make for their father's estate, supposed to be near Thirsk (an easy day's journey from Pickering), where he appeared at church and entered the Daltons' pew. He was recognised, and allowed first to sing, then to preach—an illustration of the easygoing ways of that mediaeval Christianity which has been represented by and to the ignorant as a tyrannical and hidebound system of ceremonial.

After he had been for a time an almost unwilling guest of the Daltons, the father gave him a cell, an allowance, and, with the proper dress, the recognised status of a hermit.

These details have been given because, with the exception of the Caedmon story, they are almost the first fragments of literary biography in English. The accounts of the remainder of Richard's life are less picturesque. He remained for some years in the hermitage which Sir John Dalton had given him, attaining at last complete "conversion," and it would appear converting others, sometimes travelling to do so. From the Thirsk hermitage he seems to have transferred himself to one in the Richmondshire district of his native Riding. We hear something of his friends here, especially an anchoress named Margaret Kirkby. But at last he made another move to Hampole, near Doncaster, in the extreme south of the county, and abode there for the rest of his life in the neighbourhood of a Cistercian nunnery, where he seems to have had disciples. He may have died of the first outbreak of the Black Death, which coincided with the date above given, and his sepulchre, which was carefully tended by the nuns, became famous for miracles.

The works of Hampole[15] are, as has been said, both Latin and English. The former do not directly concern us, but it is noticeable that the alliteration of which we shall presently hear so much is very obvious in them as well as in the English. They also contain perhaps the clearest exhibitions of his religious opinions. These centred round that mystical clinging to Divine Love which was the frequent, and no doubt the natural, reaction from the intense but hard intellectuality of scholasticism. Although Hampole has all the mediaeval terror of the "soft mystery" of woman's love, though he cannot reach the noble directness and passionate sanity of the author of *Cleanness,* he had an odd aversion to "rules," to the regular monkish institutions, which explains, or at any rate is a very early

15. The *Prick of Conscience* was edited by Morris for the Philological Society (1863). The E.E.T.S. added some *English Prose Treatises* (ed. Perry). Dr. Horstmann's Hampolian Thesaurus above referred to is entitled *Yorkshire Writers,* 2 vols. London, 1895-96.

symptom of, the deterioration of monachism apparent in England.

His principles also appear in his English works, but it is not with his principles that we are here concerned. The study of him would have been facilitated if his latest, most extensive, and most enthusiastic editor, Dr. Horstmann, had indulged his readers with the usual compliment of a table of contents, the absence of which is at all times troublesome, but positively bewildering in the case of a thousand large pages of small print, arranged, as far as the verse is concerned, in double columns, and consisting of scores and hundreds of separate pieces of all lengths. This edition, moreover, does not contain the *Prick of Conscience,* Hampole's chief work. This is a poem containing nearly 10,000 lines, dealing with the Life of Man, its uncertainty, and the Four Last Things. The matter has a sort of shuddering intensity which is very noticeable, and which sometimes gives direct picturesque force. The form is the octosyllabic couplet with distinct trisyllabic admixture in the *Christabel* direction. It has been pointed out already that this scheme constantly tends towards something that may be indifferently scanned as a "four-accent" verse with trisyllabic sections and a heroic of five iambs. Such things, *e.g.*—

> The b(o)ugh | es are | the ar | mes with | the handes
> And the | legges | with the | fete | that standes |

are, or are like, heroic couplets, and accordingly it has not been very unusual to claim for Hampole the use, or even by a singular want of understanding of the facts the invention, of the metre before Chaucer. This is uncritical, if *deliberate* use is meant.

His prose treatises contain nothing very remarkable as literature, though they may, with care, be taken as further stages in the chain which leads from the *Ancren Riwle* to Chaucer's *Parson's Tale.* But his minor poems, if they be his, have much more merit, and excel in this respect the *Prick of Conscience* itself. They are all sacred; but they show that the "soft mystery" of human love was not absent from, and indeed had probably, for ill or good, inspired Hampole's Love Divine. To say, as a too ardent editor has said, that their beauty and melody have never been surpassed, is unlucky; this is the kind of thing which brings discredit upon literary history and hopelessly mars its usefulness. But

Unkinde man, give kepe til me,

and

Lo leman sweet, now may thou see,

have the "unction" of our most successful hymn-writers, and certainly the poem beginning—

My truest treasure so traitorly taken,
So bitterly bounden with bytand band(e)s,
How soon of thy servants wast thou forsaken,
And loathly for my life hurled with their hand(e)s!

has a rhythm which is no common one, and which curiously reminds us of another Northumbrian poet 500 years later than Hampole—that is to say, of Mr. Swinburne.[16]

Nor can any one of these canticles of Divine Love, according to Richard Hampole, be spoken of otherwise than with admiration, while of the remaining pieces of verse attributed to him most have a certain individuality of form or spirit or both. But for the attribution to him of the revival of strictly alliterative verse there is little if any more warrant than for the ascription to him of the invention of the heroic. We can at the most (and also at the least) allow that this revival was a very reasonable consequence of the increased stimulus to literary composition in the North—always fonder of alliterative rhythm, and more rebel to strict metrical ways, than the South—of which he certainly was one of the lights and leaders.

Two other named writers, one a little earlier, one a little later than Hampole, have obtained representation in English

---

16. Swallow my sister, O sister swallow,
How can thy heart be full of the spring ?

Itylus.

and the great stanza of the *Triumph of Time*. The final *es* of Hampole's alternate lines would soon have dropped. There is no other weak ending. Cf. also the pretty lines of Eve in the second Coventry Play, "Alas! that ever the speech was spoken."

literary history, though they are decidedly less interesting, even when we take the hermit who robbed his sister of her gowns somewhat less seriously than he has sometimes been taken. The first of these, Adam Davy, occupied the rather mysterious office of "Marshal of Stratford-atte-Bowe" about the year 1312, and no doubt spoke good French of the local pattern to the persons whom he marshalled. He happened, while many worthier writers escaped it, to attract the attention of Warton, who not merely attributed to him divers sacred poems found in the same manuscript, but also the excellent romance of *Alexander,* which is probably earlier, and certainly by a much better writer. Davy's undoubted work consists of *Visions of Edward II,* which have been re-edited for the Early English Text Society by Dr. Furnivall.

Adam Davy.

Laurence Minot had a likelier subject than Adam Davy, inasmuch as he celebrated not Edward II, but Edward III in his earlier glories. His subsequent fortune has been correspondent, for he has had the honour, most unusual for a Middle English poet even of higher rank than himself, of being four times edited, and five times printed in full—by Ritson in 1795 and 1825, by Mr. Wright in his Record Office *Political Poems,* by Dr. Scholle in a German periodical, and by Mr. Joseph Hall for the Clarendon Press. The fact is the best possible evidence of the superiority of subject to form as means of gaining general attention. Minot, who wrote in 1352, who seems to have been a Northerner from his dialect, but of whom we know nothing more, is a fair, but no more than a fair, specimen of the English trouvère-of-all-work of the period. His subjects are : Halidon Hill; the capture of Berwick, which he takes as an avenging of Bannockburn; the entry of Edward, our comely king, into Brabant; the battle in the Swin; the leaguer at Tournay; the march to Calais; Crecy and the battle there; the siege of Calais; Neville's Cross; the sea-fight with the Spaniards; and the taking of Guines.

Laurence Minot.

The forms of the poems that compose this cycle of the deeds of Edward—for that is what, with all its formal variety, it comes to—are various. Halidon is told in octave eights admitting catalexis, rhymed alternately with a title couplet which is found in all the poems and a final quatrain. The Berwick sack is in sixains rhymed *aaaabb,* the lines hovering between anapaestic fours and iambic fives as so often noted; the entry into Brabant in octosyllabic couplets followed by romance sixains 886886 rhymed *aabaab;* the Battle of the Swin or Sluys in the above hovering couplets; Tournay in octaves of sixes, to the three last of which "bobs" and couplets are added, making the *Tristrem* stanza (*vide infra*); Crecy in octaves like Halidon with a couplet prologue; Calais in similar staves without prologue; Neville's Cross in long sixteen-lined stanzas of very short lines, which perhaps should be octaves of longer lines; the Spaniards in twelves of the same kind, and the Castle of Guines in the same.

These poems have historical and patriotic interest[17] in no small degree; but for literature their chief value is perhaps the way in which they show that a fairly sufficient and satisfactory medium, a ready-made poetic diction and cadence, was now at last at the disposal of the verse-writer. There is nothing in Minot's poems, though some have spirit, especially the Neville's Cross piece, and that on the naval victory over the Spaniards, with its apostrophe to the

> Boy with the black beard!

that can be said to show any very special or peculiar poetical talents in the author. He is given to expletives, he seldom or never succeeds in giving us a distinct visual picture; his very variety of metre, etc., looks more like the absence of any distinct grasp and command of one form than like a sense of general mastery. But, as has hardly been the case for three

17. Their patriotism, as is not unnatural or uncommon, becomes a little abusive now and then. It may perhaps be usefully observed in connection with them that the employment of the vernacular for political satire, etc., is a sure gauge of its literary standing. In Wright's first collection of *Political Songs* for the Camden Society in 1839—a collection extending from the reign of John to that of Edward II—not one of the four pieces for John's reign is English, only one of the fifteen for Henry III's, but nearly *half* (eight out of seventeen) of those for the Edwards. In his later and much larger collection from Edward III to Richard III for the "Rolls Series" (2 vols. 1859-1861) any language save English becomes more and more the exception.

hundred years and more, he has a fairly settled tongue and a generally accepted prosody, with its peculiarities of lilt and swing all ready to his hands; and he manages to make very tolerably good use of them. Indeed, though it may seem rather ungracious, it is not impossible to say that his chief use in literature proper is that he *explains* Chaucer—shows how the tools were ready for the workman.

Last in this chapter falls to be noticed a very remarkable group of poems, which, with another reserved for the Romance division, have been attributed to a single author by their editors, who have also in some cases indulged in much hypothesis as to that author's identity. As in all cases, the reader is here simply referred to the discussions in question on the latter point. As to the former, I should be disposed to admit as extremely probable the common authorship *of Patience, Cleanness,* and *The Pearl.*[18] *Gawain and the Green Knight* (*vide* chap, v) seems to me to be much more dubiously their brother; for the fact of their being found m the same MS. is really no argument at all, considering the almost invariable mediaeval habit of transcribing, straight on, the most heterogeneous and unconnected work. And it is also very possible to allow too much weight to the alleged linguistic resemblances. But it is not impossible that the four poems may have had a common writer, and it is certain that all are much above the average in merit.

Cleanness and *Patience.*

In the three that are to be noticed in this place, the alliterative reaction, which has been already referred to, shows itself (as it does also in the *Green Knight*) very strongly, though in differing measure and degree. *Cleanness* and *Patience,* two poems, the first of rather over 1800 lines, the other of rather over 500, each of which begins with the title-word, are written in alliterative blank verse, observing for the most part the old rule of two alliterations in the first section and one in the second, very closely though not rigidly equivalent in syllabic

18. *Early English Alliterative Poems,* ed. Morris (E.E.T.S.), [*The*] *Pearl* separately edited by I. Gollancz, London, 1891.

length, precise in the middle pause, and though not metrical, yet exhibiting a general set of rhythm towards anapaestic cadence in the first half, and trochaic in the second. This, in fact, was the general scheme of the new alliteration at its best time, as here and in Langland. Later, especially in Dunbar and Douglas, the alliteration is exaggerated, and the lines lengthened accordingly. *The Pearl,* on the other hand, though very strongly alliterated, does not depend on alliteration for its system of scansion, but is in twelve-lined octosyllabic stanzas rhymed *ababababbcbc,* these stanzas being further grouped in divisions generally of five each, the last line of each stanza in the group being a sort of refrain, which is more or less repeated throughout. The characteristics of matter and spirit are more uniform. All three poems are pervaded by a singular and very impressive mixture of devotional feeling, with poetical appreciation of things mundane as well, and by a solemn melody rare in earlier verse. In *Cleanness* the mediaeval worship of purity, enforced by vigorous paraphrases and commentaries on the Parable of the Marriage Feast, the Fall of the Angels, the Deluge, the Destruction of Sodom, the Incarnation, and the story of Nebuchadnezzar and Belshazzar, is yet entirely free from the almost insane exaltation of virginity in and for itself which is so common. There is no nobler or more passionate appreciation of the delights of lawful love in English poetry than a passage in Jehovah's denunciation of Sodom to Abraham—Milton's famous apostrophe is a coarse and diffuse example of rhetorical commonplace in comparison—and the whole poem, though quaint now and then, is full of somber energy, mixed, as in the destruction of Babylon and of the fire from Heaven, with description of great power. *Patience* has an apparently less inspiring subject; but the story of Jonah, with which the poet chiefly fills it, gives him good opportunities of which he avails himself well. The storm in particular is very good. It must no doubt be admitted that the slightly grotesque effect of continuous and regular alliteration, and the way in which it compels even poets very fertile in resource to choose the wrong word instead of the right for the mere sake of an initial letter, receive some illustration here. But the result is by no means fatal.

The Pearl.

As a whole, however, *The Pearl* is undoubtedly the pearl of the three. As too often happens, the well-intentioned and very amiable partiality of its latest editor has set some against it; but this is always indefensible. It need only be read—and it is by no means difficult to read—to show its real beauty. There can be no reasonable doubt that it describes the loss of a daughter, probably in early age, who may very likely have borne the actual name of Margaret, beloved by the Middle Age because of the charming and popular legend of the patroness saint, because of its own harmonious sound, and because of the endless plays on the meanings "pearl" and "daisy" which it suggested.[19] This

Pearl pleasant to princes' pay—

(the first line)—this

Privy pearl withouten spot—

which, with slight changes, is the refrain of the first group—is first dealt with as a gem richly set, but dropped by the owner on the ground. The father (probably) visits the spot, almost avowedly a grave, and, falling asleep of pure sorrow, is carried off to a strange region. Following a stream he sees a white-clad maiden, whom he at first partly, and then seeing a mighty pearl set on her breast, wholly recognises. He asks her whether she is really his Pearl, since the loss of whom

I have been a joyless Jeweller.

She says "Yes." But she is not lost, though he cannot now come to her. He must wait God's will awhile; she is a queen in Heaven, which (he proving dull of understanding) she explains, adding the Parable of the Vineyard and an account of the Brides of the Lamb. He has a distant vision of the Heavenly

19. Although Saint Helena and Saint Juliana have, by accident probably, the precedence of her in our earliest A.S. documents, Saint Margaret has probably a fuller series of extant Old English lives of nearly all periods than any other saint. No name was commoner, and of none do the abbreviations so often occur in familiar writing.

Est mea mens mota pro te speciosa Magota!

as the doggerel leonine has it.

City and the worship of the Lamb, and rashly endeavouring to cross the water, wakes.

It is easy to see that this poem is not faultless. The fault does not lie, as some would vainly speak, in the allegory : for allegory is always a natural and frequently a powerful ally to poetry, while it is never dangerous if kept in its own place. The only faults of *The Pearl* in connection with allegory are that there is, as is the case with the vast majority of narrative poems of the kind in the fourteenth and fifteenth centuries, far too much of a single common form—that of the *Romance of the Rose,* the following of which is actually conducted to the point of walking down the river before the adventure, such as it is, is met. But beyond this, beyond an occasional expression a little beyond reason in carrying out the minor points of allegory (it is in this that Spenser and Bunyan so far excel their brother allegorists), and beyond an occasional succumbing to the temptations of alliteration, there are singularly few weak points in *The Pearl.* The exceeding beauty of its descriptive passages, especially that of the strange region where the poet awoke, its

> Crystal cliffs so clear of kind,

and the mystic woods hanging down them, with their purple trunks and silver foliage; the melancholy clangour of the verse, never descending to a mere whine, but always maintaining dignity and sanity in the midst of its sense of the pity and the loss of it,—these can escape no fit reader. The poet who could give such expression to pathos in *The Pearl,* to passion in *Cleanness,* and who had such a mastery of the descriptive faculty as appears in all three pieces, was no mean poet.

4

EARLY ROMANCES—METRICAL

Sir Tristrem—Havelok the Dane—King Horn—King Alisaunder—Arthour and Merlin—Richard Caeur de Lion— The *Seven Sages—Bevis of Hampton—Guy of Warwick—Ywain and Gawain—Lybeaus Desconus—*The *King of Tars—Emarè—Sir Orpheo—Florence of Rome—The Earl of Toulouse—* The *Squire of Low Degree—Sir Cleges* and *Le Fraine—Ipomydon—Amis and Amiloun—Sir Amadas—Sir Triamour—King Athelstonc,* etc.—The Thornton Romances—Charlemagne Romances.

THERE has, perhaps, never been such a capital example of the danger of indulgence in literary satire by a man of the first literary genius as the comparative disrepute into which the ever (and most justly) increasing estimate of Chaucer has thrown the Early English metrical romances.[1] That Chaucer

---

1. It may be convenient to give at once in a note the titles and contents of the chief collections of these romances—collections which in themselves fill one of the most satisfactory of book-shelves :—

   (a) Ritson (J.). *Ancient Engleish Metrical Romancëes* (spelling was one of Ritson's numerous manias), 3 vols., London, 1802, containing a long and still, for all its errors and crazes, valuable dissertation, with *Ywain and Gawain, Launfal, Lybeaus Desconus, King Horn, The King of Tars, Emarè, Sir Orpheo, A Chronicle of Englelond, Florence of Rome, The Earl of Toulouse, The Squire of Low Degree, The Knight of Courtesy and the Lady of Faguel,* with, in the Appendix, another form of *Horn—Horn Child and Maiden Rimnild.*

   (b) Weber (H.). *Metrical Romances of the 13th, 14th and 15th Centuries* (3 vols., Edinburgh, 1810), containing a less valuable introduction, with *King Alisaunder, Sir Cleges, Le Fraine, Richard Caeur de Lion, Ipomydon, Amis and Amiloun,* the *Seven Sages, Octovian, Sir Amadas,* and the *Hunting of the Hare.*

himself, in the *Rhyme of Sir Thopas,* intended to pour any real discredit on the class in general, I do not myself in the least believe. He probably had at most two or three "awful" examples (upon one at least of which it would not be difficult to put the finger even now) before him. And it is permissible to be equally sceptical in respect of his alleged contempt for the matter, especially the Arthurian matter, of these romances—the passages usually quoted will not bear the construction put on them. Chaucer's own adoption of different styles and treatments and sources of material is, at best, the most negative of arguments. It is as natural for some men of genius to prefer to take new ways, to strike into the path worn by the feet of none, as it is for others to produce masterpieces in kinds already tried by their contemporaries and predecessors.

However, all that can be said positively is that if Chaucer did despise the romances, he merely exhibited that not infrequent infirmity even of noble minds which makes men unjust to their immediate forerunners—which made Coleridge talk absolute foolishness about Gibbon's style, and which induced even Dryden, with his admirable critical catholicity, to imagine that Restoration verse was not merely a good thing in another way from that of the Elizabethans, but a positive improvement upon them. No such mistake can prejudice our judgment.

(c) Utterson (R.). *Select Pieces of Popular Poetry* (2 vols., London, 1817). The first contains *Sirs Triamour, Isenbras, Degorè,* and *Gowghter.*

(d) Hartshorne (C.H.). *Ancient Metrical Tales,* containing among other things *King Athelstone, King Edward and the Shepherd, Florice and Blancheflour,* and part of the alliterative *William of Palerne.*

(e) Halliwell (J.O.). *The Thornton Romances—Sirs Perceval of Gales, Isumbras, Eglamour of Artois,* and *Degravant* (Camden Society, 1844).

(f) Hazlitt (W.C). *Early Popular Poetry of England* (4 vols., London, 1864) contains, among a great many other things, *Robert the Devil* and *Robert of Cisylle* [*Sicily*].

(g) Hales (J.W.) and Furnivall (F.J.). *Bishop Percy's Folio MS.* (3 vols., London, 1867) contains many variants of romances named, and some new ones, notably *Eger and Grime.*

Separate editions are noted *infra;* for collections of *Alliterative* Romance see first note to next chapter.

It is very difficult to place with any exactness the earlier, still more the earliest, examples of this fascinating form of composition in English. What is certain is that the Anglo-Saxon genius—for reasons too hastily pronounced upon by some, but for some reason or other—had very little inclination towards it. The admirable saga of *Beowulf,* though well enough known to have been modernised and copied long before the Conquest, seems to have found no imitators, or, at least, none that have survived—for the chance of an English original of *Havelok* is very strong. The enormous preponderance of attention given to sacred subjects, both in Anglo-Saxon itself and in early Middle English, must have had something to do with this; but the general decadence of Anglo-Saxon poetry after the eighth century must have had more. For in no country of Europe, except Iceland, was prose ready for the task until far later.

It has therefore to be admitted fully that the known beginnings of romance in English all came from French in point of substance, while their forms could not be evolved till the "shaking together" of English, Latin, and French itself had provided the new prosody. The earliest examples of the result now existing, and perhaps the only ones which can be reasonably attributed to a period before the year 1300,[2] are the three romances of *Sir Tristrem,* of *Havelok the Dane,* and of *King Horn;* and it is practically admitted that though the first and second at least must almost certainly have sprung from British soil, they only appeared in the English language as translations or adaptations from the French. Each is of interest enough for separate consideration at such length as is here possible.

In sheer intrinsic literary merit *Sir Tristrem*[3] is far from being the best of the three; in fact it is certainly the worst. But

2. By fifty years after that date many, probably most, of our verse romances must have come into existence. The famous Auchinleck MS., which contains a good score, is of this time; and in the *Cursor Mundi,* which is perhaps as early as 1320, we find reference not only to these but to others, such as *Sir Isumbras,* of which our existing copies are later.

3. Scott's memorable edition of this can never, in a sense, be obsolete; but more modern apparatus and knowledge are added in those of Kölbing (Heilbronn, 1882) and M'Neill (Scottish Text Society, 1886).

its adventitious attractions are of the most unusual kind. It is, in all probability, the first English romance in the great "matter of Britain"—the only rival, *Arthour and Merlin,* is, I think, later. It tells a story which, however it may seem to some to yield in poignancy, as in nobility of interest, to the companion loves of Lancelot and Guinevere, was even more popular in the joint days of the two, and which has maintained itself. It is identified—perhaps, indeed probably, by mistake, but still it is identified—with the interesting, if legendary, personality, and the certainly early vernacular predictions of "Thomas the Rhymer." And last, but by no means least, in almost the earliest day of the revival of Romance, it had the honour to be ushered once more to public knowledge by Sir Walter Scott.

Sir Tristrem.

With some of these attractions we must deal here in cruel brevity. The argument as to the question of authorship must be sought by those who are curious about it in the editions cited in the notes. It is enough to say that the "Thomas" cited by Gottfried of Strasburg, the chief continental handler of the story, can hardly have been Thomas of Erceldoune; that the story of Sir Tristrem was certainly current in French long before the date either of the "Rhymer" or of this rhyme; and that it is, all things taken together, a little improbable, to say the least, that, considering the absence of any certain Scottish poetry till nearly the end of the fourteenth century, anything so elaborate as this should have been composed in such "Inglis" by a Scot before the end of the thirteenth—and according to the dates usually assigned to Thomas the Rhymer (*c.* 1280) considerably before it. At any rate, the poem in its present form can hardly have come from any one who wrote north of the Tweed. That it is, as its latest Scottish editor holds, a southernised version of a work of Erceldoune does not seem to me entirely impossible. But it rests on no evidence.

The form would lead us to believe it not much, if at all, anterior to the fourteenth century, the stanza used being one of those complicated and bizarre ones which, as has been explained in the last chapter, came from the attempt to adjust Provençal-French metres to English rhythm. It resembles one previously mentioned in the arrangement of the rhymes alternately in an eleven-lined stanza broken by a short fresh-rhymed bob at the ninth line. The best argument for its being older than 1300 is that the staple line is of six not of eight syllables—for, as we have seen, the six-syllabled line or half-line somewhat anticipated its longer and more convenient amplification into eights. After the plump statement that the author was at Erceldoune and spake with Thomas, hearing a *geste* of Tristrem (which, by the way, is an odd fashion of signature, but very likely a shift to father work on a well-known name indirectly), it passes to a stanza of gnomic reflection, very common, as we shall see, in the earliest days of English romance, and then plunges into its story, the Tristrem-saga proper—the famous and fatal loves of Tristrem and Yseult being preceded in true saga fashion by a history of the unhappy contest of Rouland Rhys, Tristrem's father, with Douk Morgan.

The rather unsuitable nature of the stanza for narrative is occasionally relieved by a middle rhyme—

> They ne raught [recked] how dear it bought,

and on the whole does fairly well; but the earliness of the piece finds a certain support in its crudity. The repulsive story of the fashion in which Yseult would have paid her maiden Brengwain's self-devotion is not in the least softened, and the poet does not show himself able, as his German predecessor had been able, to bring out the unmatched attractiveness of the sylvan life of Tristrem and the Irish princess. But there are good touches, at least not lost if not actually invented by the minstrel, such as that when the luckless, if unamiable, Mark discovers his queen and Tristrem with the sword between them—

> A sunbeam full bright
> Shone upon the queen,
> At a bore [hole]
> On her face so sheen—
> *And Mark rewed therefore.*

It is not always that later poetry has succeeded in achieving or retaining a phrase so simple, sensuous, and passionate as that last line, which is almost the equal of Sappho's ἔγω δὲ μόνα κατεύδω.

Horn[4] and *Havelok*[5] are in less elaborate metrical form. The metre of both comes under the general designation of the octosyllabic couplet—in *Havelok* lengthened and "swung" by the admission of trisyllabic feet, in *Horn* shortened so as to show that the poet was still hovering, as many did for a time, between sixes (or sevens) and eights. There is also some similarity between the general subject of both, which is that favourite romance *donnée* of the heir kept out of his own. The palm, both for individuality of story and for spirit of narration, decidedly belongs to *Havelok,* which has all the notes of a genuine local saga, and not merely of a literary composition on accepted romance lines. There is in it a double wrong done—the innocent Havelok, the heir of Denmark, being excluded by his guardian Godard, while Goldborough, heiress of England, is similarly treated by her tutor Godric. But Havelok, being as a male heir more dangerous, is exposed to greater personal danger than his destined bride, for Godard, determining to make away with him altogether, hands him over to the fisherman Grim to drown. Grim treats him roughly enough, but a night fortunately intervenes, and before the actual immersion the fisher's wife sees the sacred flame-aureole, sign of kinghood, on Havelok's brow, and her husband, having also prudently ascertained by a trick that he was like to have traitor's wages for his crime, gives it up and escapes oversea to England, where he lands at the future Grimsby. Havelok, brought up as a mere fisher-boy, seeks service at Lincoln Castle, and distinguishing himself by strength and athletic proficiency as one of the "kitchen knaves" dear to romance, is chosen as Goldborough's husband by the usurper Godric, who, milder-minded or more economical in crime than his Danish counterpart, only plots to degrade not to slay his charge. Goldborough is naturally enough displeased at having to marry a scullion, but at night the mystic flame

Havelok the Dane.

4. Two versions, as noted above, in Ritson; there are also three or four more modern editions, and the whole is given in Morris and Skeat's *Specimens,* vol. i.

5. Ed. Skeat, E.E.T.S.

reconciles her to her lot. Right thus meets right, a party is formed for the young pair, and the two traitors receive their proper doom. In this, of course, there is a certain amount of romantic stock-matter, the humours and promotion of the scullion Havelok being a very favourite and early device found even in the ancient and brilliant French *chanson de geste* of *Aliscans.* But the general tenor is, as has been said, unusually vigorous and fresh. The poet strides along like a man who has a real story of his own to tell, and is not merely compounding one out of dried or bottled materials. In fact, there is no doubt that the tradition as to the origin of Grimsby was an old one in Lincolnshire; and we find Robert Manning,[6] a Lincolnshire man, in a rather quaint state of dubiety between his early familiarity with the story and the silence of his graver historical authorities on the matter. For, as has been, and will be again hinted more than once, the mediaeval mind—naturally enough, considering the vast surrounding and invading seas of nescience which bounded its islands of knowledge—rarely seems to have had any distinctively critical power of distinguishing fact from fiction, and could at most attain to surprise at not finding the former in places where no trained historical critic would dream of looking for it.

King Horn.

Horn, though a good poem, and preserved in various forms which have made it one of the best known of its kind, is less racy either of any particular soil, or of any special poetical faculty. A certain King Murray—the locality of whose kingdom is described with sufficient vagueness as "biweste"—and his wife Queen Godhild had a son Horn, who was a very beautiful child,

Fairer was none than he was,
He was bright as the glass,
He was white as the flour,
Rose-red was his colour—

6. In a long passage (ed. Hearne above cited, i, pp. 25-26); given also in Prof. Skeat's Introduction, ix, x. Manning, after duly translating Langtoft, who barely refers to Havelok, bitterly complains that neither Gildas, nor Bede, nor Henry of Huntingdon, nor William of Malmesbury, nor Pierce of Bridlington (*i.e.* Langtoft himself) says anything about the incidents of the romance.

lines which, not unfairly, give the key-note of the real, but rather conventional, prettiness which marks the poem. As Murray was riding by the seashore he met with fifteen shiploads of Saracens keen, who frankly avowed their intention—

> The land-folk we shall slay,

and began with the king. Horn's extreme beauty saves him from slaughter, but he is put in a boat, with his two companions Athulf and Fikenild, and set adrift. By luck and pluck they come safe to the coast of Westernesse, where the king gives him protection; the king's steward, Athelbrus, instructs him in knightly ways, and the king's daughter Rimenhild falls deeply in love with him. Indeed *Horn Child and Maiden Rimnild* is the title of one of the actual versions of the story. Athulf is a good friend, even withstanding the awkward temptation of a moment when Rimenhild, mistaking him for Horn, makes the most undisguised advances; Fikenild is a traitor, but his machinations, though nearly successful, are defeated, and Horn, of course, comes to his own in love and kingdom.

The fifteen hundred short lines of the poem do not allow time for it to be tedious—the great danger of these somewhat identically constructed stories—and there are passages of directness and vigour which deserve all the more recognition in that the piece, though probably translated from the French, is still very early, and can have had very few English originals to furnish the writer with stock phrases and passages. One of the straightest and best is when Horn, with his beloved's ring on his finger, meets the slayer of his father—

> Before him saw he stand
> That driven him had from land
> And that his father slew.
> To him his sword he drew,
> He looked upon his ring,
> And thought on Rimenhild,
> He smote him through the heart
> That sore him gan to smart,

which, though the last line is a little superfluous, cannot be called contemptible in so early an attempt. It is worth-while to notice the assonance in *ring* and *hild.* Assonance does not suit the English ear, and is rarely attempted in English; but it was so prevalent in the French models of the writers of the thirteenth century, and it is such a help to a novice in rhyming, that it would be strange if it did not sometimes occur.

We may conveniently take next a group of romances, in all probability not much junior to these, that is to say, dating at latest but a little within the beginning of the fourteenth century, and attributed by a German scholar, who was honourably distinguished for the union of philological and literary competence, Dr. Eugen Kölbing, to the same hand. I cannot say that I myself see any strong probability of this, but at the same time I cannot see any very serious argument against it; and its admission would add to the list of English poets a figure anonymous indeed, but more considerable in quantity of work than any other before Chaucer, and certainly not inferior to any except the equally shadowy personage, to whom, as has been said in the last chapter, the other quartette of *The Green Knight, The Pearl, Cleanness,* and *Patience* has been similarly gifted. At any rate the four romances themselves, *King Alisaunder,*[7] *Arthour and Merlin,*[8] *Richard Caeur de Lion,*[9] and the *Seven Sages,*[10] are each and all among the most interesting of their kind, among the oldest, among the most considerable in scale and subject; and whether they had a common author or not, they are equally worthy of consideration.

The history of the formation and transformation of the mediaeval legend-history of Alexander belongs to another story than that of English literature. It is sufficient to say here

7. Ed. Weber, as above.
8. Ed. Kölbing, Leipzig, 1890. It had already been printed for the Abbotsford Club (1838) by Turnbull, and like many of the romances in this chapter, abstracted still earlier by Ellis in his famous *Specimens of Early English Metrical Romances,* which (despite a tone of persiflage sometimes though seldom inappropriate) is still the best introduction to the subject, and easily procurable in Bohn's Library.
9. Ed. Weber.
10. In two forms, one given by Weber, and the other by Wright for the Percy Society (1845) with a valuable introduction.

that the English romance in question follows generally the lines of the great French *Roman d'Alixandre,* but assigns greater proportionate space and credence to the initial fables about Nectanebus (Neptanabus in the English), the Egyptian enchanter-king who revenged himself upon Philip by seducing Olympias in the guise of the god Ammon. The wonders and episodes of the later part, the Fountain of Youth, and the rest are, on the other hand, curtailed, but as it is the poem extends to more than 8000 lines in octosyllabic couplets of a good stamp. These couplets, which form the measure of all the romances now in question, and supply one of the arguments for their common authorship, show a considerable advance in ease and grip over the respective kinds of *Horn* and *Havelok.* The writer in all rejects, or, if the phrase be thought more appropriate, has not arrived at, the hard and fast French octosyllable, and allows himself *Christabel* equivalence in a very satisfactory manner. Another very noticeable peculiarity shared by some, though not all, of the group is the interposition—in such a manner as justified Weber, the poem's editor, in taking the phenomenon as implying chapter or "fytte" division—of short gnomic or descriptive prefatory remarks, which have nothing whatever to do with the narrative, as thus—

King Alisaunder.

Merry time is the wood to sere,
The corn ripeth in the ear,
The lady is ruddy in the cheer,
And maid bright in the lere,
The knights hunteth after deer,
On foot and on destrere,

which comes, apropos of nothing whatever, between the story of Alexander's coronation, as Prince Expectant and King-coadjutor, and his knighting. The whole poem is one of the most spirited of the romances, and Weber's claim for it, that it is less burdened with expletives than others, is just, and even within the mark. These nuisances, which appear with the very rise of the style, which are not absent even in Chaucer, and which in fifteenth-century work like that of Lonelich become a mere abomination, are quite rare in it, and the author's faculty of description is extremely vivid and good. Where he fails, as all English and most mediaeval poets before Chaucer do fail, is in character.

Arthour and Merlin.

Arthour and Merlin is still longer than *Alisaunder,* extending to not much fewer than 10,000 lines, not dissimilar in character from those just noticed, but less regularly and abundantly provided with gnomic introductions or "fytte" headings. It is a verse rendering of what is called the "Vulgate" *Merlin,* an early history of the court of Arthur, preceded by an account of Merlin's own birth, and of the adventure of Uther with Igraine, which seems to have been thrown into French prose before the end of the twelfth century, or not much later, and of which, besides other verse renderings, including one by the above Lonelich, only published in part (see Book iv), there is a good prose English version published by the Early English Text Society. The most interesting parts of the Arthurian story are not here, and, as in all the *Merlins,* a vast amount of space is taken up by battles with the Saxons and with Arthur's rival kings, which Malory's extraordinary literary instinct led him to omit or cut short. But, on the other hand, there are things in these *Merlins* which we miss in Malory, especially the earlier and comelier version of the enchanter's enchantment by his lady-love. Apart from the subject matter, the piece deserves commendation, inferior indeed to that allotted to the *Alisaunder,* but not small. Still, if they had the same author, he had either not yet learnt in the *Arthour* to do without expletives, or had in it succumbed to a bad habit which he had earlier resisted; and the catalogues of names are rather tedious. The great interest of the piece is that it is the first setting of the romance of Arthur (for Layamon supposed himself to be telling history) that we possess in English—the king of all stories of the land having at last come to his own after linguistic exile for a century and a half in French. Indeed there are touches about the piece which might justify a conclusion that it is decidedly older than the *Alisaunder,* and may even belong to the thirteenth, not to the fourteenth century.

Richard Caeur de Lion, the third of the group, is pretty certainly the best. It has not merely the general interest of being "matter of Britain," but the more direct appeal of being the *geste* of a great English prince, told at a time near enough to his own to have the relish and savour of popular fancy and fondness. It is rather more than 7000 lines long; and the metre is managed with a spirit of which we find few examples in *Arthour and Merlin,* and though more, yet fewer than here in *Alisaunder* itself. Even the finale, "common form" as it is, will show this—

Richard Caeur de Lion.

Thus ended Rychard our King,
God give us all good endíng,
And his soul rest and roo,
And *our* souls when we come thereto!

Here is the real *diable au corps* of the ballad-romance style—the combined faculty of speaking simply and straight, and *metring* with vigour and variety. Nor is the matter of the poem inferior to the manner. Sir Walter Scott has made it better known than most of our romances through his quotations in the *Talisman* notes, referring to the grimly humorous episodes of the cooking of the Saracen's head instead of a pig's jowl, and of the king's ferocious banquet, on the same material, to the Paynim ambassadors. A recent French historian who cried affrightedly over a certain letter of Troubridge to Nelson, "This is the laughter of cannibals," might be better justified here; yet the humour of the thing and the spirit of it quite carry off the savagery.

Here too, almost for the first time (save in that very likely contemporary proem of Robert of Gloucester which has been quoted), appears really *English* patriotism, the triumph in the Lion-heart's exploit as a king of England, which (call him Angevin or anything else) he was. The refrain "Richard our King" obviously comes from the heart; the malison on his traitor brother—

his brother John
That was accursed, flesh and bone—

is equally hearty. Never before in English do we find the real daredevil tone, rightly associated with Romance, as here—

> He [Richard] gan cry, *As arms*! Gare!
> *Caeur de Lyon*—how they fare!
> Anon lept King Richard
> Upon his good steed Lyard,
> And his English and his Templeres
> Lightly lept on their destreres,
> And flings into the heathen host
> In the name of the Holy Ghost.

On few things would it be pleasanter to dwell than on this poem of real flesh and blood, which is good in its overture as to the fair fiend "Cassodorien" (who takes the place of Eleanor as Henry's wife and Richard's mother, with, no doubt, a remembrance of the Angevin house-fairy Melusine), better in the "lion's heart" episode, but best in its fighting scenes. Indeed it is the first and best fighting poem in Middle English. But we must pass on, only observing that here also the heroic couplet, and that curious English fancy for winding up with it at a marking or turning point which is so noticeable in Shakespeare, make their appearance—

> And swore | by Je | su that | made moon | and star |
> Ayenst | the Sa | racens he | should learn | to war |

(unless indeed this is an embellishment of the editor's). The gnomic insertion occurs now and then in this poem.

The *Seven Sages* is the shortest of the four, not much exceeding 4000 lines, and like all the versions, prose and verse, of the famous Eastern collection or collections from which it is derived, it is in fact a mere series of short tales bound together by one of the usual straps—in this case the stories are told by a wicked queen to support her false accusation of her stepson, and by his Seven Wise Masters on his behalf. The general literary interest of these things and their far travel from the East is great; but though in the piece, and still more in the later *Gesta Romanorum,* they produced noteworthy books in English,[11]

The *Seven Sages.*

11. The actual English *Gesta* may not be very early, but authority seems to favour the English origin of the Latin original.

their special attraction for us is less, inasmuch as they were but translations of translations, having been beyond all doubt decanted through Latin and French, and perhaps Greek before either on their way from their Eastern homes to their English receptacles. They are, however, interesting as the earliest, or among the earliest, instances in our language of the short verse-story itself—the *fabliau* which, in a couple of generations or so, Chaucer was in the *Canterbury Tales* to make the vehicle of one of the capital efforts of European poetry. Although there is no doubt some general resemblance, of the kind almost unavoidable, to the other three, the *Seven Sages* seems to me even less likely than *Arthour and Merlin* to be the work of the same author as *Alisaunder* or as *Caeur de Lion,* for there is much less spirit in the verse, and there is present that indefinite, but to careful observers very noticeable, inability to distinguish between prosaic and poetical incidents which marks off the born prose-writer (in the bad sense) from the born poet. That some of the stories in the *Seven Sages* arc disgusting does not so much matter; the Saracen's head episodes of Richard are not precisely delicious. But the poet of *Richard* knew how to carry these off, the poet of the *Seven Sages* did not know how to carry off the others; and the difference, though not very easy to prove by example, is at once felt in the reading.

All the metrical romances hitherto noticed are beyond doubt either actually of the thirteenth century, or only a very little younger. But it is a matter of difficulty and guesswork to decide which of the much larger number that remain should accompany them, and which should be postponed till we come to the fifteenth or the late fourteenth century, from which probably the larger number of the actual manuscripts date. Thus, as noted above, we have a notice of *Sir Isumbras* in the *Cursor Mundi,* or about 1340 at latest; but our text of it—that in the Thornton MS.—is a full century later. On the whole, the best plan will probably be to notice here all the metrical romances, which may possibly be older in their original forms, if not in their present texts, than the death of Chaucer, and to keep for the company of Malory those which, like *Sir Launfal* in Chester's version, and the work of Henry Lonelich, distinctly belong to the later time by authorship if not in substance.

It is probable, but not certain, that all the English romances—even those which, like *Havelok* and *Horn* among those already mentioned, like *Bevis of Hampton* and *Guy of Warwick* among those to come, rest upon English traditions and deal with English scenes—were directly translated from French originals. Sometimes, as in the just-mentioned case of *Sir Isumbras,* we have no knowledge of such originals, and sometimes, as in the case of *Sir Amadas,* there is opportunity for confusion.[12] There may have been exceptions to the general rule of translation from French; but there is no reason to think that the rule was not general. And it was probably the exigencies of the translation—the termination of the original sense, leaving part of a line still to be filled up, and the like—which encouraged, and to some faint degree excused, the practice of stuffing and padding with expletives and stock phrases that brought the whole class into really undeserved disrepute.

Only brief observations can be made on each of these romances, but except by oversight none shall be passed over; and in face of the difficulty, not to say impossibility, of dating them with any certainty, they shall be mentioned for the most part in the company and order in which they appeared in the printed collections of Ritson, Weber, and others.

Guy of Warwick and *Bevis of Hampton,*[13] which were the first except *Sir Tristrem* to enjoy the honours of separate publication, owed those honours in all probability rather to their traditional fame, to their great size, and to the fact that both are found in the precious Auchinleck MS.—which Boswell's father gave to the Faculty of Advocates, and which is not merely the largest but one of the oldest of existing Romance MSS.—than to their intrinsic merit either as poetry or, except

12. The *Cursor Mundi* mentions this too, but with the addition of the heroine's name, Idoine. This identifies it for us with an existing French romance of the double title, quite different from our English *Sir Amadas*.

13. They were both edited for the Abbotsford Club by Turnbull, *Bevis* in 1838, and *Guy* (a mighty quarto of black letter) in 1840. The eccentric C.K. Sharpe furnished both with frontispieces in the Retzsch style, one of which, that to *Bevis,* is very comic. *Guy* has been re-edited, in both fourteenth and fifteenth century forms, with immense care by Dr. Zupitza for the E.E.T.S., and *Bevis* by Dr. Kölbing for the same society.

for the mere adventures, as story. In these last respects—to speak with all the tenderness due to such famous names—they are rather poor things, inferior to the majority of their companions, and owing almost all their charm to the mere common form, the ready-bottled herbs and essences, of the average romance of chivalry. Neither has anything specially English about it except the names, and the adventures of both are carried on mostly in countries other than England. *Bevis of Hampton,* the better of the two, owing to the lively characters of Josiane the heroine and Ascapart the giant,[14] rests upon the well-worn theme of a faithless wife, a murdered husband and father, a disinherited son, and an intruding tyrant. There is some interest in Bevis's vengeance on his father's murderer and his own wrongdoer, appropriately named Sir Murdour; and his horse Arundel and sword Morglay rank well among those favourite properties of Romance. But the kindness (somewhat "coming" and forward, but legitimately imitated from the conduct of all Paynim princesses in the *chansons de geste*) of Josiane, her courage, her fidelity, are really the salvation of the piece. *Guy of Warwick* (another and still longer tale of adventures all over the Romance world, with a huge *coda* telling those of Rembrun or Raynburn, the hero's son) lacks this attraction. Felice, the heroine here, is a cold and capricious mistress (the pattern doubtless of the Polisardas and Miraguardas of Spanish fiction), who is indeed useful to the story by constantly requiring new exploits from her suitor. It is true that he forgets all about her by the way once, and only the sight of the wedding-ring that he is about to put on another's finger reminds him at the fifty-ninth minute and second of the eleventh hour. And she is justly, though by no means interestingly, punished when Guy after marriage is seized by a craze of chastity, and determines to desert his wife and unborn child, spending the rest of his days as a palmer and hermit. There is plenty of fighting (for he has

Bevis of Hampton.

Guy of Warwick.

14. Ascapart now quietly guards the gates of Southampton with his victor and benefactor; but he was not a good giant to the end, and was killed after turning traitor.

not abjured that pleasure) in the sequel, including the famous combat with Colbrand; and Guy, at last coming home, is not recognised by Felice till at the point of death he sends her ring to her, and she receives his last breath and dies after him. The story appears to have been almost without exception the most popular of all the romances in England from a very early time, and its immense length and varied incidents give, of course, abundant scope for successful treatment. But in none of the versions which have come down to us (Ellis would make an exception for the Colbrand part) does it seem to have fallen into the hands of a poet of any power. The crowning moment of the meeting of Guy and Felice, the latter unknowing, the former conscious, is blundered with a completeness which makes us think vividly of the admirable success of the Scottish poet Henryson at the somewhat similar meeting of Troilus and the lazar Cressid. The sheer silliness which dogs the footsteps of Romance shows itself in Guy's forgetfulness, which is as absurd as his conscious succumbing to new charms could have been made natural. Almost every chance throughout the long record is consistently missed, and the undoubted popularity of the thing in verse and prose, in MS. and print, in recitation and reading can have been due to the adventures alone.[15]

Ywain and Gawain.

Of Ritson's collection,[16] the *Chronicle* does not here concern us, *Sir Launfal* we postpone, and the interesting *Lady of Faguel* (Fayel) is rather a ballad than a romance. *Ywain and Gawain* is a free adaptation of Chrestien de Troyes's *Chevalier au Lyon,* one of the earliest poems of the Arthurian cycle, which, having been also

15. The point where the poet fails least is perhaps the short passage describing the revulsion of feeling which causes Guy to quit his wife, and which comes from the sudden thought, as he gazes on his fair heritage from the towers of Warwick, of the carnage and devastation he has wrought—

    All for the sake of woman's love,
    And not for the sake of God above.

    But even this is not very well done. *Guy,* it should be said, is partly in couplet, partly in twelve-line romance stanza. *Bevis* has the same partition, but the stanzas take the shorter six-line form.

16. See note, p. 102.

paraphrased by Hartmann von Aue, has the advantage of appearing in English, French, and German. The English poet, though unknown (that prolific eidolon, the supposed author of *Arthour and Merlin,* has been credited with this also), does not compare ill with his famous fellows. The poem, which is about 4000 lines long, in couplets, has spirit and merit throughout. *Lybeaus Desconus* (which strange appellation is only *Le Beau Déconnu* with its Old French form misspelt) is also a Gawain poem, dealing with a son of that courteous knight. It is about half the length of the last, in stanzas of twelve six-syllabled lines. This is not a very good romance medium, but the poem is above the average. Its story is a variant of the "Daughter of Hippocrates"; but Sir Lybeaus is not exposed to the danger of refusing to kiss the worm's mouth, for she takes the initiative, and the transformation scene is very gracious. The *King of Tars* (same stanza, but in fairly regular eights for 1 2 4 5 7 8 10 11, and sixes for lines 3 6 9 12) gives a Christian and Paynim fighting story of average interest in not quite 1200 lines. But *Emare* (trisyllabic, *Emarè*), in the same stanza, but 200 lines shorter, is one of the best. The verse is good; the description of the cloth embroidered in the four corners with the stories of *Amadas and Idoyne, Tristrem and Iseult, Florice and Blancheflour,* and the *Sowdone of Babylon* is one of the best stock-passages of mediaeval upholstery, and the character of Emarè is touched with a distinctness and a tenderness which are none too common in these poems. It is one of the class of stories in which fathers fall in love with their daughters and are resisted. That Emarè should be set afloat in a boat by her father, blown to a friendly shore, married to the king, plotted against by her mother-in-law, again floated forth with her little child, once more succoured by good Samaritans, and finally restored to her proper place and to the chastened affection of her repentant father, is all common form, if not commonplace. What is not commonplace is the graceful fashion in which the tale is told, and the writer's abstinence from the long-windedness which is so frequent a fault. *Sir Orpheo* is *Orpheus and Eurydice* with a happy ending, for which the

Lybeaus Desconus.

The King of Tars.

Emarè.

Sir Orpheo.

Middle Ages had a possibly childish, but certainly healthy liking. It has some 500 lines in couplets.[17] *Florence of Rome* (over 2000 lines in the twelve-lined stanza) is the daughter of the Emperor. She is most unseasonably courted by Sir Garcy, Emperor of Constantinople, who was a hundred years old, and whose disqualifications are spiritedly told in this stanza—

Florence of Rome.

His flesh trembled with great eld,
His blood cold, his body unweld,
His lippes blue forthy;
He had more mister of a good fire,
Of right brands burning shire,
To beik his bonès by,
A soft bath, a warm bed,
Than any maiden for to wed,
And good encheason why—
For he was bruised and all to-broken,
Far travelled in harness and of war wroken,
He told them readily.

Florence and her father naturally object. Sir Garcy, who is not too old to fight, attacks Rome and brings it to great straits. Florence, to spare bloodshed and misery, offers to sacrifice herself, but her father will not hear of it, and dies in a sally. Two brothers, Sir Miles and Sir Emere, get the better of Garcy, and Florence marries Emere; but his brother plays the traitor during Emere's absence, carries off the faithful Florence after a false report of Emere's death has proved useless, hangs her to a tree and beats her, like the Counts of Carrion in the *Cid* story. Nor is this the last of her trials, though, of course, all comes right. This piece is rather unequal, and the *Earl of Toulouse* (1200 lines, in the same stanza) is rather slight. But the *Squire of Low Degree* (a happy title, and one which made its fortune) comes,

The Earl of Toulouse.

17. The Auchinleck version of this, which Laing printed (see first note of next chapter), is called *Orfeo and Heurodis.* Both contain charming descriptions of Fairyland, which, with the parting of husband and wife and other passages, make the piece one of the most delightful of the whole class.

in about the same length of couplets, up to its promise. The famous distich with which it opens—

> It was a squire of low degree
> That loved the king's daughter of Hungarỳ—

obeys, unconsciously no doubt, the maxims of authority as to the advantage of plunging the reader straight into the subject, and he is never let go. The introduction of the valiant squire (who, for all his "low degree," was marshal of the king's hall) is cunningly managed, not too soon after the opening nor too late for the refrain to ring in the ear—

The *Squire of Low Degree.*

> And all was for that ladye—
> The king's daughter of Hungarỳ

The garden, with the favourite mediaeval catalogues of trees and flowers, and the references to other romances, follows, and still

> The king's daughter of Hungarỳ !

rings agreeably now and then. The squire tells his love, and the lady accepts it in all honour, with stated conditions, and a warning against the steward—stewards are generally wicked. But cautious as she is, she ends with "kisses three"—one less than the pale knight gave La Belle Dame sans Merci, but not made more lucky by their sacred number. The steward sees them, and vows mischief. The king will not believe his calumny, but the steward undertakes to show the lovers together, and unluckily the squire, after taking leave of the king to seek adventures, returns under cover of night—

> To take leave of that lady free,
> The king's daughter of Hungarỳ !

The interview takes place, but the enemy is upon them. The squire cuts the steward's throat, but is overcome by numbers and imprisoned, his lady thinking him dead, because her father's men have cunningly changed his clothes with the dead steward's at her door. Her father offers her a curious catalogue of delights[18] if she will leave off mourning; but she will not,

18. This list of all the things the Middle Ages loved best—finery and music,

and after seven years the relenting king sends the squire to make him a name in Lombardy and gives him his daughter at his return. A fairy tale without fairies, but a pleasant one and well told.

The chief constituents of the next collection (Weber's, in 1810), *Alisaunder, Caeur de Lion,* and the *Seven Sages,* have been already noticed; but it contains others which must not be passed over, and one at least which is of great merit. The

Sir Cleges and *Le Fraine.*

make-weights of the great *Alexander* poem in the first volume are *Sir Cleges,* a short piece in not quite fifty twelve-lined stanzas—respectable, but of no great note—on the favourite mediaeval motive of the knight who spends his all, not in riotous living, but in generous housekeeping, and recovers it. This in the present case is partly by divine mercy (which gives him cherries at Christmas), and partly by his own shrewd wit and stout heart, avenging him on the court officials, who strive to hinder or blackmail his present of these cherries to the king. The other is a translation of the *Lai le Fraine* of Marie de France, rather *a fabliau* than a romance. The second volume, which contains *Richard Caeur de Lion,* contains also two romances of

Ipomydon.

great excellence, *Ipomydon* and *Amis and Amiloun.* The former is one of the best stories, and not the worst told, of the whole class. It is in some 2400 lines of couplets, and bears a remarkable analogy to the at present untraced "Sir Beaumains" episode of Malory. The hero is the heir of Apulia ("Pouille" or "Poile," as it meets us in French and English romance), the pupil of Sir Tholomew, one of the good old knights so common, and the suitor of the heiress of Calabria. He determines to rest only on his own merits, visits her court incognito, makes himself conspicuous and attractive by the usual mediaeval virtue of lavish giving and skill in the hunting art, and then retires to let his charms work. After a time he goes to the (then) adjacent court of Saxony, obtains the post of honorary and honourable lover to the queen, and from this

wines and foods, sports and pastimes, castles and yachts, with crews singing heyho and rumbelow, "gentyle pottes with ginger green," and "blankets of fustyane"—fills over 100 lines.

point of vantage enters for the tournament which is to decide the spousals of the Calabrian princess. He puts on daily fresh disguises of white, red, and black armour, with all things to suit; overcomes, of course, but, in true romance fashion, is not satisfied with so easy a victory. Difficulties with foes or unknown friends, Sir Camys and Sir Campanys, have to follow before all is as it should be.

Amis and Amiloun.

As for *Amis and Amiloun,* no Middle Age story is the superior of this for pathos and beauty; but it is only an adaptation of a much older French *chanson de geste,* and so interests us less here than those romances which are either English by origin, or have no known French original, or are adapted with some special difference. The third volume, which contains the *Seven Sages,* contains also *Octovian Imperator* (a story of some liveliness, but a very bad poem, in 317 six-lined stanzas, syllabled 888484 and rhymed *aaabab*), *Sir Amadas,* and *The Hunting of the Hare.* This last, like the *Tournament of Tottenham* and some others, is a burlesque of some, but no extraordinary, merit. *Sir Amadas,* which has nothing to do with *Amadas and Idoyne,* but is found, as we shall see, in another version, has rather less than 800 lines in the twelve-lined stanza. It is a sort of variant of *Sir Cleges,* but the knight recovers his fortunes not by shrewdness but by his charity to a dead corpse which he finds in ghastly conditions, it having been kept from burial by a brutal creditor. The general poetical merit of *Sir Amadas* is not great, but the situation is good, and there is one couplet which only wanted a little trimming to make it a sublime one. The knight, having seen the festering debtor, is at a feast of much splendour—

Sir Amadas.

[But]
Sir Amadas made little cheer,
For the dead corpse that lay on bier
Full mickle his thought was than [then].

The first three of the Utterson Romances—*Sir Triamour, Sir Isenbras, Sir Degorè*—are taken from early printed copies and are in very lamentable state—the twelve-lined stanzas of *Sir Triamour,* for instance, appearing by the grace of the copyist or the printer in irregular batches of threes, varying from six lines to eighteen. And the curse of prose, which, with such rare exceptions, weighed in the fifteenth century, is heavy on it. But the story, which is one of the class of queens wronged by stewards, is touching.[19] Still better in this respect, though even worse off in others, is the beautiful legend of *Sir Isenbras* or *Isumbras,* who in his domestic happiness and worldly pride forgot God, and was punished by the successive loss of possessions, children, and wife, to have them restored after he was purified by much suffering and gallant daring in deed. *Sir Degorè* (supposed to be = L'égaré, but unfortunately responsible for "Diggory") is a short romance in about 1000 lines of couplets celebrating the prowess of a "love-child." *Sir Gowghter,* which Utterson was the first to print, is a very interesting and spirited variant of the story of "Robert the Devil," in between fifty and sixty twelve-lined stanzas.

Sir Triamour.

Hartshorne's book, containing much interesting matter, and possessed of all the attractions of the Pickering Press, has always been a trial to students from its confused arrangement, its presentment of shreds and patches, and its careless editing. But it gave from different Cambridge MSS. *King Athelstone,* a spirited story of the ordeal by fire, dating from the fourteenth century, in the twelve-lined stanza; *King Edward and the Shepherd,* one of the innumerable variants of the favourite *donnée* of a king guesting incognito with his subjects; an extract from *Florice and Blancheflour,* nearly the most popular of all mediaeval stories; one from *William and the Werewolf,* which being alliterative is reserved for the next chapter; and a great number of small burlesques or *fabliaux,* the *Tournament of Tottenham,* the *Boy and the Basin,* the *Cokwolds' Dance,* etc.

King Athelstone, etc.

The Thornton Romances[20] give the English version, not a

19. Mr. Halliwell printed a MS. version for the Percy Society, and there is another in the Percy Folio. The editors of this last seem to think better than I do of the execution of this tale of King Aradas and Queen Margaret and the wicked steward Marrock; but I quite agree with their praise of its spirit and substance.

20. So called from their transcriber, a Yorkshireman, who a little before the

very valuable or extensive one, of the great story of *Sir Percevale* (143 stanzas as below); another version, in twelve-lined stanzas, of *Sir Isumbras; Sir Eglamour* (also twelves), the nearest to *Sir Thopas* of all the romances in faults, and chiefly *salvandum* because it contains the name "Christabel"; and *Sir Degravant,* in the same stanza as *Sir Percevale,* a rougher but less mawkish composition. The companion Camden Society volume by Mr. Robson, which is chiefly noteworthy for the alliterative *Auntyrs of Arthur* (see next chap.), also contains a different version of *Sir Amadas,* and a non-alliterated Arthurian romance in sixty stanzas like *Percevale* and *Degravant,* sixteen-lined, each quatrain consisting of a monorhymed octosyllabic triplet and a six.

The Thornton Romances.

Lastly, we may mention a group of Romance which in subject has least interest of all, while of its most attractive members the alliterative story of *Rauf Coilyear* belongs to the next chapter, and Lord Berners's *Huon of Bordeaux* (prose) to the next Book but one. These are the English Charlemagne Romances, of which some at least, if not most, in their earlier form must date from our present period. These are *Sir Ferumbras,* a long version of the French *Fierabras* in some 9000 lines of the six-lined stanza; the *Sowdone of Babylone,* another version of the same in an early kind of the ballad quatrain of eights and sixes—early and long (3000 and odd verses) for this form; the *Siege of Milan* and *Roland and Otuel,* each in the twelve-lined stanza and each about 1600 lines long; a fragment of an English *Song of Roland.* All these, with Caxton's prose *Charles the Great* and *Four Sons of Aymon,* which will fall like *Huon* to be noticed hereafter, have been printed for the Early English Text Society. None of the romances just named is of the first merit or interest. Indeed, the Carlovingian epic, when stripped of the intense idiosyncrasy of the *chanson* form, hardly tolerates any other save prose.

Charlemagne Romances.

---

middle of the fifteenth century included them (with much of the most noteworthy work of or attributed to Hampole, and other things) in one of the *omnium gatherum* MS. books so fortunately fashionable in the Middle Ages. It belongs to Lincoln Cathedral.

5

EARLY ROMANCES—ALLITERATIVE

Gawain and the Green Knight—The *Awntyrs of Arthur*—*William of Palerne*—*Joseph of Arimathea*—The Thornton *Morte d'Arthure*—The *Destruction of Troy*—*The Pistyl of Susan.*

THE interesting phenomenon of the revival of alliteration, the facts and causes of which in the early fourteenth century have been more than once referred to, naturally had its chief exercising ground in the field of Romance. The most remarkable of all English alliterative poems later than Anglo-Saxon times, the *Vision concerning Piers the Plowman,* falls for treatment in the next Book, and a good many others date only from the fifteenth century. But not a little interesting work belongs to the time of this chapter.

The most intrinsically interesting examples of Alliterative Romance[1] are beyond doubt *Gawain and the Green*

1. The greater part of the work mentioned in this chapter will be found in the following collections, some of which include much else. One or two pieces which occur by themselves will, as before, be noted later :
   (a) Pinkerton (J.). *Scottish Poems,* Edinburgh, 1792, which gives a version, with altered title, of the *Awntyrs of Arthur.*
   (b) Laing (D.). *Ancient and Popular Poetry of Scotland,* Edinburgh, 1822, and thrice reprinted since, including the *Pistyl of Susan* and the *Awntyrs.*
   (c) Madden (Sir Frederick). *Sir Gawayne* (Bannatyne Club, 1839), giving *Gawayne and the Green Knight,* the *Awntyrs,* etc.
   (d) Robson (J.). *Three Metrical Romances* (Camden Society, 1842), containing a third text of the *Awntyrs.*
   (e) Amours (F.J.). *Scottish Alliterative Poems* (Scottish Text Society, 1897), containing the *Pistyl of Susan* and the *Awntyrs.*

Knight[2] and *William of Palerne* or *William and the Werewolf.* The former may, like the latter, have had a French original, but none such is known, and it stands at the head of an interesting group of Gawain Romances, which it is not fantastic to associate with Cumbrian rather than Welsh or Armorican traditions, but which are certainly Celtic in character.[3] Of *Gawain* I have already observed that the identity of its author with him

Gawain and the Green Knight.

Much of the introductory matter of these books is occupied with a discussion of the authorship of these poems, into which it is impossible here to enter fully, but of which so much has been made that a slight notice of it, with the present writer's own conclusions, may justly be expected. Wyntoun, the verse chronicler (*vide* Book iv), dealing with a disputed point in Arthurian matters, cites a certain "Huchowne," describing him as "of the Awle Ryale," and saying that

He made the great geste of Arthure,
And the Awntyrs of Gawane,
The Pistyl also of sweet Susane.

This has set the speculative commentators off at almost interminable score. Huchowne (Hutcheon, Huchon, the usual French accusative-diminutive of Hugh or Hugues) has been erected into a great poet of the thirteenth century, the earliest (or the earliest next to Thomas the Rhymer) of known Scottish poets, and has been endowed with all, or more, or fewer of such early alliterative poems as are known to be or may possibly be of his time, the amplest appanage including *Gawayne and the Green Knight,* the three alliterative religious pieces noticed at the end of chap. iii, the *Pistyl,* the *Awntyrs,* an alliterative *Morte d'Arthure,* also contained in the Thornton MS., and what not. In argument for and against this the stores of dialect, allusion, diction, and the like have been literally ransacked, with the most contradictory results. Those interested in the matter may be referred to the introductions in question. We may here safely say three things—(1) Nothing is known of "Huchowne" save from Wyntoun, and Wyntoun does not say whether he was Frenchman, Englishman, or Scot, nor in what language he wrote; (2) It is not impossible that he may have written some of the poems in question, especially the extant *Pistyl of Susan,* which (*vide infra*) is at least as old as 1380; (3) There is no evidence that he wrote this or any other.

2. Re-edited after Madden by Dr. Morris for the E.E.T.S.
3. Gawain, unlike Lancelot, appears in the earliest handling of the story; and Welsh authorities always strive to put him above his rival. This is most curiously illustrated in the late Welsh version of the Graal story, *Y Seint Greal* (London, 1876).

of the interesting *Pearl* group is not, according to my notions of literary evidence, proven; but it is not impossible. The poem consists of rather more than 2500 lines, in a curious irregular sort of stanza, consisting of an uncertain number (from sixteen to twenty), mostly unrhymed, unmetred, but somewhat dactylically rhythmed "four-accent" lines regularly alliterated, terminating with what Guest has made it usual to term a "bob and wheel," that is to say, a single-foot iambic and an eight- or six-syllabled quatrain—the five-rhymed *ababa.* This scheme, which, with variations, is not uncommon, seems to show that some revivers of alliteration themselves felt that it could not be depended upon entirely alone—that it must be backed by the charms of metre and rhyme.

Even in this poem, the best of its kind, the fatal danger of alliteration—that the selection, or at worst invention, of the "rhyme-words" is too often solely determined by their sound, not their sense—makes itself painfully felt. But the author's power is very much greater than that of most of his competitors in metre or in alliteration, and the story is one of singular interest and force. It opens with a few touches suggesting the very old and popular piece (also a Gawain one) of the *Chevalier au Lyon* or *Ywain,* but soon all resemblance ceases. Gawain (who in all this group, as in the earlier romances generally, is not represented as the light o' love that the French and Germans made him) undertakes, when others quail, the adventure of a perilous "Green Knight" who enters Arthur's hall unbidden and challenges any one to give him a buffet and bide one in turn. The king's nephew fetches a swashing blow with his battle-axe and beheads the knight clean, but the trunk picks the head up, mounts the green steed with it in hand, and departs, after the lips of the severed head have given Gawain his venue at the Green Chapel on New Year's Day twelvemonth. When the appointment draws near Gawain arms himself splendidly and rides alone through England to North Wales in quest of his doom. He is royally guested at a castle where the knight welcomes him warmly, and the lady even more so, and where he is told that the Green Chapel is close at hand. His host proposes a bargain—that they shall exchange whatever they gain in hunting or otherwise—and Gawain grants it. The host hunts with great success, but Gawain stays at home. He is tempted by the chatelaine, but resists so far as only to take a kiss. He keeps his word on receiving the host's game by giving him a kiss, though he will not (as indeed he need not) tell him where he got it. A second day witnesses the same events; but on the third the lady, who now very nearly overcomes the knight's steadfastness, forces on him her girdle, which has the virtue of making the wearer invulnerable. This temptation is too much for him when he thinks of his perilous adventure, and he takes it (with "kisses three") under promise of secrecy. Accordingly when swapping-time[4] comes he gives his host the kisses, but says nothing about the girdle. The reader anticipates the result. The host is the Green Knight, though not even at the last, when in his fantastic garb he meets Gawain and deals the deadly blow, does he reveal this. Gawain flinches ("shunts") at the first stroke, but manfully bides another, which only gives him a flesh wound. He draws his sword, prepared to fight it out as the wager is accomplished, but the knight leans calmly on his axe and reveals the truth. He and his wife agreed to tempt Gawain, who came out scatheless except in his acceptance, through caution, if not exactly cowardice, of the girdle-lace, and his failure to give it up according to compact. Therefore he saved his life, but lost his blood. The knight, Bernlac de Hautdesert (who is one of Morgane la Faye's), forgives him, gives him the lace, and all ends happily. The high and yet not mawkish morality of the piece is well matched by the telling, and the romance is certainly one of our very best.

The *Awntyrs of Arthur.*

The still more curious, though as literature inferior, *Anturs* or *Awntyrs* (adventures) *of Arthur at the Tarne Watheling* (Tarn Wadling in Cumberland), but for its strong and regular alliteration, might have been put in the last chapter. For here the unrhymed *tirades* of the *Green Knight* become regular nine-lined stanzas, rhymed (rather imperfectly, it is true) *ababababc*. There is no "bob," but the "wheel" consists of a triplet and singleton rhymed *dddc*. The story opens in a strange and promising manner with the

4. This is no slang—the word "swap" is in the text.

apparition to Gawain and the Queen of a specially loathly spirit, the ghost of Guinevere's mother, to give her good advice, and this is told with some power; but the romance then declines into an ordinary fight between Gawain and Sir Galleron of Galway. We have three texts of it in the Douce, Thornton, and Ireland-Blackburne MSS. respectively; and all three have been printed in the collections referred to in the note at the beginning of this chapter. The language is in no case "Scots"—indeed, as we shall sec later, it could not be; but it is in all Northern, like that of almost the whole of the poems of this group, and in at least one form, that of the Ireland-Blackburne version, it is distinctly uncomely, not to say barbarous, though this rather suits the grisliness of the ghost.

William of Palerne.

William and the Werewolf or *William of Palerne,*[5] less original, so far as we know, than the *Green Knight,* but pretty freely adapted from its extant French model, is in plain and unadulterated "four-accent" verses, directly comparable with *Piers Plowman,* of the oldest version of which it may be ten or fifteen years the elder. The story of a missing heir fostered by a werewolf, who is himself the victim of machinations, is interesting, and the execution sometimes capital. Indeed, it is superior to the *Green Knight* itself in one point, the rejection of uncouth or manufactured words for the mere sake of alliteration.

Two important Arthurian poems, one certainly and the other very probably dating from this period, belong to the plain unrhymed and unstanza-ed variety of alliterative verse.

Joseph of Arimathea.

One of these is on *Joseph of Arimathea,*[5] and the other is the long alliterative *Morte d'Arthure* of the Thornton MS., which has had its claims put in as the "great geste" of Huchowne. The date of this MS. is, as has been said, much later than our present period; but in view of its other contents this is no argument. The *Joseph* is contained in the Vernon MS., and therefore certainly ours here.

It is of no great length—about 700 lines—and does not seem, though it is incomplete, to have been ever much longer;

5. Ed. Skeat, E.E.T.S.

it is only a paraphrase of the constantly reworked legend of its subject, and it has no special literary characteristics. Yet it has interest for us, like so much else, because it shows the set of the tide—not in this case the main set but an important "overfall"—in the alliterative direction, and the way in which the great "matters" of mediaeval interest were being at the moment handled in England.

The alliterative *Morte d'Arthure*[6] is a much bigger thing, extending to over 4000 lines, and possessed of distincter literary character. It belongs in point of matter to what may be generally called the "Brut" rather than the romance type of the Arthurian story, and busies itself, like the older versions of that story generally, with the king's wars against the Romans chiefly, ignoring the more romantic, and even the more mystical, parts of the legend almost or altogether. But it is a vigorous piece, employing its somewhat rugged and clumsy implement of verse with a sort of sword- or rather axe-play which is refreshing and effective, and calling to its aid a vocabulary well suited to the subject and style, and sufficiently individual. Few will wish for a complete literature of such poems; but we could endure several more as good as this *Morte d'Arthure*.

The Thornton *Morte d'Arthure*.

Among its actual companions it seems to have had pieces dealing with both the great classical subjects of mediaeval romance, Alexander and Troy; but the alliterative poems on the first subject which can be probably referred to this period are but fragmentary.[7] It is otherwise with the great *Destruction of Troy*,[8] which we possess in plainly alliterated verse, and which is not impossibly older than 1400. This is a huge poem of over 14,000 lines, translated with a certain amount of freedom from the popular compilation on the subject by Guido Colonna, written in a Northern or North Midland dialect, and containing no sort of identification of author or time of composition, though attempts have been made to father it on the usual

The *Destruction of Troy*.

6. Ed. Perry, E.E.T.S.
7. See note at end of chapter.
8. E.E.T.S., ed. Panton and Donaldson.

Huchowne. It is less rugged than the *Morte d'Arthure,* and a good deal less picturesque, though appearances are unfairly against the poet when he says in his penultimate line "Now the *proses* is put plainly to end," for he only means "process." On the whole, it is by no means unreadable, long as it is, and every now and then, in some of the interminable fighting, in some storm passages, in the account of the death of Ulysses at the hands of Telegonus, and in the Troilus and Briseida[9] episodes, the writer contrives to acquit himself very fairly. But it does not compare well with its chief rival in the same "matter" on the metrical side, *King Alisaunder.*

The *Pistyl of Susan.*

And so we come to the *Pistyl of Susan,* one of the smallest in bulk, but, for reasons already given and others, one of the most remarkable. It is a versification of the pleasant piece of poetical justice which, as "not found in the Hebrew" of the Book of Daniel, was turned out from the Canon into the Apocrypha of the English Bible, but is still to be found there, and was, until recent tamperings with the Lectionary, regularly read as First Lesson at Even-song in the Church of England on 22nd November. The earliest version (there are four others dating from the fifteenth century) is found in the great Vernon MS. of the Bodleian Library, one of the hugest of its kind, containing some 800 very large pages filled with religious compositions, and put by experts at not later than 1380.

Susan contains exactly 366 verses (a number perhaps not fortuitous) arranged in one of the varieties (the eight-line with bob and wheel) of the peculiar alliterated and rhymed stanzas already described. The alliteration is heavy—four alliterated words being often, and I think five sometimes, crowded into a not very long line. But it is very well managed, and the poem is distinctly above the average not merely of its class, but of mediaeval verse generally. The author follows the Vulgate narrative closely as a framework, but amplifies and embroiders

9. The retention of this form of the name is perhaps an argument for an early date. For by 1400 the authority of Chaucer would most probably have whelmed "Briseis" and "Briseida" once for all in "Cressid." Yet some think that Chaucer's *Troilus* is referred to.

in the usual fashion, and occasionally breaks in with a completely original addition. The two chief of these (of unequal value) are one of the stock mediaeval gardens, with apples and pomegranates, parrots and goldfinches as serenely mingled as in the *Swiss Family Robinson,* and a most beautiful stanza describing the parting of Susanna and her husband Joachim :

> She fell down flat on the floor, her fere when she found,
> Carped [spoke] to him kindly, as she full well couthe
> (could):
> "Iwis I thee wrathed never at my witand (witting),
> Neither in word nor in work, in eld nor in youth."
> She cowered up on her knees and kissed his hand—
> "For I am damned, I not dare disparage thy mouth."
> Was never more sorrowful segge (man) by sea nor by
> sand,
> Ne never a sorrier sight by north ne by south.
> Then there
> They took the fetters off her feet,
> And ever he kissed that sweet.
> "In other worlds shall we meet,"
> Said he no mair.

Huchowne or no Huchowne, the man who wrote that was a poet in form and in fact. Nor does his dealing "disparage" the mouth of Daniel when that youthful prophet comes to judgment and addresses the elders (indeed they richly deserved it) in language of extreme directness.[10]

10. *Note to Second Edition.*—The uncertainty of date as to the *Alexander* alliterative romances caused, in the first edition of this book, first, irresolution whether to notice them here or later, and then (by an accident, to which most writers in this kind have I suppose at some time or other fallen victims) the unintentional omission of any further notice of them. As at present accessible (the Scottish Text Society promises further publication) in the Roxburghe Club issues (ed. Stevenson), and in those of the E.E.T.S. (ed. Skeat), they consist of two short fragments and one long one. This latter (C. of Skeat, E.E.T.S., 1886) in the longest version extends to nearly 6000 lines of the usual character, giving the fabulous history of the hero from the usual starting-point of Nectanebus (see p. 113) to the Conquest of Babylon, and including the correspondence of Alexander and Dindimus (see p. 37

note). This also appears in one of the shorter fragments (B. of Skeat, E.E.T.S., 1878) while the other (A. of Skeat printed in his *William of Palerne,* E.E.T.S., 1867) deals with earlier parts of the story. None of the three exhibits remarkable poetical merit, and their authorship (plural or singular) though it has been discussed as usual, is quite unknown. The long poem is, however, interesting for comparison with the rhymed version noticed above; and, if inferior in some points, shows the superior *vigour,* as well as capacity, of the long alliterative line.

Note to Third Edition—I observe that the short piece of *Chevalere Assigne* ("The Knight of the Swan," E.E.T.S., 1868) has also been overlooked. It is not wanting either in vigour or in pathos; but the alliterative verse is even less rhythmical than usual.

INTERCHAPTER 2

THE incorrectness, or at least the insufficiency, of that view of literature and literary criticism which despises the historic estimate, and bids us look only to "the best and principal things," is perhaps nowhere illustrated in a more complete and damaging fashion than by the period of which I have endeavoured to give some account in the foregoing Book. With exceptions, rare in number and almost infinitesimal in proportional bulk, it contains nothing that can, by the widest inclusion and the kindliest judgment that retains critical competence, be described as "best" or "principal" in relation to literature at large. Whether even these exceptions—a lyric or two of the calibre of *Alison,* a passage here and there in Layamon and the Romances, the flashes of intensity in the author of *Cleanness,* the melancholy music of *The Pearl* and some of the Hampolian poems, the simple and pathetic parting of Susanna and Joachim quoted just now—whether even they reach the fringe of the best things may be questioned without excessive severity. Under a still lower and more accommodating standard this Early Middle English literature demands, in order to enjoy much of it as literature, a kind of pre-established harmony of taste in the reader, not a little acquaintance with other letters, and a certain though not a very great amount of patience and preparation in the mere rudiments. Every now and then, especially in the alliterative poems, the strange combination of elaborate pains and insufficient accomplishment or taste will positively disgust; in almost every case an impatient temper must know how to avoid, or a patient one how to endure, vast overdoses of ill-baked bread to a modicum of sack, vast stretches of literary desert to a few not always quite paradisaical oases.

And yet there is no portion of English literature the study of which can be wholly pretermitted with greater danger, none the study of which is repaid by greater increase of understanding, and even of enjoyment, in regard to the rest. It is desirable, no doubt, that the student—even that the reader, who, though he may not call himself a student, wishes to read intelligently—should read Anglo-Saxon literature; but it can hardly be said to be necessary. In certain points, and those of the most importance, some acquaintance with Middle English literature before Chaucer may be said to be an absolute necessity. Fortunately we now only preach to the converted when we insist on the necessity of understanding Chaucer in order to understand what follows him; before long, let us hope, it will be equally unnecessary to dwell much on the hopelessness of understanding Chaucer unless we have some understanding of what he followed.

Let us see, then, what the three hundred years which passed since the date of our last summary, in the first of these interchapters, had done for English literature, what they had put ready as accomplished facts for acceptance or rejection in the way of materials and in the way of tools for any one who felt the vocation of writing about, or a little after, the middle of the fourteenth century.

In the first place, though this concerns us least, and is moreover a now generally accepted fact, they had provided a language which, disguised a little by the occasional retention of obsolete forms of letters, by unsettled and capricious spelling, and by dialectic variations, possessing still a considerable number of obsolete words, and lacking as yet some of the terms of art and thought which the translators, and especially the prose writers, of the fifteenth century were to add, was to all intents and purposes English—not Old English, not Middle English, but English, with still a chip or fleck of shell in the shape of an inflection only half discarded upon it, but about to cast even these off. The notion of Chaucer as having flooded the language with French words in contradistinction to the sound Saxon vocabulary of his contemporary Langland died hard, and perhaps simulates life even yet; but its obstinacy in surviving is merely Partridgean.

If less general adhesion be given to the proposition that English metre was also, in the rough at least, fully created, that, I believe, is chiefly due to the much inferior attention which has been given to the subject. It is true that the formative period of prosody had not yet ceased, and that the genius of the four masters, Chaucer himself, Spenser, Shakespeare, and Milton (to whom it is perhaps but just to add Surrey and Marlowe), had to be applied before all the resources of English in this respect were at the command of whosoever chose—and chooses—to use them. It is true that at the actual time a revolt, and a rather formidable one, was being made by alliterative rhythm against metre. This went some way, and if Langland had had variety, flexibility, range, equal to his intensity—especially if he had had anything like Chaucer's command of phrase—it might have gone farther. But the truth is that alliteration, with its tyrannous restriction to the word which must be, not the word which ought to be, chosen, is the deadly foe of phrase itself, and consequently of style, and could not have triumphed. On the other hand, English metrical writers themselves had to unlearn something and to learn much. They had to get rid of the final *e,* a live thing once, but now somewhat like a half-dead but not severed branch on a tree. They had to get rid of the superstition of the central pause, and of strict syllabic number, which they derived, though they fought against both, from their French models, and in the first case from the grasp of the "dead hand" of Anglo-Saxon itself. But 150 years at least of steady practice, of constant pressure of metrical form, on the yielding but by no means merely passive body of older rhythm, had got the poetical capacities of the language into real shape, had made not a merely mechanical junction, but a true graft. The octosyllable and decasyllable, with the trisyllabic variance in each, were already established, a crowd of ballad and romance combinations of eights and sixes was in existence, the rhymed, loose-pivoted line of the *Moral Ode* and Robert of Gloucester, with the unrhymed double stave of the alliterators, were ready between them to produce a family of metres of greater compass than the decasyllable—the Alexandrine, the iambic or trochaic fourteener, the tetrameter anapaestic. It is true that the actual production of these in any satisfactory form was postponed for a century and more; but that is merely one of the constant accidents of literary history, and we shall perhaps be able to give some explanation of it when we come to sum up the fifteenth century itself.

Of advance in the direction of kinds and subjects we have to speak with more reserves and allowances. In some cases there is even a falling back; thus Early Middle English is entirely destitute of the sound and valuable, if not extremely accomplished, original historic prose that we find in Anglo-Saxon. Indeed, in the whole domain of prose there is at best a stationary state, at most and more commonly a distinct decline. Nor is this in the least surprising. Prose is, far more than verse, a matter of practice and copying; and by the tenth century—the best age of Anglo-Saxon prose—that language had had experience plentiful in bulk and extensive in time, if a little restricted in kind. The disorganisation which necessarily attended the remaking of the language made this practice to at least some extent useless and obsolete, while there were no models for the new tongue except Latin, inasmuch as none of the modern vernaculars (except Icelandic) had any prose worth speaking of to give it. We shall indeed see that no really good English prose appeared till a long apprenticeship in translating Latin and French had supplied this want. Meanwhile, such prose as there was, was more than ever exclusively religious.

This meant in its turn that all new kinds and subjects, whether suitable or not, had to be treated in verse, and they were so treated. It has been often enough pointed out that, to compensate for its drawbacks, verse had at least one merit, that in a non-reading age it was better suited for reading or reciting aloud to others. At any rate, its predominance is an undisputed fact, and one on which it is not necessary to dwell. Homilies and paraphrases of the Bible, narrative historical and narrative fictitious, rudimentary science, political satire, anything and everything found a vehicle in verse of kinds nearly as various as the subjects, but with the skipping octosyllable or the swinging, if not yet very smoothly swinging, fourteener for preference. Much of this verse (and that not merely in the Romance section) is pleasant and profitable to read even now. But comparatively little of it can be said to be fully accomplished as literature, and almost the whole of it is pervaded by a characteristic not new (for it confronts us almost equally in Anglo-Saxon); not in the least surprising, for it was practically inevitable; but necessarily affecting the interest and merit of the whole in an unfavourable way.

This characteristic comes from the fact that the great majority of the literature of the period is certainly, and that all but an infinitesimal part of it is probably, not original literature at all but translation. It is true that translation was not then so entirely unoriginal a thing as it is—as it prides and boasts itself upon being—now. Unkind critics have suggested that at least one reason why the mediaeval translator allowed himself such liberties was that he had not the scholarship to be faithful; kind ones may prefer to see in it at least something of native literary aspiration, and the desire not merely to tread in the exact footsteps of another. But what is certain is that in English and at this time really original writing—writing "out of a man's own head"—is so rare as to be, in important instances, almost unknown. When a man did not, as the enormous majority of the romance-writers and not a few others certainly did, merely translate more or less loosely a single precedent work, he either compiled from several or (as must have been the case with even the more original religious writers from him of the *Ancren Riwle* downwards) wrote on subjects which had been so frequently handled, and which had such a large stock of prescribed and expected commonplaces and common forms appertaining to them, that his work has almost the character of a translation, or at least compilation. Nothing is more singular, more characteristic, or more puzzling in mediaeval literature than the immense mass of its additions to the literary stock of the world, not merely in mere bulk of writing, but in new themes, new touches, new handling of all sorts—contrasted with the almost impossibility of attributing any large original increments of the kind to single persons. It is not made, it grows. The great Arthurian legend itself is only the crowning example of the kind. In a few years this passes from the barest and most unpromising scantlings first, and then from an ingenious but not specially poetical sham history like a hundred others, to the stateliest and most elaborate structure of romance that exists. And how, from whom, exactly when, exactly where all this comes nobody knows, though in the desperation of craving for knowledge men have constantly thought and asserted that they knew. Nor is this the only point of the kind in which the Middle Ages resemble the enchanted forests of which they were so fond. Nothing happens as it might be expected to happen: the land which pretty certainly furnished the materials of the legend does not furnish the language in which it is first told; the language decoys the investigator away from the real fatherland of the story. "Everything is somebody else's," as the pathetic-humorous complaint of later fiction has it.

Yet to those who can be content to acquiesce in ignorance of an authorship which is, after all, a matter of very little consequence, and in whom the artificial thirst for *Quellen,* for origins, does not master the natural one for the water or wine of literature, whether fresh-drawn from spring, fresh-pressed from grape, or transfused through a dozen vessels, provided only it be clear and well-tasted—there is little disappointment and much satisfaction in the literature, even the English literature, of this period. If the writers seldom absolutely created for themselves, they are as a rule careful never to leave any capital that may come into their hands entirely unimproved, if it be only by fresh borrowings and combinations. And it is perhaps not less reasonable and more fair to suspect that their additions were, in many cases at any rate, not borrowings at all but original gifts—that the creative fancy, too shy and distrustful of itself to go altogether alone, took its opportunity of exercise under cover and with the assistance of what existed already. At any rate, till we know to the contrary, there is no harm, for instance, in giving Layamon the credit of Argante and the elves; and if it should unluckily turn out after all that he does not deserve it, why, we can at worst transfer that credit to somebody else. The thing is important in literature, not the man.

Moreover, for those at least who are fortunate enough to take interest not merely in the thing, but in the way in which it is treated, the manner in which it is done, this Middle English period has plenty of attraction besides that chief one of prosody, which has been sufficiently brought out. Not only is the mere word-hoard regularly, if at first slowly, increasing, but the uses of it are varying, multiplying, acquiring deftness and artistic value with every author and in every book. Here we have the rough draft of a wordplay or a conceit familiar in Elizabethan writers. There we see (in a pamphlet published by Wynkyn de Worde, and translated from the French, it is true, but no doubt much older in both languages) an early form of the trap by which Goldsmith for once avenged himself on Johnson, and actually obtained an acknowledgment of his victory. Here again a familiar cadence in verse, there (it is true very rarely as yet) a memorable rhythm in prose, connects itself, for those who have the fortune to recognise the connection, with better things, or at least other things, to come. We are still in the workshop, and hardly any master workman has yet appeared, but *opus fervet* and the master himself is at hand.

Book III

Chaucer and His Contemporaries

1

CHAUCER'S LIFE AND POEMS

Life—Probably spurious Tales—Other questioned work—The arguments for and against it—Admittedly genuine work—The three periods—The *Romaunt of the Rose*—The Minor Poems—*Troilus and Cressid*—The *House of Fame*—The *Legend of Good Women*—The *Canterbury Tales.*

IT was somewhat past the middle of the fourteenth century when the long process of incubation and experiment which we have followed from the cessation of the *Anglo-Saxon Chronicle* to Hampole, Minot, and the revival of alliterative verse, culminated in a generation of positively accomplished, and in some cases positively known, poets and prose-writers. Chaucer is not the earliest of these; he is not, as is sometimes still openly said, and perhaps much more frequently thought, the only one worthy of attention. But he is by so much the greatest figure, that he deserves to give, as he has always given, name to the period, and to have precedence of those who, like Gower possibly, Langland, if Langland it was, and Wyclif pretty certainly, had the start of him in literary performance.

The life of Chaucer has for the greater part of a century had its full share of that touching, if not always intelligent, devotion which justifies the theory that the human race is not after all indifferent to its heroes. We know indeed very little about him that has even the slightest connection with literature; and we are bidden to give up the idea that he once beat a Franciscan friar in Fleet Street—which is picturesque and not impossible. We know that Cecilia de Chaumpaigne pardoned him or released him *de raplu meo;* but we have no

Life.

portrait of Cecilia, we know nothing about her, and there is no more interesting probability about the matter itself than that *raplus meus* was one of those abductions of heiresses for purely mercenary reasons which were extremely common in mediaeval times and later, perhaps as late as the days and experiences of Henry Fielding. We know the pots of wine assigned as Chaucer's allowances, the details of his court suits as a page, and a great many other even less interesting details; but for the real Chaucer, the man, the poet, we are left to the poems[1] and our own imagination, being perhaps not the more unhappy therefor.

There is no positive evidence of the date of Chaucer's birth; for that of his death, 1400, we have not only tradition but the strong circumstantial proof that his pensions ceased to be paid at that time. The birth-date used to be fixed at 1328, and is now shifted to 1340, for reasons which must be sought in the biographies. The older date suits better with the acknowledged fact that Chaucer was an old man when he died; the new with most known circumstances of his life. He was pretty certainly the son of John and Agnes Chaucer, the former a citizen and vintner of London, who had a house in Thames Street The separation between Court and City was not in medieval days by any means sharp or total, and John Chaucer was not only a citizen and vintner, but held a post in the Royal Household which necessitated his accompanying King Edward and Queen Philippa to the Continent in 1338. Nor is there any doubt that Geoffrey Chaucer himself was in close and constant connection with the Royal Family.

The first link of this connection has been presumably found in some accounts for the household of Lionel, Edward's son, which record the provision of cloth, etc., and money allowances to a Geoffrey Chaucer in 1357. Two years later, he served in the army which invaded France, was taken prisoner, and ransomed in March 1360. In 1367 he had a pension

1. Editions are extremely numerous; the standard library form is that of Professor Skeat's work (Clarendon Press), in six volumes, with a seventh containing what modern philological scholarship regards as the Chaucerian Apocrypha.

of 20 marks as valet of the King's chamber. In 1370, 1372, 1377, and 1378 he was employed on diplomatic missions abroad, the second and fourth extending as far as Italy, with practically certain results on his literary work. We cannot find space here for the successive grants, from pitchers of wine to pensions, which he received for those and other services, with their cessations, restorations, diminutions, and augmentations, all which the biographers record to the uttermost farthing. The most important and interesting of these details are that in 1374 he received from the Corporation of London a lease for life of the gate-house at Aldgate, which he actually held for many years; and that a little later he was appointed Comptroller of Customs in the port of London. His prosperity ebbed and flowed with that of the sections of the royal house to which he was more particularly attached, and was at its worst during the predominance of the Duke of Gloucester under Richard II. But though Chaucer was faithful to the latter, the accession of Henry of Bolingbroke did him no harm, as he had been attached of old to John of Gaunt. It seems that he probably died at Westminster, where he had taken a house not long before. He was certainly married; his wife pretty certainly died in 1387; and he had a son named Lewis, to whom in 1391 he very agreeably dedicated his *Treatise on the Astrolabe*. But his wife, whose name was apparently Philippa, is rather a shadowy personage, her identification as sister to Katherine Roet or Swinford, last wife of John of Gaunt, being rather probable than proved. Nor is there much positive evidence of Chaucer's formerly alleged connection with Woodstock or of his fatherhood of the Thomas Chaucer who became a person of wealth and importance later.[2] Nor is it superfluous to add a word of caution on the attempts made to take the personal descriptions in the Prologue to *Sir Thopas* as authentic. Nothing apparently will cure commentators of this rashness, not even the diminutive

2. At the same time, it is not to be too lightly rejected, for the authority is Thomas Gascoigne (the author of the *Liber Veritatum,* partly edited by the late Mr. Thorold Rogers), who was born but a year or two at most after Chaucer's death, was later Chancellor of Oxford, in which University he resided almost all his life, and was a man interested in letters, inquisitive, and usually well-informed.

figure which Thackeray has subjoined to his own pretty faithful delineation of the face of Michael Angelo Titmarsh. What manner of man Chaucer was mentally we can see with infallible certainty from his work; what he was physically is quite unimportant and utterly uncertain, though there is a fair chance that the so-called Occleve portrait, occurring in a MS. of that writer's work, may be genuine.

On the work itself (and in this case much more reasonably) infinite pains have also been spent; but here also we meet with difficulties. There was, of course, in Chaucer's time no regular "publication" of literature; and not only in that time, but for long afterwards, precise dating of work was an exception and an accident, while precise attribution of it was rarer still. In the fifteenth and sixteenth centuries, both in MSS. and early printed copies, a very heterogeneous mass of material came to pass under Chaucer's name. This mass, which it has been the business of the last century to sift, may be conveniently found in Chalmers's *Poets,* and it may, stopping short for the moment of all controversial matter whatever, be divided into four classes:

I. What is certainly, or so probably as to amount to certainty, Chaucer's.

II. What is certainly not Chaucer's.

III. What, on grounds which can be admitted by strictly literary and comparative criticism, is probably not Chaucer's.

IV. What, on grounds doubtful to such criticism, has been rejected by some.

With the matter contained in the second class, such as Lydgate's *Tale of Thebes* and Henryson's *Testament of Cressid,* we need not trouble ourselves. It never had any business where it was, and such of it as deserves notice will have that notice elsewhere. The third division, though containing some interesting work also, may be briefly dismissed. The *Tale of Gamelyn,* a capital ballad-romance in rough but spirited eights and sixes, containing a version of the story on which Shakespeare founded *As You*

Probably Spurious Tales.

Like It, is the best of the division and an excellent thing. But neither metre, language, dialect, style, nor anything else about it is in the very slightest degree Chaucerian. It belongs distinctly to the class of poetry which, whether he contemned it or not, he certainly eschewed; and it could only be his as a literary *tour de force* entirely out of character with the age. So too the less excellent *Plowman's Tale,* in eight-lined stanzas of eights rhymed *ababbcbc,* though less good than the *Gamelyn,* is equally or even more un-Chaucerian. It is a half-mystical satire, evidently written by some one who had both Chaucer and Langland before him, and who chose to throw the matter (as far as he could catch it) of the one into the form (as far as he could conceive it) of the other. Here again Chaucer could only have written the thing as a *tour de force,* as a kind of parody, in the spirit of the nineteenth, or at farthest back of the eighteenth, century, not of his own time. The *Tale of Beryn,* or *Second Merchant's Tale,* with its Prologue *The Pardoner and The Tapster,* is un-Chaucerian in metre rather than in character, but the external attribution to Chaucer is late and weak.

Other questioned work.

The case is very different with another class of work, which, unlike this last, passed the vigilant and eminently literary scrutiny of Tyrwhitt, but has during the past generation been black-marked owing to the operation of a class of argument which was, I believe, started by the late Mr. Henry Bradshaw, and which has been perfected by Dr. Skeat. The power of literary, or at least bibliographical, divination which Mr. Bradshaw possessed does not seem to have been exaggerated, any more than the "magnetic" force of his personal character. And it is impossible for any one who has the slightest knowledge of the immense erudition and the unwearied kindness of the now late Professor of Anglo-Saxon at Cambridge to speak of him with disrespect. Further, there is the difficulty that the class of argument in question, itself resting on extremely minute points of linguistics, phonetics, and other "sciences of the border," as we may perhaps call them, seems to demand an equal specialism from those who would attempt to meet it. Yet the criticism which would exclude from the Chaucerian canon such things not merely as the *Court of Love* and *The Flower and the Leaf,* but in whole or in part the existing English version of the *Romance of the Rose*, which we know that Chaucer did translate, cannot be allowed to pass quite unchallenged by those whom it does not satisfy.[3]

This criticism rests, as I understand it, upon two points—alleged differences of language, which, in the *Court of Love* especially, is said to be much later than Chaucer's time; and still more, alleged differences of rhyme. Few can lay much real stress on such arguments as that *The Flower and the Leaf* must have been written by a woman because the supposed narrator is addressed as "daughter"—an argument which would prove, among ten thousand other agreeable absurdities, that *Fatima* was not written by the author of *Locksley Hall,* and that Sir David Lyndsay was a four-legged creature.

It is said more seriously that Chaucer in his certain works never rhymes such a word as *grene,* in which the final *e* still existed, to such a word as *been,* where it was not; that he never rhymes *y* and *ye,* and so forth. And upon pleas of the kind an injunction against ticketing the incriminated poems as even possibly Chaucer's has been sought, and commonly taken as granted.

This question, of course, cannot here be argued at length, but it is far too important to be passed over altogether. And as similar arguments, *mutatis mutandis,* are applied to much interesting work of others before the Restoration, I may be allowed briefly to state three demurrers, in ascending order of what seems to me cogency, which justify, again as it seems to me, suspension of judgment in all the cases where these arguments are brought.

The arguments for and against it.

A. The first and weakest (being merely *ad hominem,* but still stronger than others) is that the black-markers should agree a little better among themselves. The English *Rose,* for

3. It does not seem necessary to dwell on all the Apocrypha, many of the pieces having very small interest. *The Cuckoo and the Nightingale* has a little, chiefly from its possible connection with *The Owl and the Nightingale,* and its possible influence on Milton's first sonnet later. It is now attributed by the Separatists to one Sir Thomas Clanvowe.

instance, has been split up, and the very parts which are granted to Chaucer by one critic on these principles are denied to him by another. A calculus which brings out contradictory results is not quite a calculus to accept without reservation.

B. The second and much stronger is that the malcontents practically beg the question. They exclude certain work from consideration to get at Chaucer's rhymes; they draw an inference from the remainder; and then they argue back to the excluded parts and declare them not genuine, when they have not themselves been allowed to give evidence. We might as well exclude the "classical" experiments in the appendix to *Enoch Arden,* because there is no trace of such scansion in the mass of Tennyson's voluminous work.

But the third argument, and by far the strongest of all, is this:

C. If a poem be in metre, rhyme, or language distinctly *older* than its alleged author's time, then it may fairly be pronounced not his, unless the habits of the age permit the supposition of deliberate archaism. But if it be *younger,* no argument can be founded upon that fact alone, because copyists may always have been responsible for the modernisation. And as a matter of fact we have but *one* MS. for the *Court of Love* and *none* for *The Flower and the Leaf*—facts of which the importance cannot be exaggerated.

These arguments do not appear to me to have received sufficient answer, and they are therefore put on record here, with the caution that I do not by any means assert that Chaucer wrote the English *Rose,* or *The Flower and the Leaf,* or the *Court of Love.* There is not evidence enough for that.[4] Moreover, Chaucer can do more than well without the poems, and the poems are quite pretty enough to stand by themselves.[5] If *The*

4. There is even evidence, of a much stronger kind than that on which the Separatists rely, against it. For instance, it may fairly be questioned whether Chaucer would have compared grass to "green wool," as the author of *The Flower and the Leaf* is made to do. He was the less Chaucer for the time if he did.

5. *The Flower and the Leaf* is put by the Separatists about 1440, in the dead waste and middle of the night of English poetry; the *Court of Love*

Flower and the Leaf is middle fifteenth century, the *Court of Love* early sixteenth, as the prevailing opinion holds, supported by at least a general consensus of the chief authorities in the philological treatment of English, then there are two unknown English poets of those two dates who have each left nothing else, and who were not everyday poets.

The works which, by the severest modern criticism, are left as indisputably Chaucer's are as follows:

A translation (whether it be in whole, in part, or in no part, that still existing) of the *Roman de la Rose*.

Admittedly genuine work.

A considerable body of Minor Poems, original and translated—*The Book of the Duchess, The Complaints of Mars and Venus, The Parliament of Fowls, An(n)elida and Arcite,* with about a score of short pieces, ballads, and what not.

The House of Fame.

The Legend of Good Women.

Troilus and Cressid.

The Canterbury Tales.

Besides the prose translation of *Boethius* and the *Treatise on the Astrolabe,* which will be dealt with in the next chapter but one.

The three periods.

Further, an ingenious, and by no means improbable, though not absolutely certain, theory has divided all this work into three *Periods*—in the first of which, represented by the *Romaunt of the Rose* and most of the minor poems, French influence predominates; in the second of which this is exchanged for Italian, as shown in *Troilus* (adapted from Boccaccio), the *House of Fame* (at least possibly suggested by Dante), and the first draft of the *Knight's Tale* (again from Boccaccio); while in the third, of which the *Canterbury Tales* are the great outcome, the poet, except for themes and motives merely, discards all foreign influence and becomes substantially English, though retaining

at about 1500, when that night saw only the broken dreams of Hawes and the cockcrow of Skelton, or about 1530, still before dawn.

his literary scholarship, both in the modern literary tongues, French and Italian, and the ancient, his proficiency in the latter as far as Latin is concerned being very considerable, and extending not merely to the compilations of the Dark and Middle Ages, but to a very fair share of the Classics proper. This arrangement corresponds very well with the known procession of the facts of Chaucer's life and with the probabilities of the case, but it is, to use the word which Mr. Matthew Arnold godfathered in English, "facultative," it can be taken or left; the examination of the work itself is necessary.

The translation of the *Roman de la Rose,* though it is incomplete and stops far short of the enormous length of the French original, yet extends to the very respectable number of 7700 lines, in octosyllabic couplets. One great literary reason for accepting it as Chaucer's lies in the nature and conduct of these octosyllables. We have seen that, as was unavoidable, they were early imitated from French, and were for some time the favourite romance-metre, though they gradually gave place to more complicated arrangements, especially the six- or twelve-lined stanza, with sixes at regular intervals between the eights. Before Chaucer, however, the octosyllabic couplet, in its stricter form, had not been well mastered by English writers, who either availed themselves more or less of the license of equivalence (which at its full stretch gives us the *Christabel* rhythm) or else fell, as indeed most French mediaeval writers themselves fell, into a *staccato* stiffness on the one hand or an over-fluent and insignificant sing-song on the other. We shall find that Chaucer's exceedingly ingenious and scholarly contemporary Gower did not avoid this latter danger. But in the English *Romaunt of the Rose* a distinct command of the measure is observable, not indeed quite to the same extent as in the probably later *House of Fame* (one of the capital examples of the metre in English), but sufficiently like that and sufficiently unlike others to justify the attribution of the two to the same hand. Fortunately the English includes the whole of the first part of the original—that written by William of Lorris—and it renders very well the exquisite touch of that original, uniting as it does the languid charm of moonlight and dream

The *Romaunt of the Rose.*

with the fresh vividness of morning and movement. Nor need we very bitterly regret the loss of a version of the far more prosaic pedantries and pleasantries of Jean de Meung.

The Minor Poems.

Of the Minor Poems, all display in various ways the learning, and in different stages and degrees the accomplishment of language and metre, which make Chaucer so delightful, while some have interest certain or probable of a biographical or historical kind. The *Book of the Duchess,* for example, which is certainly on the death of Duchess Blanche of Lancaster, first wife of John of Gaunt, gives us a date—she died in 1369—and has been—on the 1340 theory of the poet's birth—plausibly enough conjectured to be one of his earliest works, the *Complaint of Pity* (which appears to enshrine some unlucky love affair) being perhaps earlier still. The *Book* is in octosyllables much less perfect than those of the *Romaunt,* and evidently the work of a novice, while its substance is rather clumsily made up of classicism and allegory in the less happy manner of the *Rose* itself. *Chaucer's A B C* (a sort of acrostic in which each stanza opens with a letter of the alphabet in order) is said to have been written for the same Blanche. These stanzas are eight-lined (*ababbcbc*), religious in tone, and of no great poetical merit. Much better in the eyes of literature, if not in those of morality, are the *Complaints of Mars and Venus.* In the first, and probably in both, the well-known story is applied to personages who are pretty certainly identified with John Holland, Earl of Huntingdon and Duke of Exeter, and Isabel of Castile, daughter of Peter the Cruel, and wife of Edmund Duke of York, son of Edward III. Isabel was more famous for beauty than for strict propriety of conduct. But there is no open attribution in the poem, and the "Venus" part at any rate was translated or adapted from a French original by Otes de Granson. The *Complaint of Pity, Queen Annelida,* and the *Parliament of Fowls* are all mainly in the seven-lined stanza *ababbcc,* which was Chaucer's favourite among these combinations, and which acquired the name of rhyme-royal perhaps from that circumstance, though the usual explanation is that it was because of the use of the stanza in the *King's Quair.*

Of these three poems, the *Complaint,* though the least accomplished in form, is genuine in tone; and *Queen Annelida,* though ostensibly fiction, rings as of a personal sorrow. But the *Parliament* or *Assembly of Fowls* is by far the best of the three, and indeed of all the minor poems. Here in the very opening—

> The life so short, the craft so long to learn,
> The essay so hard, so sharp the conquering,
> The dreadful joys alway that flit so yerne [eagerly],
> All this mean I by love—

we feel at once the grip, the thrill, the sense of mastery and mystery which are so rare in earlier poetry. And the rest of the piece which some would have to show already Italian influence, announces Chaucer quite unmistakably in the catalogue of trees afterwards copied by Spenser—

> The builder oak and eke the hardy ash—

and that other of the birds themselves. These catalogues he was fond of applying afresh in various forms and matters, and they display his then unexampled, and seldom since approached, still seldomer outdone, faculty of making the epithet fit the noun, and transforming the bald enumerations which are one of the curses of mediaeval poetry into broad and varied examples at once of keen observation and masterly expression.

The smaller poems do not seem to require any very special notice. Some of the ballads, such as the newly recovered one *To Rosamond,* are pretty; the late and sad *Flee from the Press* has dignity and truth; and others are interesting. But Chaucer, who was for so great a poet curiously deficient in strictly lyrical gift, shows better in long poems than in short, and better in narration than in reflection. Indeed, it is scarcely wrong to say that, as regards the tone and substance of his work, he is rather a dramatist and a novelist than a poet, though he applied to the subjects which, there being as yet no novel and no play, he treated in poetic form, an unsurpassed and rarely equalled power of poetic expression. His expression is the expression of the poet; his thought the thought of the dramatist or novelist.

Hence it is—a matter rare and certainly not to be grumbled at—that, as has been just remarked, his long poems are better than his short. In the long poems of his supposed middle period he was indeed still hardly out of leading-strings—or rather he chose to wear them, for *Troilus and Cressid* is translation in little more than name, the *House of Fame* owes nothing more than hints to its original, and the *Legend of Good Women* handles the classical stories, which it takes chiefly from Ovid, with nearly as much freedom as that shown in the *Canterbury Tales* themselves.

Troilus and Cressid.

Each of the three has a charm of its own, and *Troilus* has the additional one of forming a link in a chain of writing on the same subject by a succession of writers all eminent in the history of literature, and most of them possessing far more than merely historical importance. The figure of Cressida (Briseida, Griseida, etc.), which the trouvère Benoît de Sainte-More had extracted from the dustbin of Dares and had partially, but only partially, vivified, passed, a very little further modernised, into the *Historia Trojana* (mostly pillaged from Benoît) of Guido Colonna or delle Colonne at the end of the thirteenth century. Hence Boccaccio in his *Filostrato,* applying his genius as a novelist and his talent as a poet, took Cressid, but made her something far more interesting than the passive love-thrall of Benoît. Chaucer, in turn taking her from Boccaccio, softened and complicated her trails a little, but added to the story the wonderfully vivid and individual figure of Pandarus. Chaucer's Scottish follower, Henryson, not meddling with his master's actual matter, completed the story unequally, but with marvellous touches in parts, by the *Testament of Cressid* in the fifteenth century; Shakespeare in the sixteenth dramatised, with variations, the Chaucerian part; and Dryden in the seventeenth refashioned Shakespeare. Perhaps there is no other instance in literary history of so many persons of such distinction taking and handing on the same torch so long. Nor need we hesitate to give Chaucer's own contribution to the series the credit of the most accomplished long poem yet written in English. The rhyme-royal stanzas are thoroughly beaten out; the passionate side of Cressid's character is fully developed, yet with a delicacy which is not always associated with the idea of Chaucer; the comic, and yet not farcical presentation of Pandarus is the first of its kind in English; and the scene where the lovers are made happy, though somewhat too much elaborated (as indeed is the whole poem) with the "Court of Love" scholasticism of the time, is a masterpiece. Nothing but want of technical originality and a certain absence of incident could be charged against *Troilus,* and the first of these charges, as we have seen, is more formally than really true.

The *House of Fame.*

The *House of Fame,* a much shorter poem, in rather more than 2000 lines of octosyllabic couplet, adds to the presentation of Chaucer as master by this time of whatsoever metre he chose to adopt, and strengthens the suggestion (already given by Pandarus) of his peculiar and hitherto unexampled humour. The piece is one of the dreams, curiously compounded of learning, satire, and other things, which flowed from the never-failing fountain of the *Rose* for some three centuries; and it affords opportunity for much shrewd criticism of life. But the most Chaucerian touches of all, perhaps, are put in the mouth of the eagle who carries the poet up to Heaven to see the House. This eagle is a very humorous as well as powerful fowl, and his remonstrances with the wriggling bard at his being so "noyous" to carry, together with his cool, dry comfort and reassurance against any danger of his burden's being made cupbearer to the Gods, or "stellified" or otherwise inconveniently honoured, exhibit the English thing called Humour in almost as full development as the *Canterbury Tales* themselves.

The *Legend of Good Women.*

The *Legend of Good Women,* besides the general interest of all Chaucer's verse, besides its own intrinsic attraction (for the "good women" are the most hapless and blameless of Ovid's *Heroides*), and the remembrance of its suggestion of what is perhaps, all things considered, the most perfect example of Tennyson's verse,[6] has the additional charm of presenting to

6. I read, before my eyelids dropt their shade,
"The Legend of Good Women," long ago

us Chaucer's first experiment in the heroic couplet, the main pillar, with blank verse, of later English poetry, and the medium of his own greatest work. The faint foreshadowings of this in earlier verse, the ways in which the uncertain crystallisation of our prosody now takes this form, now loses it again, have been already indicated. But, as is generally the case when a poet of the first genius hits upon a metre of the first importance, the thing, after being almost unbodied, certainly embryonic, in its first appearance, presents itself practically full-grown. The pathetic subjects of the *Legend* do not indeed give the author much opportunity for showing that marvellous suitableness of the form for comic portraiture and description which the *Canterbury Tales* display. But it is noticeable that he opens the collection with one of those ironic or agnostic, rather than positively sceptical, references to things beyond the present life which are found elsewhere (*e.g.* in the *Knight's Tale),* and which indeed may be said without paradox to form not so much a reaction from the piety of the Middle Ages as a complement or even an integral part of it. After this and some of that passionate praise of the Daisy which, common as it is in fourteenth and fifteenth century poetry, always, or almost always, hides or discloses affection for some living Margaret, one of the usual allegorical overtures (here specially interesting because it refers to the poet's own works) conveys a rebuke to him from the God of Love and Alcestis his servant for the sacrilegious remarks contained in the *Rose* and in *Troilus.* So he undertakes a palinode, and tells in turn of Cleopatra and her faithfulness to Antony, of Thisbe and Dido, of Hypsipyle and Medea, how true they were to the false Jason, of Lucrece, Ariadne, Philomene (Philomela), Phillis, and Hypermnestra—all examples of truth, deserved or undeserved, in woman. It is pleasant, as it always is, to receive the old classical stories set out with the new romantic charm, but the chief attraction of the poem is the new-born metre—the strength, command, and freshness which Chaucer shows in it, his penetration at once

---

Sung by the morning star of song, who made
His music heard below.

A Dream of Fair Women.

of the secrets of *enjambement* or overlapping, of paragraph arrangement, of the merits of a full stop at the end of the first line of a couplet, his mastery of lift and swing, the eddying internal swirl, and yet the constant onward progress of his whole rhythm.

The most like in tone to the *Legend* of all the minor poems are the chief "doubtfuls," the *Court of Love* and *The Flower and the Leaf,* though they are in the Chaucerian stanza or rhyme-royal, not in heroics, and though the *Court of Love* expresses the libel as well as the palinode. It is difficult to say which of the two is the more charming—the *Court of Love* with its statutes half ironical, half passionate, and the delightful concert of the birds at the end, with their amorous descants founded on psalm-motives; or the dreamlike vision of *The Flower and the Leaf,* with the white and green parties of Diana and Flora, and the fantastic allegory of a not extravagant virginity. Of the two, the sentiment is the more Chaucerian in the *Court of Love,* the expression and arrangement in *The Flower and the Leaf.* Perhaps the best argument for the non-Chaucerian authorship is that if they be later they take away the almost unintelligible reproach of England during the ensuing century.

The *Canterbury Tales.*

There is, however, no doubt that common fame has even more than that measure of reason which (to do her the justice too seldom done) she often, though not always, has in such cases in considering Chaucer as the poet of the *Canterbury Tales.* In these we have not only his most considerable work (even if the English *Rose* be wholly his) in bulk; not only his latest; not only work which includes in one part or another of it all the merits and beauties which can be discerned elsewhere, but work displaying a variety and a vigour nowhere else to be found, as well as evidences of original genius which do not appear even in the best of the other works. Although the *Decameron* may have furnished the bare suggestion of alternate tale-telling, although many, perhaps most, of the tales are founded in subject, and even in some details of treatment, on previous work, classical, Italian, or French, yet the whole as a whole is distinctly "new and original" in a very different sense from that of the play-bills. The entire framework, and very much of the inset tales, is studied directly from the English life of the time: the gracious lunar rainbows of the *Rose* have given place to sunlight; the abstractions of scholastic philandering retire in favour of beings of flesh and blood. For Dangier and Bialacoil, even for Cressid, the fair, frail type, and Troilus, the *amoureux transi* of all time, we have the bouncing Wife of Bath and the mincing Prioress, the stout carle of a Miller, and the Summoner as full of reality as he is wanting in delicacy. Even the pieces like the famous *Knight's Tale,* which, like the earlier poems, are taken from others, and deal with literary tradition rather than with English contemporary fact, wear a new guise and breathe a new spirit. We pass from convention to direct impression and expression, from pageantry to conduct, from allegory to fact. There is not less art; there is, in fact, more art than ever, but there is infinitely more matter, and the matter and the art have not the slightest difficulty in joining hands.

We must neglect as usual, or at least notice only by reference, a great deal of the matter which a praiseworthy zeal has accumulated in reference to the *Canterbury Tales.* It is evident on the face of it that they were not finished, and it is very probable that the successive instalments were never arranged even in a provisional order by the author. Industrious editors have accordingly, by the help of the Prologue, the interspersed introductions, and other real or imaginary hints, regrouped the tales, calculated how many more were to be told, and adjusted the stages of the journey. This is good matter for whoso likes it; whoso does not, may neglect it without scathe or demur. It is, however, not unimportant to bear in mind that, as the sure evidences of style and metre show, the book represents work of very different periods, and probably includes not a little which was originally composed without a distinct view to the whole scheme as we have it.

The simplest literary facts, as distinguished from what classical scholars call "hariolations," are that the *Canterbury Tales* consist of about seventeen thousand and odd lines of verse, and two pieces, the *Tale of Melibee* and the *Parson's Tale,* of prose, the former having, in parts, odd indications or remnants of blank verse in it. The poetical part is, with the exception of the burlesque romaunt of *Sir Thopas,* either in rhymed couplets of the kind just described or in stanza. It is divided in point of matter into a prologue, which describes the cavalcade of the Pilgrims to the shrine of Becket, and depicts each in a series of wonderful vignettes or kit-cat portraits. There are, besides *Sir Thopas* and the two prose tales, twenty-one tales in verse of very different lengths, ranging from the two thousand lines of the *Knight's Tale* to mere fragments like the *Cook's*. Between the Tales there are lesser prologues which keep up the framework, and very commonly, if not invariably, display the dramatic power of the author, and his intensely vivid observation of contemporary life at their highest. In point of subject, the Tales now vary in the widest and freest manner. The *Knight's Tale* is a regular romance of chivalry, not on the smallest scale, and belonging to the antique matter. So is the *Man of Law's Tale,* which handles in rhyme-royal a variant of the story of Emarè (p. 121). So is the *Clerk's,* which tells the story of Griselda (rhyme-royal); the *Squire's,* which "leaves half told The story of Cambuscan bold." The Prioress, the Monk, and the Nun tell legends of Saint Cecilia, of Hugh of Lincoln (not *eo nomine*), or stories of Scriptural or classical lore. All the rest are *fabliaux* of one kind or another—that is to say, Englishings, in the most original and least second-hand fashion, of the peculiar verse-stories, often, but not always, distinctly "free" in incident and language, and almost always containing a more or less satirical criticism of life, which had become popular in France about two centuries before.

The prologues are equally various in length and in immediate subject, though the tone is pretty much the same in all. The longest, the most famous, and on the whole the happiest, is the celebrated discourse of the Wife of Bath, which suggested Dunbar's only less brilliant (though more bitter) *The Twa Maryit Women and the Wedo,* and which, like it, is bitter satire on women put into the mouth of a woman, and arranged there with the curiously artful faculty of making the speaker unconsciously a self-satirist. All these prologues are full of direct and personal touches, and, with their prior, the opening piece, contain such a gallery of pictures from the life as no mediaeval writer had ever attempted. The last Shakespearian touch—that which at once makes a character personal and individual for all time, and conveys to it the abiding characteristics of humanity which belong to no time in particular—is indeed not quite Chaucer's. His characters are rather astonishingly brilliant types, individualised by the freshness and sharpness of the impression, than absolutely individual persons. It was indeed almost impossible, till the clutch of allegory had been finally shaken off, that the complete tyranny of the type should be shaken off likewise. But no poets' characters that still partake of the type are so free from its drawbacks and blemishes as Chaucer's; and many as are the great English humorists who have followed him, hardly one has succeeded in making more out of humour. This naturally shows itself in the comic tales and in the prologues, but it is not absent anywhere—not in the stately chivalry of the *Knight's Tale,* not in the pathos of the stories of Constance and Griselda.

Next to this almost omnipresent humour the great feature of the *Canterbury Tales* is the extraordinary vividness and precision of the presentment of images, whether complicated or simple. Of the former, the poem bears in its very forefront—in the figures of the prologue and the temple-descriptions of the *Knight's Tale*—unsurpassed instances. And in such phrases as the famous

> Smiler, with the knife under the cloak,

we meet, and meet almost for the first time, that gift of putting *multum in parvo* which only the greatest men of letters, perhaps in perfection only the greatest poets, possess. Pursuing this faculty still closer, we can bring it down, in at least some instances, to that unsurpassed power of making the epithet suit the noun which has been noticed already. It is evident, and interestingly evident, that this magical power of Chaucer's own words impressed, as it deserved to impress, his contemporaries and scholars more than anything else. His astonishing command of "rhetorique" (which the next age unluckily endeavoured to rival by searching for the most "aureate" words instead of the most appropriate), his "gold dewdrops of speech," were then the things that struck them most. It is true that, even in the *Canterbury Tales,* he has not quite escaped the curse of the *cliché,* of the expletive. But he has it far less than his predecessors, and often for long passages he escapes it altogether.

Lastly (for even Chaucer must be handled summarily here), we perceive in the *Canterbury Tales* the completion of his command of verse. On the subject of this verse there are many opinions, which often depend on preconceived theories. The old seventeenth and eighteenth-century notion that he could not scan is, of course, now held by no instructed person. But there are some who hold that Chaucer allowed himself nine-syllable lines, and others, or the same, that he adhered to a strictly decasyllabic basis, as, it is pretty certain, his immediate successors tried (in their floundering attempts to follow him) to do. My own opinion is that, although Chaucer had not, as till after the great dramatic period it was practically impossible for any man to do, realised the full powers of equivalence in the English decasyllable, and the full advantage derivable from extending the license of pause to every place, he had yet made great strides in this direction. I believe that wherever only nine syllables, even with the final *e,* occur, there is probably a fault in the reading; that there are occasional Alexandrines; and that, although in many instances "the" or "to" was intended to coalesce with a succeeding initial vowel, there are also instances of unquestionable trisyllabic feet. I am quite sure that the balance of the verse is managed with an almost (not perhaps a complete) freedom from that prejudice about the middle pause which, derived from the antediluvian prosody of Anglo-Saxon, and accidentally strengthened by the caesura of French and Latin verse, weighed even upon some Elizabethans, and has never been entirely shaken off by a few, even among artists and scholars in verse, to the present day. And I am sure also that this mobile and sensitive prosody is the second, just as the inexhaustible freshness and propriety of his phrase is the first, great secret of the fact that Chaucer is the earliest English poet who can, without reservations and allowances, be called great, and, what is more, one of our greatest, even to the present day.

Note to Fifth Edition—Further prosodic study has converted me to something like certainty as to the *fact* of the nine-syllable lines in Chaucer; though it is dangerous to dogmatise on his reasons for the use of it.

2

LANGLAND AND GOWER

Piers Plowman—Argument of the B Poem—Gower—The *Confessio Amantis*—Gower's reputation.

ALMOST exactly contemporary with Chaucer were two other poets, both of more than ordinary mark—one of them Chaucer's own equal, if not superior, in intensity, though far his inferior in range and in art, both curious contrasts in more ways than one with him, and with each other. The first was the author of the *Vision of Piers the Plowman*; the second was John Gower.

The now generally accepted identification of the first with William Langley or Langland (the latter being the preferred form) rests on no very definite evidence, but it has fair probability in its favour. And the adoption of it (with a caution) saves us from the inconvenience of constantly using a clumsy periphrasis for a person who will have to be often named. It is well, however, to stop short of the further adventurousness of identifying all the personal details that can be got out of the *Vision* with Langland himself—of giving him a wife named "Kitty," and a daughter named "Calote" (Colette? Nicolette?), of placing him in London, of conferring on him those minor orders which did not necessarily comport celibacy, and so forth. Once more the "prosaic heresy," as we may conveniently call that which takes poetic and dramatic utterances for statements of biographical fact, is to be sedulously eschewed. The allusion to Malvern Hills in the opening of all versions of the poem is less questionable, though it is even here to be observed that the famous and almost proverbial extent of the view therefrom would make it a fitting imagined scene for the sort of survey of England which was coming. But fair presumption, though not certainty, may be drawn from the facts that the varying legends about Langland's birth locate it either at Cleobury Mortimer in Shropshire, or at Wychwood in Oxfordshire, both of which, though at opposite sides, may be said to be in the remoter Malvern precincts, and that the dialect of the poem is said to be West Midland.

Piers Plowman.

Its extreme popularity is shown by the great number of MSS. which remain of it,[1] and by the earliness, if not the number, of the printed editions.[2] It went out of favour in the late seventeenth and eighteenth centuries, neither more nor less than other books of its kind and time; but it was recalled to attention rather earlier than most of them by Whitaker's edition (1813), the *editio princeps* of the "C" or longest text. Not, however, till the more thorough study of it during the last thirty years, in which Professor Skeat has been the main worker, was it discovered that this "C" text was not the only variant on the accepted or "B" text which had up to that time been printed.[3] There are, in fact, three families of MSS., comparison of which has established,

1. The "A" form (*vide infra*) appears in the great Vernon Collection (see p. 107). Professor Skeat—whose repeated studies and editions of the poem culminated in the issue (2 vols. Clarendon Press) which is uniform with his Chaucer, and ranks as the standard—enumerates nearly fifty others.
2. 1550, in three different forms, and 1561. Spenser, who refers to the poem in the *Shepherd's Calendar*, must have read one of these, unless his allusion at the end of December is, as some have thought, to the *Plowman's Tale.* This is to the last degree unlikely, as, if he knew this at all, he would have known it as Chaucer's, with whose works it was then printed, and Chaucer has been already disjunctively referred to in the preceding line.
3. Among others by Wright 1842, revised 1856, and again reprinted 1887. This edition (to which Professor Skeat does that justice by which he is so admirably distinguished in comparison with too many so-called scholars when they deal with predecessors) would be the best of all for general reading, if it were not printed in half lines. It also contains *Piers Plowman's Creed*, an ill-tempered but vigorous Wyclifite lampoon in some 850 lines, which the critics will not allow to be Langland's, though they put it as early as 1394.

as fairly as such things can be established, the fact that the poem was rehandled by its author with remarkable thoroughness at two separate times after the appearance of the first version; that first version itself was not the *receptus* or B, but an earlier, shorter A; and that this earliest version, from allusions in it, may very probably have been written as early as 1362. The B or main text is similarly assigned to 1377 or thereabouts, and the C or longest to 1393, or thirty years after text A. Yet further, if Langland was, as seems extremely likely, the author of the alliterative poem on the deposition of Richard II, which Dr. Skeat calls *Richard the Redeless,* he must have been alive in 1399. This would give him a literary life of not much less than forty years, and assuming, as we may fairly do (for there are no marks of extreme juvenility even in the first version), that he was about thirty when he wrote it, this would carry his life from about 1330 to about 1400. The latter, it is to be remembered, is the year of Chaucer's death pretty certainly, while if the first version of *Piers Plowman* dates from the year mentioned above, it is earlier by some years than anything that we can date with probability as among the still existing works of Chaucer.

At first sight nothing can well be more different, not merely from the *Canterbury Titles,* but from all Chaucer's work, than the *Vision concerning Piers the Plowman.* It is in alliterative verse, according to the revived form of that rhythm so often mentioned in the last Book. The lines are tolerably equal in length, and they not unfrequently fall—urged by the inevitable pressure of the growth of the language and the literature—into Alexandrines, fourteeners, and other constructively metrical shapes. But they do not *aim* at any such structure, they rigidly abstain from rhyme, and they derive their whole poetical form from the middle pause, the fairly corresponding accents, and the three alliterated words, two in the first half and one in the second.[4] The appearance of much greater antiquity than Chaucer's which this gives, and which used to mislead the

4. Langland sometimes indulges in four, but I think never puts himself out of the way for them, or for the extravagant and overloaded alliteration of five or even six words which we find elsewhere.

unwary, is assisted by a somewhat greater allowance of archaic words. But it is entirely false that, as used also to be said, Langland is more "Saxon" in his vocabulary than Chaucer. It has even been calculated by patient industry that his percentage of Latin and Romance words is, if anything, a little larger than Chaucer's; it is quite certain that if both were printed in modernised spelling, it would be at once seen not to be smaller.

The poem, despite its merit and the pains that have been spent on it of late years by interpreters, is by no means a very easy one to understand; and there are few that are more in need of an argument or a running marginal commentary. This arises from the fact that it is not one vision, nor even two, but a series of visions dissolving one into the other, often without any more attempt at coherence—of completion even in the dream-integer, such as it is—than actual dreams exhibit. It would seem as if the author, whether owing to his mysticism and its accompanying vagueness, or to his satiric intent, and the wholesome sense of danger which accompanied that, deliberately avoided rounding off his chapters and driving home his meanings. But the general scheme of the poem, which is divided into *passus*[5] or cantos, is as follows in the central or B text.

Argument of the B Poem.

A prologue of rather more than two hundred lines tells how the Dreamer, in "a summer season when soft was the sun," put on a shepherd's smock like "a hermit unholy of works," and wandering on Malvern Hills, slept by a brook side, and saw a strange vision—a high tower (Heaven) on one side, a deep dungeon (Hell) beneath, and a "fair field full of folk" between (Middle Earth). And he describes the folk and their occupations with much *verve,* digressing, in the bewildering kaleidoscopic fashion which characterises the whole poem, to a very shrewd and early version of the "Bell-the-Cat" story. Indeed, no simile

5. Of these A has twelve (perhaps originally only eight), B twenty, and C twenty-three; but even where the three, or two of them, coincide there are often great variations. Wright's B text—Prof. Skeat does not number his continuously—has 14,696 short or half lines.

is at once so apposite or so illuminative for *Piers Plowman* as that of the kaleidoscope, in respect of the way in which elaborate arrangements of word and thought suddenly and without warning fall into something as elaborate, but quite different. The first *passus* proper opens with a promise, not too exactly kept, to expound the meaning of the tower, dungeon, and field; and their obvious interpretations are given by a lovely lady in linen clothed, who is Holy Church. Her speech is allegorical and digressive in the *Rose* manner—indeed, different as is his spirit, Langland is as full of the *Rose* inspiration as Chaucer himself. The second *passus* introduces—in sharp contrast to this figure, and in answer to the Dreamer's request to be told of Falsehood as she has said so much of Truth—another lady far more gorgeously clothed. This is "Meed the maid"—reward in the good sense, bribery, etc. in the bad—daughter of False (Falsehood), and betrothed to Favel (Fauvel, the hero of an allegorical French romance of the preceding age, and here signifying Flattery). Here Holy Church vanishes, and the current of the story is deflected in the usual odd manner to the marriage of Meed, which it is decided ought to take place in London. The bridal party set out thither under the escort of Simony and Civil Law, but Soothness anticipates them, tells Conscience, who tells the King, and a warm reception being prepared for the party, they disperse, leaving Meed the maid, who stands her ground, weeping. She is at the beginning of the third *passus* courteously taken by the middle and brought before the King. The natural seductiveness of Meed, and the fact that she *may* be honestly gained, are here glanced at. She confesses her sins, uses great largesse to the court generally, and the King promises that she shall marry Conscience, who, however, refuses utterly, giving his offered bride the worst possible character, and belabouring her with Latin quotations, against which she very naturally and indignantly protests. At the beginning of the fourth *passus* this uncompromising knight declines even to kiss her, "but Reason rede me thereto." The King thereupon bids him fetch Reason, who comes, supports Conscience, and brings over the King, who at the end of the fytte says, "As long as our life lasteth live we together."

At the beginning of the fifth *passus* the dream is broken and once more joined. A notice of the Rule of Reason leads or falls, after the mediaeval fashion, into a long and vigorous passage on the Seven Deadly Sins, containing one of the most famous and brightly coloured passages of the poem, the description of a London tavern and the bibbers there. Only at the end of this *passus,* which includes some curious anticipations of Puritan nomenclature, does the personage who gives name to the poem, Piers the Plowman, make his appearance; and even then he has a double portion of the floating phantasmagoric character that marks the whole. At one moment he is a simple plowman who digs and delves, and does what Truth hight, who has half an acre to ear, and cannot leave his work. But he is also a guide to Godliness, and has a wife Dame Work-while-it-is-time, a daughter "Do-right-or-thy-dame-shall-beat-thee," and a son with a longer title still. After dialogues and doings in the sixth with Hunger and others, he emerges in the seventh *passus* as Christ Himself, opposing the venal priests of the day, and teaching a better way to salvation. This is a sort of epilogue to the *passus,* and to the first part of the poem, which resolves itself in the Dreamer's own words into a counsel to seek the help of "Do-well."

But where is "Do-well" to be found? That is the question with which the eighth *passus*[6] opens, and the second part of the poem. Certain friars, though they are quite sure he dwells among them, give no help, and a fresh dream brings to the poet's side Thought, who informs him that not only Do-well but "Do-bet"(ter) and Do-best must be sought. But he cannot tell where to find them, though Wit may. Wit in the ninth *passus* is prodigal of information about the three, about their relation to Lady Anima, and about the fact that Do-well is Obedience, Do-bet Love, and Active Benevolence Do-best. In the tenth *passus* Study, the wife of Wit, takes up the tale and confuses the Dreamer, "sternly staring" with more theology, sending him moreover to Clergy, who talks still more ("This is a long lesson," says the Dreamer, "and little am I wiser. Darkly

6. The numbers, it must be remembered, are those of the B text: in A this *passus* is the *ninth,* and in C the *eleventh.*

ye show where Do-well is or Do-bet"), and to Scripture, who similarly occupies the eleventh. Kind and Reason follow, and at the end of this *passus* the Dreamer, thoroughly bemused, meets one of the most original characters of the whole shadowy procession, Ymaginatif—his own mother-wit apparently, or human reason, not antipathetic to but stopping short of theology. The thirteenth adds others, especially "Hawkyn[7] the Active Man," who cannot keep his clothes unspotten for his daily work—an allegory more open than some. Hawkyn discourses with Patience throughout this *passus* and the next, the fourteenth, but the Dreamer, waking yet again at the beginning of the fifteenth, renews, and with reason, his wailing how it was wonder long ere he could kindly know Do-well. Nor in the long fifteenth *passus,* though according to the title "Do-well" is finished and "Do-bet" begun, can the process be said to be at all clear or satisfactory. We find, however, that the scholastic allegory of the last five *passus* is passing into simple Scripture-history and Christian teaching, and in the sixteenth Piers Plowman reappears, while both this *passus* and the seventeenth shape themselves more and more into a plain life of Christ Himself, leading in the eighteenth to the finest poetry of the whole—a splendid paraphrase of the Entry into Jerusalem, the Passion, and the Harrowing of Hell. This completes Do-bet = Love = Christ, and "Incipit *Do-best,*" which also occupies the last or twentieth. But this is the vaguest and most unfinished part of the whole, Piers Plowman after Christ's death seeming to become the Church, and the two cantos leading to no conclusion whatever.

The so-called A text is much shorter than this. Not only are there but twelve *passus,* the work stopping at the end of the so-called *Vita de Do-well,* but the individual treatment of the different points is much less developed. Not a few of the more striking episodes of the B text, such as the Bell-the-Cat fable, do not appear. On the other hand, there are some things in A which were afterwards left out or completely refashioned, including almost the whole of the last *passus.* C is longer even than B, though the extension to twenty-three *passus* is rather

7. Hawkyn = Henrykin = Harry.

misleading, the old Prologue now ranking as *Passus I,* and some of the earlier divisions of B being split up and redistributed. And there are again some omissions. These, however, are compensated by long insertions, sometimes of the perhaps treacherously biographical kind, especially one in *Passus VI* on which the biography-builders do much rely for Langland's London life; sometimes on "Lolling" and Friardom; sometimes of the more abstract philosophical kind. Indeed this later tendency has distinctly got the upper hand in C, as where, for instance, the quaint and vivid personality of "Hawkyn the Active Man" is changed into a Lorrisian abstraction called "Activa Vita."

On the whole, the presence of this abstraction in *Piers Plowman* has been too little allowed for by some of its eulogists, who have been seduced by the pictorial and dramatic force of the opening of the "Meed" scenes and others to put it rather in competition with the *Pilgrim's Progress*[8] than with the *Roman de la Rose.* There is vivid portraiture in it, and there is a good deal of sharp and practical satire. But even in the Vision proper to some extent, and in *Do-well, Do-bet,* and *Do-best* to a very much greater, the reflective, theological, and allegorical side gets altogether the better of the dramatic and pictorial. To use the image suggested by the change between B and C just noted, Hawkyn the Active Man, who is not always present even in the early part, is hardly present at all in the second; and in his place we have pale abstractions arguing and jargoning about matters of the first importance in themselves—but ill suited for such treatment.

We cannot therefore put Langland by the side of Chaucer either for range, or for directness, or for artistic sense. To say, according to the common antithesis of the books, that he is a poet of the people, Chaucer one of the Court, is very idle. The author of the *Reeve's* and *Miller's Tales* is hardly to be charged with ignorance in respect of the people; and the author of the

8. Guillaume de Deguilleville, from whose *Pélerinage de l'Ame Humaine* Bunyan, through whatever channel, certainly did derive not a little, was as a dreamer before Langland also, just as he was before Chaucer, who adapted from him the *A B C.*

passus about Meed the Maid would certainly not have thanked his eulogists for presuming him to be unfamiliar with the Court. But it is true that Chaucer, to some extent, represents the Humanist and cosmopolitan distaste for politics and for controversial theology, while Langland represents a strong turn for both.[9] It is true also, though he himself seems to have been no Wyclifite or Lollard, that much of the tendency afterwards known as Puritan appears in him, and that, to our sorrow, the iconoclastic spirit, which was in the sixteenth and seventeenth centuries to be the disgrace and curse of England, shows itself in angry remarks about church building and the putting up of painted windows. Intense, but narrow; pious, but a little Philistine—so we must pronounce him.

Nevertheless he had a great literary talent, which perhaps amounted to genius. The literary craftsmanship which succeeds in impressing on a form so uncouth as the unrhymed and only faintly metred alliterative verse the combination of freedom and order, of swing and variety, which marks *Piers Plowman*, is of that kind which must have distinguished itself whatsoever the form it happened to adopt. And although the architectonic gift, which might have enabled the poet to present a real whole instead of a series of dissolving views, is not present, yet it is astonishing with how little repugnance the reader who has once "got his hand in" accepts this apparent incoherence, and resigns himself to see the visions rise and blend and melt, the bubbles swell and gleam and break. While as for the force of individual passages—the Prologue, the Fable, the best Court scenes, the London Tavern, the Harrowing of Hell—these have never been mistaken by any competent critic who has read them.[10]

---

9. The politics of *Piers Plowman* itself are pretty distinct; those of *Richard the Redeless,* the attribution of which to Langland is one of the least doubtful of such things, are open to all. The poem (which is to be found in Professor Skeat's edition, and as "The Deposition of Richard II" in Wright's *Political Poems,* "Rolls Series," i. 368) is incomplete but extremely vigorous, though marred by the "Philistine" and ungenerous radicalism which is too frequently English.

10. The best commentary on the *matter* of Langland is, and is long likely to be, M. Jusserand's *L'Epopée mystique de W. Langland.* Paris, 1893.

Beside the shadowy and in part apocalyptic figure of Langland, the solid, well-authenticated, somewhat prosaic personality and literary work of John Gower[11] present a contrast which has its interest. Gower, after being wrongly connected by tradition with more than one family and county, was definitely established by Sir Harris Nicolas as John Gower, Esquire, of Aldington, in Kent, and of other places. His birth-year is not certain; he died, old and it is said blind, in 1408, and his tomb is one of the numerous literary illustrations of the great and recently rebuilt church of St. Saviour's, or St. Mary Overy's, Southwark, with which Gower seems to have been connected in various ways. Indeed, though married, he appears to have been in minor orders.

Gower.

His literary work even as we have it is considerable, but part of it is lost. Part also, both of what exists and of what does not, only indirectly concerns us here, being written in languages other than English. Gower is the last of the probably not small class of English men of letters between 1200 and 1400 who were trilingual—writing, and probably speaking, French, Latin, and English with equal facility. The principal existing piece of Gower's French is a set of fifty Ballades, the favourite French (*not* Provençal) form, with intertwisted identical rhymes, a recurrent refrain, and (generally) an *envoy.* But he also wrote in French one of the three divisions of his capital work, the *Speculum Meditantis,* a moral poem, in twelve divisions, on Vices and Virtues, which, after being long lost and misidentified, has been printed, in full length and dulness, at last. Another part of this, the *Vox Clamantis,* also exists, but is in Latin. It is a lively political poem in elegiacs with internal rhyme, dealing with the disturbances of Richard the Second's reign. Gower was a favourite of the unlucky but not unlettered king, and

11. An excellent and standard edition of Gower (4 vols. Clarendon Press, 1899-1902), ranking with and in a way completing Prof. Skeat's Langland and Chaucer, has at last been produced by Prof. G.C. Macaulay. The *Confessio* is in Chalmers, and in separate editions by Dr. Pauli and (cheaply, but not quite completely) by Prof. Morley. The *Speculum* is in the Oxford ed. only; the minor French works were given by the Roxburghe Club and by Stengel (Marburg, 1886); the Latin by Wright (*Political Poems,* "Rolls Series"), and in the Roxburghe.

deserted him for the rising sun of Bolingbroke. This poem contains a very striking sketch of Wat Tyler's outbreak. Later, as a Lancastrian, the poet wrote another poem of the same kind in leonine hexameters, which is called the *Tripartite Chronicle,* and is a strongly partisan account of Richard's errors and downfall. This is almost wholly historical : the *Vox* diverges into a good deal of miscellaneous matter (satire on the friars, etc.), which reminds us of *Piers Plowman.*

The *Confessio Amantis.*

The *Confessio Amantis,* the third and English part of Gower's *opus magnum,* is much less vigorous and spirited than either of these Latin poems; but while they have no significance for English literature, it has much. It was undertaken at the hapless Richard's suggestion.[12] It is an immense poem, or collection of poems, in (with infinitesimal exceptions) octosyllabic couplets, accomplished to the point of extreme fluency, but curiously lacking in backbone and vigour. It fills, in Chalmers's *Poets,* some five hundred and fifty columns, each of which at its fullest holds nearly seventy lines; but Latin arguments of the various sections take some room. Probably there are between thirty and forty thousand lines in all. The author declares his purpose of writing in "the middle way," of composing a book half of pleasure and half of learning. After a long historical and miscellaneous prologue, he opens his first book with one of the stock complaints of the woes of lovers, and proposes to make his own confession to Genius—a *Rose* personage, of course. The confessor, after a sermon, appropriately or inappropriately illustrated as usual, begins to hear his confession, and succeeds in making of it a frame for a huge series of tales from classical and mediaeval sources alike. Actaeon, Perseus, and Ulysses are succeeded by the tale of Florent, the subject of Chaucer's *Wife of Bath's Tale;* Narcissus jostles a king of Hungary; Alboin and Rosmunda have their place not far from Nebuchadnezzar. The beautiful story of Constance (*Emarè,* see *supra*), which Chaucer probably borrowed from Gower, appears; the original of *Pericles;* the tale of "Rosiphele," perhaps the

12. Its exact date is matter of guesswork. It probably took a good many years to write, but *may* have been begun as early as 1383 or thereabout.

original of *The Flower and the Leaf*; and dozens of others from all sources and of all sorts. The poem ends gracefully enough, though not altogether cheerfully, by Venus at once hearing the poet's prayer, and dismissing him from her court as too old for love, with a rosary of black beads hung round his neck inscribed *Pour Reposer*.

Grace, indeed, Gower cannot be said with justice at any time to lack; his faults are the want of strength, of definiteness, in his conceptions and deliveries, the insignificant fluency of his verse, and above all, the merciless and heart-breaking long-windedness which results from it. Even this conclusion, which is full of true and touching things (as where Venus after her operations asks the forlorn poet laughingly what love is, and he cannot answer her), is prolonged to such an extent that all the shock is expended, all the race and spirit watered down. In his own time, by himself and by Chaucer, Gower was specially called "moral." Venus, with her kindly scorn, acknowledges this gift in him, and dismisses him to its enjoyments now that he is unfit for hers. In recent days a slight imputation, not exactly of immorality, but of morality of a low kind, has in turn been cast on him. The truth seems to be that he was moral enough in the special contemporary fashion, which consisted in illustrating every point by some approved extract from authority, and by subjecting it as far as possible to the process of allegorical homilising. Although Chaucer casts, directly or dramatically, blame on his selection of such stories as those of Apollonius and Canace, this, if serious, would be rather a hypercriticism. But Gower has no passion, the "cold ointment" which Venus puts on his heart at the end of the *Confession* must, one would think, have been applied to some extent even before the beginning of it; and in his most pathetic serious stories (the humorous he hardly attempts) the sinewy directness of Chaucer, the mystical fire of Langland, are things to which he does not even try to attain.

Yet it would be a very great mistake to minimise or, like many, to pass by as negligible the contribution of Gower to English literature. Even in itself, if it has not the very highest qualities, it is far above contempt. Coleridge's rather pettish wish that Chalmers had given Lydgate instead, must have been caused either by very excusable ignorance of Lydgate's actual worth; or by a complete failure to recognise the formal superiority of Gower and the importance of his priority in time; or "perhaps, and even probably, by that capriciousness which too often mars Coleridge's criticism." The contemporaries of Chaucer and Gower, and the immediate successors who entered into their labours, made no such mistake, though in the fifteenth century they sometimes, and not quite unjustly, promoted Lydgate himself to the actual company of his masters. That, historically and as a master, Gower had a real right to be ranked with Chaucer, is as unquestionable as that Gower is vastly Chaucer's inferior as a poet. We need not attach great value to the supposed and indeed probable priority of Gower to Chaucer himself. It is sufficient that they were certainly fellow-pioneers, fellow-schoolmasters, in the task of bringing England to literature. Up to their time, as we have established by actual survey, the literary production of the country, whether in the successive vernaculars of Anglo-Saxon and Early Middle English, or in the half-naturalised foreign tongues of French and Latin, had been exceedingly rudimentary and limited. All but a very small part of it had been purely religious or ecclesiastical; of the small "profane" portion the whole of the *belles lettres* division had been in verse; and again all but a very small part of this verse had been directly translated romance. It was the function of great writers now to establish the form of English as a thoroughly equipped medium of literature, and to furnish it further, as far as they could, with matter various in kind, and with varieties of style. Even Langland, a much more interesting and striking figure than Gower to us, could have been much better spared by his own generation than Gower himself. In literary form Langland had nothing to teach : he was in fact merely rowing off-stream, if not against it, up a backwater which led nowhither. In substance he was powerful rather than profitable, offering nothing but allegory, of which there was already only too much, and political-ecclesiastical discussion, a growth always nearer to the tares than to the wheat of literature. In other words, and to vary the metaphor, he gave the workmen in the

Gower's reputation.

new workshop of English letters no new or improved tools, he opened up to them no new sources of material. He was a genius, he was a seer, he was an artist; but he was neither master nor stock-provider in literature.

Gower was both. The want of zest and race in his literary style (though he has style), and still more in his poetical medium, must not be allowed to blind us to the fact that both show an enormous improvement on such immediate predecessors as Hampole, as the author of *The Pearl,* as the author of *Cursor Mundi.* He knows his craft far better than they did; he has better tools; he can teach others to turn out work that can be depended on, while they themselves, and all those who followed them, were constrained either to have touches of genius or to be frankly inadequate if not simply intolerable. Gower, unlike Chaucer, was apparently no master of prose, and his faculty in verse was strictly limited to the octosyllable in English—in Latin, as we have said, he could write more vigorously, if also more barbarously. But so far as he went he was distinctly an example of literary accomplishment—and examples of literary accomplishment were what England then wanted first of all.

What she wanted next Gower also saw, and this too he also, as he could, provided. It was a want which the plain common sense of Caxton saw still existing nearly a hundred years later, and which was never really supplied till a hundred more had passed; a want which explains the dearth and dulness so often charged against the fourteenth century; a want which no exceptional genius could supply. The English Muses simply did not *know* enough to do much : they wanted feeding, training, educating; they were in their nonage. Now the, to us, odd and cumbrous medley, the "marine store" of the *Confessio Amantis,* was an attempt to supply these wants, to give matter and models at once : to write a book, as Gower says in the interesting exordium, which only his fatal fluency prevents from being quite excellent—

> After the world that whilome took
> Long time in oldë daiës past.

And

to touch also
The world that neweth every day.

That his efforts were not vain, the genuine gratitude of his immediate successors for his lessons in "rhethorike"—in form—testifies; and Chaucer and Shakespeare are perhaps sureties after whom it is unnecessary to produce any others as to the value of his contributions in matter.[13]

---

13. Chaucer dedicates his *Troilus* to Gower and to the philosophical Strode—identified fairly well with Ralph Strode, who flourished about 1370, and seems to have written a good deal in Latin and English prose and verse. An attempt, ingenious but purely fanciful, has been made to find the "*Pearl* poet" (pp. 102-03) in this Strode.

Note to Eighth Edition—The student should be informed that, during the last few years, the usual (but unusually long delayed) attempts have been made to split up the authorship of *Piers Plowman* between four or five or more persons. These attempts (as usual also), were rather welcomed at first by some philologists, but were coldly received by other critics, and have not stood examination. It is certain that in so large a number of MS. copies (*v. sup.*) there may or must be interpolations. But no sound textual criticism has really invalidated, and almost all sound literary criticism supports, the theory that the author of "A," "B," and "C" was one.

3

CHAUCER'S PROSE—WYCLIF, TREVISA, MANDEVILLE

Turning-point in prose—Chaucer's prose tales—His *Boethius*—The *Astrolabe*—Wyclif—John of Trevisa—Sir John Mandeville—The first prose style.

THE prose of the late fourteenth century in England is not to the mere literary taster, with one notable exception, at all comparable in interest to the verse of the same time. But it is hardly less important. For this time was in fact the beginning of English prose properly so called. Before 1350 it may be doubted whether there is a single English work in prose, with the exception of the *Ancren Riwle,* which unites the bulk and the literary quality of a book proper; and while the *Ancren Riwle* is still almost more Saxon than English in language, it belongs in subject to the division of sacred literature, which, though it is one of the noblest of all divisions, yet of necessity is less national, less idiosyncratic, than any other.

Turning-point in prose.

At the great turning-point, however, which, though it must have come sooner or later anyhow, was undoubtedly determined to no small extent by the concentration of English patriotic sentiment, owing to the conquests of Edward III, prose did not merely, like verse, make a fresh start, it made a start almost for the first time. From the later years of Edward and the reign of Richard II, date four writers of prose, each noteworthy in his own way, and three out of the four notable in something more than his own way—Chaucer the poet, Wyclif the controversialist, Trevisa the chronicler, and the shadowy personage long known, and perhaps even yet not entirely exorcised, as "Sir John Mandeville." All were translators in less or greater degree, but all also were originals of English prose writing.

The interest of Chaucer's prose works, the *Treatise on the Astrolabe,* the translation of *Boethius,* the *Parson's Tale,* and the *Tale of Melibee,* is almost entirely an interest of form; and in the last that interest is minimised and almost confined to the fitful and straggling emergence of blank verse, or something like it, at the opening. So too the *Parson's Tale,* a translation and a theological translation, does not advance us very much further than the prose treatises by or attributed to Hampole and his followers in the first half of the century. It is good straightforward English, but shows no attempt at style, while the well-worn and strictly prescribed common form of its matter expresses further limitations. The *Boethius* and the *Astrolabe* are superior. The version of the first, even if it were intrinsically less attractive, would inevitably invite comparison with Alfred's at the dawn of Saxon as this at the dawn of modern English prose, and the often noble, never contemptible, matter of the original could not and did not fail to stimulate an artist like Chaucer. But the most valuable point of the *Boethius* as an exercise for the pioneer in a new prose is the fact of the "Metres," which, especially when rendered by such a poet as Chaucer into a language with such illimitable latent possibilities as English, must needs result in far more ambitious and far more successful attempts in "the other harmony" than had yet appeared. Accordingly some of the metre passages in Chaucer's version, though quite legitimate and sound prose, attain a rhythmical as well as verbal dignity, which English prose was hardly to know again save in a few passages of Malory, Fisher, Berners, and the translators of the Bible, till late in the sixteenth century. And the whole shows that, if it had suited Chaucer to write more originally in prose, he might have effected a revolution therein at least as great as that which he did effect in verse, nay greater, seeing that he had practically no forerunners.

Chaucer's prose tales.

His *Boethius.*

The Astrolabe.

The attractions of the *Treatise on the Astrolabe* are different, but perhaps they are not less. The specially pleasant and easy address to "little Lewis my son," for whom the treatise was compiled, and of whom, unluckily, we know no more, does not so much contrast with as supplement the interest of the piece as an early scientific treatise by one of the greatest of men of letters. The astrolabe was a small pocket instrument, somewhat of the sextant kind, for taking the altitudes and positions of the heavenly bodies; and though the object of its use was astrological rather than astronomical, it has, I believe, been admitted by "scientists" of the severest stamp that the treatise itself shows an exactness of scientific acquirement up to a certain point which certainly would not be easy to parallel in any but a specialist of modern times.[1] And it is not perhaps superfluous or impertinent to add that astrology, a study which may be defined as rather extra-scientific than anti-scientific, and which at least attained a complete rigidity of scientific method, has an almost unsurpassed traditional interest for literature. To the time of Chaucer's great moderniser Dryden, it held the belief of the best informed and least generally credulous of men, and even since it went out of fashion, it has been splendidly celebrated in prose and verse by Scott and Coleridge. But in this treatise of Chaucer's, the great interest is the spectacle of an early example of the scientific application of literature and the literary handling of science.[2]

---

1. Astronomy ("*Ast.* colit astra") was part of the regular mediaeval *Quadrivium.*
2. A thing of more length than merit, the *Testament of Love,* used to be included in Chaucer's prose works, and may be found, by those who warn it, in Chalmers and in Professor Skeat's Supplement. For once the exorcists are justified of their spells. Not only does the composition (an allegorical-religious treatise on the author's quest for a "Margaret," who is less doubtfully than usual a mere *eidolon* of Grace, or spiritual truth, or the Church) contain internal evidence that it is not Chaucer's in its reference to him, but, as any one who, knowing the *Boethius,* reads it will see at once, it pillages that book and others of his in a way which, barefaced in another, would be unintelligible in himself. It is now put down (a kind of signature being discovered) to a certain Thomas Usk, a busy Londoner, who was executed with a good deal of barbarity

The work of Wyclif,[3] a prose writer only, and a "sacred" and philosophical prose writer only, is less novel, less attractive, but not less important. Little, despite his fame and the violent partisanship for and against him, is really known of the author. We do not know when John Wyclif was born or where, though the probabilities connect his birth with the place of Wycliffe-on-rees and the time of 1320-1325. He was certainly Master of Balliol (a northern college) at Oxford, in 1360; and by the confession of his opponents, was a recognised expert in theology and scholastic philosophy. He had, after giving up Balliol on his appointment to a college living, become Warden of Canterbury Hall, now merged in Christ Church; but was deprived of this post by the next Archbishop but one of Canterbury. Other preferments came to him, and in 1374 he received the Crown benefice of Lutterworth, which he held till his death, ten years later. The best-known event in his life was his summons to appear in St. Paul's on a charge of heresy in 1377, on which occasion the court was practically broken up by the turbulence of Wyclif's partisan, John of Gaunt. Into the nature and extent of his heresies we are here precluded from entering. On "Dominion," on Transubstantiation, and other points, they reached the extreme of scholastic subtlety; and perhaps the most practical part of his tenets was the establishment of an irregular order of "poor priests," who took the field at once against the corrupt friars and the extravagantly endowed prelates of the time. These poor priests, more definitely than Wyclif himself, were responsible for the "Lollardy" which, though its first-fruits in

Wyclif.

---

by the triumphant Gloucester faction in 1388. Usk did not quite deserve "hanging for his bad *prose*"; but it is not good.

3. Wyclif's English work, outside the Bible, with some not his, is to be found in Mr. T. Arnold's *Select English Works of Wyclif* (3 vols.), Clarendon Press, and Mr. F.D. Matthew's *English Works of Wyclif* hitherto unprinted (E.E.T.S.). The whole *Bible*, a composite work of Wyclif and others, was edited in 4 vols. 4to by Forshall and Madden, Oxford, 1850; the *Gospels* (very conveniently printed in parallel columns, with the early Gothic and A.S. versions and Tyndale's) by Bosworth and Waring (3rd ed. London, 1888). His very voluminous Latin works, philosophical and ecclesiastical, have been tackled by a special Wyclif Society.

the Wat Tyler insurrection came in Wyclif's lifetime, developed later, and did not call for sharp repression till the reigns of Henry IV and Henry V. Much of Wyclif's tendency in politics ecclesiastical is observed in Langland, but the latter shows no sign of any doctrinal heresy.

The English literary work of Wyclif and the Wyclifites (for a large part of the University of Oxford was saturated with his doctrine, and the complete body of Wyclifian literature is rather an earlier "Tracts for the Times" than the work of any one man) consists on the one hand of a new and complete translation of the Bible, on the other of a considerable mass of tracts and sermons intended for popular consumption. In some respects these latter are not very delightful or profitable reading. We find already in them the hard, narrow intolerance of contrary opinion and the refusal to believe in its honesty, the savage, churlish hatred of all the beauty of holiness—music (the "knacking of new songs," as the Wyclifite catchword has it), painted windows, fair architecture, and all that makes the mediaeval church gracious and precious in our eyes—the almost Iscariot-like grudging of all expense on divine worship that is not "given to the poor," the rage, at least as much political and social as theological, at wealthy and exalted bishops and abbots, the sectarian jealousy between "poor priests" and friars,—all the ugly Philistine sourness, in short, which disgraces the extreme Protestant party of the sixteenth century and the extreme Puritan party of the seventeenth. There is little room in this furious cudgel-play of partisan hatred for the serene exercise in elaborate prose which Chaucer gives us in the *Boethius,* for the scientific precision of the *Astrolabe,* for the gay and varied garrulity of Mandeville. A few lively touches of manners, a few of the less merely "teeth-gnashing" flouts of satire, a quaint phrase here and there, a racy translation of antiquity—these are the principal attractions which the Wyclifite tracts have to offer; while as for the Translation of the Bible, as it cannot compete as literature with that produced some two centuries later, so it has merely the same attraction as matter. It should be observed that there are later and earlier versions of it, the former much the more advanced in grammar and style.

Nevertheless both, as much the one as the other, were most important as contributions to English prose. Wyclif and his coadjutors brought to both their tasks—that of translation and that of tract-writing—a combination of education and of "object" which has been very rare in literary history. They were all trained in the severest science of scholastic study, the most thorough perhaps that has ever been seen. Even a Bachelorship of Divinity represented four years' training in arts, three more in the quadrivium of mediaeval science, music, arithmetic, geometry, and astronomy; and seven more still in theology. Every man who had gone through this had been in the habit of constant disputes with opponents, on the watch to note the slightest vagueness of definition, the slightest illicit process of argument. Yet these accomplished scholars were in their new venture addressing the common people first of all. Their training compelled them to be precise; their object compelled them to be forcible. In the translation of the Bible they had a wide range of the most various kinds of literature, history, poetry, oratory, philosophy, parable,—matter which still retained, after being passed through the Latin sieve, large admixture of its original Oriental elements to colour and diversify the English result. In their tracts they had above all things to be exact in aim to meet their enemies, and to be forcible to attract disciples. No better exercising ground for an infant prose, in at least some ways, could have been provided, than this combined one of translation and polemic. We do not, indeed, find in Wyclif, or in any of the immediate Wyclifites, the full consequences, which we shall find fifty years later in Pecock's *Repressor,* of a vocabulary and arrangement varying between extreme scholasticism and extreme vernacularity, but we find approaches in both directions.

John of Trevisa.

The third prose author of this time owes his position to reasons rather different from those which have preferred Chaucer, Wyclif, and Mandeville. He is neither a great poet who was an almost equally great all-round man of letters, nor an eager controversialist who has linked his name with one of the great versions of the Bible (there seems to have been an idea in Caxton's mind that

Trevisa did translate the Bible, but nothing else is known of it), nor an interesting if shadowy personality whose name is attached to a charming piece of literature. He simply produced an English version of the Latin Chronicle or *Poly-chronicon* of Ralph Higden, which had been written not so very much before his own day. Higden was a West-countryman, who was born about the last decade but one of the thirteenth century; became a monk of the Benedictine Abbey of St. Werburgh at Chester; perhaps (it is necessary to lay stress on that "perhaps") had something to do with English literature directly in the matter of the Chester Plays, and certainly wrote this *Polychronicon,* one of the usual historical surveys, "beginning at the beginning," narrowing to a rather more particular survey of Jewish and Roman history with others, and ending with that of England continued to the writer's own time. Higden is said, on the not altogether trustworthy authority of Bale, to have died in 1363. Not very long after this his book was Englished[4] by John of Trevisa, who, as the "Tre" shows, was a Cornishman, but seems to have been chiefly connected with Berkeley in Gloucestershire. He is said to have died in 1413, but his History was finished as long before as 1387. The piece has more interest for its matter, which includes much early (indeed the earliest) description of England in English, and for the evidence it gives of the now unrestrainable impulse to write about English matters generally in the English tongue, than for any special literary merit or savour. Trevisa, who seems to have been no great scholar in Latin, for he confesses that he could not always understand his original, was no genius in English. But his style is racy from its age, and agreeable for its want of pretension. In his day a man deserved almost more credit for undertaking a long work in English than most men would deserve now for abstaining from it.

The last name to be mentioned in this chapter is by far the most interesting in the special connection of English prose. But

4. Edited, with the Latin, in the "Rolls Series." As with nearly all the early historians, the interest of the work for literature can be almost sufficiently gauged by sample, and a dozen pages of extract will be found in Morris and Skeat, Part II.

the discussion of it is complicated, and obstructed by a more than ordinary amount of those teasing and extra-literary squabbles about authorship and authors which meet us so frequently. Nay, in consequence of the doubts which have been raised as to the existence of Sir John Mandeville, and the proofs (not invalid as such things go) that the real author was a French or Flemish physician of Liège, proposals have even been made to oust the book[5] altogether from English literary history and give it to French.

Sir John Mandeville.

These proposals cannot for one moment be admitted. The French version of Mandeville may be—very likely is—the oldest. It may have been—it very likely though by no means necessarily was—written by some one who was not an Englishman. But it is a book which, in the history of literature, has very little importance. French prose had been written currently on all subjects for two centuries before it; and there was nothing remarkable in its existence. No one has contended that the French author can for a moment vie with Villehardouin, or Joinville, or his own contemporary Froissart, as a prose-writer. The book has had no influence on French literary history—no great French writer has been inspired by it, none of its "notes" in the least corresponds to any mark of French. The contrary of all these things is the case in regard to the English version. Even the infidels do not place that version much later than 1400, and it may be permitted to doubt whether it is not older; for though the prose shows an advance in ease and resource on Wyclif, a great one on Trevisa, it is not much, if at all, in front of Chaucer. It is quite an admirable thing in itself; it shows, if it be a translation, that some third person must be added to Malory and Berners to make a trinity of such English translators, as the world has rarely seen, in the fifteenth century.

5. There is no thoroughly satisfactory edition. Wright's, in the Bonn Library (among *Early Travels in Palestine*), is too much modernised; Mr. Warner's, for the Roxburghe Club, is not generally accessible. Halliwell's, more than once reprinted, is the best *edition*; and Mr. E.B. Nicholson, Bodley's Librarian, is the best authority on the disputed points, which he has treated in the *Encyclopaedia Britannica* and elsewhere.

It expresses with remarkable fidelity the travelling mania of the English, and in the stories of the "Watching of the Falcon," the "Daughter of Hippocrates," and others, it has supplied romantic inspiration for generation after generation. As French it is little or nothing to Frenchmen or to France; as English it is a great thing to England and to Englishmen.

The facts as to authorship and contents are as follows. The book purports to have been written by Sir John Mandeville of St. Albans, who began to travel on Michaelmas Day 1322, journeyed in the East for thirty years and more, and after obtaining leave from the Pope, and coming home a sufferer from gout, produced his book in Latin and French and English in 1356. Later accounts have it that he was buried at Liège. Against this are the facts that no other notice of any such Sir John Mandeville exists; that the arms quoted as on the Liège monument have nothing to do with any family of the name; and that, as we have mentioned, the French version seems to be much anterior to the English, if not also to the Latin. Further, before any more serious doubts had been started about Mandeville's personality than those which arose from the marvels narrated in his book, and which had almost from the first caused it to be regarded as a capital example of a "traveller's tale,"—it had been observed that its contents were very far from original. A certain Friar Odoric may have travelled in "Cathay" (Chinese Tartary), and had his travels written down by a brother of his Order, as early as 1330. Now the resemblance between Mandeville and Odoric is striking. Further borrowings, certain or extremely probable, have been indicated from another Franciscan friar, from an Armenian named Hayton, from a German knight named Boldensele, and from others. Fart, it is true, is not accounted for, and seems to be direct personal experience; but the whole is very like a blend of such experience with matter from earlier books. And the compiler has been identified with a certain Liège physician, John of Burgundy or John of the Beard, who is said to have revealed his personality on his deathbed to a third John, John of Outremeuse. Perhaps we may not impertinently, like Prince Henry, take leave of all these withered old Johns and Sir Johns, whose identity is shadowy in the extreme and of no importance.

Once more the book is the thing; and the importance of the book, by whomsoever written, at whatsoever time anterior to the latest (the beginning of the fifteenth century) at which it can possibly have appeared, and whether translation or original, remains for the history of English prose immutable and inexpugnable. The title of "Father of English Prose," which used to be given to Mandeville, is indeed rather silly, as are all such titles, if only in that they provoke the chronological and other squabbles from which literary study has suffered so much. No one man could be "the Father of English Prose" at any time; and as a matter of fact it had, as we have seen, at this time at least four simultaneous fathers. What the *Voyage and Travaile* really is, is this—it is, so far as we know, and even beyond our knowledge in all probability and likelihood, the first considerable example of prose in English dealing neither with the beaten track of theology and philosophy, nor with the, even in the Middle Ages, restricted field of history and home topography, but expatiating freely on unguarded plains and on untrodden hills, sometimes dropping into actual prose romance, and always treating its subject as the poets had treated theirs in *Brut* and *Mort d'Arthur,* in Troy-book and Alexandreid, as a mere canvas on which to embroider flowers of fancy. It is the first book of *belles lettres* in English prose, and this is such a priority as the most ambitious of authors, identified or unknown, might be content with. And being such, it deserves a brief handling of its material and formal characteristics, such as we have given to its verse predecessors in the same supreme, and indeed only purely literary, department of literature.

The extreme attractiveness of the matter, and the delightful illustrations of old attached to it, have perhaps a little drawn away attention from the fact that the form of the book is well worthy of the substance. A summary of the life of our Lord (for it must be remembered that the book is primarily a road-book for the Holy Land) leads to a description of Constantinople and a précis of the tenets of the Greek Church. Then we cross the "Brace of St. George" (Sea of Marmora) and come to Asia Minor, where Cos gives us the "Daughter of Hippocrates," and Rhodes another wild tale, and Cyprus an account of hunting leopards. Jerusalem itself follows, and "Babylon" (which it must be remembered is always Cairo in the Middle Ages), and a long account of Egypt and of Arabia, and how roses came into the world, and of Jerusalem again, and of whole Palestina. Only after this do we get into the true Utopian El Dorado of Mandeville, with the "Watching of the Spar-hawk" in an Armenian castle (what time the Ark still was visible on the top of Ararat), and the Customs of Ind, and the great Cham of Cathay, and the royal State of Prester John, and the four floods that come from the Paradys Terrestre. There is hardly a page in the book which is not full of interesting detail, of romantic suggestion, of fact sublimed and opalised by imagination, or by the mere process of continuous report from lip to lip and book to book.

The first prose style.

But the great interest for us is that here, and here for the first time distinctly, the subject and the idiosyncrasy of the author produce between them a *style.* There are approaches to a style in Chaucer; but he was kept too close to his text in *Boethius,* to his subject in the *Astrolabe.* Wyclif might have reached one; Trevisa probably could not; Mandeville did. His object being to produce his effect by the accumulation of interesting marvels, with few models before him except the arrangements of the Bible, he mostly affects short sentences, and has a trick of beginning each with "And." This conjunction is dear to the story-teller, because it has a sort of arresting and exciting effect upon the hearer, by promise of something fresh; while the long periodic sentence, besides requiring greater practice, is apt to weary hearers as opposed to readers. The vocabulary is simple and rather modern, with few obsolete or archaic words, as indeed might be expected, whether the book was really the work of a cosmopolitan traveller or that of a mere homekeeping forger of letters. Few books of the time, when the spelling is completely modernised, have so little uncouthness about them. And one thing (rarely to be said of any author, rarest of one mediaeval in time) is that this author knows exactly when he has said enough. Nothing tempts him to the fatal loquacity of nearly all writers between the Dark Ages and the Renaissance, and he will even apologise for the Sparrowhawk discussion which tells the reason of the woes of Armenia. "This is not the right way to go to the parts that I have named, but for to see the marvel." To see the marvel of the rising of literary prose style in English there is no better way than to read Mandeville.

INTERCHAPTER 3

SHORT as is the period which has been covered in the preceding Book, and few as are the names which it contains, we have at last reached in it one, the importance of which has, in great part at least, not to be pleaded for. At no time during the present century—at no time, indeed, during the last five centuries, except, and that not universally, for a short interval during the eighteenth—would the right of Chaucer to a place, and a great one, in English literary history have been contested; while, silly as the title of "Father of English Prose" may be, the fact of its having been long ago awarded sometimes to Mandeville, sometimes to Wyclif, is a piece of evidence in itself. Yet there is no need for this to break the good custom of these interposed summaries; indeed, one at the present juncture may have special value.

For it is impossible to appreciate too clearly the exact position of Chaucer in poetry, while that of himself and his contemporaries in prose certainly has not always been appreciated with even the least clearness—if Professor Earle had any justification for saying, not more than a few years ago, that "there exists a general impression among educated Englishmen that our prose dates from the sixteenth century."[1]

Even to appreciate Chaucer with exactness and propriety is by no means a matter of course; yet without such an appreciation it is impossible to get the parts of the history into true proportion and connection. At no time have competent readers failed to perceive his abounding humour, the shaping faculty which enables him to make every character at once an individual and a type, the "gold dewdrops of his speech," the sweetness of his

1. *English Prose,* p. 369.

music. Perhaps we have outgrown (there is at any rate no excuse for us if we have not) the idea entertained even by Dryden that this sweetness is "rude," that there is something untutored and infantine about it. But it may be doubted whether even yet, whether even among persons who may boast some acquaintance with him, an accurate estimate of his position in regard both to the past and the immediate future prevails. It so happens, oddly enough, that the first part of this has been expressed with extreme propriety of fact, and in words that could not be bettered in another language in reference to another person, by a writer who probably had never heard of Chaucer, and would have regarded him as a savage if he had. Boileau's famous couplet—

> Villon sut le premier dans ces siècles grossiers
> Débrouiller l'art confus de nos vieux romanciers—

is, as it stands, a sort of Helot among critical utterances. The *siècles* were not *grossiers;* Villon was not the first to "disembroil" poetical art of any kind; and what he did had nothing whatever to do with the *vieux romanciers,* but was the infusion of a modern spirit into forms already arranged for him as exactly and neatly as any art could be arranged. But the second line expresses precisely what Chaucer did in English, and what gives him, if not his chief title to admiration as a poet, his chief place in literary history. He, in fact and in deed—

> Débrouilla l'art confus de nos vieux romanciers.

It already existed in plentiful quantity, and now and then in no inconsiderable degrees of accomplishment. But it was all in the shape of *brouillon*—of rough draft. Men had practised the octosyllabic couplet for centuries, but they had never succeeded in writing it with a sure mastery at once of vigour and of variety, of smoothness and of strength. They had got safely through very intricate stanzas, but no one of them had any stanza so under his command as to write anything at all approaching the best passages—indeed practically the whole—of *Troilus.* They had now and then stumbled upon the great heroic couplet itself, but they had hardly known it when they saw it, and had invariably let it slip again, even if they perceived its character. Nay, in his own day, some men were even relapsing from the point that art had reached on the earlier stage of "rim ram ruf"—on the rhythmical prose of alliteration, either simple of itself or awkwardly bedizened, like a true savage art, with feathers and gawds of inappropriate stanza and rhyme.

All this Chaucer *débrouilla*—set straight, copied out fair, and left the copy so transposed as a testimony for ever, and a point to which men might return, but which, once gained, they never could really lose. He was no doubt powerfully backed on the more artistic side by Gower, but Gower had, in English at least, little strength; and he was far more powerfully backed on the other by Langland, but Langland had, or chose to have in this respect, an inferior and antiquated art. In the union of the two Chaucer stood alone, and fortunately he was quite able to stand alone.

To such an estimate the demur may be made, "If he did so much, how was it that outside his own work so little resulted—that nearly a century and a half had to pass after his death before any real advance was made?" To this, of course, no absolutely complete answer can be given. The most philosophical view of the philosophy of history never pretends to explain all the facts, especially in regard to "the times and the seasons." The best explanation why there is no poet in English—even in Scots—who is the equal of Chaucer, between Chaucer himself and Surrey, is that, as a matter of fact, no such poet appeared. But we can give some side-explanations, some, as it were, marginal notes on this, and we can at any rate see that things were much better as they were. If Chaucer had not appeared when he did, the language might have got into ways too slovenly for it to acquire a real *Ars poetica* at all, might have succumbed to the rigid syllabic prosody of French (there was some danger of this for a long time to come), or have gone off "rim-ram-ruffing" into the wilderness. But since he appeared when he did, his work was necessarily exposed to the drawback that it was composed in a language which had still not acquired its complete modern form. The final *e,* a troublesome and by this time a useless thing, which meant anything and everything and nothing, had to be shed; some other structural changes had to be gone through. Above all, the language had to pass under certain modifications of sound which have never yet been fully explained. In this welter Chaucer could not be equalled; Spenser could not come till it was over. But through it all Chaucer's work remained, above the welter itself, a pattern and a beacon at once.

The influence of Gower, infinitely less as is his value for us, was probably not so very much less than Chaucer's for his own contemporaries. The third great poetical figure of the time exactly reverses these conditions. Langland is for us a true, nay a great, poet; his reactionary aberrations in form can do us no harm, and his apocalyptic obscurity adds something of a zest to our reading of him. These would not have been the best of influences on his own age, which was urgently in need of formal correction, and was not at all in need of incitements to allegorical meandering. But, as a matter of fact, he does not seem to have exercised much, if he exercised any, influence, and what he had was in the direction of political and other satire, not that of poetry proper. Even the alliterators did not usually follow his straightforward reliance on alliteration and accent, but confessed their sense of insufficiency by calling in more and more the aid of stanza and of rhyme.

The formal importance of the age in prose is hardly less, though its productions have far less intrinsic interest. The excursion of prose beyond the narrow limits of theological matter which had so long confined it was one great thing; the use of it to address the common people, who had hitherto been only accessible by verse, was another. That the third limit—translation—which had been imposed upon it still remained, was no drawback for the time. Very much more importation of vocabulary; very much more experiment, like that of Pecock in the next age, with term-forging; very much more copying of the more accomplished prose forms of French and Latin, were necessary before the resources of style could really be at the command of the English prose-writer in miscellaneous subjects. But the return to vernacular writing in history, more than two hundred years after the pen had left the hand of the last annalist of Peterborough, meant a very great deal; the application of the genius for letters of such a man as Chaucer to scientific exposition in the *Astrolabe,* to philosophical exposition in the *Boethius,* meant a great deal more; perhaps the example of prose narrative of the easy, interesting, not first of all instructive kind in Mandeville meant most of all. This fascinating shadow, whatever else he was, and whatever else he did, was the spiritual father of Malory and Berners, of Lyly and Sidney, of Defoe and Fielding, of Miss Austen and Scott. They were still long to be "bodiless childfuls," but they were now "bodiless childfuls of life," and Sir John, if ever any other, gave them that life.

Lastly, we must not forget, though considerations of weight have necessitated a mere allusion to it as yet, that the third great kind, the kind which is not essentially prose nor essentially verse, but partakes of both—to wit, Drama—was by this time certainly born in English. It was as yet in swaddling clothes; perhaps we must not be too absolutely certain that any single piece now actually in our possession existed in the form in which we have it now.[2] But there is no reason for doubt that this momentous and important kind—which was to absorb the greatest genius of the first really complete age of English literature, which was to confer inestimable benefits upon both prose and verse, and was to be the first literary kind to engage, apart from some consideration of profit, the attention of a great audience—had for some time left the use of Latin and become common in the vernacular. It was still, as has been said, in swaddling clothes, it was performed and composed in ways unfavourable to a rapid, accomplished literary development, it was limited in subject, awkward in form; but it was the drama—the direct ancestor of the great Elizabethan drama itself—and its presence in the list of literary kinds is a matter of the first importance.

In short, the literary work of the Middle Ages proper in England was now complete, and, with a good fortune rare and

2. The well-known *Harrowing of Hell* is possibly as early as *Alison,* but it is faintly dramatic, and there is a long interval between it and other things.

almost unparalleled, what they had given was caught up, summed, uttered in perfect form by a poet of the greatest genius, and a prose writer of no small talent. Perhaps this good fortune had in a manner to be paid for by the relapse in poetry which the next century saw. But even this was a rest as well as a relapse, and meanwhile prose the unresting, if also the unhasting, was making advances as steady as they are unmistakable.

Book IV

The Fifteenth Century

1

THE ENGLISH CHAUCERIANS—LYDGATE TO SKELTON

Contempt for fifteenth-century literature—Lydgate—Occleve—Bokenam—Audelay and Minors—Hawes—The *Pastime of Pleasure*—The *Example of Virtue*—Barclay—The *Ship of Fools*—The Eclogues—Skelton—His life—His poems.

Contempt for fifteenth-century literature.

FEW sections of English Letters have been more abused or more disdained than the literature, and especially the purely English poetry, of the fifteenth century. The contemptuous ignorance of M. Taine extended even to the Scottish poets, who have been more generally excepted from condemnation; and less excusable under-valuation of these same has been made by critics, at least to the language born, such as Mr. Lowell and Mr. Lounsbury. Even those who do not commit the unpardonable or inexplicable error of belittling or ignoring Dunbar and Henryson have usually a short shrift and a long drop for the English writers of the time, and especially for the English poets.

Of these disdains literary history knows nothing; and nothing is to be passed over by her unless it is at once devoid of intrinsic attraction, and of no importance as supplying connections and origins. Even from the first point of view, slighting of the *Twa Maryit Wemen and the Wedo,* of the *Testament of Cressid,* of the *King's Quair,* of Malory and Berners, of the *Nut-browne Maid,* and the carol "I sing of a maiden," must convict the slighter either of invincible bad taste, or of ignorance that cannot be too soon corrected. From the second, the period which shows us the progress in, and the final stoppage of, the blind alley of alliteration, the strange failure to make the improvement that might have been expected on the magnificent advantages given by Chaucer, the process, slow but sure, of elaborating the machinery and amassing the capital of English prose, the probable beginning of the ballad, the spread and popularising of the drama,[1] and the certain and glorious ending of romance, need not be ashamed of itself in any company which knows and observes the laws of literary history.

The poets, both Scotch and English, of this century were wont to leash with Chaucer and Gower in the triplet of masters whom they acknowledged and hailed with reverence John Lydgate, the "Monk of Bury." Very little is known of the life of this voluminous, somewhat undistinguished, but by no means unpleasant or uninteresting poet, who has had decidedly hard measure in the way of presentation to modern readers, though the Early English Text Society has begun to devote a portion of its too small resources and its too largely drawn upon labour to the task.[2] The latest certain date in his life is 1446. As the dates of his orders are—sub-deacon, 1389; deacon, 1393; and priest, 1397, he may have been born about 1370. He appears to have enjoyed the advantages of the three greatest European Universities of his day—Oxford, Paris, and Padua—and his knowledge both of ancient and modern literature must have been pretty complete for the time. He taught rhetoric at Bury St. Edmunds, and it must be remembered that Rhetoric,

---

1. For reasons given *post* it has seemed better to reserve the dramatic matter, which might have made some appearance even earlier, and has a fair claim to a place here, for the next Book, so far as the main text is concerned. See also Interchapters iii (*supra*) and iv (*infra*).
2. Until this reissue, which has already given the *Temple of Glass* and other things, was begun, Halliwell's edition of the *Minor Poems* for the Percy Society, and the *Story of Thebes,* and some smaller pieces given by Chalmers in his Chauceriana, formed the accessible Lydgate, illustrated by four-and-twenty pages of bibliography, which Ritson devotes in his *Bibliographia Poetica* (London, 1802) to "this voluminous, prosaick, and drivelling monk," as the critic, with his usual sweetness, describes his subject.

which had for many centuries, legitimately or illegitimately, extended itself in the sense of the Art of Prose Literature, had by this time absorbed poetics likewise, and that in the fifteenth century especially "rhetorike" and (in French) *rhétoriqueur* are words almost interchangeable with "poetry" and "poet." Unluckily, as from the days of Martianus Capella[3] downwards rhetoric and ornate diction had been closely connected, this also became confounded with poetry, and the main objection to fifteenth-century verse next to, or indeed connected with, its prolixity and dulness, is its addiction to "aureate" terms—that is to say, bombastic classical or pseudo-classical phraseology.

In this Lydgate is not quite such a sinner as some of his contemporaries and still more his successors. He could now and then catch something at least of the propriety of language which is one of his master Chaucer's glories, and he was also less to seek than any other of that master's purely English followers in versification, though he too shows some signs of that curious confusion of poetic tongue which came upon his time.

Lydgate.

The early printers, Caxton, Pynson, and Wynkyn de Worde, in whose time Lydgate still ranked as one of the *di majores* of English literature, were not unkind to him; but the mania for early printed books as such has made these editions entirely inaccessible, save in public libraries, to the lover of literature who is not a millionaire. At last the E.E.T.S. reprints have reproduced a fair body of his work, much of the current abuse of which is only an echo of the violence of Ritson, a critic seldom to be undervalued when he praises, but too often merely to be neglected when he blames. The *Thebes* poem, which was obviously intended as a pendant to the *Knights Tale,* gives the more canonical history of the wars which are taken for granted as precedent in Chaucer's poem, consists of between four and five thousand verses in couplets (*vide infra*), and begins as a *Canterbury Tale* with a prologue,

3. This crabbed, but to fit tastes not unpleasing, writer paints the breast of Rhetoric as *exquisitissimis gemmarum coloribus balteatum,* gives her arms which clash *velut fulgoreae nubis fragore colliso bombis dissultantibus,* and assigns to her a *vox aurata*—all transparent allegory.

references to Ospringe and other localities, and an invitation by the host to "Dan John" to tell it. In this piece the characters of Statius and those of Boccaccio are both drawn upon, and the story is sufficiently well told, though with too many speeches and involutions, and with little share of Chaucer's orderly and artful action. The most noteworthy thing about it, however, as about most of the poetry of Lydgate, of Occleve, and even of Hawes, not to mention smaller men, is that strange loss of "grip" in versification which has been more than once referred to. How far this is due to careless or ignorant copying or printing cannot be said with confidence until a much larger amount of Lydgate's enormous work has been competently edited from the MSS.; but attempts to make him out an elaborate and harmonious metrist are little less than preposterous.[4] The truth would rather seem to be that Chaucer was too far in advance of his time both in ear and in perception of the capabilities of the language; that his followers completely failed to adjust pronunciation and versification, and to understand versification itself, while their failure was made worse by rapid and uncertain changes in the language, as the dialects blended, as the final *e* fell off, and as the very vowel-sounds altered. Certain it is that in Lydgate, still more in Occleve, and more or less in all the others of this chapter, while the line sometimes loses all rhythmical sufficiency, though it does yield ten syllables to the finger, it at many other times fails to respond even to this mechanical test, and simply sprawls—a frank and confessed nondescript or failure.

These faults appear, but somewhat less, in the *Complaint of the Black Knight* and the other smaller poems caught in the

---

4. If Lydgate is really responsible for the following lines in an account of Henry VI's entry into London (*Minor Poems*, p. 3), no bathos and no bad verse can have been inaccessible to him—

> Their clothing was of colour full convenable:
> *The noble Mayor clad in red velewet* (!)
> The Sheriffs, the Aldermen, full notable,
> *In furrèd clokys the colour scarlett.*

Observe that "In furrèd clokys, scarlet in coloùr," is an obvious change, and makes a very fair line.

great "Chauceriana" net. The rhyme royal of the *Complaint* seems to have acted as a sort of support and stay to the backboneless writers of this time. In the other shorter poems, and in the pleasant piece of *London Lickpenny*—perhaps Lydgate's best-known thing, but grudged him, sometimes on the unkind ground that it is too good, sometimes for philological reasons, to which it may be objected that the accepted text acknowledges itself to be posthumous and rewritten—there is naturally much more variety and liveliness. Not that there is a lack of contention even here. It is exceedingly rash to take the confessions of youthful follies and peccadilloes which Lydgate makes in his *Testament,* just as Occleve does in his *Male Règle,* and many other poets of this and other ages elsewhere, for solid biographical documents. The chief of Lydgate's other works are the *Temple of Glass,* the very title of which is redolent of fifteenth-century allegory; the *Falls of Princes,* perhaps his most popular book in his own day, adapted from Boccaccio, and itself serving as model to the famous miscellany of the *Mirror for Magistrates* in the sixteenth century; a *Troy Book,* one of the numerous versions of Guido Colonna's plagiarism from Benoît de Sainte-More; an extraordinarily quaint Englishing of Deguileville's *Pilgrimage of the Life of Man,* interesting both for itself and for its foreshadowing of Bunyan; a most dismal *Assembly of Gods,* even more religious than moral, and making both its themes disgusting; part of a translation of the *Secreta Secretorum; Proverbs;* the *Court of Sapience;* a *Life of Our Lady;* a *Chronicle of English Kings;* Lives of his patron at Bury St. Edmunds; and so forth. These are but a few of the enormous number of works attributed to him. But the general value of Lydgate is not hard to fix. He is a scholar not a master, a versifier rather than a poet; an interesting figure in a time of groping and transition, and perhaps not so very unlike other figures in other times.

Thomas Occleve[5] (there seems to be as good authority for this as for the somewhat uglier form "Hoccleve") is, and probably will continue to be, inseparably connected in literary

5. The first two volumes of an edition have been issued by the E.E.T.S. under Dr. Furnivall's editorship.

history with Lydgate, of whom he is a much less voluminous and rather less accomplished double. He was often given to autobiographic details of the preciser kind, and from two of these we gather that he must have been born about 1368 (*where* is guesswork, the nearest locality in spelling being Hockcliffe in Bedfordshire). He entered the Privy Seal Office when he was about twenty, and we have abundant records of payments to him for parchment, ink, and wax used, as well as of salaries and pensions. He was always expecting a benefice or "corrody" (annuity charged on ecclesiastical revenues); but nothing came till 1424, when he was quartered, to an extent not exactly defined, on the Priory of Southwick in Hampshire. We may have something of his as late as 1448, and he may have died a little later, say 1450.

Occleve.

Occleve's principal work is an English version or adaptation in rhyme-royal of one or more Latin originals, under the title of *De Regimine Principum,*[6] preceded by a long introduction, partly autobiographic and wholly moralising. The enthusiastic address to his "master dear" Chaucer, of whom, be it remembered, one of his MSS. preserves the most probably authentic portrait, is the most interesting thing in this lugubrious and desultory work, of which the versification frequently sprawls and staggers in a fashion beside which even Lydgate's is well girt and neatly moving.

Among the smaller pieces attention has chiefly been given to the above-referred-to piece, entitled *La Male Règle de T. Occleve,* which seems to have been written when the poet was coming to forty years, *after* which age of wisdom, however, he married—for love, he says. This poem has the invariable characteristics of such regrets for lost youth, together with the less usual peculiarity that the poet represents himself as not merely a ne'er-do-well, but a very poor creature—a valetudinarian, "letting I dare not wait upon would" in his very escapades, a coward, a glutton, vain, weak, lazy, but with none of the nobler vices. If the thing had been better done we

6. Edited for the Roxburghe Club by Wright in 1860, and E.E.T.S. 1897.

might have taken it for his humour; but the poorness of the verse,[7] with a Chaucerian flash or two such as—

> Excess-at-board has laid his knife with me,

is rather a warrant for truth. A singularly weak *Complaint of Our Lady before the Cross,* where the subject strikes no spark out of Occleve's flabby nature; a feebly violent onslaught on Sir John Oldcastle and the Lollards; certain *ballades,* pious or political, which are no *ballades* at all, Occleve being apparently too weak to keep up to the rhyme-and-refrain scheme, may be noticed. The *Letter of Cupid to Lovers* is a little better. Not so much can be said of *Occleve's Complaint* and *Occleve's Dialogue,* though the latter may have an attraction for some in its querulous garrulity. But the tale which it introduces—a versification from the *Gesta Romanorum* about the Emperor Jereslaus's wife—and a later *Story of Jonathas,* are not bad of their kind, while the poem which comes between them, and which is connected with all that have been mentioned since the *Complaint, Ars Utilissima sciendi mori,* is, in a different vein, their equal. It is, like most of the work of this time and of this poet, merely a translation, though of what original is not quite certain. But there is a much healthier and manlier tone in it than in the puling regrets of the *Male Règle* for wasted health and feeble follies gone. The fifteenth century thought much of Death, and the thought was here, as elsewhere, tonic. The whining poltroon of the retrospect of life faces the prospect of death with no sham philosophy, and if not without fear, yet in humility and faith.

For those, and perhaps only for those, who desire to appreciate at first hand the strange paralysis of humour and harmony, of grace and strength, which came upon the successors of Chaucer and Langland, it may be worth-while to turn over the work of Osbern Bokenam (= probably Buckenham),[8] whose *Legends of the Saints,* in some 10,000 lines of decasyllables variously arranged in Chaucerian fashions, have had the very

7. Occleve, says Dr. Furnivall, "is content so long as he can count the syllables on his fingers." This is generous rather than severe.

8. "Dr. Bokenham of Bury" occurs, however, in Roger North.

undeserved honour of two reprints,[9] chiefly, it would seem, because they represent the not very common dialect of Suffolk.

Bokenam.

Bokenam, who, as we learn from a note in the MS., was a Suffolk man, a Doctor of Divinity, and an Austin Friar of Stoke Clare, tells the lives of Saints Margaret, Anne, Christina, the Eleven Thousand, Faith, Agnes, Dorothy, Mary Magdalene, Katharine, Cecily, Agatha,[10] Lucy, and Elizabeth of Hungary, in verse of rather more smoothness than some of his contemporaries could manage, but of a *saltlessness,* an absence of flavour, sparkle, piquancy, bite, which is desperate and almost inconceivable. Not St. Margaret and the Dragon, not St. Katharine and the Wheel, not even that lovely legend of St. Dorothea, which might draw poetry from an expert in phonetics, can inspire Bokenam with anything beyond the mildest prettiness of expression, and this he very seldom reaches. The most interesting thing in the whole book is the statement in the same end-note that Thomas Burgh had the poem copied in Cambridge in the year of Our Lord 1447, at the cost of thirty shillings—which sum can seldom have been either worse spent or more hardly earned either by town or gown in that locality.

Indeed, after making every allowance for the attempts, estimable if not delectable, of Lydgate and Occleve to keep English poetry alive during the first half of the fifteenth century,

Audelay and Minors.

it is impossible not to be struck, not merely with the extremely moderate success of their own efforts, but with the paucity of any attempt to support them among their contemporaries. What we may call the Apocrypha of *Piers Plowman,* the *Creed,* and the *Tale* (*vide supra*) may belong to the beginning of this century as well as to the end of the last. So may the verses of the Shropshire poet, Audelay,[11] who, like Langland himself, was a

9. By Stevenson for the Roxburghe Club, and by Horstmann (Heilbronn, 1883).

10. "Agas" in the English, a form identical with the original of "haggis."

11. Ed. Halliwell, Percy Society, 1844. A selection only. The MS. is dated 1426, and Audelay lived and wrote as late as the reign of Henry VI. He has "bob and wheel" stanzas, sometimes alliterated and sometimes

reformer without being a Wyclifite. To the first quarter of the fifteenth century belong William of Nassington, a Yorkshire writer of sacred verse, who perhaps belongs to the tradition of Hampole; and Hugh Campden, another translator, the author of the moral romance of *Boctus and Sidrac*. The hapless Prince Edward, son of Henry VI and Margaret of Anjou, before Clarence stabbed him in the field by Tewkesbury, underwent the minor pain of having a moral poem on the *Active Policy of a Prince* written for him by a certain George Ashby, Clerk of the Signet to his mother, and an aged Chaucerian. One of Caxton's books is a verse translation of Cato's *Morals*, by Benedict Burgh, done about 1470; and the last quarter saw some curious alchemical verses by George Ripley and Thomas Norton. But this, and perhaps a little more of the same kind, purely curious and appealing only to the robuster kind of curiosity, is all that bridges in England the space between Lydgate and Occleve in the early part of the fifteenth century, and Hawes and Skelton in the beginning of the sixteenth. There is, it is true, some anonymous matter of far greater interest which may represent this interval, and which will be dealt with in a later chapter. But even this is but scanty in amount.[12]

Hawes.

Very little is known of Stephen Hawes, and that little does not include the date either of his birth or of his death. He is said to have been a gentleman of birth, an Oxford man, a pretty considerable traveller, a master of modern languages, a man of great memory (seeing he could repeat by heart the works of Lydgate), and the possessor of a critical faculty somewhat smaller, inasmuch as he made that voluminous person equal in some respects with Geoffrey Chaucer. It is said with probability that he was Groom of the Chamber to Henry VII; he was able to write verses to congratulate Henry VIII on his accession; and it seems likely that he died

not, Romance sixains, a system composed of triplet octosyllables separated by single lines, monorhymed throughout the poem, etc.

12. I know the writers mentioned in this paragraph, after Audelay and Nassington, mainly at second hand. [*Fifth Edition*. This knowledge is now first hand throughout.]

in Suffolk in early middle age, certainly before 1530, and probably about 1523.

Wynkyn de Worde printed collections of the poems of Hawes—the *Pastime of Pleasure,* by which he is now almost solely known, in 1509, with some more pieces and the *Example of Virtue* in 1512. The *Pastime* was reprinted by Wright for the Percy Society,[13] unluckily with some omissions. Mr. Arber long ago promised a reprint of the *Example of Virtue,* the contents of which were abstracted in Mr. Henry Morley's *English Writers.*[14]

The *Pastime of Pleasure.*

The text has at last appeared in the *Dunbar Anthology.*[15] It is not nearly so long as the *Pastime.* Hawes has been said to belong to "the Provençal school," a statement, of course, entirely erroneous, and due to the confusion between Provençal and French, which was at one time excusable, but has long ceased to be so. He is, in fact, a Chaucerian who has deepened one particular colour of Chaucerism by recurrence to the *Romance of the Rose* itself, and still more to the heavier following of its allegory in the fourteenth and fifteenth centuries by French and English writers. The *Pastime of Pleasure,* or the history of Graund-Amour and La Bel Pucell, is, like Gavin Douglas's contemporary *King Hart,* simply an allegory of the life of man. The hero passes the meadow of Youth; chooses the path of Active Life, neglecting the Contemplative or Monastic; is introduced to the Seven Daughters of Doctrine (the *Trivium* and *Quadrivium*); meets La Bel Pucell, determines to obtain her, but is exposed to some danger by the misguidance of a comic slanderer of women, Godfrey Gobilive; destroys a three-headed giant and seven-headed ditto, so forcing his way to La Bel Pucell; is received by the Virtues, and married to his beloved by Law. He lives happily with her till Age strikes him with infirmities and the vice of Avarice. Contrition comes in time, however, before Death, and he is buried by Mercy and Charity and epitaphed by Fame.

---

13. 1845. The Abbotsford Club added the short *Conversion of Swearers* in 1865.
14. vii. 75-81.
15. London, 1901, pp. 217-95.

Thus presented in its bare scheme or skeleton, the poem may well seem (to use a Drydenian phrase) but a cool and insignificant thing. Nothing is more dead to us, hardly anything perhaps seems more certain of no resurrection, than this bald yet childish form of allegory, which lacks alike the vivid passages, the attractive, dreamlike transformations, and the fiery intensity of Langland, the gorgeous romance of Spenser and his perfect poetic skill, the amiable humanity and vivid novel-interest of Bunyan. In the two last of these cases—perhaps even in the first—the allegory, though ever present, is present in the background; it will come when called, but does not obtrude itself; in Hawes it is pitilessly obtrusive at every step. Further, the poet is singularly ill provided with the means of his art. He is far from being such a "dull dog" as Occleve; he has perhaps more flashes of poetry than Lydgate. But either the venerable Wynkyn was false to the central principle of all good printing, "Follow copy even if it flies out of the window," or else Hawes was less able to keep up any standard of correct and musical versification than even these his predecessors. Both his rhymes-royal and his couplets (both are used in the *Pastime*) are subject to the strangest lapses, to fits of a kind of verse-giddiness or epilepsy.

The *Example of Virtue,* which is wholly in rhyme-royal, is a very much duller poem, perhaps because it is even more nakedly allegoric than the *Pastime of Pleasure.* The usual invocation of the unequal three—Chaucer, Gower, and Lydgate—is followed by the usual dream. Youth is escorted by Discretion, voyages over the sea of Vain Glory to an island where are the castles of Justice, Nature, Fortune, Courage, and Wisdom; is engaged to Cleanness; is tempted by Lust, Avarice, and Pride; fights with a three-headed dragon (Hawes cannot spare the three-headed dragon); is new-dubbed Virtue; marries Cleanness, and is finally translated with her to Heaven. The three are once more invoked, and the poem ends. Of course, in both these poems there is a certain faint adumbration of the *Faërie Queen*—its outline without its glorious filling-in, its theme without its art, its intellectual reason for existence without any of its aesthetic

The *Example of Virtue.*

justification thereof. It is not improbable that Spenser did know Hawes; but if so he owed him a very small royalty. The merit of this poet is that he manages occasionally to lighten his darkness with flashes, to refresh his desert with flowers, of by no means mediocre poetry. We owe to him one of the oldest forms, if not the oldest form, of the beautiful saying—

> Be the day weary, or be the day long,
> At length it draweth to evensong.

For which and other things he may be forgiven such intolerable matter as the following, which deserves its place as a general example of the worst side of fifteenth-century poetry—

> And if the matter be joyful and glad,
> Like countenance outwardly they make;
> But moderation in their minds is had,
> So that outrage may them not overtake.
> I cannot write too much for their sake
> Them to laud, for my time is short
> And the matter long which I must report.
>
> *Pastime of Pleasure,* CAP. xii. last stanza.

It is between Hawes and Skelton that we may perhaps most conveniently mention a third writer, who is even more of a mere curiosity than Hawes himself, but as characteristic of his time as either. This is Alexander Barclay,[16] the Englisher of the famous *Narrenschiff* of Sebastian Brandt. As far back as Bale's time (that is to say, in the age just after his own, and partly overlapping it) there was a doubt whether Barclay was a Scot or an Englishman. The spelling of his name would incline to the former hypothesis, which also has early authority of the positive kind; but no connection of any sort is known between Barclay and Scotland, all his associations are with the South and South-west of England, and the spelling (always a very untrustworthy guide) is after all merely the pronounced form of "Berkeley." His literary

Barclay.

16. Warton has given a rather full account of Barclay (iii. 189-203, ed. 1871), and Ritson is as usual to the point in four pages of the *Bibliographia Poetica.* But the long introductions to the modern editions mentioned below are the things to consult.

qualities are scarcely such that the two divisions of the island need fight very keenly for him. He must have been born somewhere about the beginning of the last quarter of the fifteenth century, and pretty certainly had a University education. The only allusion traced in his work is to Cambridge,[17] but Scots more often went to Oxford, and Oxford had more connection with the West Country. He was certainly for some time chaplain of the College of St. Mary Ottery, in Devonshire (the future birthplace of Coleridge), and seems there to have translated the *Ship of Fools*,[18] which Pynson published in 1508, dedicated to Bishop Cornish of Exeter. He may have had poetical employment at the Field of the Cloth of Gold, was a monk at Ely, and after the dissolution of the monasteries obtained livings in Essex and Somerset under Edward VI, as well as later, just before his death in 1552, that of Allhallows, Lombard Street.

Barclay's work was extensive, but chiefly translated. He "did" Gringore's *Castle of Labour* before the *Ship,* and after it some more, though not wholly, original Eclogues, of which the *Citizen and Uplandishman*[19] is the one most easily accessible in full. Divers other works, some of them extant, are assigned to him, and he seems in one, *Contra Skeltonum,* to have made a formal onslaught on a poet at whom his existing poems contain more than one fling.

Barclay seems really to deserve the place of first Eclogue-writer in English, if anyone cares for this fortuitous and rather futile variety of eminence. His Eclogues, moreover, are not merely rather more original, but deserve at least to be called less jejune than the *Ship.* This latter owes its fame partly to its rarity before the reprint referred to in Note above, partly to the famous and really admirable woodcuts which it contains. The

---

17. Trumpington, also mentioned, would prove nothing, because Chaucer had made it a place of literature.
18. Very handsomely reprinted, with the woodcuts, by T.H. Jamieson (Edinburgh, 2 vols. 4to, 1874).
19. Ed. Fairholt, Percy Society, 1847, with extracts from the others. The Spenser Society reprinted all, and *The Mirror of Good Manners,* in black letter folio, 1885.

first "fole"—the possessor of unprofitable books—has a certain savour of promise which is unluckily but seldom fulfilled afterwards. Still, mainly thanks to the illustrations and to the general sympathy with Puck in seeing and saying, "Lord, what fools these mortals be!" it is possible to make one's way through the long catalogue which fills from two thousand to two thousand five hundred stanzas of rhyme-royal. The individual line is rather an interesting one, showing a sort of intermediate stage between the would-be rigid decasyllable of Lydgate and Occleve and the long rambling twelves or fourteeners of the mid-sixteenth-century poets. Sometimes Barclay permits himself a full Alexandrine; oftener (in fact, in the majority of cases) he lengthens out his line with trisyllabic feet, so arranged as sometimes to take very little keep of the iambic basis. This same line is found in the Eclogues, arranged mainly in couplets, but with, insertions in stanza, such as the allegorical octaves describing the *Tower of Virtue* in the Fourth Eclogue. In the first three (paraphrased from Aeneas Silvius) the speakers are Coridon and Cornix, in the fourth Codrus and Menalcas, in the fifth (the *Citizen and Uplandishman* [countryman]) Augustus and Faustus. They have for almost pervading subject that rather monotonous grumbling at the vices, follies, and ingratitude of courts which was the natural result of the Tudor concentration of the fountains not merely of honour but of profit in the sovereign, and of which we find more than an echo in Spenser.

The *Ship of Fools*.

The Eclogues.

No more curious instance of literary contrast could possibly be provided than that which is supplied by the writer who is always coupled with Hawes, and sometimes with Barclay, his enemy. The birthplace of John Skelton[20] is given with the very sufficient variants of Cumberland and Norfolk; his birth-year must have been somewhere about 1460, and so in a not uninteresting way he takes up in the cradle the torch which Lydgate and Occleve dropped in the tomb. He was pretty certainly a Cambridge man, and was M.A. in 1484. His earliest poem is thought to be one on the death

Skelton.

20. Re-edited London, 1736; in Chalmers; and ed. Dyce, 1843.

of Edward IV, which is noteworthy, like Dunbar's *Lament for the Makers,* for a Latin refrain, melancholy in tone. Caxton in 1490, and in the preface to his *Aeneid,* speaks of Skelton's scholarship with reverence, and tells us that he was Poet Laureate in the University of Oxford. This title, which Skelton also enjoyed from Louvain and Cambridge, has caused mistakes which seem even yet not to be universally cleared up. Perhaps it is too much to speak of it as a "degree"; it was rather, in old Oxford language, a "position" in rhetoric and poetics (then practically confounded) which necessitated a verse-thesis. It had nothing to do, except accidentally, with the modern sense of "Poet Laureate," which practically comes into existence with Ben Jonson and the seventeenth century.

His life.

Skelton seems to have been one of the numerous literary *protégés* of Lady Margaret and her son Henry VII; he took orders in 1498, when he must have been no longer a young man, and was tutor to Henry VIII. At this time Erasmus follows Caxton as his encomiast. He became rector of Diss, in his (probably) native county, Norfolk, before 1504. Up to this time, when he was far advanced in middle life, he seems to have been continuously prosperous and well-reputed. He lived twenty-five years longer, during which he became a complete Ishmaelite. The beginning of his trouble seems to have been that he married. At any rate he was suspended for this offence (or perhaps not for marriage at all) at some time not clearly known, and seems to have gone to London. The King favoured his old tutor, but either from jealousy or sheer quarrelsomeness, or, as his partisans maintain, reforming zeal, he fell foul of Wolsey, whose friend he had previously been. A series of satires on the minister made it necessary for Skelton to take refuge in the sanctuary of Westminster, where he died in 1529, probably near his full term of days, and only a year before the former friend, now foe, on whom his pupil, and Wolsey's master, somewhat ungratefully revenged him.

One point which distinguishes nearly, not quite, all Skelton's verse from that of Hawes is that it is thoroughly alive. The *Crown of Laurel,* a stately, sterile, eminently fifteenth-century piece, mainly in rhyme-royal and aureate language, does indeed meet us in the forefront of his work and inspire doubt and dread—

> Aulus Gellius, that noble historian,
> Orace also with his newe poetry,
> Master Terence, the famous comicar,

are lines likely to "strike a chill." But if Skelton was not equal to "new poetry" himself, he could at any rate rebel against the old; if he could not write musically, he could at any rate take refuge in the doggerel of talent and almost of genius. Even this very poem, with its addresses to various young ladies of high birth, contains, in the short staccato metres that Skelton loved—to Margaret Hussey ("Merry Margaret As Midsummer flower"), to Isabel Pennell ("My maiden Isabel, Whose mammy and whose daddy Brought forth a goodly baby"), to Gertrude Statham ("Mistress Gertrude, With Womanhood Endued"),—very pleasant examples of better things. The *Bouge of Court* retains the dim and dreary personages—Dread, Suspicion, Disdain, Favell, etc.—of allegory.

His poems.

The real Skelton, taking the order of his works as usually printed, emerges first in a very long, very boisterous, very rude, and in part rather childish and ignoble, but curiously spirited and fresh, ballad of triumph over the Duke of Albany, who ran away shamefully with a hundred thousand "tratland Scots and faint-hearted Frenchmen" beside the water of Tweed. Here—in almost the shortest possible lines, anapaestic in general character and for the most part of two feet only, rhymed in couplet, and with language sometimes almost inarticulate in its bubbling volubility, strongly alliterated, using the repeated beginning of the line freely—Skelton crows and whoops at the defeated enemy with a heartiness that may not be chivalrous, but is certainly unfeigned. *Speak Parrot,* in rhyme-royal, is an odd mixture of the author's favourite half-gibberish doggerel with "aureate" language and "rhethorike"—indeed, it is impossible not to see a deliberate satire on the second in both constituents. The above-mentioned *Dirge on Edward IV* is, of course, quite serious, couched in twelve-line stanzas of decasyllables decidedly Occlevian in their character, with the refrain *Quia ecce nunc in pulvere dormio. Against the Scots,* a song of triumph for Flodden, is a duplication of the other crow, but rather more ignoble because the triumph and the tragedy were both greater. This is partly in "Skeltonics," partly in octosyllables. *Ware the Hawke*! is pure doggerel satire; and then a few serious pieces introduce us to what is perhaps Skelton's most vigorous, though certainly not his most elegant, work, the *Tunning of Eleanor Rumming.* This is a more than Hogarthian sketch, in language which might make Swift or Smollett squeamish, of the brewing and drinking of a certain browst of ale by a country ale-wife and her customers. It is wholly in the Skeltonian dimeter or monometer, which, it should be observed, has a tendency now and then to fall into six-syllabled iambics or seven-syllabled trochaics for longer or shorter breaks, the centre of the verse shifting precisely in the same fashion as in the *Genesis and Exodus* or *Christabel* metre, of which, in fact, this is undoubtedly a shortened and doggerelised variant for satiric purposes. In this form it pervades Skelton's two chief political satires against Wolsey, *Why come ye not to Court* and the *Book of Colin Clout,* as well as the *Book of Philip Sparrow,* his most whimsical and graceful thing, a long desultory mourning for the pet bird of Mistress Joan Scrope.

In these, and in Skelton's minor poems, the chief of which are a *Lament on the Death of the Earl of Northumberland* and a morality called *Magnificence,* we see a fertile, restless, and ingenious spirit entirely unprovided with the proper means of expression, and just falling short of the intelligence and originality necessary to elaborate such means for itself. It is impossible not to recognise in the "Skeltonics" an attempt, crude and clumsy it is true, to get away from the intolerable dulness and dryness of the stanza-decasyllable, as it appears in Hawes and the earlier fifteenth-century poets. To this day it is difficult to see why this fit of stuttering should have come upon English. At the beginning and at the end of the 150 years of it (to pass over Skelton's younger contemporaries Wyatt and Surrey for reasons) we find Chaucer before and Sackville afterwards making the seven or eight-lined stanza-decasyllables the instrument of music, sweet or stately, merry or sorrowful, at their pleasure and with no sort of difficulty. Between them (to borrow a phrase from Mr. Swinburne of another matter) it seems almost impossible for an English poet to "clear his mouth of pebbles and his brow of fog."

Probably at no time would Skelton have been a great poet in the serious and passionate way—probably, at all, his genius would have inclined to comedy and to satire. As it is, he holds a position with Butler as the chief English verse-writer who has deliberately preferred to be burlesque to the verge, and in his case considerably over the verge, of grotesque and doggerel. In comparing the two men, whose powers, natural and acquired, do not seem to have been very different, while their tempers were also not dissimilar (Skelton inclining rather to the jovial, Butler to the saturnine), it is impossible not to remember that Butler came just after, as Skelton came just before, the enormous, the incalculable advances made by the Elizabethan period, not merely in language and metre, but in everything, small and great, that pertains to the business of poetry. And we ought to give the author of *Philip Sparrow* and *Eleanor Rumming* and *Why come ye not to Court* a substantial allowance for the fact.

2

THE SCOTTISH POETS—HISTORICAL, POLITICAL, AND MINOR

Lateness of Scottish Literature—Barbour—Wyntoun—Blind Harry—Minors—Lyndsay—His life—His works—The *Satire of the Three Estates*—Minor poems.

ALTHOUGH the literary eminence of the quartette of poets who will be discussed in the next chapter is unquestioned, even the earliest of them (taking him to have been James the First) was not the first known poet of Scotland. That position, assigned by tradition or imagination, first to Thomas of Erceldoune, and then to the still more shadowy "Huchowne," belongs historically to John Barbour, Archdeacon of Aberdeen, and author of the *Brus,* which was finished in 1375. The reasons of this extraordinary lateness, and the still more extraordinary lagging of prose (of which, except laws, letters, and a few translations,[1] etc., we have nothing till the *Complaint of Scotland* hard on the middle of the sixteenth century), are too conjectural to be argued out here. Attention can only be called to the following facts, which (though some of them are even now sometimes attacked) are absolutely indisputable. They are these: that the establishment of a separate kingdom in any sense corresponding to what we call Scotland was very late; that this kingdom when established consisted of, or rested on, the *debris* of four different nationalities and

Lateness of Scottish Literature.

1. The Scots New Testament (S.T.S.) is not earlier than 1520, nor Bellenden's *Livy* than 1533; but Sir Gilbert Hay's version of *L'Arbre des Batailles* (S.T.S.) goes back to 1456; and a certain "John of Ireland" to 1490.

languages— those of the Picts, of the Scots of Dalriada, of the Britons of Strathclyde, and of the Anglo-Danes of Northumbria; that the literary chances of the last, where only an English literature could have arisen, were ruined by the Danish invasion, and not recovered till, after the Norman conquest of England, English was everywhere undergoing a process of moulting which made literature impossible; that even in the comparatively halcyon times of the Alexanders, English (ail the Scottish writers up to Douglas invariably call their language "Inglis," and if they use "Scots" at all, mean Gaelic by it) was yet unformed; and that from the latter half of the thirteenth to the latter half of the fourteenth century the War of Independence, and the turbulent State in which Scotland emerged from it, made literature improbable, if not actually impossible.

Barbour.

At any rate, whether it be strange or not, that we have nothing earlier than Barbour, the author of the *Brus,*[2] is a fact and indisputable. His identification with the Archdeacon rests testimony of his immediate successor, Wyntoun, and of the Archdeacon we have divers documentary notices. These do not include the date or place of his birth. The former is guessed at as about 1320. Our first notice of him is thirty-seven years later, when in 1357 Edward III granted him license to corne, with three scholars, to Oxford to study, to stay there and exercise scholastic acts, and to return to Scotland, where, it must be remembered, there was as yet no University. Seven years later he had a similar safe-conduct to the same place, and at other times others to go to France, also for the sake of study. The other references, which are numerous, refer chiefly to payments of pensions, etc., and do not concern literature. He died in March 1395.

Besides the *Brus* there have of late years been assigned to Barbour, and taken away from him by turns, a fragment of a Troy Book and a very large collection of *Lives of the Saints.*[3] In

2. Frequently edited. The Scottish Text Society's issue by Professor Skeat (Edinburgh, 1894) is the one I have used.
3. Also in the Scottish Text Society's issues. Ed. Metcalfe, Edinburgh, 1896.

dialect and metre these are similar to the *Brus* itself; but they are naturally less interesting, being simply members of a very large class, and treating common matter in common form, while the *Brus* stands quite by itself. Even as a historical document—though it takes some remarkable liberties with fact, confusing Bruce with his own grandfather, making him refuse an offer of the crown from Edward, etc.—it is not despicable. It was written (we have the exact date in a passage of its own) less than fifty years after Brace's death, and by a man who was probably nearly ten years old at the date of that death, so that he had ample opportunity for communication with direct witnesses. That Barbour takes, as every mediaeval writer, almost without exception, invariably did take, license of embellishing, altering, supplying, omitting, to suit his own notion, of the story, is not so much probable as certain, but it is not material. As a poet, Barbour, if not taking very high rank, is very far indeed from being despicable. His famous and often-quoted outburst about freedom does not seem to be, by any means, a mere commonplace, and many of his descriptive passages (the pursuit of Bruce by John of Lorn being only one of them) fully rise to the level required. It would be absurd to compare Barbour to Chaucer or to Langland, but, with a little less elegance, he has more spirit than Gower.

Wyntoun.

Poetry was not the strong point of his younger contemporary and immediate successor in the verse-chronicling of Scottish history, Andrew Wyntoun, Canon of St. Andrews and Prior of St. Serf in Lochleven. His birth- and death-dates are not known, but he certainly held his priory from 1395 (Barbour's death-year) to 1413 at least; and he was alive six years later, for he notices the death of Robert Duke of Albany in 1419. 1350-1420 would therefore (as he speaks of old age having mastered him) be a probable life-date. The title of "Original Chronicle" which he gave to his work[4] does not, as Dr. Irving[5] seems rather oddly to have thought, claim

4. Edited in part by D. Macpherson (1795) and in whole by Laing (1872-79). A thorough revision has since been made by Mr. Amours for the S.T.S.

5. *History of Scottish Poetry*, p. 116.

"originality" in our common modern sense—indeed Wyntoun very frankly quotes many authors down to Barbour. It signifies that he began at the beginning—*origo*—after the wont of the mediaeval chronicler. His verse is less poetical than Barbour's in spirit but a little more accomplished in form, attaining the trisyllabic swing of the *Christabel* metre sometimes with very good effect, as witness the line in his often-quoted account of Macbeth and the Weird Sisters—

> *Lo* ! yon | der the thane | of Crum | bauchty | [Cromarty],

And another in reference to the Maid of Norway—

> To Nor | way and Scot | land both right | wise heir.

He has not a few passages interesting for matter—as far as manner goes the interview between the Devil and St. Serf (Book v, chap. xii) is a very fair specimen. It is from him that we have the well-known and interesting piece "When Alexander our King was dead," which, however, can hardly be contemporary with the event it commemorates.

The transition, from Wyntoun's easy amble of manner (not seldom degenerating into a mere pedestrian verse) and hig placid chronicling, to the next writer on this special list is

Blind Harry.

not a little curious. Barbour had been patriotic beyond all dispute, and he had not been over-squeamish about dressing up the facts of history to better advantage in the garb of romance. Wyntoun, with more sense of history, had been patriotic too; but neither showed any violent animosity against England, and an Englishman must compare with some compunction the international courtesy of Laurence Minot and theirs. Both were cosmopolitan, and the method of Barbour himself was rigidly critical, as compared with Blind Harry,[6] or, as modern punctilio prefers to call him, "Henry the Minstrel," the poetical biographer of the other great hero of the War of Independence. The author himself is a very obscure person. The *locus classicus* about him is a passage of the same Latin-writing historian, John Mair or Major, who is our authority for the authorship of the *King's Quair*. Mair says that Henricus, blind from his birth, executed

6. Scottish Text Society, ed. Moir.

the poem in his (the historian's) infancy, which is judged to have been *cir.* 1460. We have only one MS. of it, and that is dated 1488, while we have some records of payments to Henry as late as 1492, and Dunbar includes him among the Dead Makers in 1508. The last three-quarters of the fifteenth century would therefore seem to have been his date; and the text of his poem, if not directly taken down from his dictation, to have been at least contemporary.

Sir William Wallace consists of nearly 12,000 lines in heroic couplets, often very spirited, and generally correct enough in construction, but observing the sharp French caesura at the fourth syllable. It purports to be based on a Latin book by John Blair, Wallace's own chaplain; but no such book is known to have existed, nor is it referred to by any authority, except such as have obviously derived their knowledge from Harry himself. Nor does it need more than the slightest examination of the poem to see that it is in substance, though not in form, a true *chanson de geste,* having only the remotest foundation in history, and weaving its story perhaps out of some popular traditions, but mainly out of the poet's own head or the heads of his unknown predecessors. It is well known that the authentic documents for Wallace's history are extremely meagre. Barbour never mentions his name. But Wyntoun, long before Harry, says that great *gestes* of him existed, and suggests that a "great buke" (the opposition is not unnoteworthy) might be written. It is by no means improbable that Blind Harry took the hint directly from the good prior of St. Serf. By his time the national animosity between Scots and English, according to a custom odd at first sight but not unintelligible, had grown much more fierce than during the actual Wars of Independence in the previous century. And Harry's verses are inspired by the hottest flame of this. The presence of indignation and the absence of information combine in him to make an exceedingly spirited romance, which was naturally and deservedly popular in Scotland from the very first, but which, of course, has the slightest—if the slightest—pretence to historical importance. The ghostly apparition of Fawdone, in the finest passage of all, is not more a thing of the imagination than the still more famous fishing story with which the poem opens, or the stock incident (very freshly and excellently told) of the visit of the Queen of England to Wallace, and her mediation with her no less cowardly than ferocious husband. But it was all perfectly right and proper, according to the laws of the class of composition to which Blind Harry's work belongs; and it is a compensation or the extreme lateness and comparative scantiness of Scottish iterature that it was thus able to produce the latest, and very far indeed from the worst, example of the national folk-epic which blends traditions of all sorts, adds commonplaces from he general stock of fiction, and makes the whole thick and slab with original sauce, in order to exalt and consecrate the deeds of a popular hero.

Minors.

It may be not inconvenient here, before coming to the last of the batch of historical poets or verse-writers who form the staple of this chapter, and who in this case extend beyond the fifteenth century proper, to note very briefly the minor poets of this and the other class who complete the list of the makers of the fifteenth century itself, as we have them on the authority of Dunbar and ethers. The chief of these was Walter Kennedy, Dunbar's contemporary ad antagonist in the "flyting" *(vide infra),* who took his degree at Glasgow in 1476, and is spoken of not as dead but dying in the *Complaint of the Makers,* published therewith. There are poems of Kennedy's in existence, but mostly unpublished, and said to be of no great merit. Others who are not mere names are Richard, or Sir Richard Holland, a Douglas's an, who wrote about the middle of the century the *Book of the Howlat,*[7] alliterated and rhymed, describing a general council the Birds, with the Peacock as Pope-President; and Clerk of Tranent,

7. This is in the Scottish Text Society's *Alliterative Poems,* ed. Amours. Everybody knows the two short lines—

O Douglas, Douglas, Tender and true!

which end the wheel of stanza 31, and the whole passage dealing with Lord James and the heart of he Bruce is good. Otherwise not much can be said for the poem, which is a mere variation of the *Parliament of Fowls.*

who is spoken of as having made the "Anturs of Gawane" *(vide supra).* To him may be due the existing *Golagros and Gawane,* an alliterative rhymed poem of the Gawain Northern cycle *(ante,* p. 129, and *post,* p. 252). Mersar, two Rowls or Rolls, and others are but shadows, and only a single poem seems to remain by Quentin Shaw, a poet who is not only mentioned by Dunbar, but picturesquely introduced by Gawain Douglas—

> Quentin with ane huttock[8] on his head—

as one of the Scottish poets worthy to show cause against even Chaucer, Gower, and Lydgate. And to the poets who are thus without, or nearly without, poems, a list of poems at present unattached to poets might be added, showing more evidence of the literary working in Scotland which began so late and was to die away, all but completely, so soon.

Lyndsay.

It is probable that among these forgotten, scarcely known, and too often still disdained writers, there was more than one who was a better poet in the strict sense of that term than "Sir David Lyndsay of the Mount, Lord Lyon King of Lyndsay Arms," who, at the cost of a slight stretch of chronology, may best be mentioned here. But Lyndsay is an interesting, and though not a fully yet a fairly known personality, while they flit as shadows; he has left an abundant supply of work,[9] frequently interesting in itself, and generally characteristic of his time; and in one particular he has the rare good luck to have left the only example, not merely in Scottish but in English literature, of an early *sotie* or political farce-satire in dramatic form. If he had given us nothing but the *Satire of the Three Estates,* Lyndsay would be a remarkable figure in English literature; as it is, he has left much else.

He is supposed, rather than known, to have been born at The Mount, near Cupar, in Fife, somewhere about 1490; but daims (also guesswork) have been put in for Garmylton or Garleton in East Lothian, an estate which certainly belonged

8. *i.e.* a hood, probably like that in Chaucer's portrait, and copied from it by fifteenth-century poets, as those of the eighteenth copied Pope's nightcap.

9. Ed. Laing, Edinburgh. 3 vols., 1879.

to his father and to him. The family was an offshoot (whether legitimate or not is uncertain) of that of Lyndsay of the Byres.

His life.

He may, rather than must, have been the "Da. Lyndsay" who was an incorporated fourth-year student at St. Andrews in 1508-09. He certainly had not merely a regular salary in the Royal Household, but a "play-coat of blue and yellow taffety" in 1511, and played before King James IV and Queen Margaret. He is said to have been present at the famous scene of the apparition to the King before Flodden, which is enshrined in *Marmion*. And he was master-usher, or master of the household, to James V from his earliest childhood. In 1522 he was a married man, and his wife Janet Douglas was accustomed to sew the King's ''sarkis" with double hanks of gold thread. James's very early nominal coming of age at his twelfth year caused the removal of Lyndsay, who retired to his estate of Garmylton and "commenced poet." But four years later James emancipated himself from his still real tutelage to Angus, and almost at once promoted his old master to knighthood and the office of Lyon King, which then involved very important diplomatic duties. In discharge of these Lyndsay went to England, France, the Netherlands, and Denmark. He held a chapter of his heralds in January 1555, and seems to have died between that month and the following April.

Lyndsay's works consist of the above-mentioned *Satire of the Three Estates,* of a *Dialogue between Experience and a Courtier,* and of the *History of Squire Meldrum,* all long poems,

His works.

with a considerable number of shorter ones. Of the long poems, *The Dialogue* (or *The Monarchie)* consists of more than 6000 fines, chiefly octosyllabic couplets, and gives the history of the world, with comments in the dismallest manner of the fifteenth century. The *History of Squire Meldrum,* in the same metre, is an exceedingly pleasant romande biography of a real person, a sort of cross between Quentin Durward and the Admirable Crichton, whose prowess against Englishmen and others in the field, and his courtesy to ladies in the bower, are very lovingly depicted. The most noteworthy of the three, however, (though, in common with Lyndsay's other poems, it is disfigured by the extraordinary coarseness of language which marks most of this early Scottish poetry, and which, except for a very brief time at the Restoration, and then chiefly in anonymous writings, has never been matched in England), is the *Satire*. This, as its length, not far short of 5000 lines, makes inevitable, is not a single piece, but, on the model of the French compositions, which no doubt suggested it, a set or pentalogy of five different pieces: the First part of the play proper, the First and Second Interludes, the second part of the play, and the Third Interlude, while there is a preliminary interlude of between two and three hundred lines more which has been thought spurious, but with no apparent reason, and which is certainly not less vigorous than the rest, though it is if possible even coarser.

The Satire of the Three Estates.

The main play is a "morality" of the familiar kind (see next Book), but with the allegory deflected from its usual ethical tenor to a political bent, Rex Humanitas being tempted by Wantonness, Placebo, and the Vices in the habit of Friars, and saved by Correction, Gude Counsel, and the Virtues. It is in the second part that the Three Estates make a direct appearance; while the Interludes, not losing sight of the moral, enforce it with more farcical and general satire. It has been customary to regard Lyndsay as a partisan of the Reformation, and so, in the merely literal and grammatical sense, he certainly was. But it does not appear very certain that he was a partisan from any doctrinal side.

This sharp satire on abuses in Church and State, perhaps mixed, as satire so often is, with some selfish consideration, appears also in all, or almost all, Lyndsay's minor poems, which, if not over numerous, are very interesting. They scarcely reach a dozen in number, and, as has been said, grace of poetic style and thought is by no means their prominent characteristic. But they all have a certain accomplishment of phrase and form which is extremely noteworthy in contrast with the staggering State of English in both ways at the time, and more noteworthy still when we remember that the Scottish Muse was about to fall almost barren for centuries, while the English was in some fifty years' time to become the fruitful mother of the best poetry in the

Minor poems.

world. And they are all interesting, more or less, in matter. The *Dream* (which is in plain language a begging letter to the King) is in rhyme-royal, and the body of it is simply part of that vast and dreary common form of fifteenth-century allegory through which, as throughout this Book, we have to make our way. But the begging letter by itself has some very interesting biographical touches, reminding James how his master-usher had carried him in his arms and tucked him up in bed; how he had told him not merely "of Hercules the actis honorabill," and much other improving matter, but the Prophecies of Rymour, Beid, and Marlyng, and tales of the Red Etin and the Gyre Carling, for which posterity would very cheerfully give twenty *Dialogues between Experience and a Courtier.* The *Dream* itself ranges from the centre of the Earth (*i.e.* Hell) and the description of Paradise, to the relations between France and Scotland and the State of Argyle and the Out Isles, which would appear not to have been Paradise at all. The piece, with all its parts included, considerably exceeds 1000 lines, and ends with a direct Exhortation to the King's Grace (in nine-line stanzas, with a different one as *coda)* which is manly and sensible. In fact, both Dunbar and Lyndsay deserve the highest credit for the absence of "assentation" in their addresses to their patrons, James the Fourth and Fifth, though neither father nor son seems to have profited very much thereby.

This manly tone is renewed in the *Complaint of Sir David Lyndsay*—some 500 lines in octosyllabic couplets—which is again biographical and again suppliant, but does not hesitate to mingle probably unpalatable advice with supplication. Nor is the *Testament and Complaint of the Papyngo* (the King's Parrot), which is about the length of the *Dream,* and chiefly, but not wholly, in rhyme-royal, very different, being directed largely against various abuses in Church and State, especially the former. The *Answer to the King's Flyting* (the *Flyting* itself is lost) partakes of the studied coarseness of this singular form of poetical amusement. But Lyndsay's practical honesty makes him still more attentive to warning the "Red Tod of St. Andrews" against vice and disorder than to exercises in curious ribaldry. Another court poem, probably not without special meaning, is the *Petition* of the King's old hound "Bagsche" to his successors in favour, Bawtie and others, for "ane portion in Dunfermling," concluding with good advice. The poet's most important attempt in pathetic poetry, the *Deploration of Queen Magdalene,* the fair and ill-fated French princess who was James's first wife, and to whom the climate of Scotland was almost at once fatal, is meritorious but hardly successful, Lyndsay being unable to extract from the rhyme-royal that plangent note which it so readily yields to true poets. He is happier, though still not consummately happy, in the comic handling of the *Justing between Watson and Barbour* and the *Supplication in Contempt of Side Tails* (trains), as well as in the rather famous anticlerical *Kitty's Confession,* to which the *Description of Peddar Coffis*[10] is a kind of pendant. Lastly has to be mentioned the *Tragedy of the Cardinadl,* a ferocious attack on the dead Beaton in the style of the *Fall of Princes.*

10. *i.e.* "pedlar knaves," in senses both literal and transferred.

3

THE FOUR GREAT SCOTTISH POETS

The *King's Quair*—Henryson—The *Testament and Complaint of Creseide*—The *Fables*—*Robene and Makyne*—Minor poems—Dunbar— *The Twa Maryit Wemen and the Wedo*—Other large poems—Gawain Douglas—His life—His original poems—His *Aeneid.*

IT has constantly been remarked as a most curious and partially unaccountable phenomenon, that while Chaucerian poetry, as soon as Chaucer's own hands failed, gave nothing but third-rate work or worse in England, it produced in Scotland work in some cases of very high quality indeed. Such account as is possible of the reasons for the general lateness of purely Scottish literature has been given in the last chapter. In this we shall give an account of the four chiefs of Scottish poetry when it did come—James the First, Robert Henryson, William Dunbar, and Gawain or Gavin Douglas.

Criticism of the strenuously inert kind has played its usual games with the literary work of James Stewart, first king of the name in Scotland. After by turns attributing to him and taking away from him *Christ's Kirk on the Green, Peebles to the Play,* etc., it has recently attacked his claims, which for nearly four centuries had been undisturbed, on the *Kingis Quair* itself. Once more this history does not trouble itself with otiosities of the kind. It is sufficient that the *Kingis Quair* (*quire,* book) is attributed to James by John Major or Mair, not an impeccable historian, but fairly near the time, and likely to know; that it is also given as his in the MS., which seems to be still more nearly contemporary; that no other attribution of the poem has any early authority; and that nothing is to be gained by disturbing the accepted tradition. It is indeed unwise to try, as other freaks of the same tricksy spirit have done, to force the dramatic details of the poem too closely, or closely at all, into line with the historical events of James's life, or to insist that the locality of the poem is Windsor, the heroine Joan Beaufort, and so forth. For us it shall be sufficient that the unbroken and till now unopposed tradition of four centuries has given the *King's Quair*[1] to James the First of Scotland, and that though we cannot say on positive evidence that he did write it, absolutely no facts have been produced showing that he did not. With regard to *Christ's Kirk on the Green* and *Peebles to the Play,* two very lively and spirited, though slightly coarse, narrative ballads of a "Burnsish" cast, the case is different. Early attribution hesitates—a fatal thing—between James the *First* and James the *Fifth* as the author of *Christ's Kirk on the Green,* and its tone is much more suggestive of the "goodman of Ballengeich" than of his fierce but knightly great-great-grandfather. Also, though it is very difficult to speak of the older Scots with any certainty, the language certainly seems more recent than the early fifteenth century.

The *King's Quair.*

On the contrary, the *King's Quair,* if not by James, must be by some unknown Scottish poet who was under the fresh and full Chaucerian influence. This James would naturally have been, seeing that he was born in 1394, captured at sea by the English in 1405, and kept in an honourable captivity in England till 1424, in which year, having married Joan Beaufort, Henry V's first cousin, he was allowed to ransom himself and return to Scotland. There he was crowned at Scone, ruled his turbulent realm with some justice, considerable ability and love of learning, and very great harshness, till 1436, when he was assassinated by not quite unreasonably wrathful rebels in the monastery of the Black Friars at Perth, despite (or not) of the heroism of

1. Ed. Skeat, Scottish Text Society. The arguments against James's authorship have been carefully examined and replied to by M. Jusserand; but it was really unnecessary, for not one of them is even plausible.

"Kate Barlass." There was, if a slight variation of dialect, a complete unity of literary sentiment between England and Scotland at the time, and the increasing study of the French *rhétoriqueurs* had not yet, as it was to do in Scotland even more than in England, *aureated* the vocabulary with too cumbrous a garment of brocaded diction. The piece, which is in stanzas of rhyme-royal (said indeed to be so named from it), has the drawbacks from which even Chaucer's own minor poems are not free, of the common form of the *Rose* tradition—the sleep, the dream, the vision of Paganly divine personages, the Deadly Sins, the Wheel of Fortune, and the rest. It has none of the direct dramatic faculty of Chaucer in the *Tales* or of Dunbar, none of the intense romantic power of Henryson's *Creseide,* or the idyllic grace of his *Robene and Makyne.* But it has very much of the dreamy elegance of the *Rose* itself, in the passages describing how the weary dreamer looks out into the castle garden, and sees the gracious apparition of his love with golden hair, tricolour plumes in it, and a single ruby glowing on her breast; the interview with Venus (that which follows with Minerva is a little owlish); the fine episode of Fortune; and the final boon of red gillyflowers brought him by the bird of Venus, the turtle-dove, with an encouraging inscription on the leaves. On the whole, if *The Flower and the Leaf* be not Chaucer's, it and the *King's Quair* may be ranked as the two most graceful, scholarly, and elegant poems of the French-Chaucerian tradition to be found in English. The *Ballad of Good Counsel,* which is also ascribed by good authority to James, and is the only other piece bearing such attribution, is also, though in another kind, strongly Chaucerian, its refrain being—

> And for ilk inch He will thee quit a span,

and breathes the same mixture of pious humility and moral wisdom which appears in *Flee from the Press,* etc. Both pieces, the *Quair* and the *Ballad,* are thus distinctly "school-work," owing almost everything, as far as mere originality goes, to Chaucer. But they are school-work of the best kind, standing to their masters as Luini's to Lionardo's in painting, and showing the highest ability in execution.

Henryson.

Few poets whose personality is certain, and whose work is both eminent in merit and not inconsiderable in bulk, have a more shadowy record than Master Robert Henryson, schoolmaster in Dunfermline, as he is entitled in editions of his work printed some sixty or seventy years after his death. It may, in fact, be said that Dunbar's reference to that death in the *Complaint of the Makers,* which was written about 1506—

In Dunfermline he has done down,
Good Master Robert Henryson[2]—

is the only certain and positive reference that we possess to him. For it is not certain, though it is highly probable, that he is the Venerabilis vir Magister Robertus Henryson who was incorporated in the University of Glasgow (then scarcely ten years old) in 1462; and all attempts to identify him with the Henrysons or Hendersons of Fordell in Fife have quite failed.

About his works,[3] however, there is no reasonable doubt. They consist of two poems of some length, the *Testament of Creseide* and *Orpheus and Eurydice;* of a collection, with prologue, of Aesopic fables in Scots; and of rather more than a dozen miscellaneous minor poems, of which the chief is the somewhat famous *pastourelle* of *Robene and Makyne.* The total bulk is not large, but the merit is, for the fifteenth century more particularly, very high, and the variety of the directions in which it is shown is extremely remarkable. Of the two long poems, *Orpheus and Eurydice* is partly in rhyme-royal, partly in couplets, with a *ballade* in ten-line stanzas interposed and a "morality" in couplets. If it stood alone it would not create any very special position for its author. There are much better Middle English poems on the same subject; and this is only a fair Chaucerian exercise, not better than the best of Lydgate, though much better than the worst of Occleve.

2. Readings vary.

3. Ed. Laing (Edinburgh, 1865). Professor Gregory Smith has issued (1906) the first vol. of a new edition for the Scottish Text Society.

Very different is the *Testament of Creseide*[4] (sometimes subdivided into a "complaint" and a "testament" proper), which undertakes to complete Chaucer's *Troilus,* and, not adopting the story of the jilted prince's speedy death, to give that of Cressida's punishment. After a vigorous prologue, describing how the poet in middle age, and a cold night, mended the fire, "beikit him about," "tuik ane drink his spirits to comfort," and a book, the *Troilus*—

The *Testament and Complaint of Creseide.*

To cut the winter night and make it short—

he resolves to tell the sequel. Diomed, satiated with Cressida, deserts her as she has deserted his rival. She takes refuge with her father, Calchas, and will not show herself in public, but in "ane secret oratoir" angrily reproaches Venus and her son. Cupid, highly indignant, summons the council of the Gods[5] to determine the punishment for this blasphemy, and it is referred to a committee consisting of Saturn and the Moon. Little mercy is to be expected from these two cold deities; and there is singular force in the description of the sentence pronounced by Saturn. Passing down where careful Cressid lay, and placing a frosty wand on her head, he deprives her of all beauty and joy. Cynthia strikes her in addition with the incurable and loathsome signs of leprosy. The doom takes effect at once, and she has to seek the spital-house, where (in a nine-lined stanza) she makes her complaint. One of her wretched companions, not unkindly, bids her make virtue of necessity, give up useless wailing,

And live efter the law of lipper-*leid* (= *folk*).

So she goes forth with clapper and begging-dish. As she sits forlorn by the wayside, a gallant company rides by from Troy, Troilus among them. And then comes the crowning passage of the poem. Their eyes meet; but her bleared vision

4. This can be found in Chalmers's *Poets* and in Professor Skeat's Chauceriana.

5. It is not superfluous to say that Mercury is "full of rhetoric," and has "a *hude* Like to ane Poeit of the auld fashioun"; see note on Quentin Shaw in the last chapter.

does not recognise her former lover, and it is impossible for him to know Cressida in the ghastly creature beneath him. The stanzas describing this situation are nearly perfect. She receives his guerdon, is told by one of her comrades who he is, utters one last complaint, and sending him a ruby ring he had once given her, dies.

The two great passages of the doom of Saturn and the meeting would of itself give this poem rank with, if not above, the best work of its century, but the whole is not unworthy of them. Only in Sackville is the power of tragic effect which rhyme-royal eminently possesses brought out with equal fulness, and Sackville is less terrible than the Saturn piece, and less pathetic than the lovers' meeting.

The *Fables*.

The powers of this remarkable stanza in the lighter way are not generally held to be as high as those in serious verse; indeed, its great inventor or naturaliser in English usually deserted it for octosyllables or heroics when he was bent on comedy. But Henryson has been not much less happy in his use of it for Aesop than in the *Creseide* poem. His prologue is again personal, though less vivid; his fables are—The Cock and the Jasp (jasper); The Uplandish Mouse and the Burgess Mouse; a Fox series—Sir Chantecleer and the Fox, The Fox confessing to the Wolf, The Parliament of Beasts; The Dog, Sheep, and Wolf; The Lion and the Mouse; The Preaching of the Swallow; The Fox, the Wolf, and the Cadger; The Fox, the Wolf, and the Moon's Shadow; The Wolf and the Wether; The Wolf and the Lamb; The Paddock (Frog) and the Mouse. Many of these are told at considerable length, extending to some hundreds of lines, and the *moralitas* of each, as we should expect in this most moralising of all centuries, is prolonged to forty, fifty, sixty, or even more lines, but the general treatment is not at all heavy.

Robene and Makyne.

There is, however, no doubt that *Robene and Makyne* = Malkin ("Maudkin" not "Marykin," as is sometimes said), the best known of Henryson's poems from its fortunate inclusion in Percy's *Reliques*, is, if not the best, superior to all except the *Testament*. It is the Old French *pastourelle*, or shepherdess wooing-poem, with a difference. In the first part the usual order of things is inverted, and Makyne woos in vain the impassible and clownish object of her love. She is, in fact, "*Merry* Makyne" by grace of the perpetual epithet only. But the God of Love avenges her: the moonlight and the "sweet season" work on Robin, and he in turn solicits her favour. But she has been heard and healed, and every fit reader of the poem has praised the simple, but inimitably felicitous touches with which, in no undignified spirit of "tit for tat," but with the straightforwardness of the heart-whole, and not without a touch of solemnity, she reminds him of the old saw—

> The man that will nocht when he may,
> Sall hauf nocht quhen he wald;

and to a second despairing plea of the soft dry night, the warm balmy air, the secret greenwood, replies—

> Robin, that world is all awa,
> And quite brocht to an end—

and goes home no longer merely technically "merry," but blithe enough "among the holtis hoar," with (as we may supplement the description) chin no doubt slightly upturned in the moonlight, leaving the luckless fool "in dolour and in care."

Minor poems.

The remaining members of this small but admirable collection of verse are less interesting, though much above the standard of their time. The *Garmond* (Garment) of *Good Ladies* has been much praised, but its allegory—"Her hat should be of fair-having"; "Her sleeves should be of esperance"—too frequently takes an excursion beyond the agreeably quaint into the tediously grotesque. The *Bludy Serk*—the shirt of a knight who was desperately wounded in rescuing a lady from a giant, worn by her after his death—is better, but it is not improved by the inevitable *moralitas* (spared us in *Robene and Makyne*), likening the lady to man's soul, the giant to Lucifer, and the knight to Christ. The *Abbey Walk* is interesting for its opening couplet—

> Alone as I went up and down
> In ane Abbaye was fair to see—

and its possible association with the actual Dunfermline; while it morals on the refrain—

> Obey and thank thy God of all—

with a right musical and pleasant piety. The rest, except a rather coarse and not very clever gibe at *Some Practice of Medicine,* are mostly religious-philosophical, and the best of them is the *Three Dead Pows, i.e.* death's-heads, which address man, warning him of his end. This is also given to Patrick Johnston.

Dunbar.

It is usual to rank William Dunbar as the chief of all this group, and in fact the greatest Scottish poet except Burns. Nor is there much reason for quarrelling with the estimate, since Dunbar, though he has perhaps nothing equal in their own kinds to the above-noted passages of the *Testament of Creseide* and to *Robene and Makyne,* has a larger collection to show, both of good and of excellent work, a somewhat wider range, and above all, a certain body and fulness of poetical wine which is not so evident in the pensive though not uncheerful schoolmaster of Dunfermline. We know a little, if not very much, more about Dunbar than about Henryson. He was certainly a Lothian man, probably allied not merely in name to the great family of the Earls of Dunbar and March, founded in the eleventh century by Cospatrick, and now chiefly subsisting in its northern or Morayshire branches. The year 1460, with the usual *circa,* is accepted as his birth-date. He went to St. Salvator's College, then the only one in the University of St. Andrews, took his B.A. in 1477, and his M.A. two years later, being, it seems, destined for the Church. He appears, both from his own account and that of others, to have been for a time a Franciscan friar, preaching and begging all over England and in France as well as in Scotland. But in the French phrase he "threw the frock to the nettles," and appears to have been employed by James IV, on diplomatic duty not merely in England, but in almost all parts of the Continent. One of his best and best-known poems welcomes Margaret of England on her coming to Scotland as the King's bride in 1503—he was specially attached to her service; and in 1508 he had some of his principal poems printed and published by the first Scottish printers, Chepman and Millar. Records of gifts and pensions to him exist up to June 1513, and then we hear no more of him. Flodden came in September of that year, and it has been thought that he too may have fallen in the "dark impenetrable ring" round his master. He was certainly dead in 1530, for Sir David Lyndsay says so; but this is all we know.

The Twa Maryit Wemen and the Wedo.

The poems known to be by, or reasonably attributed to, him are tolerably numerous, but not very bulky, none exceeding some 600 lines, while most are quite short. The entire number in Dr. Small's edition[6] is 101, of which eleven are given as "attributed," while seven, having been, as noted above, printed in the poet's own lifetime as his, have a higher degree of certainty than any of the others in text. The two most considerable are *The Twa Maryit Wemen and the Wedo* and the *Friars of Berwick,* the latter only "attributed," but displaying a *verve* and an accomplishment of form not known to be possessed by any other Scottish poet of the time. Both are very strongly Chaucerian, and the *Friars* is in Chaucerian "riding-rhyme"; the other piece is perhaps the most accomplished specimen of that revived alliteration which has been previously discussed. Dunbar does not limit himself to three alliterations, often giving four or even five, and he is somewhat less distinct in his middle pause than Langland. On the other hand, his whole verse, which averages thirteen or fourteen syllables, has a distinctness and evenness of rhythm which are only found in parts of *Piers Plowman.* The matter of the poem is an ultra-Chaucerian satire on women. The three personages are represented as all young and all pretty; they are drinking freely in a goodly garden on Midsummer Eve, and the poet achieves a triumphantly contrasted picture of physical beauty in scene and figure and of moral deformity in sentiment. The Wife of Bath, the undoubted model of these three young persons, is neither mealy-mouthed nor strait-laced, but she is always good-natured. Dunbar's wives and widow combine sensuality

6. For the Scottish Text Society; also editions by Dr. Laing and by Dr. Schipper.

with ill-nature in a way not elsewhere to be paralleled in English literature till we come to the rakes of the Restoration. Yet the ugliness of the picture is half redeemed by the mastery with which Dunbar makes them expose their own shame, and sets their figures for us with a touch of grave irony worthy of Butler, and less purely caricatural in style than *Hudibras.* The *Friars of Berwick* is a version of a well known *fabliau,* in which two friars, treated with scant hospitality by a woman who in her husband's absence has made an assignation with her lover, revenge themselves upon her (though not to extremity), taking advantage of the husband's unexpected return. It is therefore much less of an original and more of a commonplace than *The Twa Maryit Wemen,* but the story is told with the true *brio* of the *Canterbury Tales* themselves.

Other large poems.

Next to these two may be ranked the *Golden Targe,* the *Flyting of Dunbar and Kennedy,* the famous *Dance of the Seven Deadly Sins,* and *The Thistle and the Rose.* The first of these is a typical fifteenth-century poem, allegorical in tone and very "rhetorical" in language, with the usual praise of Chaucer, "Rose of rhetors all," and "light of our Inglis," as well as of the "sugared lips and aureate tongues" of Gower and Lydgate. The *Targe* is in nine-lined stanzas; *The Thistle and the Rose,* in rhyme-royal, is of the same stamp and style, but adjusted to convey a welcome full of grace, good sense, and good taste to the youthful Margaret, the "rose" married to the "thistle." Many who know nothing else of Dunbar's, know the *Seven Deadly Sins* from its early inclusion in anthologies. The vigour of its lurid pictures has not been exaggerated, nor the real command of metre (Romance eights and sixes) which the poet here as everywhere displays, and which contrasts so strikingly with the staggering gait and palsied grip of his English contemporaries. The *Flyting,* one of a group of such things, is a curiosity no doubt, but a curiosity of a kind which could perhaps be spared. Literary Scots at all times, up to the eighteenth century, admitted, as has been said, a coarseness of actual language which is rarely paralleled in. literary English; and these "*flytings*" consisted of alternate torrents of sheer Billingsgate poured upon each other by the combatants. There is not much doubt that many of the strange terms of abuse used are mere gibberish, coined for the occasion, but there was considerable legitimate accommodation in Scots for the purpose, and the poem, like others of its kind, is at worst a quarry for lexicographers.

Of the very numerous minor poems must be mentioned the touching and interesting *Lament for the Makers,* "when he was sick," with its passing-bell refrain of *Timor Mortis conturbat me,* and its list of poets, most of whom are shadows of shades; the lively if irreverent *Ballad of Kind Kyttok,* and her reception at Heaven's gates; the *Testament of Mr. Amiro Kennedy,* a macaronic pendant to the *Flyting;* two rhetorical pieces on the Lord Bernard Stewart, living and dead; a sharp satirical description of Edinburgh Session; a quaint contrast of merry Edinburgh and distressful Stirling; the very vivid if not very decorous *Dance in the Queen's Chamber,* which, with other poems to the Queen, shows that Margaret had the full Tudor tolerance of broad speech; the not unamusing *Poem to ane Blackamoor*—"My lady with the meikle lips"—a negress who, as a rarity, had been imported to be maid to the Queen. The rest are pious or profane, personal or general, rhetorical or direct. But they are nearly always out of the common way of literature of their time; and the contemptuous fashion in which they have been sometimes spoken of is not a little surprising.

Gawain Douglas.

The last of the four poets to be mentioned here is also the least, though he has an interest of his own. Gavin or Gawain Douglas was the third son of Archibald Douglas—"Bell-the-Cat"—fifth Earl of Angus, and of Elizabeth Boyd. It is not known at which of the numerous seats of the Douglasses he was born; but the date must have been somewhere about the juncture of the years 1474-75. He matriculated at St. Andrews in 1489, was a "determinant" (= Bachelor Elect) in 1492, a Licentiate or incipient Master two years later. He took orders, and at once obtained various preferments, the chief being the benefice of Prestonkirk or Linton in East Lothian; while in 1501 he was made Dean or Provost of St. Giles's, Edinburgh. In this same year he finished the *Palice of Honour.* Between this and the year of Flodden, 1513, in the summer of which he finished his *Virgil,* we hear little of him. As readers of Scottish history know, his two elder brothers fell in the battle itself, which broke the heart, though it did not actually see the death, of Bell-the-Cat his father; while his nephew, son of the Master of Angus, killed at Flodden, very speedily gained the heart of Queen Margaret, who, though a widow and a mother, was not much more than a girl in age. By this marriage Gawain not merely became in the future, through the Countess of Lennox and Darnley, a collateral ancestor of the whole royal house of Great Britain and Ireland, but was brought into very immediate connection with the chief person in the state, the Queen Regent, who at once gave him the rich Abbey of Aberbrothock or Arbroath, and shortly afterwards the brevet-keepership, as we may say, of the Great Seal. But Margaret's hasty marriage to the head of a powerful but dreaded house was extremely unpopular, and Gawain Douglas reaped from it more trouble than profit. He was never confirmed in Arbroath by the Pope; an attempt of his niece by marriage to make him Archbishop of St. Andrews, and therefore Primate of Scotland, was frustrated by the address and interest at Rome of another candidate; and though Douglas, in 1515, obtained the Bishopric of Dunkeld, this appointment also brought him endless trouble, and he was actually imprisoned by the new regent Albany for an offence apparently somewhat analogous to the English Praemunire, in obtaining the Pope's letters without the King's, *i.e.* the Regent's, sense. The Pope, however, resented this very decidedly, and as Albany's severities towards Queen Margaret were also attracting the displeasure of her brother Henry VIII, Douglas was liberated, and after some further difficulty was consecrated to Dunkeld. He did not, however, enjoy it very peaceably—peaceable enjoyment of anything was hardly possible then in Scotland—and his death in London, where he was negotiating against Albany, coincided with hostile measures against him taken by Archbishop James Beaton, and removed him from evil to come. He died at the house of his friend Lord Dacre, and was buried in the Savoy. We have his will and a considerable number of public documents about him.

His life.

Douglas was not an old man—forty-eight only—when he died; and for the last ten years of his life he had been incessantly engaged in public and private business. But his work in literature—no doubt all composed in the quiet time between his ordination and Flodden—is not inconsiderable. Besides what we have, we know that he translated some Ovid, and it is possible that he did other things. His existing work[7] consists of the *Palice of Honour, King Hart,* and the version of the *Aeneid.* Critics of weight[8] have held up Douglas, on the strength of this *Virgil,* as representing, or at any rate anticipating, the new movement in poetry, that which incorporates the classical and modern tradition, and so as occupying a position at least historically more important than that of his more intensely and poetically gifted contemporary Dunbar. With all due deference, this may well be deemed a mistake. Even in the selection of Ovid and Virgil, Douglas, though he may have been slightly further affected by the classical influence "in the air," did not go very much further than Chaucer a century and more before him. And in the manner of his work, both original and translated, he is not modern at all. He is with Hawes, even with Lydgate; not with Wyatt and Surrey.

His original poems.

In order to come to a just estimate of this, though the *Virgil* itself will give us sufficient data, it is before all things necessary to consider his original poems, the *Palice* and *King Hart.* Douglas, like his other countrymen just mentioned, is a better manager of "our Inglis" (it is believed that he himself first uses "Scots" with the national differential) than Hawes; but the *Palice of Honour* and *King Hart* are in scheme and tone absolutely on a par with the *Pastime* and the *Example.* No later Renaissance sunrise-colour is on them: they are lighted only by the setting moon of the *Rose.* Indeed, neither in Hawes nor in Lydgate, neither in Occleve nor in the stiffer work of Dunbar, is there a more essentially fifteenth-century poem than the *Palice of Honour.* It has a prologue and parts; it is written in "aureate"

7. Ed. Small, 4 vols. Edinburgh, 1874.

8. See W.J. Courthope, *History of English Poetry,* i. 374, one of the few passages in this excellent book with which I cannot agree.

language of at least eighteen-carat "rhetorical" value; it has entire stanzas (nine-lined ones rhymed *aabaabbab*) consisting of mere catalogues of names. The May morning, the stock, though no doubt quite sincere, classing of Chaucer, Gower, and Lydgate, with an interesting note of "Dunbar yet ondeid," the vision, the heathen mythology and the historical characters, the bare, childlike allegory everywhere intruding itself, are unmistakable. Nobody who knows the *Romance of the Rose,* as Guillaume de Lorris started it nearly three hundred years before Douglas's death, can possibly mistake the quality. As usual in these poems, the story, apart from the allegory, is slender. The poet offends Venus (whose lusty countenance and "topaz" hair have been thought to be a compliment to the youthful Margaret), and is sentenced to a palinode and a journey round the world in company with the Muses. They at last reach the slippery Rock of Honour with its Palace at the top, are introduced to much historical and allegorical company, and the poem ends abruptly by one of the common devices for waking. The common form for this is relieved not merely by the singularly abundant vocabulary which distinguishes all these Scottish poets, but by a distinctly poetical imagination and no small descriptive power.

King Hart, the date of which is unknown, is duller. The hero is simply the Heart of man; and the poem is one of the innumerable allegories of Life. He has five servants—the senses; is captured by Dame Pleasance, liberated by Pity, captures Pleasance in turn and marries her, is visited by Age, deserted by his wife, etc., and at last mortally wounded by Decrepitude. It is impossible to understand Mr. Small's assertion that this is "a work which in its execution is quite original." The stanza is the Chaucerian octave.

Undoubtedly, however, if Douglas had left nothing but his two ostensibly original poems, he would not stand nearly as high in historical repute as he does stand. It has been said that the idea of him as a strictly Renaissance writer, because he translates Virgil, is a mistake. Douglas, it is true, was no bad scholar; he certainly knew Latin well, and he may have known Greek. But Virgil comes out of his hands as he might have come out of those of Chaucer, almost as he might have come out of those of Benoît, with the sole exception that Douglas is faithfuller. He does not embroider on is text. But his version of that text looks backward and not forward. He accents classical names with an entire indifference to quantity. His vocabulary and phraseology are Romantic, not Classical. He substitutes the irregular charm of the Middle Ages for the exact, the impeccable, though the somewhat frigid, correctness of Virgil. Nor is this all. The fifteenth century, as we have seen, particularly affected prologues, and Douglas has given us a Prologue to each of the books of the *Aeneid,* as well as to the thirteenth *Aeneid* of Mapheus Vegius, which he also translated.

His *Aeneid.*

And these prologues are, as indeed might be expected, by far the most interesting part of the work. The text is translated into riding-rhyme of very fair Chaucerian quality, and displaying Douglas's usual correctness of ear and his justness and colour of language. But in the Prologues he gives himself, as was natural and permissible, a much freer field. Their interest is not to be judged from the First, which is itself in couplets, and after a very "aureate" laudation of Virgil as "Chosen carbunkil"—

> Lanterne, lodesterne, mirror, and *a per se*—

engages in a severe criticism, not very graceful in tone and most awkwardly clothed in verse, of Caxton's *Aeneidos.* This extends to several hundred lines. The Second is very short—three stanzas of rhyme-royal—and not very notable; nor need much be said of the Third—five stanzas of nine lines each. It is not till the Fourth that the poet allows himself really to expatiate; but he does so here, with good effect, in nearly forty "royal" stanzas on the strength of Love, the incommodity and remedy of the same—it has been observed that he translated the *Remedium amoris,* though it is lost. The very first stanza hits successfully that clangorous note of the rhyme-royal which has been observed upon, and this note is well sustained throughout. The Fifth, short, nine-lined, and with another fling at Caxton, is less notable; and the Sixth (octaves) is chiefly noteworthy for its matter, a curious discussion of various poetical and philosophical accounts of Hell. But the Seventh and Eighth are each, in its different way, of very high interest indeed. The Seventh, in couplets, contains a vigorous description of Winter attractive in itself and as an instance of that copious and vigorous vocabulary which all these poets show, and curious to contrast with Thomson. The Eighth has a curiosity still higher; for here Douglas indulges in that very quaint combination of alliterative and metrical prosody which was still sometimes attempted at this time, and has achieved, perhaps, the most remarkable example of it. The stanza somewhat resembles that of *Gawain and the Green Knight,* but is regularly arranged in a form of thirteen lines bobbed and wheeled. The first nine are heavily alliterated, differing from those of *The Twa Maryit Wemen* by having strong not weak endings, and rhymed *ababababc;* then comes a triplet, rhymed, of three iambics with equivalence, and then a final line *c* of four syllables only. The vocabulary of the piece is, outside the "Flytings," the most crabbed and fantastic even of these Scottish poems, and not a few of the words can merely be guessed at. The tenor of the whole is satirical on the state of the world.

The Ninth, beginning in six-lined stanzas, but soon passing into couplets, is still ethical in tone; and the Tenth (in five-lined stanzas) theological; while the Eleventh deals with chivalry, both sacred and profane. The Twelfth, "ane singular learned prolog" of the description of May, again ranks among the best, and is in couplets;[9] and there is a similar one on June for the egregious Vegius his work.

It is, let it be repeated, much more on these Prologues (where he has evidently set his mind upon giving specimens of his powers in various matters and forms) than on his two long pieces that the estimate of Gawain Douglas should be based. That estimate cannot be of the highest, for the poet has too little detachment from the mere literary forms and fashions of

9. Here is a fine passage :

For to behald it was a gloir to see,
The stabylit windís and the calmit sea,
The soft seisoun, the firmament serene,
The lowne illumynat air and fyrth amene.

his time, and is far too much under the prevalent delusion of the identity of "rhetorike" and poetry. But it should be relatively and by allowance high. He has in a very eminent degree that feeling for nature by which the poets of his country have ever since been honourably distinguished; he has a very good mastery of metrical form, and he perhaps shows the good side (it must be allowed that he also shows the bad) of the "aureate" or *rhétoriqueur* language better than any poet, either in English or in French, of his time and school.

4

LATER ROMANCES IN PROSE AND VERSE

Sir Generydes, etc.—*Sir Launfal*—The verse *Morte Arthur*—*Golagros and Gawane* and *Rauf Coilyear*—Malory—Lord Berners—Caxton's translated romances.

THE difficulty in distinguishing the romances[1] of the fifteenth century from those of the fourteenth has been already referred to. With rare exceptions, it is doubtful whether we possess anything, originally of the fifteenth, in verse which is really of great merit. *Bevis of Hampton, Guy of Warwick,* the Charlemagne stories, and the rest continued to be copied or rehandled; and though it pleased Chaucer to make fun of the style, this does not seem to have had much effect on its popularity. In particular, the Arthurian legend, which, except in the Northern or Gawain division, appears not to have attracted very much attention in the fourteenth century, recovered, to our eternal advantage, much of its popularity in the fifteenth. The non-Arthurian romances, verse and prose, of the time are but of small interest. A fair example of them is *Sir Generydes,* which must almost to a certainty have been originally French, but of which no French original is known, while two different English versions—one in octosyllabic couplets, printed by Dr. Furnivall for the Roxburghe Club, and one in rhyme-royal, printed by Mr. Aldis Wright for the E.E.T.S.—are in existence. *Sir Generydes*[2] is a fair example of the common form of the romance of chivalry, but has little more (though certainly no less) individuality than the average

Sir Generydes, etc.

1. For the chief romance-collections, see notes, pp. 104 and 128.
2. I use the E.E.T.S. edition.

nineteenth-century novel. *Torrent of Portugal*,[3] a shorter story of the same class, is in *Sir Thopas* metre; *Octovian*, a wicked mother-in-law story, mentioned before as possibly earlier, is, as printed by Weber (there is another version), in a slightly modified form of that stanza, rhymed *aaabab*, with the *b* lines shortened, instead of the usual *aa* long, *b* short, *cc* long, *b* short.

The best romances in verse not strictly ballad-romance (see next chapter), and the worst, belong to the Arthurian division. At the head of the former we may put, despite its libel on Queen Guinevere, the beautiful poem of *Sir Launfal*,[4] adapted and much improved by Thomas Chester, who probably lived in the second quarter of the fifteenth century, from a poem of Marie de France, centuries older and not improbably metamorphosed before it came into Chester's hands. The discredit of making the Queen play the part of Potiphar's wife, of which there is no trace in the better Arthurian legends, is not his. But the actual story of Launfal, with his fairy love, his unfortunate divulging of their passion, his punishment and his pardon, is one of the most exquisite of all mediaeval tales, and is quite charmingly told by Chester in the *Sir Thopas* metre doubled. The beauty of which this stanza is capable, especially in the doubled form, where the rhymes run *aabccbddbeeb*, each *b* line being short, is nowhere better shown, nor its complete freedom at its best from the ding-dong, sing-song monotony which beyond all doubt it often puts on, and which Chaucer has so wickedly immortalised.

Sir Launfal.

Not far below *Launfal* in poetical merit, and of the first interest as having almost demonstrably served as direct original to Malory (*vide infra*), is the *Morte Arthur*, which Dr. Furnivall printed more than forty years ago,[5] a piece of some 4000 lines, arranged in quatrains rhymed *abab*, which not uncommonly spread into sixains or octaves of the same arrangements.

The verse *Morte Arthur.*

3. Ed. Halliwell, London, 1842. Re-edited for the E.E.T.S. by Dr. Adam.

4. Printed in Ritson's first volume.

5. London and Cambridge, 1864.

Lancelot of the Laik,[6] a poem in heroic couplets, and in Sects or some other extremely northern dialect of English, is ascribed to the end of the fifteenth century, and if so, is the latest Arthurian poem of the genuine kind (before the legend began to be merely "translated," as we find it in Spenser) that we possess.

Meanwhile one of the most conscientious, but of the very dullest, of the vast army of dull versifiers of the time had busied himself with the great matter which, perhaps at the same time, was taking in a sense almost final form in prose at the hands of a very different person. "Herry" (Henry) Lonelich, skinner, a subject of King Henry the Sixth, was evidently as pious as his namesake and master, and in his different vocation as ineffective. His *Merlin* is not yet accessible in print, save for an extract of Dr. Kölbing's.[7] His *Holy Grail* has been twice printed by Dr. Furnivall,[8] and is one of the most curious books in existence, the wonderful interest and charm of the matter, which might have been thought likely either to stir a translator into genius or compel him to silent despair, being approached with a cheerful doggedness of incompetency difficult, if not impossible, to parallel elsewhere. Hardly any other story could possibly survive such a translator; no other translator, one would hope, could have failed to catch fire from such a story. But except from his matter, which flames like the infant Havelok in the rude hands of Grim, there is no spark of illumination in Lonelich, who thumps out his couplets by the help of "sikerly" and "everidel," of "verament" and "echone," in a manner well-nigh intolerable.

In the way of alliterative romance we have to put to the credit of the century in all probability, or rather certainly, two very interesting poems in Scots, *Golagros and Gawane* and *Rauf Coilyear*.[9] For neither of these have we MS. authority, though

6. Ed. Skeat, E.E.T.S.

7. In his edition of *Arthour and Merlin.*

8. For the Roxburghe Club and the E.E.T.S. Some prefer "Lovelich."

9. *Golagros and Gawane* has been reprinted by Pinkerton in *Scottish Poems,* 1792; by Laing (a great rarity) in 1827; by Madden, with other Gawaine pieces, in 1839; and by Mr. Amours in *Scottish Alliterative Poems,* cited

we know that both did exist in the Asloan MS.; and our printed *Rauf Coilyear* is as late as 1572. But we have an allusion to this same poem by Gawain Douglas as early as 1503, and *Golagros and Gawane* was published by Chepman and Millar among the incunabula of the Scottish press in 1508. Both are in the thirteen-line alliterated and rhymed stanza with wheel (*v. supra,* p. 192). *Golagros and Gawane* belongs evidently to the Cumbrian branch of the Arthurian legend, and presents some very close resemblances to the latter part of the *Awntyrs of Arthur. Rauf Coilyear,* on the other hand, belongs to the other great family, and, so far as we know, is the only original Charlemagne poem in English. It is one of the numerous and generally interesting family of the "King and the Tanner" class, the king's unknowing associate here being a "collier" (*i.e.* charcoal-burner), and the king, as has been said, no less a person than Charlemagne. It is a very spirited poem. Nobody has succeeded in identifying the author of either this or *Golagros;* but it is not at all impossible that both may have one poet, and most probable that he lived at the end of our century, and was one of Dunbar's "makers." If so, he was by no means the worst of them, and not very far from the best, except Henryson and Dunbar himself.

Golagros and Gawane and *Rauf Coilyear.*

Practically nothing is known of the author of the greatest of all English romances, prose or verse—of one of the greatest romances of the world—a book which, though in mere material a compilation, and sometimes cleaving rather closely to its multifarious texts, is, despite the occasional misjudgment of unhappy criticism, a great and original book. Caxton, the printer (*vide infra,* chap. vi)—who, instead of, like most early printers, giving us early editions, and mostly bad ones, of the classics, which were quite safe, gave us, to the infinite advantage of England, early models of composition in English, and preserved to us, in this instance at least, an English text which

---

above. There is also a German reprint. *Rauf Coilyear* can be found in Mr. Amours's volume, in one of the volumes of the E.E.T.S. *Charlemagne Romances,* and also in Laing's several times reprinted *Ancient and Popular Poetry of Scotland* (last edited by Small, Edinburgh, 1885).

might but for him have perished—tells us that the *Morte d'Arthur* was translated in the ninth year of King Edward IV (that is to say, in 1470, fifteen years before he himself published it) by Sir Thomas Malory, Knight. Caxton's follower, Wynkyn de Worde, in the second edition of 1496, makes the name "Maleore." Malory or Mallory is both a Yorkshire and a Leicestershire name, but there are absolutely no materials for identifying Sir Thomas; the later suggestions that he was a Welsh priest, not an English knight, are baseless guesses, and we do not know in the very least why, when, or where he executed his book. What we do know, from the verse *Morte* and from Lonelich, is that a strong revived interest in the Arthurian Legend came in about the middle of the century, and this is to all appearances one of the fruits of it.[10]

Malory.

If so, it is incomparably the most precious. It is probable that, though among the laborious and respectable, but rather superfluous, inquiries into origins, none has yet been discovered for the "Beaumains" story and for a few other things, Malory "did not invent much." The fifteenth century was not an inventive time, and there was much better work for it to do than second-rate invention. Then and then only could the mediaeval spirit, which was not quite dead, have been caught up and rendered for us with a still present familiarity, with the unconscious but unmistakable touch of magic which approaching loss reflects, and in English prose, which, unlike English verse, still had the bloom on it—the soon-fading *beauté du diable* of youth and freshness.

Criticisms have been made on Malory's manner of selecting and arranging his materials—criticisms which, like all unsuccessful exercises of the most difficult of arts, come from putting the wrong questions to the jury—from asking, "Has this man done what *I* wanted him to do?" or "Has he done it as *I* should have done it?" instead of "Has he done what *he* meant to do?" and "Has he done this well?" Malory might perhaps, though in his time it would have been difficult to get

10. The book, frequently printed up to the seventeenth century, has also been repeatedly reprinted since the beginning of the nineteenth.

all the texts together, have given an intelligent *précis* of the whole Arthurian Legend, instead of which he selected his materials rather arbitrarily, and indulged in what looks to some critics like incomprehensible divagation, and not much more comprehensible suppression. He might have arranged a regular epic treatment of his subject, instead of which it is often difficult to say who is the hero, and never very easy to say what special contribution to the plot the occasionally inordinate episodes are making. What he did do consists mainly in two things, or perhaps three. He selected the most interesting things with an almost invariable sureness, though there are one or two omissions; and he omitted the less interesting parts with a sureness to which there are hardly any exceptions at all. He grasped, and this is his great and saving merit as an author, the one central fact of the story—that in the combination of the Quest of the Graal with the loves of Lancelot and Guinevere lay the kernel at once and the conclusion of the whole matter. And last (his great and saving merit as a writer) he told his tale in a manner which is very nearly impeccable.

There is one practically infallible test by which all but the dullest and most incompetent can be convinced of Sir Thomas's skill in this last direction, the comparison of his narrative of the last scenes of all with that in the verse *Morte Arthur* above mentioned, which was in all probability his direct original, and which was certainly written just before his day. Take the death of Arthur itself, or the final interview of Lancelot and the Queen, in both; compare them, and then remember that Malory has been dismissed as "a mere compiler." It is possible that his art is mostly unconscious art—it is not much the worse for that. But it is nearly as infallible as it is either unconscious or thoroughly concealed. The pictorial power, the musical cadence of the phrase, the steady glow of chivalrous feeling throughout, the noble morality (for the condemnation of Ascham and others is partly mere Renaissance priggishness stupidly condemning things mediaeval offhand, and partly Puritan prudery throwing its baleful shadow before), the kindliness, the sense of honour, the melancholy and yet never either gloomy or puling sense of the inevitable end—all these are eminent in it. It has been said, with perhaps hardly too great whimsicality, that there is only one bad thing about Malory—that to those who read him first he makes all other romances of Chivalry disappointing. But the fancy may at any rate be fairly retorted, for if any one is so unfortunate as to find other romances of chivalry disappointing, there is Malory to fall back upon. Merely in English prose he is a great figure, for although his medium would not be suitable for every purpose, it is nearly perfect for his own. Merely as the one great central storehouse of a famous and fertile story his place is sure. But apart from all these extrinsic considerations, it is surer still in the fact that he has added to literature an imperishable book.

Lord Berners.

The second great writer or translator of Romance in prose during this period, John Bourchier, Lord Berners, was born, a little before the probable date of the writing of Malory's *Morte d'Arthur,* in 1467, and was the son of Humphrey Lord Berners, who fell on the Yorkist side at the battle of Barnet. He may have been a Balliol man; he certainly saw much both of war and diplomacy in the later years of Henry VII and the earlier of his son; he was Chancellor of the Exchequer in 1516, and from 1520 onwards Governor of Calais. It would seem that his literary work all dates from this last period of his life, which closed in 1533. His *Froissart* began to appear in 1523, and he also translated (though the books did not in some cases appear till after his death) the great romance of *Huon of Bordeaux,* that of *Arthur of Little Britain,* later in date and lower in kind, Guevara's *Dial for Princes,* a book which has been thought, not without some reason, to have had much influence on the development of Euphuism, and another Spanish allegoric-chivalrous romance, the *Castle* (originally *Prison*) *of Love.*[11] In his work from the Spanish he appears to have used not the originals but French versions.

11. Not to be confounded with the very much earlier book of the same name translated from Bishop Grostête's French a little before or a little after 1300, and edited by Dr. Weymouth for the Philological Society. This is religious, and of some linguistic, but very little literary, interest. As for Berners's own work, the *Froissart* was reprinted by Utterson in

In a late stage of writing, prose, and indeed verse, translations have very little interest, and are merely or mainly makeshifts for the use of those who cannot read the originals. In the early stages, especially of prose writing, their value is very different, and this constitutes the attractions of our fifteenth and early sixteenth century prose, borrowed as it almost always is in matter. And Lord Berners ranks with Malory as its most gifted practitioner. His *Froissart* gives him the greatest opportunity, and he has availed himself of that opportunity to the utmost. His style would not, of course, be suitable for every purpose or even for many purposes, but in his combination of rhetorical and "aureate" language with simpler forms, in his faint retention of poetic diction with a perfect adjustment to those needs of prose fiction or of romantic history which are nearer to those of poetry than is the case with any other division of prose, he is certainly unsurpassed, and it may be doubted whether he has been equalled, though Mr. William Morris sometimes ran him hard. The *Huon,* representing a late French rehandling of one of the most romantic of the *chansons de geste,* has the fault, common to most such rehandlings, of long-windedness and surplusage; but still it gives Berners good opportunity, and he takes it admirably. The part which Mr. Lee has isolated in his second volume as "The Story of Esclaramonde" might very well be taken as an introduction to this kind of romance by novices, and they are to be pitied if they do not go on. Even *Arthur of Little Britain* well represents the beginning of the later and more extravagant romances, of which the *Amadis* group are the best known: and Spenser almost certainly knew and used it.

Between the *Morte* and the *Froissart* Caxton and his successors had made very large additions to the stock of romance in English. The *Histories of Troy,* more than ten years before the printing of Malory, *Reynard the Fox,* the *Golden Legend, Paris and Vienne,* the *Life of Charles the Great,* the *Four* translated

---

1812, with some reduction and modernisation by Prof. Macaulay for the "Globe" Series, 1895, and completely by Prof. Ker in the "Tudor Translations." *Huon* has been edited by Mr. S.L. Lee for the E.E.T.S. Utterson also reprinted *Arthur of Little Britain* (1814).

Sons of Aymon, Blanchardyn and Eglantine, Godfrey of Bulloigne, the *Aeneidos,* which so did vex Gawain Douglas—being Caxton's own contribution, a very considerable one, as most of them were translated as well as printed by himself. We shall speak of Caxton's prose style later: here we are chiefly concerned with the romance substance of his work. There is little doubt that these late romances, especially the prose ones, had an immense effect on the first generation or two of readers of printed books, while perhaps their diffusion in print, as well as the fact that the versions selected for reproduction or translation were nearly always late and very seldom of the best, may have also contributed to that strange disgust with them which is not entirely to be accounted for by the mere pedantry, innocently consequent on the revived study of the classics directly, or by the touch of religious and Puritan dislike of romance, which soon supervened. At the same time, this crop of romances, and the attention paid to it, had also beyond all question much to do with the heroic enthusiasm of Elizabethan days, and with that after-glow of chivalry itself of which the noblest and most undying monument is the *Faërie Queene.*[12]

Caxton's translated romances.

12. Although as much room as possible has been given to the romances, far more would be required to do them real justice. Indeed, the division branches off into almost infinite sub-varieties—for instance, the curious series of *Visions* of Hell and Purgatory, of which the *Visions of Tundale* (fifteenth century), ed. Turnbull (Edinburgh, 1843) is a good example. The minor *Prose* romances are, as a rule, of much less interest, as may be seen from the standard collection of them by W.J. Thoms, 2nd ed. 3 vols. London, 1858. To the *Verse* may be added the English *Partonope of Blois* (Roxburghe Club, 1862), which may date from *c.* 1430, and is a fair version, in loose octosyllables, of its beautiful story; the Scots *Clariodus* (Maitland Club, 1830), in very wooden heroics, which is possibly fifteenth century; and the curious *Buik of Alexander the Great,* in Scots octosyllables, printed in 1580 and reprinted by the Bannatyne Club in 1831.

5

MINOR POETRY AND BALLADS

Date of Ballads—The *Nut-browne Mayde*—"I sing of a maiden"—The Percy Folio—*Graysteel.*

BAD as the reputation of the fifteenth century is for poetry in England (and indeed in most countries except Italy), it will have been seen that there are notable individual exceptions. And a still better face is put upon the matter when we come to what is called minor poetry, and especially to Ballads.

In a history, and especially a short history, of this subject dissertations on purely speculative points are out of place, and perhaps in no case is this more so than in regard to the origins of Ballad literature generally and the date of English Ballad literature in particular. There may be said to be here, as generally, three main opinions, or groups of shaded opinion: the first assigning a remote, and if possible even contemporary, origin to ballads that have any pretence of history, and as ancient a one as possible to those which are purely romantic; the second postponing the date to comparatively, or in some cases quite, modern times; and the third, which endeavours to assign not merely a general middle term but a particular age in which the literary sentiment, as yet not absorbed by a literary class, existed fluidly and at large, and found its special bent in ballad-making. It may be observed in passing that the second, while disagreeable to sentiment, is also quite contrary to probability, and has scarcely any direct evidence to support it. Between the first and third, opinion rather than demonstration

Date of Ballads.

must decide, but it is not impertinent to remark that besides the opposition on their surface, a very important order of difference is involved, which may be indicated by the question, "Are romances and early epics conglomerates of ballad, or are ballads disintegrations of epics—romance-episodes worked up into ballad form?"

To the present writer the balance of probability, for reasons too numerous and intricate to be more than partially and generally stated here, seems to incline to the supposition that the fifteenth century was the special time of ballad-production in England; while not probability merely, but something like direct evidence, shows that during this time and the early sixteenth the romances, while they were lengthened in prose, underwent a pretty general process of shortening and modifying in verse. Among the facts pointing to these conclusions may be advanced the change during the fourteenth century from French and Latin to English as the vehicle of avowedly political poems dealing with the events of the day, and therefore dated; the famous ballad of *Chevy Chase,* the oldest of its class, if not of all our ballads, which in its primitive form certainly dates within a decade or so of the battle of Otterbum itself; the general language and colour of the ballads, which is scarcely ever of a tone more archaic than that of 1400; and lastly, the testimony of the famous Percy Folio, the most important single collection of antique ballads that we have. It is known that, as far as actual writing goes, the folio is not older than the middle of the seventeenth century, and that some of the texts contained in it are not older than that date. But the majority are very much older, and yet pretty certainly not older than the fifteenth. In the balladised versions which this MS. contains of romances like *Sir Launfal, Sir Degarè,* and a dozen others, which are pretty certainly of fifteenth or early sixteenth century date, we get not merely interesting direct evidence of the process which the romances themselves were at this time undergoing, but inevitable collateral suggestions of the ballad influence, which beyond all reasonable doubt was creating as well as reshaping. Like the oldest of our ballads, the oldest of our carols also date from this time; and while in England proper formal poetry of substance is undoubtedly at a lower level than previously, regular as well as irregular lyric is at a distinctly higher. Except *Alison* and the best of its companions, there is indeed nothing so good in this division of English literature before the fifteenth century as the two best things of that century's own, while it has others not inferior.

These two best things, both anonymous, are the famous ballad of the *Nut-browne Mayde,* and the less famous, but not less exquisite carol of Our Lady, beginning "I sing of a maiden."

The *Nut-browne Mayde.*

For the first of these we have a much earlier authority than Percy, indeed, as is generally known, it was modernised by Prior long before the publication of the *Reliques,* and had actually been reprinted critically in a very remarkable work, the *Prolusions* of Capell, the Shakespearian scholar, in 1760. It appeared first in Arnold's *Chronicle,* a book published at Antwerp in 1502. It cannot be necessary to say very much about so well-known a thing; yet it has as a rule been rather under—than over-praised. The ring and swing of the metre, of which no previous example seems to exist,[1] and which argues very considerable development of the language, the felicity of the alternate refrain, the singular skill with which the variation of equivalent feet, disyllabic and trisyllabic, is managed so as to prevent monotony, and the adaptation of the whole to the sentiment, imagery, and incident, are not less remarkable than the tenderness and sweetness, never in the least mawkish, of that sentiment itself, the dramatic management of the story, and the modest cogency of the moral. The piece is, as its own time would have said, a very "margarite" of English verse for that time, and indeed a pearl of poetry for ever.

Nor is the shorter, simpler, and far less known carol[2] inferior in charm; indeed, in the quality properly called

1. Unless it be the "E.I.O." doubtfully attributed to Hampole (No. vii, *Religious Pieces in Prose and Verse,* E.E.T.S. 1866).
2. First printed by Wright for the Warton Club in 1855 (p. 30 of *A Collection of Carols);* reprinted by Mr. Bullen in his *Carols and Poems* (London, 1886).

exquisiteness it is even superior. The best of the Caroline poets, our chief masters in this quality, would have been in danger of over-elaborating it, or of faintly "smirching" the ineffable grace of the lines—

He came also still
  Where his mother was,
As dew in April
  That falleth on the grass.

He came also still
  To his mother's bower,
As dew in April
  That falleth on the flower.

He came also still
  Where his mother lay,
As dew in April
  That falleth on the spray.

In no previous verse had this Aeolian music—this "harp of Ariel" that distinguishes English at its very best in this direction, alike from the fuller but less unearthly harmonies of Provençal, Italian, and Spanish, from the sharper sound of French, and from the less elfish though still fairy sound of German—been given to the world.

If nothing equals these things, others come near them. We may compare the older part of the Percy Folio both with some other English things and with some minor and anonymous Scottish poetry of the time. A complete detailed analysis, even in the most compressed form, of the contents of the "Manuscript"[3] is impossible here; but some remarks on the most important groups, and a few individuals among those of its contents which certainly or probably date from the period with which we are now dealing, can hardly be without value. It contains, in the first place, a group of Robin Hood Ballads, which, of course, share in the general uncertainty pertaining to all notices of that celebrated person or eidolon. It is possible that some

3. Ed. Hales and Furnivall, 3 vols. and supplement, London, 1867.

of these are in the oldest form as old as the fourteenth century; but probable that most of them date from our time. In the second place, we have a large group of broken-up, modernised, and, it must be added, for the most part vulgarised, Arthurian ballads or short romances: *King Arthur and the King of Cornwal, Sir Lancelot of Dulake, The Turk and Gowin* (Gawaine), *The Marriage of Sir Gawain* (the famous tale of the Loathly Lady), *Sir Lambwell* (Launfal), *Merlin, Arthur's Death, The Green Knight.* Closely connected with these is a still larger group, in which the same process has been applied to miscellaneous romances of adventure, some of which we possess in longer forms and some of which stand alone in the shorter. Such are *Sir Cauline* (one of the finest), *Sir Degree* (Sir Degarè), *Sir Triamore, Sir Eglamour, Guy and Amarant, Guy and Colebrand, John the Reeve,* and others. Another and extremely important class consists of the Historical Ballads, of which, as it happens, very importantly, the great majority concern the fifteenth and early sixteenth century: *The Siege of Rouen* (Henry V's), *The Murder of the Princes, The Rose of England, Bosworth Field, Lady Bessie, Sir Andrew Barton, Flodden Field, Scottish Field, Musselborough Field* (Pinkie), and others. Lastly, there are the more romantic ballads, such as the *Heir of Lynne,* the *Nut-browne Mayde* itself, and many more, which gave Percy's book, extracted from this folio, its main charm.

Graysteel.

An interesting and not unfairly representative specimen of the contents of this invaluable collection is the once extremely popular romance of *Sir Eger, Sir Grime* (Graeme?), *and Sir Graysteel,* which, till the contents of the MS. were made public, had only been known from a printed and watered-down eighteenth-century version abstracted by Ellis. The piece is probably not very early—we hear nothing of it before the end of the fifteenth century—but it is most likely one, and a happy one, of those instances whereof several have been noted in the last chapter and in this, in which the fifteenth century gathered up and reshaped for the last time the best traits of the earlier romance. Winglaine, the Belle Dame Sans Merci; her opposite the Lady Loosepain (not such a pretty name as Nepenthe, but not different in meaning), all graciousness and grace; the well-meaning but rather venturous than strong Sir Eger; his faithful friend Sir Grime; the mysterious Graysteel in his Forbidden Country—all these make an excellent tale told in some fifteen hundred couplet verses, with no great poetical accomplishment (indeed, most of the Folio texts are degraded by centuries of careless and tasteless copying), but by no means ill.

It is only by reading and re-reading (a very pleasing task) such books as this edition of the Percy Folio, as Laing's above-cited *Ancient and Popular Poetry of Scotland,* as Mr. W.C. Hazlitt's *Early Popular Poetry,* as the (also above-cited) works of Utterson and Hartshorne, and as Mr. Wright's Collections of *Political Poetry* for the "Rolls Series," and his *Carols* for the Percy and Warton Societies,[4] that the general character and substance of fifteenth-century and early sixteenth-century poetry can be properly appreciated. Even after these gleanings, pretty abundant but frequently duplicated, there is probably not a little still in MS.; yet what we have suffices. We see in it only occasional evidence of very distinct poetic gift, and still seldomer much command of accomplished poetic form; but we also see that vernacular verse was thoroughly established by this time, that there was a popular taste for it, if a rough, uncultivated, and easily satisfied one; and that it was being applied to all sorts of subjects in all sorts of spirits. In other words, the soil was being well stirred and the seeds were being plentifully and widely scattered. It did no harm that some time was to pass before anything more than a wilding harvest came.[5]

---

4. See also J.A. Fuller-Maitland, *English Carols of the Fifteenth Century* (London, *n.d.*).

5. The *Ballads,* after much piecemeal editing for a hundred years, have at last been put in a standard edition by the late Professor Child's monumental collection, *The English and Scottish Popular Ballads,* 5 vols. in 10 parts, Boston (Mass.) and London, 1882-98. But I should be loath not to find room for citation of the first book which gives our early poetry of this kind with wide range and real scholarship, Ritson's *Ancient Songs and Ballads,* 1790, 3rd ed. [Hazlitt] 1877.

Note to Eighth Edition.—There is now a most valuable additional aid to the study in Messrs. Chambers and Sidgwick's *Early English Lyric* (London, 1907), a collection largely from MS. sources.

6

MISCELLANEOUS PROSE

Importance of fifteenth-century prose—Pecock—His style and vocabulary—Fortescue, Capgrave, Fabyan—Caxton—Fisher—His advances in style—More—Latimer—Coverdale—Cranmer.

Importance of fifteenth-century prose.

THE prose of the fifteenth and early sixteenth century—or, in other words, the prose from Fortescue to Fisher—supplies, with the almost sole exception of the work of Malory and Berners, which has been treated above, little or nothing that is delectable to the mere literary consumer. But to the student of literary history it is one of the most important periods of the whole subject. It is, in fact, the great exercising-ground—the great school-time—of English prose: the period in which the nearly unconscious experiments of Chaucer and Wyclif and Mandeville were expanded and multiplied, sometimes with an almost conscious purpose of developing prose style, and always with the practical effect of so doing, by writers in the most widely diverging branches of literature—history and law, political and ecclesiastical controversy, sermons, letters, philosophy of a sort.

Pecock.

Reginald Pecock, Bishop of St. Asaph and Chichester, and author, among much other work, Latin and English, of the *Repressor of Over Much Blaming of the Clergy,*[1] is an interesting person from more points of view than one. His very life was dramatic enough, and moralled the

1. Ed. Babington, "Rolls Series," 2 vols., London, 1860.

favourite moral of the century—the effects of the Wheel of Fortune—with singular force. As is usual with men of his time, we know neither his birthplace nor his birth-date; but the former was probably Wales, and the latter pretty certainly the end of the fourteenth century. He went to Oxford and became Fellow of Oriel in 1417, soon afterwards taking orders. There was no dispute about his erudition. In 1431 he was made Master of Whittington College, London, and thirteen years later appointed to the bishopric of St. Asaph. Up to this time, when we may suppose him to have been about fifty, all things had gone smoothly with him. But he was soon to experience the reverse of the wheel, which came about in a manner not entirely clear, and probably due as much to the violent party politics of the time as to his personal faults.[2] It is, moreover, evident that Pecock, both in sermons and in his works, adopted that most perilous of all courses, the attempt to justify orthodoxy and authority by paradoxical and irregular kinds of reasoning. He met the complaints against the bishops by preaching at St. Paul's Cross that bishops were not bound to preach; and the *Repressor* attacks Lollardy with arguments which his enemies either seriously thought, or affected for their own ends to think, as heretical as the views he combated. He had been befriended by the good Duke Humphrey of Gloucester, but after Gloucester's murder he seems to have made friends with Margaret and Suffolk, and obtained, in 1450, his translation to Chichester. Suffolk was extremely unpopular, but as Pecock was not arraigned for heresy for seven years to come, it seems excessive to connect his fall with the favourite. However, it was distinct enough when it came, whatever the cause. He was accused of treating authority disrespectfully in his works, as well as of heresy in setting up reason (though on the orthodox side) as the criterion of religious truth. He was condemned, had the choice of recantation or the secular arm, recanted abjectly, handing his books to the executioner to

2. He had, however, excited the most violent personal and religious antipathy. Gascoigne's *Liber Veritatum* (*vide supra*, p. 149) is permeated with a sort of refrain of execration of "Reginaldus Pecock, Wallicus origine, episcopus Assavensis."

burn, resigned or was deprived of his bishopric, and probably spent the short remainder of his life in strict confinement at Thorney Abbey.

His style and vocabulary.

The extreme importance of Pecock's position in the history of English prose—a position which, from its original and representative character, will save us much repetition if it be dwelt on here—consists mainly in two points: the effect upon style which the purpose of his books enabled, or rather obliged, him to attempt and partly to produce, and his vocabulary. As regards the first point, it must be remembered that, though there may have been gross ignorance and intellectual sloth among the lower friars and monks, the educated and academic clergy of the fifteenth century were, with certain allowances, trained with much greater intellectual keenness and severity than any class of men at the present day; the much-sneered-at scholastic discipline providing and enforcing an intellectual *askesis* to which there is no modern parallel. But all this training went on in Latin, and the problem was how to conduct a dispute on the same lines in English. Wyclif had been an adept in scholastic argument, but when he had occasion to employ it he had mostly used Latin, and his English works were mainly, though not entirely, addressed to the vulgar. The lapse of more than half a century had made it not merely possible, but desirable to change the general *venue* from Latin to English; and to address clergy and laity at once. It is very probable that this divulgence helped to irritate Pecock's enemies against him: but that is beside our present point, which is, that having undertaken to conduct arguments of scholastic theology in the vernacular, he had to adapt that vernacular itself to the strictly accurate thought, and the precise terminology, required by scholastic habits. He did not entirely succeed, but he succeeded in a degree really surprising, and one which could not but enlarge the powers of English correspondingly. Beside the mere narrative of Mandeville and Trevisa, the popular scientific exposition of Chaucer's *Astrolabe,* and the popular invective (for it is often little more) of the average Wyclifian tract, there now took its place downright argument in English, the setting forth in vernacular dress of the long-proved technicalities and terminologies of the schools in a tongue understanded of the people.

The vocabulary which Pecock adopted or invented for this purpose has special interest. It is on the one side necessarily more technical than Chaucer's, and on the other hand it is deliberately more archaic and vernacular. In particular, we sec in it abundant examples of a process of thoroughgoing "Teutonification" of Latin, Romance, and even Greek forms, which would have almost satisfied the champions of "ungothroughsomeness" for "impenetrability" in our own times. Pecock has "about-writing" for "circumscription" of a coin; "aforebar" and "beforebar" for "prevent"; "alight" not in the modern sense, but = "alleviate"; "apropre" for "appropriate" (an instance of a general tendency of his to cut off Latin suffixes); "beholdable," an audacious Anglicising of "theoretic"; "closingly" for "inclusively"; "customable" for "habitual"; "endly" for "finally"; nay, he even retains the old English "undeadly" for "immortal." And that these and a vast number of other vernacularities were deliberate is shown by the fact that he has no horror of foreign terms as such, where he cannot get a vernacular form, though when he can find or make the latter he always prefers it. In fact, though this compound of forms that never took permanent place in the language, with archaisms on the one hand, and Latinisnis on the other, makes Pecock's pages look very harsh and obscure, it is clear that his scheme was a possible one; that it actually did exercise English in form, and enrich it in matter to no small degree; and that, though the classical reaction of the Renaissance prevented much of his vocabulary from receiving final letters of naturalisation, a good deal more than has actually been naturalised might have been admitted with no disadvantage.

Fortescue, Capgrave, Fabyan.

No other of the early fifteenth-century prose writers—*i.e.* those born certainly or probably within the verge of the fourteenth, or but a little later—equals Pecock in original and representative character, or Malory in charm. But John Capgrave and Sir John Fortescue, at least, deserve to keep here their traditional places, if only because each admitted a new subject—law in the one case, original history in the other—to the liberty of English prose. Fortescue, whose not certain birth- and death-dates are usually given as 1394 and 1474, was a member of the famous western family of his name, an Oxford man, a lawyer, and in 1442 Chief Justice of the King's Bench. He was a Lancastrian throughout the war; but after Tewkesbury rallied to Edward IV, though he had to make a distinctly ignominious recantation in print. Of his very numerous works, some of which are in Latin, the most important in English is the rather well-known *Governance of England,* one passage of which, the famous contrast between the unruly independence of the Englishman and the slavish cowardice of France, is equally notable and characteristic. Capgrave, born in 1393 at Lynn, died in 1464. He was a monk, and wrote most voluminously in both languages. His *Chronicle of England* is his main title to admission here. No two styles could well be more different than his and Pecock's, the former being not indeed incorrect, but devoid of character, singularly free from archaic obscurity and archaic relish alike, suited fairly for plain business-like narration, but hardly for anything else; and on the whole more like Mandeville, with the zest and poetic quality taken out, but the short simply-linked sentences remaining, than like any other of his predecessors. Allowing for the advance of some fifty years, the style of the next historian of note, Robert Fabyan, who represents the second half of the century as the Prior of Lynn does the first, is not unlike Capgrave's.[3]

Caxton.

The importance of Caxton in English prose was by no means merely ministerial, merely limited to the fact that he was the introducer of Malory's immortal book, and of a little other good matter to the English reading public, or that he was the first practitioner of the great art of printing among us. For very much of his extensive work was not merely printed, but written by himself; and though it is

3. Fortescue's chief work has been edited by C. Plummer, 1885; his whole works by Lord Clermont. Capgrave's *Chronicle* is in the "Rolls Series," ed. Hingeston (1858); his long verse *St. Katharine* has been given by the E.E.T.S. The standard edition of Fabyan is Sir Henry Ellis's in 1811.

perfectly true that the matter was, save in an infinitesimal degree, translated, yet that in the circumstances, as was pointed out before, does not diminish his claims. It was impossible for any one of intelligence to render Latin or French into English without exercising the youthful language in the airs, the graces, the crafts of its elder. There is no more interesting passage of its kind than that where Caxton, in the prologue to the *Recuyell of the Histories of Troye,* tells us how "I, having no great charge of occupation, took a French book and read therein many strange and marvellous histories, wherein I had great pleasure and delight, as well for the novelty of the same as *for the fair language of French, which was in prose so well and compendiously set and written, that methought I understood the sentence and substance of every matter.*" One sees at once the sentiment and the aim not of Caxton merely, but of a dozen and a hundred known and unknown translators of French and Latin in these early days, seeing "the fair language of French," or the grave and stately language of Latin, reflecting how destitute English, at least in prose (for they had no doubt about their Chaucer, even if they did a little unadvisedly couple Gower and Lydgate with him), was of such fairness, such gravity, such stateliness, and determining, so far as in them lay, to give readers in the vernacular not merely the bare matter, but the matter with some art. Nor is Caxton himself to be by any means lightly spoken of for accomplishment in this respect. He tells us here and elsewhere of his difficulties in adjusting his broad and rude Kentish dialect (we know that Kent, near as it was to London, was up to the fourteenth century certainly farther from a literary dialect than Northumbria itself), how he tried to make a prose style that should do for prose something not too far below what Chaucer had done for verse. To a very great extent he succeeded, though he sometimes exceeded in the direction of literalness. Take him with Pecock, who was probably not twenty years his senior, and we see that his form, if not quite so interesting to the historian, is far more adapted for general literature; take him with Malory, who was probably of his own age, and we find from a different point of comparison the same result. It is clear that Caxton was in at least two senses a man of letters, that he had the secret of literary craftsmanship.

The middle third of the fifteenth century appears to have been less fruitful in the birth-dates of persons important in literature than any period of equal length for the last six hundred years at least. Indeed between Caxton, who was probably born about 1415, and Fisher, who was (again probably) born just about half a century later, it would not appear that a single writer of the slightest importance in the history of English prose first drew in English air. But the last thirty or thirty-five years of the century did something to clear away the reproach with Lord Berners (1467-1532), Fisher himself (1465-1535), Sir Thomas More (1478-1535), Sir Thomas Elyot (1488-1546), and the early controversialists and Biblical translators of the Reformation, among whom, from the point of view of prose, Cranmer probably and Latimer certainly take the first rank. Of Berners we have spoken; the others must have some notice here.

Fisher.

Justice to Fisher's character as a man, an ecclesiastic, and (with allowances for a certain want of strength) a politician has been done for a long time; indeed, even at the times when anti-"Popish" feeling ran highest in England, his fidelity to honour and conscience, and his hapless fate, had preserved him from obloquy. But it was not till the republication of his English works by Mr. Mayor for the E.E.T.S.[4] that it was possible for justice to be generally done to his position in the history of prose. He was a Yorkshireman, was born at Beverley, and was educated at Cambridge, where, through his connection with Lady Margaret, the mother of Henry VII, he had much to do with the founding of Christ's and St. John's Colleges. His patroness made him her confessor in 1502, the next year he became the first incumbent of her professorship of divinity, while in another twelvemonth he

4. 1876. Good judges had, however, always appreciated Fisher, and he duly figures in the remarkable *Specimens of Prose Writers* (3 vols., London, 1807), to which George Burnett gave his name, but of which Burnett's friend, comrade at Balliol, and fellow—"Pantisocrat," Southey, was the real inspirer.

was made Bishop of Rochester and Chancellor of his University. For many years he was an active bishop, a great friend to the new classical learning, and a *persona grata* at the courts both of Henry VII and his son. The affair of the divorce alarmed his conscience, and he seems to have been the dupe of the "Maid of Kent"; while his election to the Cardinalate, after he had been imprisoned for treason, so irritated the passionate king that he beheaded Fisher as a practical repartee.

His advances in style.

Fisher's English works as yet published consist of a long Treatise, practically made up of Sermons, on the Penitential Psalms, a funeral Sermon on Henry VII, another on Lady Margaret, a third against Luther, and a fourth preached on Good Friday, with two little tractates written in prison, a Spiritual Consolation to his sister Elizabeth, and the Ways to Perfect Religion. Thus almost the whole of his work is oratorical at least in profession. But this matters little, for the whole literature of the time was so saturated with the idea of "rhetoric" that everything took more or less the rhetorical if not oratorical turn. And Fisher's rhetoric never has the very least touch of the impromptu about it. On the contrary, he is one of the very earliest English writers in whom we can discern the deliberate selection and practice of certain means and methods wholly to achieve style. He has got beyond the painful effort of Pecock to forge a vocabulary and arrange a syntax capable of conveying the effects of Latin argument in the vernacular. He is not, like Caxton, endeavouring dimly to get in English results (what, he does not quite understand) as pleasant as those of French. He has already discovered, and deliberately experiments for, rhetorical effect, with the peculiar resources provided by the double dictionary—Teutonic and Romance—of English, as well as by the more general devices of cadence, parallelism, and the usual figures of speech. The simple but extraordinarily effective plan of coupling a "Saxon" and a Latin word, which is so noticeable in the Authorised Version of the Bible, and which may have arisen before the rhetorical advantage of it was perceived, from the mere convenience of addressing one term to "lered" and the other to "lewed" folk, appears in him constantly "Wood" [mad] and "cruel," "horrible" and "fearful," "bruckle" [brittle] and "frail," "end" and "conclusion," and a thousand more stud his pages. Further, he has discovered the effectiveness—more dangerous and more likely to surfeit—of the triplet—"fasting, crying, and coming to the choir," "worldly honours, worldly riches, and fleshly pleasures." Inversion, a device so naturally suggested by the different order of Greek, Latin, and English, has no secrets for him, and, as inversion always does, suggests cadence. He is aware of the assistance given in colouring and varying prose effect by the admixture of long and short sentences; and it is scarcely too much to say that we find in him, and for the first time, examples of the rhetorical, as well as of the logical, construction and use of the paragraph. Side by side with his classical grace he has something of the vernacularity of Latimer, and he makes use of the quaint mystical and allegoric comparisons, which the Middle Ages elaborated from Scriptural and patristic use, with a felicity which occasionally does not come much short of that of the greatest rhetoricians of the seventeenth century. In fact, were it not for the spelling and for the obligatory Latin quotations, he is altogether wonderfully in advance of his time.

More.

Fisher's great companion in misfortune, Sir Thomas More, holds a less distinguished position in the strict history of strictly English literature than is generally thought. His famous *Utopia* was never Englished by himself at all, nor by others till some time after his death. It is therefore quite preposterous to quote it under his name as belonging to English prose; we might as well include Homer, Froissart, and Machiavelli as English writers. His extensive polemical writing is not remarkable in style, and is spoilt by the violence which pervaded both sides in Reformation controversy. To speak of him, therefore, as "the Father of English prose" is to apply a silly phrase in a fashion monstrously unhistorical. Even the *History of Richard III*, which is his chief claim, and (if his) a sound one, to a place in the story of style, has been much overpraised. The eulogies of critics like Hallam were probably determined by the fact that it is an early and not unhappy example of the rather colourless "classical" prose, of which a little later we shall find the chief exponents to be Ascham and his friends at Cambridge. It is, of course, a good deal better than Capgrave, and it is free from Pecock's harshness and crudity of phrase. But as it cannot on the one hand compare for richness, colour, and representative effect with the style of Berners, one of the two best writers of prose nearly contemporary with More, so it is not to be mentioned with that of Fisher, the other, for nice rhetorical artifice and intelligent employment of craftsman-like methods of work. But it is much more "eighteenth century" than either, and this commended it to Hallam; while More's pleasant wit and great intellectual ability naturally set it above the work of mere translators or compilers. Sir Thomas has a secure place in English history, and no mean one in that very interesting history of works of distinction composed in Latin, since the arrival of the vernaculars at years of discretion, which has yet to be written. But his place in the strict History of English literature is very small, and not extraordinarily high.

Latimer.

As Fisher occupies the most commanding position among the divines of the time in reference to original and skilful handling of English style, so the opposite side furnished the most remarkable and successful examples of what could be done by carrying out his principles. Tyndale, the next competent translator of the Bible to Wyclif, is more noteworthy for his hapless fate and for a vigorous controversial pen, than for distinct literary merit; but Latimer, Coverdale, and Cranmer must be better spoken of. Hugh Latimer[5] indeed—who was born in 1489 of a family of Leicestershire yeomen, was educated at Clare Hall, Cambridge, became Bishop of Worcester in 1535, and was burnt in 1555 at Oxford—holds a very important and somewhat peculiar position, ranking with Bunyan, Cobbett, and in a lesser degree Defoe, as the chief practitioner of a perfectly homely and vernacular style. Such a style naturally connects itself with an intense egotism; and Latimer is as egotistic, though not as arrogant,

5. Latimer is well presented in two little volumes of Mr. Arber's invaluable Reprints, *The Ploughers* and *Seven Sermons*.

as Cobbett himself. He was a thoroughly honest and a thoroughly practical man, no partisan in the bad sense (that is to say, in the way of winking at practices by friends which he would have stormed against in foes), with all the taste of the common people for vivid homely illustration, and sometimes, as in the universally known description of the paternal household, capable of extraordinarily graphic presentment of fact. Beyond the range of personal description and shrewd, unadorned argument or denunciation his literary gifts would probably not have extended in any case very far. But as a popular sermon-writer in his own days, or as a popular journalist in these, he had in the one case, and could have had in the other, but very few rivals and no superiors. Nor is it improper to notice that his raciness and vernacularly were specially useful as correctives of the rather monotonous correctness which the imitation of Ciceronianism in English was likely to bring in.

Coverdale.

The merits of Coverdale and Cranmer are rather matters of imputation and lending than of certain attribution by right, the claims of the one resting on his supposed principal share of the merits of the early Tudor translations of the Bible, those of the other partly on this, but still more on his reputed authorship of a large part of the Edwardian Liturgy. Miles Coverdale, who was born in Yorkshire about 1488, and educated at Cambridge, became a Protestant exile on the Continent, and was busy on more versions than one of the Scriptures, chiefly in the fourth decade of the sixteenth century. He became Bishop of Exeter in 1551, and though he suffered imprisonment in the Marian persecution, was not restored later, dying in 1569 as merely an incumbent. If (which does not seem to be absolutely certain) he was the actual translator of the Bible of 1535 which goes by his name, there is no doubt that some of the best phrasing, for sound and sense, of the great Authorised Version is originally due to him. His prologue and other editorial matter certainly seems to contain not a little of the peculiar music which has always been associated with the English Bible, and which the revisers of a few years ago showed such extraordinary ability in removing whenever they had an opportunity. It must, however, be said that even for this quality there are advocates of Tyndale's claims in opposition to Coverdale.

The praise claimed for Cranmer—that of being the chief author of the Collects and Prayers of the Anglican Liturgy—is even higher, inasmuch as the matter, though necessarily showing common forms of phrase and common stocks of matter, is more original. Cranmer was born in Nottinghamshire in 1489, became a Fellow of Jesus College, Cambridge, took a great (at least large) part in the affair of the divorce, and without holding any bishop's see previously, was appointed direct to the Primacy at Warham's death in 1532. He was burnt at Oxford in 1556. His character as a man does not concern us. But it is only fair to say that the considerable body of his doctrinal and controversial works displays, as far as the matter will admit, a command of melodious word-arrangement not much inferior to that which is to be found *passim* in the Liturgy. The truth seems to be that this peculiar style—the swan-song of Middle English transferred from verse to prose—was less the property of any individual man than abroad in the air at the time; and that it found utterance whenever fit voice and fit matter came together, from Malory to Cranmer and from Berners to Coverdale. Hardly ever afterwards could the touch of archaism be attained without deliberate *pastiche*; never before could the writers boast the possession of a full vocabulary and a tolerably exercised practice. The rude vulgarity of partisan controversy, the learned dulness of argumentative exposition, often mar this music; but where, as in the Prayer-book, the matter indited is of the best, then the style is of the best likewise—of such a best as was never again to be naturally produced, and hardly ever to be imitated by the most loving and delicate art.

Cranmer.

INTERCHAPTER 4

THE general lessons of the fifteenth century[1] are rather unusually easy to disentangle; indeed, the very want of intrinsic, and so misleading, interest leaves these lessons all the more exposed.

In poetry we have little or no progress to chronicle, and a surprisingly small amount of positive achievement, this latter being found almost wholly in the small group of the better Scottish poets and in the anonymous writers of ballads and carols. Negatively the century may be said to have done at least one very good thing—to have shown by the repeated practice of persons, sometimes possessed of actual genius, that the revived alliterative schemes, even crutched and bolstered with rhyme and stanza arrangement, would not do. Also, in pursuing another branch of the same poetic maze of "passages that lead to nothing," it may be said to have shown very clearly the danger of a too stiff and elaborate poetic diction. Otherwise its poetical practice, in the higher and more regular poetic kinds, was a rather touching, but for the most part hopelessly unsuccessful, attempt to make one good custom corrupt the world, to continue Chaucerian form and Lorrisian matter long after the latter had lost any real connection with poetic power, and without the gifts of language, of humour, of study of nature and humanity, which had given value to the former.

Yet there had more than possibly arisen during this very time—there had to a certainty come into far more extensive

1. As in the case of Middle English, there is no single book to which the student can be referred for this period; the section appertaining in Mr. G. Gregory Smith's *Transition Period* (Edinburgh, 1900) will be found most useful.

use than ever before, a kind of popular and only half-literary poetry, which was gradually to supply solvents for this stiffness, breath and life for this lack of inspiration, to stir the blood of the great new literary poets of the next age like a trumpet, to give Shakespeare himself scraps worth decking his own fabric with, models for his own unapproachable and inestimable lyrics, and last, but far indeed from least, by the very irregularity of its apparently artless art, to maintain and to extend that sort of liberty which is the glory and the essence of English poetry. It is a curious thing that this liberty has been, throughout our history, in much more danger than the political freedom which has occupied historians at such length, simply because the attempts on it have been made not by tyrants from without but by mistaken persons from within. Even now there are folk who will not face the plain fact that Chaucer allowed himself trisyllabic feet, but try to get him into the hard-and-fast dungeon of the decasyllable by slurs and elisions and all manner of unnatural tricks. His own immediate successors no doubt tried to tell their syllables as exactly as they told their beads. But the blessed liberty of the ballad was beside them all the time, and served as an alternative to and a protest against their theory.

Very closely connected with this matter is the already noted change of pronunciation which certainly went on throughout the century, though we are in the profoundest ignorance of its details, and can only dimly appreciate its results in the new verse of Surrey and Wyatt afterwards. A good deal, no doubt, was due to the increasing disuse and at last total abolition of the final *e,* with the consequent substitution of plurals in *s* for *es* and the like, the dropping of the infinitive *en,* and all the rest of it. For it must be (though it is not always) remembered that a process of this kind is a very far-reaching one. You cannot merely cut a syllable off a word and leave the sound-value of the rest as it was. The lopping and topping, in at least some cases, must affect the balance of the word, shift its centre of gravity, alter its relations to other words in the verse or the sentence. The strange tricks played, for instance, by Wyatt with the syllable *eth,* and his apparent belief in the propriety of rhyming it by itself, without any regard to what comes before, must have ultimate reasons of this sort, though we may, even as in a glass darkly, have difficulty in seeing what they were. So, too, the increasing isolation of the country and the language, as both strengthened the disuse of the glib trilingualism which distinguished such a man as Gower, must, with other subtle and obscure influences of the same kind, have had effect. We see something of this effect in the half-defiant, half-despairing doggerel of Skelton, as well as in the patient plodding of Hawes.

The details of the uprising of the great hybrid between poetry and prose—Drama—we still, for the same reasons of convenient juxtaposition, reserve to the next Book; but more even than in the last Interchapter it is important to observe that its earlier forms were now perfectly familiar to the English nation, if they had as yet (till the very close of the period) scantily commended themselves to the regular practitioners of English literature. The mystery and miracle-play had perhaps for centuries—certainly for some century and a half—been practised by the not always rude mechanicals of probably every great town in the kingdom. The farce-interludes, originally introduced to prevent the effect being too solemn, springing naturally out of such scriptural incidents as the Tower of Babel, or grafted without too much violence, as in the famous "Mak" scenes of the *Second Shepherds' Play,* had gradually detached themselves, and constituted almost an independent kind. The Morality was simply the dramatisation of the *Rose* allegory—the favourite matter of the time thrown into what was fast becoming its favourite form. That religious feeling after the Reformation exaggerated the dislike of Catholicism for dramatic performance as such, and did not maintain the exceptional tolerance for religious drama, mattered little. The excessive earnestness and sternness of the time required casement in some direction, and found it in this; nor was it till nearly a century and a half after the close of our period that Puritanism could have its way with the drama.

Of prose, as the details given in the last chapter sufficiently show, it is possible to speak with less allowance. That the period gives one of the best books in English literature may be partly, though it certainly is not wholly, an accident; that the translations, not yet final, but substantively formed, of the Bible and the adaptations of the Liturgy at its close have supplied nearly four centuries since with models of exquisite cadence, of enchanting selection and arrangement of vocabulary, is, if not an accident, the result of a concatenation of circumstances not all of which—not even the most of which—are literary.

But it is no accident, it is of the essence of the literary history and development of the time, that the resources, the practice, the duties, the opportunities of prose continue during the whole course of the period steadily to expand, to subdivide themselves, to acquire diversity, adequacy, accomplishment. That this is done for the most part through the medium of translation and compilation does no harm, but on the contrary does a great deal of good; that a certain amount of the practice is in the nature of not always successful experiment is nothing to be ashamed of, or to be annoyed at, but, on the contrary, a fair reason for satisfaction and pride. No single secret of the greatness of English literature exceeds in importance the fact that Englishmen have never been satisfied to import or to copy a literary form bodily from any other language or country, as Spain adopted Italian artificial poetry, and as France adopted the Senecan drama; and this has of itself necessitated constant and very often unsuccessful experiment before the right kind or the right adjustment has been hit upon.

It is scarcely too much to say that the fifteenth century, with a few years backward into the fourteenth and onwards into the sixteenth, plays the same part in regard to English prose that the thirteenth century, with probably (for our knowledge is dimmer here) a few years backward into the twelfth century and certainly more than a few forward into the fourteenth, plays in regard to English verse. The necessary stocks of material, some of which will have to be rejected, are accumulated; the necessary plant and methods of working, not a little of which will have to be perfected, are slowly and painfully elaborated. Additional lateness in time, and perhaps less difficulty in kind, give us indeed a more perfect result in Malory's prose than we can find in the verse of any poet between Layamon and Hampole; but *mutatis mutandis* the historical position is the same, and the historical gains and results not so very different. No single prose writer, not even Hooker, was in any near future to do for the one what Chaucer in the later fourteenth century did for the other, but that again was a consequence of the necessities of the case.

It is not the least of the advantages and pleasures of that historical study of literature which has, with halting footsteps, it is true, at last followed the historical study of politics and social development, that it provides these "condolences," these "vails" in the seemingly dullest period of the actual literary course. The airy generaliser may flap his wing disdainfully at the fifteenth century and hurry to pastures more succulent; the merely indolent person may decline the labour necessary to acquaint himself with it. But both will do what they do, and decline what they decline, at their peril. Nor, while criticism accompanies history, is there any peril on the other side. There is not the least danger of any but pedants—that is to say, the same genus as the generalisers, but a different species of it—neglecting Shakespeare or Spenser because they take the pains to read Barclay and Bokenam. Yet shall those who decline to take notice of Barclay and Bokenam run no small risk of not fully understanding even Spenser, even Shakespeare.

Book V

Elizabethan Literature to the Death of Spenser

1

PRELIMINARIES—DRAMA

Unbroken development of Drama from Miracle Plays—Origin of these—The Miracle-Play cycles, etc.—Non-sacred episodes—Moralities—*The Four Elements*—Other Interludes—John Heywood and *The Four PP*—*Thersites*—Other Interludes—Their drift—Bale's *King John*—*Ralph Roister Doister*—*Gammer Gurton's Needle*—*Gorboduc*—Other early attempts—The demand and the supply—Early plays by Gascoigne and others—Disputes as to plays—Difficulties in their way.

Unbroken development of Drama from Miracle Plays.

THE outburst of English Drama is so pre-eminently the glory of the Elizabethan period of literature proper, that it has seemed on the whole better to take no detailed notice in the preceding Books of the early experiments—not very early, not very numerous, and not of the first importance in literature—which we possess in that literary kind. Among other advantages of Drama of postponing the treatment of these to this special place, not the least is the emphasis which can perhaps best be given by such an arrangement to a protest against certain sentences of the late Professor Morley's—sentences astonishing in so careful a student of literature and so attached a lover of the drama. "The Modern Drama," says Mr. Morley,[1] "did not in any way arise out of the Miracle Plays. Miracle plays did not pass into morality plays; nor did moralities afterwards pass into the dramas. The modern drama arose out of the study and imitation

1. *English Plays*, p. 2.

of classical plays in schools and universities." Of these assertions the first three must be directly traversed, and the fourth largely corrected. The modern drama *did* arise out of the Miracles. The Miracles *did* pass into the Moralities. The Moralities *did* pass into modern dramas. And though the imitation of the ancient classical drama, and its performance in schools and universities, coloured, shaped, generally influenced, the modern drama most momentously, this drama no more arose out of them than Spenser arose out of Virgil, or Hooker out of Cicero.

Origin of these.

According to the system adopted in this book, we need concern ourselves little with the thin and dubious subject of the earliest mediaeval drama in Latin, and in the vernaculars other than English. It is sufficient to say that at last, probably about the tenth century, the extreme disapprobation with which the Church had always regarded dramatic performances—a disapprobation justified not only by the moral scandals of the ancient theatre but by its direct association with the persecution of Christianity—gave way very partially and very slowly, in obedience to the well-known principle of enlisting strong human tastes, as far as could be lawfully done, on the side of religion. Whether, as is sometimes and plausibly contended, this was partly the result of a natural and imperceptible development of the dramatic side of the Church services themselves may be left undecided. It is sufficient to say that we have from France Latin mystery or miracle plays which may be of the eleventh century, Latin mixed with a little French nearly as early, and plays wholly in French which are as old as the twelfth. It is possible, from notices that remain, that there may have been English, or partly English, plays, if not of this same century, at any rate of the thirteenth. But those that we have are much later, the earliest[2] of them not

2. This is usually taken to be the *Harrowing of Hell*, first printed by Halliwell, and assigned to the reign of Edward II. It is an interesting piece in not quite 250 lines of octosyllabic couplet, but rather rudimentarily dramatic. A prologue introduces it; Christ and Satan interchange some half-score speeches of summons and refusal; the janitor runs away, and our Lord,

being older than the fourteenth. And whereas at least two famous examples remain of purely secular French plays from the thirteenth, nothing of the kind is found in English till the end of the fifteenth, if not even later. Further, though we have a few miracle plays proper—that is to say, plays the subjects of which are taken from the lives of the saints and the acts ascribed to Our Lady—the majority of them are mysteries, *i.e.* dramatisations of the sacred history. Those which were wont to be performed by the guilds or trades of the towns remain to us in four large collections and a few other batches and single examples. Of these some account may now be given.

The Miracle-Play cycles, etc.

The four great collections,[3] known by the names of their place of performance, are the York, Wakefield (also called Towneley, from the former owners of the MS.), Coventry, and Chester plays. The first extends to forty-eight pieces, and *may* go back to the middle of the fourteenth century; the second to thirty, the MS. being a century later; the Coventry (same date) to forty-two; and the Chester (of which we have no MS. older than the end of the sixteenth) to twenty-four. We have also one of a Newcastle cycle, one of a Dublin, an East-Anglian version of *Abraham and Isaac,* one Norfolk "Sacrament Play," besides the so-called "Digby Mysteries," and the oldest of all, the *Harrowing of Hell,* which has been thought to be possibly as old as the first quarter of the fourteenth century. The details of the performance of these, though very far from uninteresting, concern the history not of literature but of the stage. It is enough to say that they were usually divided among

binding Satan, is welcomed by, and graciously answers, the patriarchs in turn.

3. These are now accessible in the following editions: *York,* ed. Miss L.T. Smith, Oxford, 1885; *Chester,* ed. Deimling, Part I, E.E.T.S., 1892; *Towneley,* ed. England and Pollard, E.E.T.S., 1897; *Coventry,* ed. Halliwell, Shakespeare Society, 1841 (reprint in hand for E.E.T.S.); *Digby,* twice edited by Dr. Furnivall for the New Shakespeare Society in 1882, and for the E.E.T.S. in 1896. A most excellent selection from all these, with others from the *Harrowing of Hell* to early sixteenth-century pieces like *Thersites* and Bale's *King John,* will be found in Mr. A.W. Pollards *English Miracle Plays* (Oxford, 1890).

the handicrafts of a town, and performed by them on large movable stages or storied wagons in different open places. Of their strictly literary character some account is necessary.

As may be presumed from the great numbers contained in each collection, the individual play is very short as a rule, indeed rather an "Act" of the whole than a separate drama. But there is great diversity of length. For instance, the very interesting *Second Shepherds' Play* of the Towneley or Wakefield set has between 700 and 800 lines; the first of the York set does not go beyond 180. The metre in which they are written is extremely various. We find both rhyme and alliteration—the two being sometimes combined; long and short lines; lyrical stanzas of the most various and complicated kind, couplets, octosyllables alternately rhymed, and other variations—no single metre predominating with anything like the same distinctness as that shown by the octosyllabic couplet in the French analogues and originals.

Non-sacred episodes.

A very little examination of these plays will show the astonishing fallacy of the proposition that the modern drama did not grow out of them. Miss Toulmin-Smith has drawn attention to the interesting fact that the York or Northern cycle of mystery plays bears a remarkable resemblance, in order and choice of subjects, to the invaluable Scripture-history paraphrase in verse called the *Cursor Mundi* (*vide* p. 91), also Northern, and probably not much anterior to the cycle itself in date. In fact, the development of verse-stories, sacred and profane, into prose tales on the one hand and dramas on the other, which we find exemplified in French, beyond all doubt took place after a similar fashion in English. And almost from the first in both languages we find the strict throwing of the Scripture history into narrative "by personages," as the instructive French phrase has it, incessantly diversified by, and gradually breaking up into, episodes and interludes of chiefly farcical matter, which are only indirectly connected, or not connected at all, with the main subject. Instances of indirect connection are to be found especially in the story of the Ark and of the Tower of Babel, both of which were fixed on almost from the first as opportunities for comic by-play and digression. The great instance of the sheer addition is the famous *Second Shepherds' Play* above referred to, where the rogueries of "Mak," the sheep-stealer, are simply though not unnaturally superadded to the Gospel story of "While shepherds watched their flocks by night." So the Magdalene legend gives the germ (of which authors eagerly avail themselves) not merely of comic, but of absolutely romantic treatment. In other words, *Secunda Pastorum* of the Towneley and the Digby *Magdalene* simply give us comedy and tragedy, or at least romantic drama, ready to hand, as additions in each case to the Bible matter. When these things, especially the farce parts, had once been given as zests and relishes, they were sure to be expected as a main element of the banquet, and by degrees to be presented by themselves.

Moralities.

So again, nothing can be stranger or (except in so far as matters partly of opinion can never be said to be absolutely true or false) falser than the statement that the Morality did not arise out of the Miracle Play, and did not in turn hasten the modern. Drama, having by means of the miracle play, and the miracle play only, taken regular rank as a department of literature, and especially of popular literature, was bound to undergo in the order of its appearance the various changes which passed over literature generally. In other words, and descending from the general to the particular, it was certain to experience, and to show traces of, the overwhelming spirit of allegorising which came upon Europe in the late fourteenth and throughout the fifteenth century. It did show them very strongly indeed, and the result was the Morality. This naturally did not altogether supersede the Miracle Play proper; but it took place beside it, the Biblical personages of the older form giving place to personified abstractions exactly as the knights of romance proper gave way to the Grand-Amours and King Harts of allegorical romance. The titles of the Moralities given in Mr. Pollard's excellent selection of this division of Drama—*The Castle of Perseverance, Every Man, The Four Elements, Magnificence*—will, without going further, suggest and almost fully explain the nature of this class of composition, and the list could be largely extended from French, and not a little from English, sources. Generally speaking, the Morality either morals the whole life of man after the fashion of Hawes and Douglas, or selects a particular vice or virtue for similar treatment. In form it does not differ much from a miracle play, though, being as a rule later, it shows the metrical and other changes of the time. Yet it maintains that singular indulgence in lyrical arrangement which has made some, hardly with exaggeration, call the Miracle Play itself the chief storehouse of formal lyric in Middle English.

This variety of drama has generally undergone, and must be said to a great extent to deserve, the reproach of being one of the very dullest divisions of literature. The fearful prolixity which attacked all letters during the fifteenth century did not spare it, and though English Moralities are perhaps shorter than French, the *Castle of Perseverance* above referred to extends to the very respectable, or disreputable, length of 3500 lines. By degrees either the name began to carry a damaging connotation with it, or the thing was felt to require relief. At any rate, the Interlude—it is not known exactly how or when—arose in its place. There is no certainty as to the extent to which the proper meaning of the term "interlude" attaches to this class of composition; but it continued, in name and substance both, to be composed for reading, if not for acting, in the remoter parts of England (especially Wales) till within the nineteenth century. Many interludes are simply moralities; but the obviously correcter meaning of the word corresponds closely to the French *farce,* and is so used of the interludes in Sir David Lyndsay's great Morality-*Sotie* (*vide ante,* p. 227). The farce-interlude naturally continued that farce-episode of the Miracles and Mysteries which has been already noticed; and though the regular French fashion of weaving mystery, morality, *sotie,* and farce in a tetralogy does not seem to have obtained with us, the Interlude gradually detached itself more and more from its companions.[4]

4. It is important and interesting to notice that in the work of the last of the "giant race before the flood," Shirley, we have actually subsisting examples of the Interlude proper, and its resultant play, in the *Contention of Honour and Riches* and *Honoria and Mammon.*

We shall see this very distinctly if we take the plays contained in the two first volumes of Hazlitt's *Dodsley,*[5] most, if not all, of which are of the Interlude kind. *The Four Elements* is of the kind nearest to a Morality, and indeed almost confusible with that. The characters are the Messenger (showing traces of classical influence), Nature (*Natura Naturata*), Humanity, Studious Desire, Sensual Appetite, The Taverner, Experience, Ignorance, "and if ye list ye may bring in a Disguising." As usual in this class of play, the *dramatis personae* so clearly betray the whole course of the action that one does not quite see what need there was for it, and rather understands the frequent disinclination of the early dramatist to provide these tell-tale *dramatis personae* at all. Humanity is coached by Nature, and more in detail by Studious Desire; becoming a little tired by this improving company, he is bewitched by Sensual Appetite, whom The Taverner seconds very zealously. Then come in Experience and Studious Desire, who talk Geography. Humanity is fought for by them on the one side, by Sensual Appetite and Ignorance on the other, and is left undecided, pleading his case with ambiguous arguments to the returning Nature. The whole of this piece, like most of the early dramas, is versified in a sort of doggerel which takes for basis sometimes a longer line, sometimes a shorter, and may be called, rather for convenience than strict exactitude, doggerelised heroic or Alexandrine and doggerelised octosyllable. The whole class of metre exemplifies the same influences which show themselves in Skelton and have been already discussed. The piece dates probably from the first or second decade of the sixteenth century.

The Four Elements.

Calisto and Meliboea is a rendering of the famous Spanish satiric medley of the *Celestina. Every Man* and *Hick Scorner* are again moral interludes, but with a difference, the first inclining to the general lines of the Morality as above given, the second a very early example (it was printed by Wynkyn de Worde) of the invective so frequent in English against the deboshed youth

Other Interludes.

---

5. 15 vols., London, 1874-76.

who returns from foreign travel all the worse for it. Allegorical characters, however, are almost as freely introduced in the one as in the other, and the metre is still doggerel. *The World and the Child* and *God's Promises* are, the first a pure Morality, the second a cross between Morality and Mystery. On the other hand, *The Pardoner and the Friar,* which is one of the works of John Heywood, the chief named author of this stage of drama, has nothing allegorical about it, but is a lively satire on the two professions with plenty of rough humour and horse play.[6]

John Heywood and *The Four PP.*

John Heywood was a Londoner possessed of some property. He was educated at Broadgates Hall, Oxford, and is said to have been a friend of More. He seems to have been a consistent Roman Catholic, and after some trouble in Edward's reign became one of the few literary favourites of Mary, and exiled himself after her death, dying at an uncertain period some twenty years after Elizabeth's accession. His son Jasper Heywood was also a man of letters. John, besides being a dramatist as far as his time admitted, was a writer of epigrams and proverbs. '*The Four PP* is a really amusing farce in doggerel shorts and longs, wherein a Palmer, a Pardoner, a Pothecary, and a Pedlar tell tales of their own and each other's trades, and compete which shall tell the greatest lie—the prize being won, as many know who never read the play, by the Palmer's assertion that he never saw a woman out of temper. The fun is rather infantine, and the literary merit not great; but the advance on any previous dramatic matter in going direct to character for the interest, and the incidental allusion to places and manners, make it important.

Another piece, trivial in itself but important for our purpose, is *Thersites,* which seems by some allusions to the birth of

6. Fairholt's Percy Society ed. of Heywood's *Wit and Folly* gives plentiful extracts in its Introduction from his other works, *The Play of Love, The Play of the Wise Men, The Husband, Wife, and Priest,* which all more or less answer the description in the text. His *Proverbs* and *Epigrams* were reprinted by the Spenser Society, 1867. The whole *Works* appear in two vols. of Farmer's *Early English Dramatists* (London, 1905-06).

Edward VI to be dated pretty exactly at 1537. It is a sort of Morality of Boasting, in Interlude form and with concrete characters instead of abstractions—to wit, Thersites himself; Mulciber, a smith; Mater, a mother; Miles, a knight; and Telemachus, a child. Mulciber, at Thersites' request, makes him arms, the dialogue including a great deal of play on the word "sallet," as, but much more briefly, in Shakespeare.[7] The braggart's mother begs him not to endanger himself, but he scorns her and brags ever more loudly. He engages in combat with a snail, and after much vaunting and horseplay claims the victory, because the beast draws in its horns. Miles, who has supervened, suggests himself as a worthier antagonist; but Thersites runs away and hides behind his mother, who succeeds in protecting him. Then Telemachus brings a letter from Ulysses, and the mother is forced by her ungrateful son's violence to pronounce elaborate burlesque charms on the pair, till Miles returns and drives Thersites off!

Thersites.

All this is, of course, excessively childish, but we must remember that it was the actual childhood of the drama, that the mere gain of live persons for abstractions was immense, and that, after all, these plays were still a mere expansion of the burlesque interludes and passages in the miracles. The drama was only in a go-cart, but it was learning to walk.

The *Interlude of Youth* relapses upon general characters, but endows them with greater life and individuality than is usual in the Morality scheme; and the same may be said of the not very differently named *Lusty Juventus,* which, however, is both interludes, longer and heavier. *Jack Juggler* forms a curious pair with *Thersites.* There we had classical names for a modern farce; here a classical drama, the *Amphitryon,* is travestied, though only to the extent of the misfortunes of Sosia, not those of Amphitryon himself. The title-hero plays the part of Mercury out of mere mischief, to tease and annoy Jenkin Careaway. The piece is one of the liveliest of its class, and shows the beneficial effect which the imitation and engrafting of the classical drama on

Other Interludes.

7. 2 *Henry VI,* iv. 10.

the native stocks was producing. But it also shows most unmistakably that the modern play did not arise out of imitation of the classical drama alone, or even principally. The *Nice Wanton* is noteworthy for being neither allegorical nor the dramatisation of any known story—for though the names Dalilah and Xantippe are used for the light heroine and the shrew her mother, no incident or condition associated with the names themselves is brought in. Xantippe has three children, Barnabas, Ismael, and Dalilah, of whom the first is a good child, and the two others ne'er-do-wells, who are easily seduced by the Iniquity[8] of the piece, and both come to the worst of ends. The *History of Jacob and Esau* is simply the Bible story dramatised, no longer according to miracle-play conditions, but to those of the interlude-morality. And *The Disobedient Child* has once more an attempt at originality. It is the dramatised story of an imprudent marriage, by which the bridegroom offends his father, and only obtains a violent shrew for a wife. There is not much dramatic ability about it, but it displays more attention to style and literary language than most, and is, indeed, said to be the work of a Cambridge man, Thomas Ingeland.

Lastly, the *Marriage of Wit and Science* returns to the pure Morality scheme as regards plot and personages, but is regularly divided into acts and scenes, and has some attempt at orderly dramatic presentation. The *New Custom*, the *Trial of Treasure*, and other pieces of the same kind do not add anything very new to the list of varieties obtainable from the above analysis.

Their drift.

But we can see quite sufficiently from it how, just as the Morality is the Miracle or Mystery, with Qualities, Virtues, Vices, personified States of Life, and so forth substituted for Scripture characters, so the Interlude is the Morality, sometimes merely changed in name, more often lightened in the farce direction as regards handling, and adapted to a very wide range of subjects—scriptural, moral, classical, social, and what not—with a constantly increasing

8. Here a "Vice" in both senses—clown and tempter. The Vice, as is well-known from the Shakespearian use, was often merely or mainly the former.

tendency towards the adoption of the regular classical division of acts and scenes, and towards the independent selection and working out of dramatic stories, invented or borrowed, in such a fashion that the resultants must fall, not into the arbitrary divisions of Mystery, Morality, or Interlude, but into the natural ones of Tragedy, Comedy, and that mixed kind which is perhaps most conveniently, though rather improperly, named "Drame" in French. There is still no reason for displacing from their position as early, if not certainly the earliest, representatives of comedy, tragedy, historical drama, and farce, the famous pieces entitled *Ralph Roister Doister, Gorboduc, King John,* and *Gammer Gurton's Needle.* Romantic drama, an original kind and a high one, was naturally not so early, and we do not meet with real examples of it before Lyly and Peele.

Bale's *King John.*

Of these, Bishop Bale's *King John,*[9] which has been dated about 1547, is the least important, and its right to be regarded as the first of our historical dramas has even been denied, on the plea that it is only a didactic interlude with a historical subject. This seems a little hard, for Bale is surely entitled to the credit of seeing that the didactic interlude—that is to say, the play in the only state it had then reached—was capable of being applied to historical subjects, and so becoming the historic play in time. His object here, as in all his other literary work, was no doubt polemical—to advance the cause of the Reformation by exhibiting the patriotic objection to the power of the Pope; and his play does not exhibit much dramatic grasp. But he had already written Protestant mysteries, and evidently had a pretty clear inkling of the popularity and possibilities of the drama. In particular the way in which the *personifications* in *King*

9. Ed. Collier, Camden Soc., 1838. Bale, a Suffolk man, born near Dunwich in 1495, went to Jesus College, Cambridge, took orders, married, fled to Germany in 1547, became Bishop of Ossory in 1552, fled again under Mary, and on returning received from Elizabeth a pretend at Canterbury. He died in 1563. Bale was not a very bright example of a Reformer in all ways, but he wrote a good deal, including a bibliography (one of the first) of English literature, and no less than twenty-two plays, of which five only, in whole or part, survive. These, except *King John,* are sacred-moral in type.

John—Dissimulation, Private Wealth, Usurped Power, become *persons*—Stephen Langton, Cardinal Pandulph, the Pope—is a thing which, whether definitely intended or not, is of the widest reach and suggestion. He chiefly employs the long slinging rhymed doggerel which, as has been noted, is the standard metre of this entire class of transition plays.

Ralph Roister Doister.

The three others are of more importance. *Ralph Roister Doister,*[10] the oldest and most accomplished in its own class, is the work of Nicholas Udall, successively headmaster of Eton and Westminster, who must have written it about or before 1550. Udall was a Hampshire man, and is supposed to have been about forty at his death in 1556. He was educated at Corpus Christi College, Oxford, and was a good scholar as well as a harsh master (he whipped poor Tusser, the doggerel verse writer on husbandry, very much), a translator, and the author of some Latin plays on sacred subjects. But he would now be merely a name but for *Ralph Roister Doister,* the intrinsic merit of which is considerable, though it has been denied, and which as a *point de repère* in English literary history is simply of the first importance. It is indeed almost by itself sufficient to correct erroneous notions as to the parts respectively played by the Interlude and the classical play in the formation of the modern drama. A man who wrote *Ralph Roister Doister* without knowing or having heard of Plautus would no doubt be a genius of extraordinary originality; but a man who, knowing Plautus, and not having the traditions of the Miracle, Morality, and Interlude stage before him, imitated Plautus precisely after the fashion of *Ralph Roister Doister* would be an unintelligible portent. The plot, though simple, is far more complex, and, above all, far more regular, than that of any mere Interlude, but the play is wholly built on Interlude lines. Matthew Merygreek, an ingenious improvement upon the "Vice" of the earlier plays, out of mischief induces Ralph, a brainless braggart and simpleton beau, to pay court to Christian Custance, the betrothed of an absent merchant, Gawin Goodluck. The

10. In Hazlitt's *Dodsley,* iii. Also separately in Mr. Arber's *Reprints.*

discomfiture of the gull, who is actually beaten off by Custance and her handmaids, the by-play of those handmaids themselves, the misunderstanding with Goodluck created by false reports, and the reconciliation, make a very fair dramatic scheme, which is carried out in rhymed doggerel of the middle length, not so short as that of most Interludes nor so long as that of *Gammer Gurton's Needle.*

Gammer Gurton's Needle.

This still more famous piece,[11] which contains (though some say it only borrows) one of the best convivial songs in the English language, was acted at Christ's College, Cambridge, in 1566. Its author, or supposed author, John Still, was a member of that college, and is guessed to have been born at Grantham about 1534, being thus a very much younger man than Udall, and, in fact, a member of another generation. In 1570 Still became a beneficed priest, in two years more Dean of Bocking, successively Master of St. John's and of Trinity, Vice-Chancellor of his University, and Bishop of Wells, where he died in 1608. He had lived to see the English drama (of which he had, *ex hypothesi,* written one of the first complete examples, and the first to be acted at either University) arrive at its highest perfection; and it is said that when Vice-Chancellor he had to protest against the very practice, that of acting *English* plays at Universities, which he had initiated. The play, though a broad farce in tone, is arranged as a regular comedy, and the losing and finding of the needle which has been employed to mend the garments of Gammer Gurton's man, Hodge, is carried on by Hodge and the Gammer; Tib, her maid; Cock, her boy; Diccon the Bedlam (mad beggar), the Vice or mischief-maker of the play; a neighbour, Dame Chat, and her maid, Doll; Master Baily, another neighbour, and his servant, Spendthrift; Doctor Rat the Curate; and Gib the Cat. The language is mainly dialect, and the vehicle, as observed above, is doggerel rhyme of the longest form—extending to fifteen or sixteen syllables. It is written with spirit and managed with skill, but unfortunately the language is of the coarsest kind—coarse even for this class of play, the authors of which are rarely refined. The magnificent

11. Hazlitt's *Dodsley, ibid.*

drinking-song of "Back and side go bare, go bare," introduces the second act, has nothing particular to do with the action, and may be older than the play.

Gorboduc.

It is impossible to imagine a greater contrast to this jovial piece than the tragedy of *Gorboduc,*[12] or, as it is otherwise called, *Ferrex and Porrex,* which was published, though surreptitiously, a year before *Gammer Gurton's Needle* was performed, and had itself been acted five years earlier, in 1561. In the second and authorised edition, which did not appear till 1570, the name was changed as above given. The authorship has generally been attributed to Thomas Sackville and Thomas Norton, and though some champions of Sackville have tried to claim the whole for him, this is rather a mistaken partisanship. The rich and stately melody of the *Induction* and the *Complaint of Buckingham* (*vide infra*) certainly neither suggests nor requires to be eked out by the wooden dulness of this dreary play, which is simply of interest and importance (and it has a great deal of both) historically and not intrinsically.

In structure *Gorboduc* is a regular play on the strictest model of Seneca the tragedian, with a slight concession to the popular taste in the matter of "dumb shows." Gorboduc himself is King, and Videna Queen, of Great Britain. They have two sons, Ferrex and Porrex, who quarrel, and four dukes, Cornwall, Albany, Logres, and Cumberland. Each prince has a counsellor, and each has a parasite. There is a messenger to tell Ferrex's death, and a messenger to tell the Duke of Albany's rebellion. The chorus consists of four ancient and sage men of Britain, and there are a secretary and a counsellor to the King to make up the tale of pairs or quartettes. No action happens on the stage, and the whole play, with the exception of the choruses (the stanzas of which bear some marks of Sackville's hand), is couched in correct but ineffably dreary decasyllables, in which the sense usually lapses with the line, and the whole stumps on with a maddening, or rather stupefying, monotony.

12. See *Works of Thomas Sackville,* ed. Sackville-West, London, 1859.

The full importance of *Gorboduc*, and of the imitations of the Senecan drama generally, will be better seen later, when we come to the actual period of Elizabethan drama proper; meanwhile it will be best to give some account of the productions of the "twilight" period—the first twenty or four-and-twenty years of the Queen's reign, when irregular and tentative experiments on the mixed lines of the Interlude in the broad sense and the classical play were frequent, and when the taste for dramatic entertainments was constantly growing, but when no one had as yet hit on a really promising vein to work. It is a division of literature which is not very easy for the historian. Little of it is of any intrinsic value; a great deal has disappeared, or has never been printed; of what is actually open to study most is anonymous, or practically so; and the real dates of nearly all the plays are very uncertain, owing to the interval which usually elapsed between performance and publication, and the invariable habit of writing up popular plays from time to time by the stock poets of the different companies.

Other early attempts.

Despite all the pains which have been spent on this very popular matter, the growth of the theatre proper—that is to say, of an establishment for the production of stage plays only—is still obscure. As generally happens in such matters, the most reasonable plan is to acquiesce in uncertainty on non-material points, and to recognise and hold fast by the material ones. For some two centuries probably, the acting of plays in one way or another by town guilds, by "servants" at court, by "servants" of the great houses, which were in effect minor courts, by monastic and collegiate-clerical households, etc., had been constantly increasing; and from the beginning of the sixteenth century onwards the appetite of the population generally had been thoroughly awakened. By degrees the trade performances, though they did not for some time disappear, dropped; and the monastic troops (if we may use the word) were cut off by the Dissolution; but the "children"—choristers of the great churches that survived the Reformation—and the "servants" of great houses remained. And yet, again, by degrees

The demand and the supply.

these "servants" formed themselves into regular companies, who, though they might retain for protection the name of some nobleman, were not really any longer members of his household, but gave themselves up entirely to satisfying the demand for plays. This demand had to be met on the producing side as well as the performing, and so came into being the profession of the dramatist, generally combined with other literary functions, but sometimes not so, and often including the vocation of actor, though sometimes also not.

Early plays by Gascoigne and others.

The most important name of the dramatists of the early part of Elizabeth's reign, next to that of Sackville, is that of George Gascoigne,[13] some notice of whose life and other work will be found below. His dramatic production includes two pieces, both translations or adaptations from the Italian, *The Supposes*—a prose comedy, the first of the kind in English, from Ariosto, and *Jocasta,* a tragedy Englished (with Francis Kinwelmershe) not from any of the classical plays of Laius' line, but from Lodovico Dolce's *Giocasta.* But many other persons known and unknown fell into the new way. The *Cambyses* of Thomas Preston, Fellow of King's College, Cambridge, and Master of Trinity, is said to be as old as *Gorboduc* itself. It is founded upon Herodotus, but is written partly in eights and sixes, partly in doggerel, has a Vice or purely comic character named Ambidexter, three comic ruffians, Ruff, Huff, and Snuff, and is altogether a curious compromise between an interlude and a regular play. The *Damon and Pythias* of Richard Edwards, acted three years later, and written by a Christ Church man, who was Master of the Children of the Queen's Chapel, is a more sober production in long doggerel, with hardly more than one comic episode or interlude, which turns on the favourite legendary character of Grim the Colher of Croydon. The short and curious *Appius and Virginia* by "R.B.," which has been thought to come between these, is not in doggerel but in regular fourteeners, or eights and sixes, rhymed sometimes in couplet, sometimes in quatrain; and the

13. Gascoigne's *Works,* ed. Hazlitt, London, 1868. Most of the others mentioned are in his *Dodsley,* vol. iv. *sqq.*

inevitable admixture of comedy, or rather horseplay, is unusually small. But the best piece of this kind and period is the *Tancred and Gismund* of Robert Wilmot, which was acted before the Queen in 1568, and republished in 1592. The blank verse of this (which was originally rhymed in quatrain), though much "stopped," is less wooden than that of *Gorboduc;* the fire of the original story in Boccaccio, which is so admirably revived in Dryden's version, is by no means absent; and the chief fault is the absence of any really dramatic action, and the alternation of the dialogue between tedious set speeches of enormous length and snip-snap stichomythia. But with these drawbacks *Tancred and Gismund* is the most poetical play before Peele and Lyly, if not before Marlowe. Of somewhat similar character, though nearly twenty years younger, and therefore belated in the dawn of the drama proper, is the odd *Misfortunes of Arthur,* performed at Greenwich Palace in 1587, and composed by a society of wits, among whom was no less a person than Francis Bacon, though the chief writing is said to have been due to Thomas Hughes. The verse of this—and indeed the tone generally—bears a strong relation to that of *Tuncred and Gismund.* It has a chorus in elaborate stanzas, dealing with the death of the King, as related by Geoffrey rather than Malory, but introduces Welsh names (such as Angharad), which must have been due to Hughes's reading in his native language, and is altogether, if not exactly a successful play, a respectable literary curiosity. The stately gloom which seems so natural to, or so well affected by, this period of the eve of greatness is, out of Sackville, nowhere better shown than here.

Disputes as to plays.

Yet we have pretty certain evidence that these plays, and others, printed and unprinted, still extant, are but a small part of the actual theatrical production of the first twenty or thirty years of Elizabeth's reign. The lists of names that survive prove this, and prove further that almost every kind of literature, sacred and profane, classical and romantic, historical and imaginative, was being dramatised. But the historical bickerings about the whole question of stage plays prove it almost better. Full fifteen years before the appearance of the first plays of the

University Wits in the early years of the eighth decade of the century, these bickerings appear. The Church had always suffered the theatre anything but gladly; and though the Puritans disagreed with the Church in almost all ways, here they went beyond her. The Corporation of London, like its analogues in most other towns, distinctly inclined to the ultra-Protestant party; and it was owing to the obstacles thrown by it in the way of stage-playing that the first regular theatres were, about 1576, built just beyond the City bounds, in the privileged district of Blackfriars, in Shoreditch, and elsewhere. And how strong the feeling ran both for and against plays at this time, from which we have no plays worth speaking of, is shown by the notable history of Stephen Gosson,[14] whose *School of Abuse*, an invective, partly delivered against poetry in general, but mainly against dramatic poetry, survives, though most of the literature which occasioned it is lost, who was himself a "University Wit" of a generation before Peele and Lyly, who succumbed to the fascination of the stage, wrote plays, acted in them, was converted from them by religious denunciations, dedicated his pamphlet, it may be presumed without permission, to Sir Philip Sidney, and thereby drew down on himself, though Sidney with characteristic courtesy does not name him in it, the famous *Apology for Poetrie* (*vide infra*, chap. iv).

Difficulties in their way.

Still, active as was the demand, plentiful in a way as was the supply, and high as feeling ran in regard to the theatre generally, the entire work of this long period—it must have been nearly forty years from *Ralph Roister Doister* to *Tamburlaine*—is surprisingly rudimentary. The drama, though divesting itself gradually of some of its extremer crudities, made remarkably little progress towards any really fresh, vigorous, and promising form. It is easy enough to see now that writers, even if they had possessed more genius than any of those of this date show, might naturally have been hampered and

14. The plays of Gosson (1555-1624), *Catiline's Conspiracies, Captain Mario*, and *Praise at Parting*, must have been written long enough before 1579, the date of the *School of Abuse*, to allow for his conversion, and probably just after he took his B.A. at Oxford in 1576.

bewildered. The mediaeval forms, of which the latest phase was the Interlude, were slowly but inevitably passing into discredit, and were indeed quite incapable of serving as vehicles to any "intricate impeach" of character-drawing, of romantic interest, or of plot.[15] The classical, or at least Senecan, model which was forcing itself upon all Europe was alien from the English spirit, and unable to give voice or shape to English conceptions of drama. And what is more than this, even if there had been a style of play to give, there was as yet no style of verse to give it in. The impossible doggerels, longer and shorter, were indeed, as well as the fourteener, giving way to blank decasyllables; but the right mould of these had not been found. The writers, bewildered at the absence of their usual guide-rope, rhyme, feared to drop into absolute prose if they did not pull the verse up short at the end of the line; there was moreover, owing perhaps to mistaken deduction from Chaucer's practice, perhaps to transferred classical teaching, the superstition about middle caesuras, that we find in Gascoigne, and long afterwards in Dr. Johnson. The Chaucerian tradition, though not fatal, was unfavourable to trisyllabic feet; and altogether the measure lacked the spring, the variety, the characteristics of oil and break by turns, which suit the dramatic wave.

15. More study than has yet been given is deserved by the curious productions entitled *Three Lords and Three Ladies of London*, etc., which were published in a group by Collier and included in Hazlitt's *Dodsley*. Their original dates are very uncertain; but they belong pretty clearly to the end of this present period; and in them we see the butterfly struggling to get out of the chrysalis in the oddest, but the most suggestive, manner.

2

PRELIMINARIES—PROSE

Elyot—The *Governour*—Cavendish—Leland—Cheke—Wilson—Ascham—His *Letters*—*Toxophilus*—The *Schoolmaster*—Their characteristics.

THE middle stage between that older literature which continues till a period well, but not very far, within the sixteenth century, and Elizabethan literature proper, is at least as clearly marked in prose as in verse or drama, and it contains matter of perhaps greater intrinsic interest than is the case with drama at least. We have seen how with Fisher English prose reached, and perhaps for the first time, the state of deliberate and conscious practice of the devices of style, and how yet farther advance, conditioned in the most momentous manner by the nature of their occupation, appears in the work of the early Tudor translators of the Bible.

Contemporary with these latters were some other writers who have obtained a place, from which it is not necessary to oust them, in the history of English literature—Sir Thomas Elyot, Leland, Cavendish, perhaps a few more.

Elyot.

The attraction of the first is indeed rather one of matter than one of manner, and it might be difficult to give any reason except the fact that it has been twice reprinted in the nineteenth century[1] for the position held by *The Boke named the Governour,* still more difficult to account for the reprinting itself. Sir Thomas Elyot, who was born before 1490, was the

1. In 1854 by Mr. A.T. Eliot, and in 1883 by Mr. H.H.S. Croft (2 vols., London). The latter is the edition used.

son of a judge, and though not a member of the famous Cornish family of his name, appears to have been a West Countryman, his forebears having been connected with the district round Yeovil. He must have been well educated, but does not seem to have gone to either University, and though a student of medicine, is said not to have been a practitioner thereof. He came early into the possession of a good estate near Woodstock, and settled there; but was made by Wolsey in 1523 Clerk of the Council—an office which seems to have metaphysical connection with literature. He published the *Governour* in 1531, and seems to have been recommended by it to diplomatic employments, in which he spent the rest of his life. He died in 1546, having four years previously been elected M.P. for Cambridge.

He wrote a medical work called the *Castle of Health,* a Latin Dictionary, some dialogues, and other things; but his fame, such as it is, rests on the *Governour.* This is one, and in England one of the first, of those curious treatises, partly of politics, partly of education, which the study of the classics, and more particularly of Plato, multiplied at the Renaissance in all countries, and not least in our own. Ascham, Lyly, Mulcaster, and many others take up from their different points of view, more and less scholastic, the theme which Elyot set them the example of handling. Incidentally the book is remarkable, because it contains the earliest version yet traced of the famous, but too probably apocryphal, story of Chief-Justice Gascoigne and Henry V when Prince of Wales—a pious invention very likely to flatter the powers that were. In the history of prose style Elyot is commendable rather than distinguished; free from obvious and glaring defects rather than possessed of distinct merits. He is rather too much given to long sentences; he has little or nothing of Fisher's rhetorical devices, and while the romantic grace of his not much older contemporary Berners is far from him, so also is the deliberate classical plainness of his not very much younger contemporary Ascham. He is principally valuable as an example of the kind of prose which a cultivated man of ordinary gifts would be likely to write before the definite attempts of Ascham and his school.

The *Governour.*

George Cavendish, of the Suffolk Cavendishes, gentleman-usher to Wolsey, and the Cardinal's biographer, does the same service in showing the style of a contemporary less cultivated, but perhaps of greater natural powers, than Elyot, and not possessed of the special literary gift of Berners. We might almost call Cavendish a prose Berners—and his account of the greatness, decline, and fall of the Cardinal has something of Berners's charm.

Cavendish.

On yet another hand, John Leland continues for us the useful, and at this time really important, function of the "literary hodmen," as they have been contemptuously and ungratefully termed. He was a Londoner, born about 1500; and after being thoroughly educated at St. Paul's School and at both Universities (Christ's College in the one, All Souls in the other), he travelled for a long time on the Continent and assimilated all the learning of the day. This was the time, 1533, when Henry VIII's Renaissance fancy for learning had not been checked or stunted by 1515, of a fair stock. He entered St. John's College, Cambridge, in 1530, and learnt Greek from his scarce elder Cheke, becoming Fellow of his college early, and before very long University Reader in Greek and Public Orator. He dedicated *Toxophilus,* in 1545, to Henry VIII, and under Edward became tutor to the Princess Elizabeth, and Secretary of an Embassy to Germany. Nobody quite knows how, without any overt recantation, he not only remained unmolested under Mary, but was actually made her secretary; while he was also favoured by his old pupil after her accession. His second chief work, the *Schoolmaster,* was written late, and not published till after his death in 1568. Even this brief story shows that he must either have had extraordinary luck, or have been not entirely destitute of the "willow" character which infected almost all public men in Tudor days. There are also indications in his very pleasant *Letters* that he was by no means free from the rather shameless tendency to beg which was common to all but a very few scholars throughout the Renaissance. But these epidemic, or rather endemic, vices of the time excepted, Ascham appears to have been a very agreeable specimen of a

Leland.

Ascham.

good type of Englishman: humorous, except for a touch of Puritan prudery in regard to art and literature; learned, and much more ready to teach others than to pride himself upon his learning; affectionate to his friends and family; zealous for his country and his country's language. The famous phrase in the *Toxophilus* about "writing this English matter in the English speech for Englishmen," is no mere figure of rhetoric or bit of jingle, but a sentence to which the author adheres as far as possible throughout his work, all the really important constituents of, which, the *Toxophilus,* the *Schoolmaster,* and the *Letters,* have already been named.

His *Letters.*

Each of the three has its separate interest in the history of English prose, and the three together give their author a very important place in that history. The *Letters,* as is natural, rank lowest, yet very far from low. In the first place, when we compare them with the Paston collection,[2] the only really considerable body of English epistolary correspondence earlier, we find—not merely or mainly as a consequence of the fact that we are dealing with a professed scholar instead of with a family group of men and women of the upper rank indeed, and of fair education, but of no special bent towards literature—a very distinct advance in command over the language for miscellaneous purposes. But we also find something more. At first the letters, even the familiar letters, even those to ladies and close personal friends, are written in Latin—the language which, as Ascham elsewhere candidly confesses, and as we can well understand from the general practice of the Renaissance, came much easier to him to write than English. But by degrees this changes. The same deliberate purpose which led him to write the *Toxophilus* in the mother tongue, assisted beyond all doubt by the same general unconscious "atmospheric" influence which was not

2. This famous and interesting series, first published by Sir John Fenn a century ago, and definitively edited in three vols. by Mr. Gairdner, has in literature rather less importance than it possesses in political and social history. In fact it may be said to lack the one kind exactly because it possesses the other, consisting of simple straightforward communications of fact and business from entirely unliterary persons.

peculiar to him, induces him by degrees to put his work, even of the most informal kind, in English, to write news of his German tour to his Cambridge friends in that language. He shows, in short, a sense of the fact—so slowly borne in upon English men of letters, even so much later and greater as Bacon and Hobbes—that English was not a mere makeshift, a mere engine of condescendence to children and grooms, but a vehicle of literature, not, indeed, perhaps quite so perfect (no man *circa* 1550 could be expected to admit that) as Latin or Greek, but capable of being immensely improved, and deserving of the pains necessary to improve it. But Ascham's chosen means of improvement, his aims, his ideal of English style naturally appear best in his more formal and ambitious treatises. It is very lucky that there is so long an interval between the composition of these, and that their subjects are so different. *Toxophilus* is the work of a man of thirty, devoted to what was at once his own favourite recreation, and still one of the mainstays of the national greatness. Of course there is a good deal in it which is very remotely connected with archery. The author would not have been a humanist, or even a human being, if he had not aired a good deal of his acquaintance with the new-found and certainly not too much prized Plato, if he had not allowed large scope to the passion for education which characterised all his literary generation, and himself very particularly. There are many more tolerable gaps in English literature than the loss of that *Book of the Cockpit*, with which, much later in life, he intended to accompany it. But even by itself *Toxophilus* gives us a happy picture of that blending of instruction with pastime, which, by one of the greatest of the many pieces of good luck which have distinguished English history, occupied the minds and ideas of the men who superintended the transition from monastic to lay studies in England, and carried out the views of Walter of Merton, and the two Williams of Wykeham and Wainfleet, in succeeding centuries, with a fortunate development.

Toxophilus.

The *Schoolmaster* is naturally more serious, yet not too serious. Something of the old largeness appears in the first book, dealing as it does generally with the bringing-up of youth; nor does this disappear by any means wholly in the second, with its preciser subject. On the ready way to the Latin tongue Ascham may go wrong; he does so go often, as in his polemic against romance, his fatal patronage of the pestilent heresy of imitating Greek and Latin prosody, not merely in feet but in metres, and other things. But in general he is an early and an eloquent defender and apostle of the true English education, in classics and in the vernacular for book-learning, in body-culture and healthy pastime as well as in book-learning itself.

The *School-master.*

And one at least of the errors just noticed was only a corruption of the best and central principle of his work in prose—the borrowing of all possible assistance from the classical tongues in the formation of a good English style. In doing this he stops rigidly short of classicising the vocabulary. Cheke does not dislike a mere Latinism, or Wilson an "ink-horn" term, more than Ascham does. Like both, and even more than both, he hates the modern foreign languages, and seems to be actuated by a positive and almost personal jealousy—not entirely groundless, when we remember how great the influence of French had been, how great that of Spanish and Italian was, and was to be, both in verse and prose—of their colouring and guiding. He retains, and even a little abuses, the specially English device of alliteration; and has a fancy which sometimes almost approaches the puerile, for arranging his sentences in strings or piles of half-parallel, half-antithetic clauses, after a fashion which we also find far back in the Middle English period. Indeed, some have even argued for a kind of "Euphuism before *Euphues*" in Ascham himself; and some seeds of it are no doubt, and necessarily, to be found in him. But, on the whole, his ideal of an English clause, an English sentence, an English paragraph is struck out on classical models—clear, not too long, but, on the other hand, not broken up into snip-snap, with no special rhetorical figure very apparent, and with the old poetical cadence and colouring carefully avoided, but sometimes fairly balanced, arranged not seldom with a weighty, yet lucid, sententiousness, and not very seldom rising with

Their characteristics.

some cunning to a climax which permits the rounding off of the paragraph with real rhetorical effect. Ascham's is, in short, the first accomplished plain style in English—the first, that is to say, that, while deliberately aiming at a certain amount of rhetorical effect, rigidly eschews the production of that effect by any such means as elaborate, highly-coloured, or quaint vocabulary, by unusual and invented tricks of arrangement, or by anything that can come under the phrases (often loosely used, but intelligible) of ornate, poetical, or impassioned prose.

The classical turn communicated to English prose by this knot of scholars more particularly, and encouraged by others from both Universities, was yet further promoted by the continuing habit of translating from the classics, and from modern writers in Latin. The authors of these translations, except in a few cases, mostly later than the present time, such as those of North and Florio (which had great direct influence on English prose, and were themselves notable examples of it) hardly fall to be noticed here. But the influence of their practice is unmistakable. The great innovation of Euphuism (*vide infra,* chap. vi) was rather an unconscious than a deliberate revolt against it; the carrying out of the system produced in Hooker perhaps the most accomplished writer of strict prose (as distinguished from the half-poetical vehicle of Malory and Berners) that appeared in English up to the end of the sixteenth century; and even the great authors of the first half of the seventeenth were deeply influenced by the tradition of classicising.[3]

3. To this period belong the later Tudor chroniclers, the chief of whom is Holinshed (1525-1578), a Cheshire man, it is said, by birth, and a Cambridge man by education, certainly one of those printer's hacks, or gentlemen of the press, to whom literature has owed something. Holinshed's close connection with the matter of Shakespeare, the divulgation of large passages of him by Shakespeare's commentators, and perhaps the fact that his Christian name was Raphael, have conciliated to him an almost disproportionate amount of esteem. But though he has no extraordinarily literary qualities, the "race" and the archaic fashions of his manner are irresistibly pleasant to us.

3

PRELIMINARIES—VERSE

The state of poetry *c.* 1530—Good effect of Italian—Wyatt's life—Surrey's—Wyatt's forms and subjects—Those of Surrey—The main characteristics of the pair—Wyatt's rhyme and rhythm—Surrey's metrical advance—*Tottel's Miscellany*—Other miscellanies—Verse translations—Churchyard—Whetstone—Tusser—Turberville—Googe—Gascoigne—His *Instructions*—His poems—The *Mirror for Magistrates*—Sackville's part in it.

THE same character of transition and introduction which appears in the prose and the drama of the latest years of Henry VIII, of the short reigns of his son and elder daughter, and of at least the first half of the long one of his younger, appears likewise in the department of poetry proper. Nay, it is perhaps even more remarkable there, for reasons easily obvious to any one who has read the preceding Books and chapters with care. Up to 1580, at or about which year the History of Elizabethan Literature, in the great sense, begins, drama was, and had been from its very origin, merely though steadily in the making; it had never reached any form that could be called artistically complete. Prose, with some examples far more absolutely excellent than any that drama could show, and with a much quicker and steadier progress, was in the making too; and had never reached perfection, save in partial and peculiar instances and forms. But poetry had, as we have seen, gone through curious successions of *maxima* and *minima.* After it had assimilated the great blend of language and prosody fashioned during the earlier part of the Middle English period, it produced in Chaucer a poet of the first class, who stood in

The state of poetry c. 1530.

a sense, though not in all senses, practically alone. It made a curious relapse from metrical upon alliterative prosody, and had produced good work in that. It had seen the singular outburst of Scottish Chaucerian poetry. It had provided a sort of underground growth of ballad. But in England itself it had, after Chaucer, fallen off, as far as the production of literary poetry of great merit went, in a manner which has still rather to be accepted than accounted for; and the inability of the poets to sing had driven them to endless and strange varieties of squeak and drone.

Good effect of Italian.

However Ascham and his fellows might dislike and dread and denounce Italian influence, there is no doubt that the way of safety was first opened to English poetry in these its straits by Italy. The sonnet—not alone, but chiefly—was the means of inducing English poets to gird up their loins, to settle the poetical accentuation of their language, to discard doggerel for regular metre, to arrange a poetic diction which should be neither stiff with the "aureate" verbiage of the rhetoricians, nor clownish with the vernacular of the doggerellists. Perhaps mere accident, perhaps the political and ecclesiastical stress of the years between the Reformation and the accession of Elizabeth, may account for the interval which elapsed between the composition and the publication of the chief documents exhibiting this new influence. But there is no explanation, except a purely fatalist one, for the fact that fully twenty years more elapsed between the actual publication and the following of the example to any good effect.

Wyatt's life.

If there has ever been any mistake about the order of the two poets who heralded modern English poetry, it must have been a very strange one, the dates and facts about Sir Thomas Wyatt's Henry Howard, by courtesy, Earl of Surrey, being altogether, too clear and (despite their occasional uncertainty) too relatively certain to excuse the slightest confusion. Both were shortlived; and so it happened, not merely that Wyatt was considerably the elder, but that he died when Surrey was still quite a young man. The father of Wyatt, Sir Henry, was a person of distinction in Kent (sometimes called a baronet, though of course not in the modern sense of the word), and the poet was born at Allington Castle in that county, in the year 1503.

He was sent to St. John's College, Cambridge, at the preposterously early age which was one of the crotchets of the Renaissance, entering at twelve, taking his Bachelor's degree at fifteen, and his Master's at seventeen. He seems to have married very early too, was a gentleman of the King's bedchamber, a friend of Anne Boleyn, and knighted in 1537. He had his share of the imprisonments which were the lot of Henry's courtiers, and perhaps, if he had lived, might have shared Surrey's fate. But he did a good deal of diplomatic work as ambassador in Spain and in the Netherlands, and died, being undoubtedly removed from the evil to come, in 1542, on his way to Falmouth, where he had a mission to meet the Spanish Ambassador and convoy him to London.

Surrey's birth-date is not known, but it is guessed at 1517 or 1518, probably in the spring of the latter year. He was grandson of the victor of Flodden, and his mother Surrey's. was Lady Elizabeth Stafford, daughter of that Duke of Buckingham who fell a victim to Wolsey's jealousy. He was thus of almost the noblest blood in England, and at fourteen he was nominally wedded to Lady Frances de Vere, of a strain nobler still. They came together in 1535, Surrey meanwhile having boon a sort of companion to the King's illegitimate son, the Duke of Richmond. He seems to have been rather a lively youth and young man, and got into frequent minor difficulties with the law. But nothing at all serious is brought against him; and his lamentable fate when he was barely thirty was due simply to the delirium of jealousy and bloodthirstiness which came upon Henry in his last days, and which, if he had lived a little longer, would have finished the English nobility. A ridiculous charge of high treason was brought against Surrey, and supported by more ridiculous charges of quartering the royal arms. He was condemned and beheaded in January 1547, nine days before Henry himself went to his own place.

There is no certainty at all as to the order of the work either of Wyatt or of Surrey, though certain poems of both date themselves fairly by reference to known events. This matters the less, however, in the case of men whose lives, as has been seen, were short, who represent very clearly results of the same influences, and who, as not merely from probability, but from Surrey's lines on Wyatt's death, we know, stood to each other half in the relation of master and pupil, half in that of fellow-pupils in the same foreign and chiefly Italian school. It will be well first to give a brief account of the actual work of each, and then to make some remarks on their common or peculiar characteristics.

Wyatt's forms and subjects.

It is not for nothing that a sonnet stands in the forefront of the collection—haphazard as that collection, no doubt, is—of Wyatt's poems. For, various and remarkable as are the Points of novelty in the work of the pair, the introduction and practice of the sonnet forms perhaps the most remarkable of these. And for some time the sonnets (with characteristics to be noted presently) continue—to give way at last to other (almost entirely love) poems in rhyme-royal, in octosyllabic couplets and quatrains, in a shortened rhyme-royal with an octosyllabic instead of a decasyllabic base, and in some fanciful stanzas, the base of which, following Skelton, though in more orderly fashion, goes as low as six syllables. A five-line stanza of heroics appears, and also eights and sixes, which may have been originally intended either for that form or as fourteeners with middle rhyme. Moreover, there appears also a curious form, which was very much favoured by all the poets of the mid sixteenth century, though the objections to it are great, the alternate Alexandrine and fourteener rhymed in couplets. There are also rondeaux and other lyrical forms, though few and cautiously attempted; and last of all we find certain epistles of a satirical kind and certain translations of the Psalms, couched in heroic quatrains arranged with curiously interlaced rhymes, as well as sometimes in definite *terza* and *ottava rima.*

The forms and contents of Surrey's poems, with one notable exception, are not very different from those of his master—sonnet, quatrains, interlaced heroic-couplets, the jog-trot fourteener and Alexandrine, in which he even translates Ecclesiastes and the Psalms. The subject is mostly love, and satire is absent. But the added item, which is of the very first importance, is a translation of the second *Aeneid* in blank verse, of which there are no known earlier examples in English, though, as has been noted in its place, there are signs of something like it in Chaucer's prose *Tale of Melibee.* We can only guess how the idea came to Surrey or to some other unknown person, if (which there is no reason to suppose) he borrowed it. Although there is no blank verse in French up to this date (or indeed, except as a curiosity, since), rhymeless verses were attempted a little earlier than Surrey's date in Italian. It is, of course, very likely that these gave Surrey, as they gave the Spaniards, the hint; but it is not quite impossible that this hint was not needed. It was a common and natural effect of the worship of the classics to look down on rhyme as a barbarous thing; and it was not a very extraordinary audacity for a man, translating what was then thought the chief poetic achievement of antiquity, to resolve to imitate Virgil directly in not using this savage gaud. Nor, when alliteration had long been borrowing rhyme and stanza from metre, would it be unnatural for metre to borrow rhymelessness from alliteration. Nor is it absolutely impossible that Surrey would have gone the entire length of the next generation and have attempted not merely unrhymed English verse, but unrhymed English hexameters, if the language had been sufficiently under his command. It was lucky that it was not; for though it is impossible, as every fresh attempt shows, that the hexameter can ever rank in English as anything but a rather awkward *tour de force,* we might have had some trouble in getting rid of it, whereas in blank verse decasyllables Surrey at once endowed the language with its most natural, though latest won, and for certain purposes most effective, variety of verse.

Those of Surrey.

"If the language had been more under his command," it has been said; and the words will aptly introduce one of the two chief points for notice in the poetry of Wyatt and Surrey. It has been repeatedly indicated in the last Book that either one cause or one concomitant of the weakness of fifteenth-century poetry in the pair. England was that the poets more and more lost this control of language. The reasons are not positively known, and cannot be dogmatically laid down; they have little or nothing to do with individual genius, though it certainly would appear that Chaucer's English is in a state of premature and forced perfection to which his successors could not attain, and which, before any fit heir appeared, had become archaic. It would appear likewise that the completion of the constitution of English proper, the final severance from the Continent, and the changes of which the disappearance of the final uttered *e* is the most remarkable, had brought about, or had at least been followed by, some not clearly intelligible change in the whole tonality and vocalisation of the tongue. The new pronounced English was not adjustable to Chaucerian prosody, and it did not find what it wanted in alliterative verse. The results were that extraordinary stumbling and plunging, that driving of the chariot as if with locked wheels, which we have noted in Lydgate, in Occleve, and even in Hawes, and from which Skelton only escaped (when he did escape) by a series of clumsy gambades in doggerel. Yet this doggerel did good by teaching the language at least to move with some flexibility, if with little elegance, and now came Wyatt and Surrey with the severe *manege* of the sonnet and the rest to get it into something like graceful movement in regular form.

The main characteristics of the pair.

What hard work they had to do, and to what extent they were still beaten by the antinomianism of the language in its state of flux, will best be shown by printing and rhythm Wyatt s first sonnet (which is by no means a specially terrible example), with foot- divisions and a few quantifying accents:

Wyatt's rhyme and rhythm.

The long | love that | in my | thought I | harber
And in | my heart | doth keep | his re | sidence,
Into | my face | presseth | with bold | pretence,
And there | campéth | display | ing his | bannér:

She that | me learns | to love | and to | suffér,
And wills | that my | trust and | lust's[1] neg | ligence
Be rein | ed by rea | son, shame, | and rev | erence,
With his | hardi | ness tak | és dis | pleasùre,
Wherewith | love to | the hart's[1] fo | rest he | fleéth,
Leaving | his en | terprise | with pain | and cry,
And there | him hi | deth and | not áp | peareth. |
What may | I do ? | when my | master | fearéth,
But in | the field | with him | to live | and die,
For good | is the | life | end | ing faithfully.

There are several things to lie observed in this—the way in which the advantage, if not necessity, of a final couplet forced itself on these very earliest practitioners of the English sonnet, the remnant of the allegorical personification of the fifteenth century, and others. But the chief of all is the nervousness and uncertainty of the quantification and rhyme. We have already left the sheer verse-prose of Lydgate and Occleve at their worst, as well as the mere doggerel of Skelton at his best. But the poet still hobbles, at times painfully. In one line, as we see above, he is driven to make "takes" a disyllable, and to put an entirely non-natural quantification upon "hardiness," and "displeasure," which should simply change places in a nonsense verse. More surprising perhaps—for this liberty of stress is frequent in Chaucer, and continues to Spenser and even to Shakespeare—is the mistiness which seems to beset him in the matter of rhyme. It is clear that the first, third, and fourth rhymes of the sestet are on the *eth* only, yet he cannot resist the double rhyme "feareth" and "appeareth," though it not merely conflicts with the single rhyme of "fleeth," but itself introduces a quite false rhythm into the lines, making them in effect feminine-rhymed nine-syllable lines, and not decasyllabics at all.

But these stumbles were inevitable in picking the way up the steep and stony path from the abysses to which English poetry had descended, and the very stumbles themselves are

1. Printed in Tottel "luste's" and "harte's," but I do not think any metrical value was meant to be given to the *e*.

gain, inasmuch as they warn the stumbler to pick his way more carefully next time. Wyatt has the plain, straight (and also strait) ways of the sonnet and his other forms to guide him; he has the enormous advantage of fresh models, different from the thousand-times-borrowed ones of a century and more past; and above all, he has the gift of poetic phrase, which we meet again in him after many days.

Into a bitter fashion of forsaking

is perhaps better than any single line in southern English since Chaucer; and when we meet with such single spies we know that they will come in battalions soon.

Surrey's metrical advance.

Wyatt found an apt pupil in Surrey, and there is, in fact, more progress between these two almost contemporary writers than we find after them in the more than thirty years between Surrey's death and the *Shepherd's Calendar*. Henry Surreys Howard perceived the absolute necessity of advance accepting a certain rhythmical standard for a word, and not varying its values and balance entirely at the pleasure, or rather the need, of the poet. There is even in him a rudimentary discovery, or rediscovery, of a matter of still greater importance, the power which an English poet possesses of varying the harmony and composition of his line by shifting the place of the pause. Neither he nor Wyatt, indeed, has arrived at the final secret, the license of trisyllabic substitution; the most they can do in this way is a clumsy elision of the vowel in article and preposition. But it was just as well that too many liberties should not be taken at once, and that the decasyllable as such should be reformed into melody before it was expanded by license into an hendecasyllable, a dodecasyllable, or even more. For the temptations of doggerel were still about, and were only too much indulged in the eights and sixes and in the "poulter's measure,"[2] the compound of Alexandrine and fourteener just noticed. If any one had at this time indulged himself in the

2. Said to be (cf. our "baker's dozen") so-called from the habit of poulterers giving twelve eggs to one customer and fourteen to another, according to fear or favour; see Gascoigne (p. 39, ed. Arber), who seems to have invented the name.

license of the dramatic or Tennysonian tribrachs, the result must pretty certainly have been chaos, and the language would never have had its period of discipline at all. As it was, there is reason still to marvel at the change which—no doubt half, if not all, unconsciously—these two "persons of quality"—one a busy diplomatist, the other a careless man, or rather youth, of pleasure—achieved. It may be that neither Wyatt nor Surrey has left any perfect poem, that nothing of either's is as sheer poetry equal to the best work of Sackville; but their gain in form is almost incalculable.

Tollel's Miscellany.

The circumstances of the publication of the poems of the two were peculiar. It had become the habit of printers and working men of letters to make and issue, with or without permission, "miscellanies" of poetical pieces, *Tottel's* sometimes attributed to their authors, *Miscellany* sometimes not, and sometimes again (as was sure to happen) attributed wrongly. In the middle of the seventeenth century especially this joint custom of MS. collection and miscellany publication led to a great deal of confusion. To this day some of the most famous pieces of English verse— Jonson's "Sidney's Sister," Bishop King's "Like to the falling of a Star," and others—are in a state of contested, if not exactly dubious, title between two or more claimants, while in the same or other cases the genuine text is very much a matter of guesswork. The publication of the chief works of Surrey and Wyatt with pieces by other persons of distinction at Henry VHI's court—the unlucky Lord Rochford, Lord Vaux, Wyatt's friend Sir Francis Bryan, and others—was due to the printer Richard Tottel, and to a Huntingdonshire scholar, Nicholas Grimald, who has been thought to be an Italian and a Grimaldi. This is by no means necessary, for different forms of the name, ranging from Grimoald to Grimwald, are found in different countries and tongues during the Middle Ages. Grimald, who was a member of both Universities, lecturer at Christ Church, chaplain to Ridley, etc., was born in 1519, and was therefore very little younger than Surrey, whom, as well as other authors of the famous

Tottel's Miscellany, he may have known. But the book itself[3] did not appear till 1557, eleven years after Surrey's death and fifteen after Wyatt's. The editor contributed (at least in the first edition, for he left most of them out in the second) no small number of pieces of his own, and there was in both a considerable contingent from "uncertain authors." Few of the uncertainties, or of the works of the minor lights mentioned above, are of great value; and Grimald himself generally writes stuff which is only distinguished from the average work of the previous generation by being invariably serious in form, and by showing a metrical regularity which, if only singsong and uninspired, is at any rate strictly observed. This is what is meant by the printer's apology for "the stateliness of style removed from the rude skill of common ears"—for "style" was then generally, and here clearly, used as including "metre," and the context plainly shows that the contrast Tottel was thinking of was with doggerel and ballad measures. And he was quite right. It is true that for a very long time Wyatt and Surrey have held their proper place in general literary history and criticism; but there have been occasional attempts, if not exactly to degrade them from it, to glance at them as mere reformers of form. The retort is, of course, quite obvious, and entirely fatal to the sneer. It was reform of form that was wanted, for the simple reason that for a century and a half form of any meritorious kind had practically ceased to exist. At first the "stateliness of style" may have been all too near to stiffness, and no one with absolute inspiration may have been ready to take the prepared instrument. But the instrument was at last prepared.

The poetical work of the period, before the appearance of the *Shepherd's Calendar* and after *Tottel's Miscellany,* divides itself naturally under three heads: 1. Subsequent miscellanies; 2. Individual poets or translators of minor rank; 3. Sackville. An extreme purist might urge that the three, or at any rate the first and the third, are one. For Sackville's poetical work, which stands in such startling contrast to the wooden verse of *Gorboduc,* appeared in what was practically a miscellany, the *Mirror for Magistrates.* But it will be better and clearer to

3. Ed. Arber.

divide the subject in the order above named, and not to mention the *Mirror* till we come to Sackville himself. The two first heads will not delay us long.

It is somewhat curious that *Tottel's Miscellany,* the popularity of which we know from the rapidity with which the second edition followed the first (itself reprinted in six weeks or so), with fresh issues in 1559, 1565, and 1574, as well as others later, and from the imitations of it, waited some time for these imitations. Few things indeed are more significant than the long "waits" between the writing and the publication of the poems contained in it, and the still longer ones before any dared to emulate it, when we contrast them with the rush and huddle of new and ever new poetry in the last half of the Queen's reign.

Other miscellanies.

The first actual successor[4] was published nearly twenty years after Tottel, in 1576, and its name, *The Paradise of Dainty Devices,* followed as it was by others, showed the influence of Euphuism, the period of Lyly, as compared with the sober *Songs and Sonnets* of the earlier book when Ascham had represented English prose. It was the work of a man then dead, the dramatist and musician Richard Edwards. It contains a mixture of work of the former and the then present generation, Lord Vaux figuring beside Lord Oxford, the courtier of the old King's time by the courtier of the still fairly young Queen. Kinwelmersh, Hunnis, and other respectable men of letters of Elizabeth's day also make show, and there is one piece the initials of which (not given in the first edition) may be Walter Raleigh's. The book, though very popular (it was reprinted once a year for three years, and repeatedly afterwards), was not much of

4. All the more important of these miscellanies up to the Queen's death were reprinted together by Collier in 1867; but the issue was private and very small, and the book hardly ever occurs in catalogues. Mr. Arber, besides *Tottel,* has given (in his "English Scholar's Library") Robinson's *Handful of Delights;* Mr. Bullen *England's Helicon,* and Davison's *Poetical Rhapsody.* Park's *Heliconia* (3 vols., 1815) contains, besides the *Handful,* the *Gorgeous Gallery,* the *Phoenix Nest,* and the large and interesting anthology, rather than miscellany, of *England's Parnassus.*

a *Paradise,* nor its devices very dainty. But they were, as their pretty if affected title might seem to warrant, better than those of the absurdly named and dully filled *Gorgeous Gallery of Gallant Inventions* which followed two years later, and seems to have been collected and partly written by Owen Roydon and T.P. (Thomas Proctor). The mania for alliteration which beset the writers of this time so strongly was particularly strong in T.P., who, outdoing even Churchyard (*vide infra),* distinguished himself by printing a production proclaimed to be "Pretty Pamphlets by Proctor." The willow song—

Willow, willow, willow, sing all of green willow—

appears here. *England's Helicon* and the *Poetical Rhapsody* are infinitely better, but they come after Spenser.

Verse translations.

Next to the miscellanies, the verse translations make a great figure in the poetical production of this time, though again it cannot be said that they attain to high poetical merit. In any case, no doubt, the popularity of the translations classics would have brought them about; but the action of Surrey, whose authority was so great in other ways, made them certain. The translators,[5] however, were by no means bold enough to follow his example of blank verse as a matter of course. They preferred as a rule the too often clumsy fourteener, which, just as it was much later going out of fashion, gave us the splendid Homeric paraphrase of Chapman. There was little splendour about the earlier examples, but the first of them had great influence in other ways, being a version of Seneca's *Troades* by Jasper Heywood, son of John, Fellow first of Merton and then of All Souls, and in Elizabeth's time a Jesuit. This play was issued as early as 1559, two years only after *Tottel's Miscellany,* and by the same printer. He followed it up with two others, the *Thyestes* and *Hercules Furens,* and the example being caught

5. They have not had quite their share of the otherwise indiscriminate devotion of reprinters, Stanyhurst's rather later and extremely mad *Aeneid* having almost alone the honour to be recently given (in Mr. Arber's "English Scholar's Library." Golding's *Ovid* has a stately reprint). The translators of Seneca besides Heywood were Neville, Studley, Nuce, and Newton.

at, the whole ten Senecan plays were issued together in 1581. Rhyme-royal, the quatrain, and other stanzas are used for the chorus; but the ambling fourteener serves as the staple.

This was also the metre of Phaer's *Virgil,* which appeared, as far as the first seven books went, the year after Tottel, and was finished partly by the author, partly after his death in 1560 by another hand. Phaer was a Pembrokeshire man, a member of the University of Oxford, a lawyer, and a doctor. There is merit in his version (which shows a consciousness of trisyllabic substitution and its advantages), as there is also in the companion *Ovid* of Arthur Golding, a man of property and good connections, who was born about the middle of the fifth decade of the century, and lived till its close. He did prose as well as verse translations; but the *Metamorphoses* was his chief book, and this appeared in 1567, again in fourteeners. The verse translators cannot indeed boast, as the prose can, that they had a distinct and important influence on the development of style in their own sphere, but the two helped in the practice, the exercise, which was the business and the benefit of this particular time.

The individual authors of the period other than Sackville partake of that character of curiosity which distinguishes the whole of it, and which repels some tastes as much as it conciliates others. The chief names are Churchyard, Whetstone, Tusser, Turberville, Googe, and, above all, George Gascoigne, the type, and at the same time the most eminent, of the whole. It is almost enough to say, on the one hand, that to no single one of the six is ascribed even the smallest piece of verse which has made its way into the memory of the general. On the other hand, all have importance to the historian, and Gascoigne is, as has been said, very decidedly the typical man of letters of the first half of the great Queen's reign.

Churchyard.

Thomas Churchyard, first born and last to die of all the group, was a Shropshire man, born at Shrewsbury about 1520, and so not much younger than Surrey, a juxtaposition which makes all the more striking the fact that he did not die till the first year of James I. It would appear that he took the portion of goods that belonged to him and went to court early enough to become "servant" to Surrey, in those conditions of honourable and gentle service and education which flourished for some time to come. The connection was continued long after his chiefs death by his contributions to *Tottel's Miscellany.* But long before the appearance of that book Churchyard had seen other and hotter service in the Netherlands (1542) and Scotland (1545), had been taken prisoner in a second Scotch campaign (1548), had travelled, had served in Ireland (1550), in Lorraine, in the Netherlands again, at Calais, or at least Guines, just at the period of its loss. He had begun a long series of mostly petty individual contributions to literature when he was about thirty; but his historical importance begins with his contribution to Tottel in 1557, and to the *Mirror for Magistrates* (see below) in 1558-59. After several more years of fighting and writing he collected his work, or some of it, under the alliterative and exact title of *Churchyard's Chips,* modestly accounting in prose for the selection of the same. Fighting he continued till the siege of Zutphen in 1572, just thirty years after he had first taken arms; writing he never left off till the close of his long life, the later part of which was spent in court service. So late as 1604 his *Good Will,* a poem on the death of Archbishop Whitgift, preserved, in a manner which must have seemed odd enough to the hearers of Donne and the survivors of Spenser, the lolloping verse, the curious antithetic alliteration, the wooden scheme of the poets of this later transition. Churchyard has been affectionately taken up, more than once, by men of letters as a curiosity; and it must be admitted that worse writers than he have had the honour of complete editions, which he has lacked.[6]

In George Whetstone, whose date of birth and death are both unknown, we have another example of the type so common at this time, and of the characteristics of alliteration, of a sort of survival of allegory, and of a kind of composition which,

6. *Heliconia* contains some things of his—including the Whitgift piece, and Collier reprinted (in a very few copies) the *Chips.* But this is little for a man whose bibliography fills nearly ten columns in Hazlitt's *Handbook.*

though advanced beyond the mere rudiments, is still stiff and wooden. The earliest dated thing that we have of his is the *Rock of Regard,* 1576, a miscellany mostly in whetstone verse; the latest is supposed to date from 1587, and is a pamphlet on the execution of Queen Mary "and other notable traitors." The only things of Whetstone's at all generally known are his play of *Promos and Cassandra* (a dull thing, but in *Dodsley)* and his *Remembrance* of George Gascoigne, which has commonly,[7] though not always, accompanied reprints of that poet. He was rather fond of these poetical obituaries or remembrances,[8] of which about half a dozen are known; and lie also wrote prose tales, chiefly collected in a *Heptameron* (the title, of course, suggested by Margaret of Navarre) *of Civill Dyscourses.* These prose tales, indeed, which played so important a part in the furnishing of subjects to the dramatists, were almost as much a feature of the time as the poetical miscellanies and verse translations. The largest and best known is William Painter's *Palace of Pleasure* (alliterative again), which appeared in 1566-67.[9]

Tusser.

Of the two T's, Tusser and Turberville, the former is not a poet at all, but a verse-curiosity. He is our only, or almost our only, English Georgic poet, and his poetry frankly acquiesces in doggerel. His life, which seems to have dated from about 1515 to 1580, began in Essex, was passed at St. Paul's and Eton (where Udall, as previously observed, beat him much), at Cambridge, at court, and lastly on a farm in Sussex, where he cultivated and rhymed. His *Five Hundred Points of Good Husbandry*[10] published in 1573, consists of quatrains in rolling anapaestic tetrameters besides interludes and oddments in other metres.

7. As, for instance, in Chalmers's *Poets,* vol. ii, and in Mr. Arber's Reprint of the *Steel Glass.*
8. *Heliconia,* vol. ii contains one on the Earl of Bedford.
9. This huge compilation from the chief French and Italian novel collections has had the honour of two reprints, one in 1813 by Haslewood, and one in 1890 by Mr. Joseph Jacobs.
10. It had appeared as "One Hundred" only in the year of Tottel. Being full of folk-lore and other extra-literary interest, it has been several times reprinted.

George Turberville, on the other hand, was a poet—certainly the best poet of the time (always excepting Sackville) next to Gascoigne, and perhaps Gascoigne's equal. He was a Dorsetshire man, who must have been born about 1530, and was not dead ten years before the end of the reign, who went to Winchester and New College, did some diplomatic work in Russia, and seems to have been of independent fortune. Like most of his contemporaries, he was specially addicted to translation in prose and verse from ancients and moderns. But in 1570 he produced a volume of *Epitaphs, Epigrams, Songs, and Sonnets.*[11] Turberville has not much power of continued poetical flight, but there is in some of his lyrics a genuine and unforced sweetness which is extremely agreeable, and at this time very rare.

Turberville.

His friend Barnabe Googe,[12] who is thought to have been born about 1540, and who died in 1594, cannot be complimented on much lyrical gift; but some Eclogues of his Googe importance, and in his *Cupid Conquered* he has some of the appeal of a predecessor—though afar off—of Spenser. He came from Lincolnshire, and was a son both of Oxford and Cambridge, a client of Burleigh's, and a particularly active and miscellaneous translator, of extreme Protestant tendencies in his selection of books to translate. The most obvious oddity of Googe's original poems, the extraordinary fashion in which the lines are divided—for instance, decasyllabics being split up into fours and sixes, and Alexandrines into quarters—is thought to have been due to the mere mechanical shiftlessness of the printer, who had a small page and large type. Googe, when he is not simply flat, often sins by the use of the bombastic and fustianish style, which was common, and at which Shakespeare laughs with such merciless good-nature.

Googe.

11. Reprinted in Chalmers, vol. ii.

12. See Mr. Arber's *Reprints.* Of Googe's translations, the *Popish Kingdom* (from the *Regnum Papisticum* of Naogeorgus or Kirchmeyer) had the honour of an extremely handsome black-letter reprint in 1880, the editor being Mr. R.C. Hope. It is in fluent and freely alliterated fourteeners, but its literary interest is very small.

Among these shadows and others more shadowy still—the very "Henry Pimpernel and old John Naps of Greece" in English literature—George Gascoigne gives us at least something like a substantive figure.[13] His life, though not Gascoigne so long as Churchyard's, was nearly as typical, and his work was much better. Like most of the men with whom he is here associated, but even more than most of them, Gascoigne was a person of birth, breeding, and education. He was the son of a Bedfordshire knight, Sir John Gascoigne, and was connected on his mother's side with Frobisher the seaman. He was a Cambridge man, his college being Trinity, and, like most University men perhaps for some three centuries, finished his education at the Inns of Court—in his case, Gray's Inn and the Temple. He was born about 1537, and can have been hardly of age when he entered Parliament, sitting for Bedford in 1557. He must have begun to write verse very early, but printed nothing for some years. His translated or adapted tragedy and comedy already referred to (p. 298) were acted in Gray's Inn Hall in 1566. He married in 1567, served in the Netherlands in 1572, and onwards to 1574, and in the first of these years published, or had published for him (there was often a little innocent make-believe about these things in those days), a collection of poems styled *A Hundred Sundry Flowers,* which in the later issue of 1575 was divided into *Flowers, Herbs, and Weeds.* He had to do with the Kenilworth Revels in 1575, and next year published his *Steel Glass,* a regular satire of considerable length in blank verse. He died in October 1577. Besides the works already mentioned, Gascoigne is noted for the first translated prose tale from Bandello (a style so much followed by Painter and others), and for his very important *Certain Notes or Instructions concerning the Making of Verse or Rhyme in English.*

These *Instructions,* being criticism not creation, escape the drawbacks of the other work in regard to intrinsic merit,

13. Poems in Chalmers, vol. ii, and more completely by W.C. Hazlitt; the *Steel Glass,* the *Complaint of Philomene,* and the *Notes* in Arber's *Reprints.* There is a good study of Gascoigne by Dr. Schelling of Philadelphia.

and hold a secure position, comparable in English, though, of course, with great abatement of scale and genius, to that held by Dante's *De Vulgari Eloquio* in Italian. They are very short; and although Gascoigne had a long past of English behind him, it will readily be apprehended by intelligent readers of the foregoing pages that his actual knowledge of English poetry was not great. The study of Anglo-Saxon was indeed reviving in his time, but it did not affect ordinary men of letters for many generations to come. Nor do Gascoigne or his contemporaries and followers seem to have been acquainted with any Middle English writers before Chaucer, though *Piers Plowman* was not an unknown book. Gascoigne himself only glances at alliterative metre in the terms of Chaucer's own scoff at it, does not mention a single poet by name except Chaucer himself, and as his followers, the later Elizabethan critics (see chap, vi), also did, though still more decidedly, confines himself mainly to a rhetorical abstract of the Art of Poetry, dwelling successively on the necessity of fresh invention and the avoidance of commonplaces, on the importance of "keeping the measure," and not (for instance) slipping from poulter's measure—Alexandrines and fourteeners—to fourteeners by themselves; on quantity, accent, and metre generally; on the disadvantage of polysyllables, and the impropriety of coining words for rhyme's sake; on the danger (a caution very specially needed, as we have seen) of excessive alliteration and of inusitate word-inversion; on the pause; on rhyme-royal and other stanza forms; and on "riding rhyme" (the heroic couplet). The most really noticeable thing about the whole is Gascoigne's assumption (all the more important because he is evidently not satisfied with it) that the decasyllable must be confined to strict iambics and (with an easement, it is true, as to rhyme-royal) to the middle pause. We have seen how this undue, but for the time salutary, restraint was arrived at; we shall see how it was removed.

His *Instructions.*

Gascoigne's practice, as compared with that of his neighbours, certainly does not discredit the maxim that "every poet should contain a critic." Except Sackville, he is the best poet of the group, and he goes far beyond Sackville in the one point of variety. The blank verse of the *Steel Glass* is indeed marred by the at this time universal fault of *staccato* movement—the lines being far too often concluded within themselves in sense, and the monotony being increased by the poet's acceptance of the middle pause, and by his abuse of the practice of beginning successive lines with the same word.[14] Yet though not vivid, it is generally vigorous, and sometimes even incisive. The lyrics and stanza poems escape this drawback, and, though the author recks his own rede about excessive alliteration but ill, attain very commonly to prettiness and not seldom to pathos. The same mark of a certain childishness is still on the verse; but it very often has the grace as well as the immaturity of childhood.

His poems.

There is nothing childish about the few and noble verses of Thomas Sackville.[15] They were published in a curious book which, except in the pages contributed by Sackville himself, has very small literary, as compared with its historical, interest. The *Mirror for Magistrates* was planned in the reign of Queen Mary by *trates.* William Baldwin, an Oxford man, a priest, a scholar, a schoolmaster, and a printer, who seems to have been born not long after the beginning of the century, and George Ferrers, a member of the same University, of Lincoln's Inn, and of Parliament, a writer on legal and historical subjects, as well as of interludes, who died in 1579. The book, which was intended to be a sort of supplement to Lydgate's version of Boccaccio's *Falls of Princes,* is said to have been printed in

The *Mirror for Magistrates.*

14. It is of the first interest to notice how this practice, which is so effective for good in the mobile-centred and complex-footed verse of Tennyson, aggravates the monotony of strict decasyllabics with the immovable middle pause.

15. Sackville's drama has been already dealt with. His life only touched literature in those two early passages of it. He was born (his father, Sir Richard Sackville, was Chancellor of the Exchequer) about 1536, at Buckhurst, and is supposed to have been a member of Hart Hall, St. John's College, Oxford, and of the Inner Temple. He was made Lord Buckhurst in 1567, K.G. in 1589, Lord Treasurer in 1599, and Earl of Dorset in 1604. He died at the Council table four years later.

part as early as 1555, but was interfered with by Gardiner and did not attain license for publication till 1559. It contained nineteen "tragedies" by Baldwin, Ferrers, and Phaer(?), Sackville not being yet a contributor. His two pieces, the *Induction* (not to the general work but to such "tragedies" as lie might write) and the *Complaint of Buckingham,* appeared in the second and enlarged edition of 1563, to which Churchyard also contributed. To complete the general story of the book, in 1574 John Higgins issued a fresh batch, taken from earlier times between Brutus and Caesar, and four years later Thomas Blennerhassett added pieces dealing with the first thousand years of the Christian era. Baldwin's and Higgins's, but not Blennerhassett's, parts were united, (still with new matter) in 1587, and at last, in 1610, the whole, again with additions, came together. Consisting, as the book does, entirely of tragical stories from English history, and covering, as its various issues do, almost the whole period during which, as we shall see, verse-history was a specially favourite form, it cannot lack a certain interest. But its merit as poetry is almost entirely confined to Sackville's contributions.[16]

Sackville's part in it.

They are short enough. *The Induction* and *The Complaint of Henry, Duke of Buckingham* (Richard Ill's victim, not Wolsey's) occupy between them less than 200 stanzas in rhyme-royal, or rather more than 1300 lines. The language, as part in it comports with the metre and with the design of the book to supply a sort of sequel to Lydgate, is a little archaic. There is even an attempt, doubtless also deliberate, to keep up fifteenth-century style both in personifying allegory and in a sort of modified "rhetoric." But hardly a single stanza, certainly no single page, can be read by a poetically-minded reader without his being well aware that an entirely new music is sounding in his ears, a music of which perhaps a faint, far-off anticipation may be discovered in the "Cressid" stanzas of Henryson already so highly praised, but which is now fully organised in diapason. This is by no means due merely, though it is in part, to the fact that the

16. The athletic Haslewood grappled with the whole in his three-volume reprint (1815), but the adventure has not been re-attempted.

writer has entirely shaken off the metrical palsy of the fifteenth century itself, and has, moreover, emerged from the swaddling-clothes of the transition prosody. Even his archaism does not make Sackville stiff; even such uncomely survival-catchwords of poetic diction as "hugy'' do not make him stale or flat. He has thoroughly saturated and informed his old stanza with the vigour and variety of the new line which the poets from Wyatt onwards had been gingerly and tentatively fingering at. He has not the slightest need of the clumsy stop-at-the-end with which they are wont to stay themselves like skaters in their noviciate, who bring themselves up by digging in a pointed stick for fear of slipping, and never dare strike out. It cannot be expected that he should have mastered (as indeed nobody did till Shakespeare) the crowning secret of English verse, the glorious liberty of the ubiquitous pause. But he already knows how to vary it, avails himself fully of the license as to the middle place granted even by Gascoigne to his metre, and rings the changes not merely upon it, but upon stopped and unstopped lines, with a master's audacity and sureness.

Nor is this all. His merely formal improvements no doubt help him to attain, but by no means wholly account for, the new music referred to above. It has been said that the fifteenth century itself was strongly impressed, more strongly than the Middle Ages themselves, with the terror of death—that

> Timor mortis conturbat me

was more than a mere literary catchword with it. But this mere terror is here changed, in English verse for the first time, to that greater and nobler Renaissance melancholy, the sighs of which served as wind to blow the organ music that distinguishes the best European poetry generally, and the best English poetry in particular, from about 1550 or later for a hundred years onwards, and the last echoes of which die away in the poetic prose of Browne and the Pindaric verse of the better part of Cowley. The *Induction,* where Sorrow in person leads the poet to the infernal regions and shows him the doleful places; the *Complaint,* with its story of civil war and public treason and private treachery and royal ingratitude, lend themselves, of course, very well to the play to be played on this pipe, but it must be remembered that they equally well invite the mere doleful dulness which the poets of the fifteenth century too often permit themselves. Sackville is not quite so far from this in the *Complaint,* where the difficulty of telling actual historical details confronts him, as he is in the *Induction,* where poetry has free play; but he is far from it in both, and absolutely at the other pole in the first piece. Passages in it have been made familiar by many histories and anthologies, but the whole of its 500 lines or so ought to be known by every one who desires to acquaint himself with the full range of the powers of English poetry. Campbell, whose naturally excellent taste was still vitiated by eighteenth-century fallacies, could see little in it but gloom, though he admitted its poetry. The truth is that the poetry should make us forget the gloom, or rather remember it only as the vehicle, the occasion by which the poetry is exhibited. Sackville never lets mere "dismals" get the upper hand; it is always the poetry of the dismal that he keeps before us. And this is the gift that we find before perhaps only in Chaucer, the gift of making the subject, whatever it is, quite subsidiary—a mere cup in which to present to us the wine of poetry, a mere canvas on which to display its colours and forms. The cup and the canvas are indeed necessary; we could not have the picture or the draught without them. But they are merely inseparable accidents: the property is the poetry.[17]

17. *Note to Second Edition.*—If the poem on St. Mary Magdalene [published by the E.T.S. (ed. Sommer, 1899), since the first edition of this history appeared and attributed to a certain Dr. Thomas Robinson, Dean of Durham] be rightly dated "before 1509," it belongs to the matter of this chapter. And if so it would deserve notice, not for its poetical merit, though it has some in the florid style which characterises late Elizabethan work, but because of its stanza, an octave consisting of seven decasyllabics and an Alexandrine, rhymed *ababbacc.* As this not only anticipates Spenser in the Alexandrine termination but Giles Fletcher in the actual arrangement, it would be, if really of the above date, very remarkable indeed. But this attribution, and the evidence for fixing the date, are very far from certain, and the style of the poem suggests a period at least a quarter of a century later. It may be well to add in reference to the mere Alexandrine ending of

a stanza that, as Guest pointed out *(English Rhythms,* p. 669, *note),* it may be found as far back as Sir Thomas More.

Note to Third Edition.—Since this note was written its suspicions have been confirmed by the cancelling of Dr. Sommer's attribution and the dating of the poem at "about 1621."

4

SPENSER AND HIS CONTEMPORARIES

The Leicester House circle—Sidney—His life—The sonnets—The *Defence of Poesy*—The *Arcadia*—Spenser—The "classical metre" craze—Other poets of Sidney's circle—Watson—Greville—Warner—The sonneteers of 1592-96—Constable—The satirists.

The Leicester House circle.

THE gossiping and personal side of literary history has always attracted rather excessive than insufficient attention. And it has naturally not been neglected in the endeavours to account for the sudden transformation, about the year 1579-80, of English literature from a rather dreary nursery ground, in which not very numerous and extremely unskilful workers were laboriously carrying out horticultural experiments, to a very garden of the Hesperides. A good deal will be found in some books about a certain "Areopagus" at Leicester House, the equivalent of the famous French *cénacles* of earlier and later times. We must not, of course, make too much of this. Spenser had certainly found his way, if not fully, before he was ever introduced to Leicester, and there is little or no evidence that the Leicester House influence counted for anything at all in the just dramatic outburst.

Sidney.

But the *coterie* just mentioned did play a part, important, though not to be exaggerated, in the new development. It included Sidney, Spenser, the future Lord Brooke, Harvey, Dyer, and others, with the occasional accession of notable foreigner, such as Giordano Bruno, and the participation of ladies, such as Sidney's sister, the Countess of Pembroke, was the chief. Nor is there any reason to doubt that Sidney was in reality, as well as in position and rank, its centre and head. His genius was indeed inferior to Spenser's by a long way. But it exceeded that of any other of the members, and it is peculiarly noticeable that it looked in more directions than one. For a young man—he was but just over thirty when he died—living in a time with, so to speak, no literary background, with no master to imitate, no blazing popularity to envy and seek to share, it is no mean thing to have left the *Arcadia,* the *Defence of Poesy,* and *Astrophel,* with minor things accomplished, and with a sort of tradition of established influence which is inferior to that of few in our literature. The tradition might have been a fond imagination or the work of flattering parasites, but the work is there to support and justify it. The work may be flawed, tentative, unequal, but the tradition is justly to be counted in as no mean makeweight.

Philip Sidney was born in 1554. His father was Sir Henry Sidney, afterwards Deputy of Ireland; his mother Lady Mary Dudley, sister of Leicester and daughter of the beheaded queen-maker who was for a time Duke of Northumberland. He gave an early example of those public-school friendships which have counted for so much in English history, with Fulke Greville at Shrewsbury; but the pair were not undergraduates together, for Greville went to Cambridge and Sidney to Christ Church. But it was probably owing to Greville that Sidney, when, after much foreign travel, he settled in London, came in contact, probably about 1578, with Gabriel Harvey, and through Harvey with Edmund Spenser. Sidney's heroic death at Zutphen did not take place till October 1586, and though his attention to literature must have been broken by more than one employment, he had the best part of ten years (for he returned from his travels in 1575) to work in.

The actual achievement in his books[1] is high—much higher than has sometimes been allowed; but the genius of Sidney was fine rather than vigorous. What is most eminently

1. An edition of Sidney's *Works* has been begun by M. Feuillerat (Cambridge, 1912). Dr. Grosart in 1873 collected the whole *Poems*;

remarkable in him, and what most justifies the reputation he achieved with his contemporaries, is the extraordinary way in which his performance, under all its disadvantages, covers almost the whole ground, in criticism or in creation, of Elizabethan literature. He wrote no dramas (unless the juvenile *Lady of May*[2] be called a drama), and in his *Defence of Poesy* he takes what we now see (with the easy cleverness of posterity) to be the wrong side about the kind of drama to be cultivated. But he made no mistake about the fatal folly of Gosson's objection to drama and poetry generally, and in the immortal words about "Chevy Chase" he gave, all unknowing it, the motto of English poetry. Nay, he did more than this, for in his practice of verse, though comparatively scanty, occasional, and utterly unrevised, he indicated and essayed in many forms the lyric which was to be one of the coming age's chief exploits, and he struck the note which was to be the note of the poetry of that age generally. So too, though his prose consists only of the tiny critical tractate of the *Defence* and the large but rather formless romance of the *Arcadia,* he managed here also to exhibit the coming events with a wonderful precision of shadow. In form this prose is not great; the nearest approach to mere flattery in regard to him is the attempt, countenanced by no less a man than Drayton, to represent his style as a deliberate counterblast to the extravagances of Lyly. On the contrary, there is nearly as much "Euphuism" in the *Arcadia* as in *Euphues,* though it is Euphuism with a more definitely Spanish difference. But it is true that the *Defence* exhibits a much more sober scheme of prose; and it is also true that in throwing the *Arcadia* into the form of the prose romance Sidney was anticipating by generations, and almost by centuries, the shape into which certainly the most copious, and some of the most exquisite, developments of English prose were to be cast.

Astrophel and Stella has been several times separately reprinted. So has the *Defence.* Dr. Sommer in 1891 reprinted handsomely the first edition of the *Arcadia.*

2. A sort of masque, said to have been written for Elizabeth at Wanstead in 1578, and appended to some editions of the *Arcadia.*

The *Apology for Poetry,* or *Defence of Poesy,* as it was successively named, must, from the known date of Gosson's pamphlet, have been composed about 1580 or the next year. The same period, during which Sidney is known to have made a long stay at Wilton with his sister, probably saw the composition of most of the *Arcadia,* which in its turn contains a very large proportion of the *Poems*. The date of the writing of the *Astrophel and Stella* sonnets is uncertain. Penelope Devereux, who was pretty certainly Stella, was already married to Lord Rich when Sidney married Frances Walsingham in 1583, but all attempts to date the sonnets exactly are guesswork.

Their form is that specially English scheme in which the triumphs of Shakespeare were to be achieved, and which is arranged in three quatrains and a couplet; while the rhyme arrangement vacillates. The uncertainty, however, of the period is shown in the occasional adoption of Alexandrines instead of decasyllables as the base verse—an undoubted mistake, as the Alexandrine in English is too long a line to adapt itself in bulk to any complicated stave.

Many minor details show, as this does, the immaturity of the writer, and the fact that he was writing, so to speak, in the dark, or only with the dim lights of Surrey, Wyatt, and Sackville to help him. But the stuff is of the best. The final line of the first sonnet—

> Fool! said my muse [to me,] look in thy heart and write;

the splendid soar of the opening of the seventh—

> When Nature made her chief work, Stella's eyes,
> In colour black why wrapt she beams so bright?

the famous "Moon" sonnet, familiar from many anthologies, and exhibiting in the most interesting fashion the superiority of the opening couplet—of the first jet—to what follows; the enigmatical "I might," on which many hypotheses have been built; the various "Sleep" sonnets, exercises in a most favourite tourney of the age; the interesting

> I never drank of Aganippe's well;

the brilliant extravagance of the "Edward the Fourth" piece; and the stately music of the hundred and seventh and hundred and tenth sonnets—

> Stella, since thou of right a princess art,

and

> Leave me, oh love, which reaches but to dust,—

these things, with many others, make up a tale which in the circumstances is merely astounding. The songs included in *Astrophel and Stella,* with one exception, are a little inferior to the sonnets, but they are not less interesting, inasmuch as the effort to secure a lyric medium is obvious, and though not quite successful, is not wholly defeated. The heavy thud of the best work of Googe and Churchyard, even of Turberville and Gascoigne, is gone. We do not yet quite "sing," but we have quite got rid of the fatal drop into unquestioned "saying." And in all Sidney's verse—the *Arcadia* fragments, the Psalm versions, etc.—this sense of the broken ice, of the fleeing winter, of "Lent coming with love to town" at last, is the pervading charm.

The Defence of Poesy.

The virtues of his prose are different, and have teen partly anticipated. The *Apology* or *Defence* (first printed as the former in 1595) has so far an interest of style that it is in parts straightforwardly and vigorously written. But its interest of matter far outruns this. Gosson (see note *ante*) had exhibited the clash of the two currents of the day which had most force in them—the scholarly and literary impulse on the one hand, and the Puritan "craving for righteousness," as some call it (the intense desire to make somebody else uncomfortable even at a slight sacrifice to yourself, as it is phrased by others). Sidney, a scholar, a poet to the bone, and an experienced politician, young as he was, must have felt the danger, and may have attempted a sort of *modus vivendi*; yet much of the *Apology,* in its exaltation of the classical theories, is merely an echo of what had been said twenty years earlier by the Pléiade in France, if not of the common form of the Renaissance in all countries. It is unlucky, no doubt, that he joins the heretics who say that verse is only an accident of poetry, and that he condemns that very mixture of tragedy and comedy which at the moment in two different countries, Spain and England, was raising and to raise the drama to such a height as it had never previously attained. But no one can be more wise than destiny.

The *Arcadia* is, except in scale, less interesting if only for the tolerably sufficient reason that it is excessively difficult to make out exactly how much of it is Sidney's at all. He wished, it is said, on his deathbed, to burn it. But his sister would not consent, and as *The Countess of Pembroke's Arcadia* it was published in 1590. It is an obvious following of the late Greek romances and the Spanish *Amadis* series, in the spirit which was at the same time or a little later, to bring forth Honoré d'Urfé's *Astrée* and the enormous roll of French imitations. It is thus principally noticeable in scheme as an instance of the impulse towards prose fiction which has affected all ages, though it never came to anything till long after Sidney's death. The high heroic spirit it displays captivated all good wits in its own and the following generation. But it is a "*Tendenz*-book" rather than a book in itself, and it illustrates the eager striving which animated Sidney's circle with less success than *Astrophel and Stella.* The mannerisms of its style, which have puzzled and misled commentators, appear, as has been said to be directly imitated from the Spanish.[3]

The *Arcadia.*

It may be thought that too much space is given to Sidney. Yet his personality does seem in some strange way to have rayed out more influence than that of any man of his generation. And his positive achievement has been more often belittled than exaggerated. Indeed, if Edmund Spenser himself had died when Sidney did, and if nothing of his survived but what was published before that date, there would be poetical justification for calling Sidney the greater, though the less accomplished, poet of the two.

---

3. See p. 271 *sq.* of Mr. David Hannay's *The Later Renaissance* (Edinburgh, 1898).

Very little is known, though a good deal has been laboriously inferred and conjectured, about Spenser's parentage and his early years generally. There is no reasonable doubt that he was of a family of Spensers settled near Burnley in Lancashire; but he was born in London about 1552. He appears to have been a Merchant Taylors' boy, and certainly matriculated at Pembroke Hall Cambridge, in 1569. He seems to have been poor, and was assisted from charitable funds. But if (and there can be no reasonable doubt of it) the translations from Petrarch and Du Bellay into English blank verse, which appeared in the same year in Van der Noodt's *Theatre of Voluptuous Worldlings*, and which in 1591 were, with alterations from blank verse to rhyme, reprinted as his, be genuine, they are evidence that he was a very promising scholar. He remained at college for the then usual seven years, taking his Bachelor's degree in 1573, and his Master's in 1576. He was not fortunate enough to change his sizarship for a fellowship; and seems to have left Cambridge for the North with very dubious prospects. He had, however, made friends with a man somewhat older than himself, Gabriel Harvey, a Fellow of Trinity Hall. By 1578 Harvey had, in some way or other, secured the patronage of the powerful favourite Leicester, and he wrote to Spenser to come and share his good luck. Whether, as is at least probable, this was the origin of Spenser's introduction to Sidney, Leicester's nephew, or whether, as suggested above, Fulke Greville had made the Cambridge literary group known to his schoolfellow, is impossible to say, and does not matter; indeed, the two things are quite compatible. But Spenser was unquestionably from this time enlisted in the Leicester House set, and he seems to have been sent by Leicester to France in the autumn of 1579. Next year he was made secretary to Lord Grey of Wilton, Deputy of Ireland, and with him was present at the famous Smerwick business, where a crew of Spanish and Papal filibusters were put to the sword, on the 10th of November. He did not leave Ireland with Grey, but received various offices there, and in 1588 obtained, or rather bought, an allotment of some three thousand acres of the forfeited Desmond lands in County Cork at Kilcolman, where he proceeded to reside, buying also the office of Clerk of the Council of Munster. In 1589 he went back to England, being now under the protection of another favourite, Raleigh. He spent at least part of two years in London, frequenting the Court and playing the part of suitor, not without some grumbling. But he obtained a pension of £ 50 a year, a considerable sum for the time and sovereign, against, as tradition has it, the influence of Burleigh. Three years later, at the mature age of forty-two, but with poetical results worthy of twenty, he married a certain Elizabeth, probably Elizabeth Boyle. He went back again to London in 1595; but the end of his days was not far off. In 1597 he returned to Kilcolman with his wife and three, soon to be four, children. He became Sheriff of Cork in September 1598, and immediately afterwards Tyrone's rebellion broke out, Kilcolman was burnt and Spenser fled, first to Cork and then to London, where, in January 1599, he died, there is no trustworthy evidence from what cause.

Spenser's life, though the facts are scanty, is not uninteresting, and it is not quite unimportant to know that he shared the strenuous and varied living of his great time; but he might not have done this and yet be one of the foremost figures of English literature. His plans and projects were numerous and early; not a few of them seem to have been actually carried out, though no remains exist. But his exile in the hills of the North, though it seems to have witnessed an unhappy love-affair with the "Rosalind" of the *Calendar,* gave him time to exercise poetical genius. Nearly ten years had passed since he showed what he could do as a mere boy in Van der Noodt's book, when this his first real work appeared, ushered and commented on by one "E. K.," "from my lodging at London this 10th of April 1579," dedicated to Sidney and addressed by the editor to Gabriel Harvey.

About this "E.K." disputes have arisen. One monstrous theory has been started to the effect that it was Spenser in mask—a theory of which all that can be said is that, if it be true, Spenser, instead of being, as he is generally taken to have been, one of the noblest and most high-minded of English men of letters, was a shameless self-puffer. Indeed, the style and general tone are unlike Spenser's, and argue very little original genius or even talent in the writer. That Spenser may have supplied some of the information is very probable, and would not be in the least discreditable. Meanwhile "E.K." is identified, in fair likelihood, with a certain Edward Kirke, a contemporary and friend of Harvey and Spenser. He supplies a good deal of elaborate ushering, some not useless glossarial and other exposition, a few comments, harmless if nothing more. If he is to be believed, he wrote other commentaries on works of Spenser's which have not come down to us.

As for the *Calendar* itself, it is a collection of twelve eclogues, one for each month of the year, and mostly, though not always, in dialogue. There is no prevailing metre, the first eclogue being in the six-line stanza; the second in the famous metre which, as we have seen, is found as far back as the *Genesis and Exodus* of the thirteenth century, but which Coleridge thought himself to have invented, and certainly re-invented, in *Christabel;* the third in another six-line stanza of shorter lines; the fourth divided between elegiac quatrains and a lyric stave; the fifth half Chaucer, half *Christabel;* the sixth in octaves; the seventh in the rather lolloping eights and sixes which the earliest Elizabethan poets had loved; the eighth partly in sixains, partly in eights and sixes, treated with more freedom than before; the ninth again in the *Christabel* form; the tenth in a different sixain; the eleventh again in quatrains and a sort of Pindaric; and the twelfth in the sixains of the first. Each has at the end one or more "emblems"—a variety of the "posies" so much affected by the Elizabethans.

The general scheme of the poem or poems was taken naturally from preceding eclogue-writers—Theocritus, Virgil, and the moderns, Mantuan, Marot, and so forth. The language (as ought to have been seen from the first, and indeed was partly) is not a natural dialect of any kind or district, but partly imitated from Chaucer, partly seasoned with Northern words. It is much cruder and more unskilfully archaic than the exquisite vocabulary which Spenser was soon to work out for the *Faërie Queene*; and is chiefly responsible for Ben Jonson's too cavalier sentence that Spenser "in imitating the ancients writ no language."

The *Shepherd's Calendar*[4] does not contain any of the finest passages of its author's poetry, but it at least shows the existence of an instrument on which the finest passages of poetry could be played. For the next ten years Spenser was busy on other things as well as on poetry, and it was not till the 1st of December 1589 that the first three books of the *Faërie Queene* were entered at Stationers' Hall. They appeared in the following spring. In 1591 a volume containing *The Ruins of Time, The Tears of the Muses, Virgil's Gnat, Mother Hubbard's Tale, The Ruins of Rome, Muiopotmos,* and the *Visions,* and including, as has been said, a revision of the twenty years earlier *juvenilia,* was published. It is worth noticing that Spenser here for himself, as Kirke had earlier done for him, gives a list of promised books which never appeared. This phenomenon is by no means uncommon in literature, and it may be set down with equal probability to an active imagination outrunning possibility, and to a ruthless critical temper which would not allow anything that it did not think perfect to appear. This volume was generally entitled *Complaints,* Spenser at this time being in melancholy mood, and *Daphnaida,* which followed, exhibits the same drift. His marriage changed his tone remarkably, and 1595 saw the *Amoretti* sonnets, the *Epithalamium,* and *Colin Clout's Come Home Again;* while at the very earliest of 1596, the completion of the *Faërie Queene,* except the odd cantos, was published, with the glorious *Four Hymns,* and the *Prothalamium,* not like the *Epithalamium* on himself, followed. He published nothing more, his prose *State of Ireland* not appearing till long afterwards. There are no Spenserian Apocrypha worth mentioning, save *Britain's Ida,* a pretty poem, but quite obviously of a later cast, in the key of the imitations of Shakespeare's two earlier poems and Marlowe's *Hero and Leander.*

Almost the whole of this later work (with, in the case of the 1591 volume, exceptions for some evidently early things

---

4. The title was undoubtedly taken from a book extremely popular in divers languages with the generation before—a work of astrological, medical, moral, and miscellaneous information, the early English form of which has been reprinted by Dr. Sommer, London, 1892.

not quite perfectly revised) stands on the same level and deserves the same praise. The towering bulk and the substantive interest of the *Faërie Queene* give it the necessary supremacy among its smaller peers. But if they stood alone without the epic and without the *Calendar,* we should undoubtedly be deploring the unkind fate which had prevented the poet who gave us these from giving us anything greater. The 1591 volume and *Daphnaida* rank much nearer to the *Calendar* than the rest of the minor works; their positive beauty is not of the absolutely commanding order. Yet there is a certain advance in the mastery of mere verse, in the faculty of communicating "cry" and echo. And in *Mother Hubbard's Tale* there has been generally and rightly noticed the exhibition of a satirical faculty which is not subsidiary, which is complementary, to the faculties displayed in the *Faërie Queene.*

But the others are of far higher quality. The *Prothalamium* for Lady Elizabeth and Lady Katherine Somerset is a delightful poem; but it naturally lacks the personal passion of the *Amoretti* and the *Epithalamium,* the former the best early sonnets in final couplet form next to Shakespeare, the latter by common consent unsurpassed in its own kind, as are the *Four Hymns* in theirs. These poems, which it is very desirable to take together, express a peculiar Renaissance note, the union of intellectual and sensual rapture, as no others do. And their form corresponds to their matter. The poet can by this time do anything he likes with rhyme and rhythm, with language and metrical scheme. No bead-roll of the greatest poems in English, which disregards conditions of mere bulk, can omit the *Epithalamium* and the *Four Hymns.*

Nevertheless the *Faërie Queene,* the best known, is also the best of Spenser's work. In this great poem, which some have put first for actual greatness, and which can hardly in any competent estimate yield the place for charm, if not for majesty, among long poems in English, Spenser displays at the very full all the gifts and graces which he showed in his minor work, and more. The *Calendar* and the *Sonnets,* the *Epithalamium* and the *Hymns,* are but the chapels and chantries of the cathedral of the *Faërie Queene.* Rather strange attempts have sometimes been made to belittle the achievement, which is the most striking and the most pervading in the book, the invention of the Spenserian stanza. Some have even said that he "took it from the Italians," which in any sense which is not next to nonsense is simply false. Others have dismissed it as a simple putting of an Alexandrine on to the eight-line stanza. The fact is that it is one of the crowning achievements of poetical inspiration in form. It stands alone in the combination of individual beauty and faculty, with suitableness to a long connected poem. Naturally, and it might seem inevitably, the latter quality is found in nearly all verse forms to exist in inverse ratio to the former. The Spenserian almost alone combines the two; and while the single stanza is often as complete and as beautiful as a sonnet, the whole flows with an evenness and absence of break which not the most ingeniously arranged "sonnet-sequence" has ever attained.

The poet's success in language is certainly more contestable; but not much diminution can be allowed in the credit due for it. The extreme and sometimes rather rugged archaism of the *Calendar* has been smoothed away, and Spenser's immense advance in melody at once makes it easy for him to select only beautiful words, and unnecessary for him to carry archaism beyond a slight degree. It is but now and then that there would be any difficulty in printing a stanza of the *Faërie Queene* in modern spelling without a single strange word, though no doubt the poet sometimes sees his account in using licenses both in vocabulary and spelling.

With such a metre and such a lexicon marvels in verbal music become almost easy. Hardly any two stanzas of this enormous work will be found exactly to repeat each other in cadence. The secrets of varying the caesura of the line and of using or abstaining from *enjambement* or overlapping, which have been by turns ignored, recovered, and abused, and on which rests practically the whole art of rescuing any metre from monotony, were perfectly well-known to Spenser, and as cunningly used by him as by any of his followers. Nor can he be said to be ignorant, though he employs them rather less, of the other two great metrical secrets, the use of trisyllabic feet and the distribution of words of varying weight and length over the line.

As for subject, Spenser's was a great one; and it was capable, even in his own time, of being regarded from curiously diverse points of view. Half told as the tale is, it is impossible to be certain how far Spenser had a fixed plan of adjusting the whole to that slightly concealed allegory of the state of England which, though too much attention may be paid to it, the poem does contain. Then was more than the mere courtiership of the time in the obvious glances at Queen Elizabeth, not merely in Gloriana, but in Belphoebe, and perhaps to some extent in Britomart. We may wish that there were less colour for the hint of Leicester in Prince Arthur, and of Queen Mary in Duessa, and it may seem rather idle curiosity to inquire whether Artegall really has anything to do with Lord Grey of Wilton, where Raleigh comes in, and so forth. There can, however, be no doubt that there is a certain amount of double meaning of the kind, that it interested contemporaries, and that it was intended to lead up to some sort of end. Indeed, the general story of the chief characters, though very slowly and with vast overlayings, does make some progress even as it is amid the completer *historiettes* of the adventures of the several Knights of the Virtues, and the almost bewildering panorama of beautiful pictures which the poet calls up at every step, and which no doubt constitute the main interest and delight of the poem to modern readers.

To Spenser, moreover, as to all the great men of his great generation, virtue and vice were not commonplaces in any sense that admitted of their being despicable or negligible. By a redoublement of his allegory—not so much the allegory, which had not yet entirely relaxed its very tyrannous hold on the later Middle Ages, as that which must always maintain its grasp on poetry—the *Faërie Queene* was also intended to be a picture of Life, of Conduct, worked out by the treatment of certain great Virtues or excellences. Holiness, Temperance, and Chastity, Friendship, Justice, and Courtesy, are celebrated in the books actually existing. Magnificence, in the full Aristotelian sense (though he must rather have meant

Magnanimity), was intended, we learn, at once to provide the special subject of another, and, as exemplified by Prince Arthur, to appear in and dominate them all. But of the actual distribution of the last six books no trustworthy testimony remains, and only tradition vouches for the fact that they, or some of them, perished in the sack of Kilcolman. Only the odd "cantos of Mutability," intended to be attached to a book of Constancy, survive; and as they are not inferior (they contain the gorgeous procession of the Months and Seasons) to the very best of the earlier work, it is pretty certain that what we have lost would be no disappointment if it were found. Indeed it is, for many sound reasons of poetical criticism, extremely probable that Spenser proceeded on the plan of indulging his genius by the composition of great fragments such as this, and, instead of hastily cobbling up a context, left them till he could worthily work them into the larger whole.

It is not true that such passages, though they are not perhaps very difficult to identify and separate nowadays, form the sole or even the chief attraction of the poem. On the contrary, they are never so beautiful as in their proper places; and the *Faërie Queene*, more than almost any other poem, demands and deserves to be read as a whole if its full charm is to be comprehended and enjoyed. But there is no reasonable doubt that the accessories of Spenser's scheme have become of more importance in poetical appeal than those things which to him were perhaps the chief. We shall never, if we are wise, forget that he is, as Milton called him, "our sage and serious Spenser," but wisdom will still insist that we regard him first of all as the poet and prophet of Beauty—the beauty of heaven and of earth alike.

This is perhaps the best place to notice a strange craze already referred to, which seems at one time to have been in danger of seriously infecting Spenser—the projected "reform" of English verse by the production of actual classical metres, especially hexameters.

This was a general and, strange as it may seem, a not quite unintelligible mania of the Renaissance generally, and had been tried in other countries besides England. The reason of it is perfectly plain. The eager spirits of the day in both France and England had outgrown the good old verse of their respective nations; they thought (and rightly) that the recent verse was not very good, and being as yet novices in comparative criticism, they jumped to the conclusion that what they justly admired in Greek and Latin poetry might be reproduced, or at least rivalled, by the use of an identical prosody. It was certain that such a learned body as the Sidneian clique would at least not reject this notion *ab initio*, and for a time it seems to have received a favourable hearing there. Ascham, a delightful prose writer but of a most unpoetical turn, had advocated the thing long before, and Thomas Drant, another St. John's man of a younger generation, had left certain posthumous "rules" on the subject.

The "Classical metre" craze.

This mania was taken up, either from crotchet or sincerely, by many in- and outside Sidney's circle, including the meritorious critic Webbe (*vide infra*), and by none more than by Gabriel Harvey, who had become Fellow of Trinity Hall. Harvey is one of those intrinsically unimportant persons who by accident have acquired a very considerable place in literary history; and there have even been fierce battles over the question whether he was a pedant or not. If not, it is very difficult to know to whom the adjective can apply. He was a genuine scholar in his own way—pedants very often, though not invariably, are. He deserves much thanks for having managed to put Spenser in the way of a preferment which enabled him to follow his genius instead of languishing as a poor scholar or hiding himself away as a country curate. It is not so certain that Harvey was wholly to blame for the distaste which he showed to the London Bohemian school, which will be shortly noticed; the great Marprelate dispute in which he was mixed up is still so mysterious in parts that it is very difficult to form any but the most guarded judgment on any matter connected with it; and it is certain that his principal literary antagonist and reviler, Thomas Nash, was at least as unscrupulous as he was clever.

But Harvey is condemned out of his own mouth. It is not Nash but himself who informs us that he thought the *Faërie*

Queene—the greatest poem that English literature had yet seen but one, if with that exception, and the greatest poem save three or four, if with these exceptions, that English literature was to see—a fantastic trifle, much inferior to nine pseudo-classical "comedies," probably something like Daniel's later ones, which Spenser had also written, and which he had the good sense never to print. And again, it is not Nash, nor any one who trusts to Nash, but Harvey who tells us that he believed in the hexameter craze, that he exemplified it in many preposterous examples, and that he tried to force it on his contemporaries.

It is not certain how far Spenser himself was seriously carried away by this lunacy. Some have seen nothing but irony in the somewhat guarded and fair-spoken replies which he makes to Harvey on the subject, and it is certain that his own attempts in the style are few and rather laboriously ineffective, with a touch of genius in them, than hopelessly mad and bad. But we may perhaps see in his attitude rather that of an honest perplexity striving to adjust itself to what his elders and betters seemed to like, but convinced of their error by native genius, than any deliberate *persiflage*.

At any rate, he did little in the kind. Others were less wary, and Richard Stanyhurst, an Irish gentleman, achieved one of the most preposterous books of English literature in his version of Virgil. Nor did the craze die soon. It was formally revived after some years, and with some differences, by an exquisite poet in true English verse, Thomas Campion, and formally denounced by a true though less exquisite poet, Samuel Daniel. It animated, as we shall see, the interesting if limited body of Elizabethan critics. And the echo it may be found long afterwards in Milton's curious heresies about rhyme—heresies which may be set down in part to an innate genius for blank verse striving to assert itself, but which, seeing that Milton could write as beautifully in rhyme as without it, may be more safely imputed to the singular cross-grainedness, the innate nonconformity, which mark the author of *Paradise Lost* in almost every relation of life and literature.

Besides Sidney, Spenser, and their *gracioso* Harvey, the Leicester House circle included divers other men of letters.

Other poets of Sidney's circle.

Sir Edward Dyer, a very great friend of Sidney's and one of the pall-bearers at his funeral, but an older man, has the accidental interest of having been born at Sharpham Park in Somersetshire, the birthplace nearly two centuries later of Fielding. He was an Oxford man, a traveller, a diplomatist and courtier, and he outlived Elizabeth, dying in 1607. He had a very great reputation in his time as a poet, but his remains are small, and only one of them, the famous and excellent, but not superexcellent,

My mind to me a kingdom is,

has obtained much place in the general memory. Abraham Fraunce, a *protégé* of Sidney's, was a Shrewsbury boy and a Fellow of St. John's College, Cambridge. His name occurs with fair frequency in the literature of the time, and he appears to have been a good scholar, but the most interesting thing about him is that he quoted the *Faërie Queene* two years before it was published.

More important than Dyer, and much more important than Fraunce, was Thomas Watson, a rather short-lived bard who died in 1592 at the age of thirty-five, but who, save for a certain frigidity, would take a high place, and who perhaps, considering his earliness, deserves no low one as it is.

Watson.

Watson,[5] who was a Londoner by birth and an Oxford man by education, translated the *Antigone* into Latin in 1581; but next year he produced an English verse book of great mark, the *Hecatompathia,* or *Passionate Century of Sonnets.* This, it is important to observe, was the very first of the great Elizabethan sonnet-collections, for Sidney's, though written, did not appear till years afterwards, and it was the tenth, not the ninth, decade of the century which saw the regular sonnet outburst. Watson was dead before this, but after his death another sequence, the *Tears of Fancy,* made its appearance, and he did other work.

5. Ed. Arber.

It is just possible that if Watson had lived a little longer (though he was outgrowing the ripest poetical age when he died), or if he had been born a little later, the frigidity above referred to would have been melted. It appears to be the result, not so much of any want of natural heat in the poet, as of his mind being somewhat sicklied o'er with learning. As was the case with all these early Elizabethan poets of the great age, except Spenser, he could not wear this learning lightly, and he hardly dared use a phrase or form a wish if somebody Greek or Roman, somebody French or Italian, had not authorised the proceeding. That the sonnets of the *Hecatompathia* are not quatorzains, but a long eighteen-line form, of a class which the Italians had wisely rejected, does not matter much. The form is not so successful as the quatorzain, but neither Watson nor anybody else could tell that till he had tried it. It is more fatal that each piece has a prose commentary and discussion of itself, pointing out its originals and its special features, with parallel passages and all the most approved apparatus of classical editing. The *Tears of Fancy* are couplet-tipped quatorzains, after what is the specially English model; but they do not gain much in freedom. Perhaps nowhere do we feel, so much as in reading Watson, the enormous benefit which was conferred upon English literature by the lawless excesses of the playwrights—some of them, Shakespeare at their head, men of no University culture at all.

It cannot be said that the last (and except Spenser and Sidney by far the greatest) of this set who remains to be noticed offers any exception to this caution. Fulke Greville,[6] who was exactly Sidney's contemporary, was born at Beauchamp Court, Warwickshire, in which county his father represented a good family, while his mother was of the illustrious house of the Nevilles. He and "Astrophel" entered Shrewsbury together, and though they were parted during their University sojourn, the friendship continued, and the two served together, when they were twenty-three, on an embassy to the Palatinate. Greville was heir to great wealth, and increased it by buying lucrative offices. He was a favourite of the Queen—who, no

---

6. *Works,* ed. Grosart, 4 vols. privately printed, 1870.

doubt, did not like him less because he seemed to have no fancy for marriage. He was knighted in 1597.

At the opening of the new reign, Grenville, who had already received many gifts from Elizabeth, had Warwick Castle, which has remained with his descendants, bestowed on him. In 1614 he became Chancellor of the Exchequer; and in 1620 was ennobled as Lord Brooke of Beauchamp. Eight years later he was, it is said, stabbed by a servant in his house, the name and site of which are perpetuated by Brook Street, Holborn. In his youth he seems to have been the friend of most of the best men of his time from Sidney to Bacon; in his age he appears, though not certainly, to have acquired a character for avarice and moroseness. Almost nothing of his considerable work was published during his lifetime, the chief exception being the play of *Mustapha,* 1601. Some of his poems appeared in 1633, his *Life of Sidney* in 1652, and more poems in 1670. He was thus a practitioner in all three kinds, poetry, prose, and drama, and it is probable, though not certain, that his best work was early.

The plays *Mustapha* and *Alaham,* which could not possibly be acted, show the influence of the coterie in their form, which is that of the Senecan drama chiefly, and have a double portion of that special characteristic of Greville which will be noticed presently, as have his longer poems or poetical tractates on *Monarchy* and other things. But *Coelica* is one of the earliest, and certainly one of the most remarkable, of the fashionable sonnet and song collections to a real or imaginary mistress. Some of the things in it are purely delightful, the best of all being that beginning

I, with whose colours Myra dressed her head.

But as a rule delight, except of a very peculiar kind, is not the sensation which Greville is apt to excite. Like Donne, his junior by some years, though with less exquisite exceptions to the rule of his incompleteness, he is an example at once of the immense capability and of the desperate dangers of the Elizabethan cast of thought, and (till the dramatists had broken down many of its trammels) of the Elizabethan conception of literature. Greville would not write for the vulgar, and, as has been seen, he scarcely condescended to give it any opportunities of judging his work. From first to last there seems to have been on him a sense that literature ought above all things to be scholarly in form and elegant in substance, that it ought not to deal with trivial things, that "words to the wise," cryptic raptures, enigmatical sentences were the things to attempt. Not merely the "abstruser cogitations" in verse, in which Lamb had perhaps a slightly paradoxical though no doubt also a genuine delight, but his simplest prose works, exhibit this characteristic of laboured remoteness as do hardly any other things in English. In both he is eccentric, unpopular, impossible, but not uncharming.

Warner.

A few individual poets and two interesting groups of poems have still to be noticed as properly contemporary with Spenser, Shakespeare and Drayton and Daniel being kept for later treatment. The chief of the former was William Warner, a poet who had his resurrection rather too early, and who perhaps on that account (he figures in Chalmers's *Poets*[7]) has had rather less attention than he deserves. Warner, who was probably born in 1558, and certainly died in 1609, was born in Oxfordshire and educated at Oxford, became an attorney, attached himself in some way to Lord Hunsdon, perhaps translated the *Menoechmi,* and certainly wrote *Albion's England,* 1586, and *Syrinx,* 1597. The latter, a collection of prose stories, is not of much importance; *Albion's England* has a good deal. At first sight it falls distinctly into the earlier and ruder class, being written in fourteeners, which, however, the poet did not divide, as his only modern editor has for convenience sake ruthlessly divided them, into eights and sixes. It anticipates Drayton and Daniel; and it shows some similarity to Spenser, not in its verse, but in its attention to the history of England; while it has a further likeness to Drayton in trying to do for the history very much what the *Polyolbion* does for the topography of the island. There is little of the new learned grace or of the new passion about the thing; but it has many vivid touches,

7. Vol. iv.

some passages of rhetorical force, and a general sense of power.

The poets other than Warner, with two exceptions, were not better executants than himself, and were much smaller men. Thomas Howell, an outsider of the Sidneian group, who wrote from 1568 to 1581 things almost sufficiently designated by their titles—*The Arbor of Amitie,* his *Devices,* etc.—belongs to a lower division of the same class with Turberville and Googe. Humphrey Gifford, whose *Posie of Gillyflowers* appeared in 1580, has much more original force, could do the ballad measure well, has a spirited war-song, and some skipping anticipation of the *Nymphidia* measure. Much below either is Matthew Grove, whose poems were published in 1587, but must have been written somewhat earlier. Yet the care which has been expended in reprinting these[8] is not lost, because nothing can be more valuable than to have, at such periods as these, specimens of the ordinary run of verse. When such verse comes to be written, as in our own time and in others, by hundreds of volumes every year, it ceases to possess this interest altogether, and, except in the case of some singular cataclysm, is not likely to recover it. But some would except from these remarks the pair above referred to—Richard Barnfield (1574-1626) and Robert Southwell (1560?-1595). The former,[9] a Staffordshire squire, wrote not a little, but his memory is chiefly attached to *The Affectionate Shepherd* (1594), an amatory poem of classical or Italian rather than English inspiration, some others of no very dissimilar character, and one exquisite thing, the famous

As it fell upon a day,

which used to be ascribed to Shakespeare. Southwell,[10] a Jesuit priest, who was imprisoned and executed as a traitor, has also, but more certainly, left one splendid poem, *The Burning Babe,* and other religious pieces, which, in spirit if not in form, are much above the average.

---

8. All three appear in Dr. Grosart's *Occasional Issues.*
9. Ed. Arber.
10. Ed. Grosart.

The two groups which have been referred to above as necessary to complete the survey of poets strictly contemporary with Spenser are the sonneteers and satirists. Both, in their close connection with each other, and in their apparent adoption of fashionable styles, show that immaturity which is still characteristic of the time; each in different ways shows that time's abounding faculty.

The sonneteers of 1592-96.

It is not possible to decide with absolute certainty what induced the sonnet outburst of the last decade of the sixteenth century in England, and especially of its middle years. The form—"non moins docte que plaisante invention italienne," as Du Bellay calls it—was no novelty in the colder climes of England and France; it had taken both by assault nearly two generations earlier with Wyatt and Mellin de Saint-Gelais. But it is perhaps the best testimony to Sidney's real importance in English literature, that it was not till after his death, and till his sonnets were gradually divulged, that thc sonnet outburst came. There was no mistake about it when it did come. Sidney's poems became known to the general in 1591, and the earliest form of Constable's (see below) next year. In 1593 appeared three remarkable collections, wholly or mainly in sonnet form, the *Parthenophil and Parthenophe* of Barnabe Barnes, the *Licia* of Giles Fletcher, and the *Phillis* of Thomas Lodge.[11] Lodge will reappear as a satirist, as a dramatist, and also as a pamphleteer. The chief achievement of Fletcher is to have been the father of two poets better than himself; and the sonnets of neither are very remarkable, though they testify to the powerful influence in the air. Barnes, though he did other work in prose and verse (a *Treatise of Offices,* a *Divine Century of Spiritual Sonnets,* a play called the *Devil's Charter*) must stand or fall by *Parthenophil.* It has been variously judged, and can never by a sane judgment be set extremely high, seeing that the author has no measure and would sometimes be much the better for having some. But it is a good specimen of the poetical

11. All these, with most of those to be mentioned presently, except *Zepheria,* are in Dr. Grosart's *Occasional Issues.* Several, including *Zepheria,* are in Mr. Arber's *English Garner.*

intoxication of the time, which contrasts so curiously with the unintentional sobriety of the Googes and even the Gascoignes.[12]

These pioneers of the sonnet seem to have encouraged followers, for the next year, 1594, was very fertile in similar books. William Percy, a cadet of the house of Northumberland, and an Oxford man, published *Coelia* (the trick of framing the set of sonnets as an address to a real or feigned mistress established itself at once). Two major poets, Drayton and Daniel, who will have separate notice later, issued, the first *Idea,* the second *Delia.* An anonymous collection, *Zepheria,* has not only intrinsic merit, but is one of the few Elizabethan books which represent very strongly and directly the French Pléiade influence. Willoughby's *Avisa,* (nothing is known of Willoughby or of Avisa, but the book has been drawn into the Shakespearian comment-vortex), though not formerly consisting of sonnets, belongs to the group in other ways. But this group's most characteristic constituent was the fuller form of Constable's *Diana.*

We know a very little more about Henry Constable[13] than about most of the interesting and obscure personages of the time; but we do not know very much. He was probably of the

Constable.

distinguished family still seated in the Holderness district of Yorkshire; he may have been born about 1554 (some say in 1562); he seems to have taken his degree at St. John's College, Cambridge, in 1579; and he was a friend of the Bacons; but he was a Roman Catholic, and, as such, inevitably a member of an Opposition which in those days was exposed to things more unpleasant than mere exclusion from office. How he can, as some say, have formed part of Queen Mary's household in Scotland is not clear, seeing that he cannot have been more than fourteen at the date of the

12. Barnes's birth- and death-dates are unknown. He was a friend of Gabriel Harvey's, and, as Harvey's friends were wont to be, much mixed up in the literary asperities of the time, being for instance bitterly lampooned by Thomas Campion. But we have no real knowledge about him.

13. *Poems,* ed. Hazlitt, London, 1859.

battle of Langside; but he certainly spent much of his middle life in exile abroad; and when he revisited England towards the end of the Queen's reign, he was thrown into the Tower, whence he only emerged after James's accession, and then not at once. He died before 1616 (some say in 1613). His verse was very highly esteemed by his contemporaries. It consists of the twenty-eight sonnets (twenty-three only had been printed in 1592) of *Diana,* the title of which, if it be necessary to seek any special origin for a thing which might have had so many, was probably suggested by the famous *Diana* of Montemayor; of another thirty or more, obtained from MS. on profane, and some seventeen on spiritual, subjects; of four prefixed to Sidney's *Apology* when it was printed, and of four contributions, not sonnets, to *England's Helicon.* The note of the whole of this work is a remarkable elegance and scholarly perfection, less "translunary" perhaps than the brightest comet or rocket effects of Elizabethan poetry, but steadier, more sustained, and in correcter taste.

Alcilia, by "J.C." in 1595, contained sonnets by name which are as far from the sonnet nature as those of *Avisa,* but which are, as verses, sometimes pretty, though usually slim. And 1596 made up for the comparative sterility of its predecessor by giving not merely Spenser's admirable *Amoretti,* but three cycles by persons of whom next to nothing is known, *Fidessa* by Bartholomew Griffin, *Diella* by Richard Lynch, and *Chloris* by William Smith. *Fidessa* is the best of the three. Robert Tofte added *Laura* in 1597, and *Alba* in 1598. The general characteristics of these sonnets will be best given in the Interchapter summarising this Book. But the poetic impulse which they show was diffused over all the later years of the reign, and it is not least well shown in the last and best of the Elizabethan Miscellanies, *England's Helicon* (1600) and Davison's *Poetical Rhapsody* (1602).

The tendency of the Elizabethans to write in schools, and after for some time neglecting a model that lay before them, to copy it in flocks, is only less exhibited in the curious group of satires which coincided with the sonnet outbreak. Wyatt, if he had not quite hit, had gone very near to, the regular satire form, and Gascoigne had actually achieved it; but their examples for a time produced no effect. It is still very uncertain what credence is to be attached to a MS. ascription of Donne's *Satires* to a date as early as 1593; and Donne's work will be best treated together and in the next Book. But Lodge, so often mentioned, and to be mentioned, most certainly issued *A Fig for Momus,* satirical in substance and in form couplets, as early as 1595; which makes the challenge of Joseph Hall, afterwards Bishop, to "follow him who list, And be the *second* English satirist," a piece of rather ill-tasted jactation. Hall published his *Virgidemiarum* in 1597, and was followed by Marston the dramatist with *Satires* accompanying his *Pygmalion's Image* in 1598, and *The Scourge of Villainy* in 1599. Guilpin's *Skialetheia,* Tourneur's *Transformed Metamorphosis,* and a few other things belong to the same school and nearly the same date.[14]

The satirists.

It is a school not to be contemned if we look at its members; less estimable, perhaps, if we look at this particular division of their works. Almost all are tainted with a very great coarseness, and injured by a singular and still not quite intelligible harshness of verse, which is most plausibly explained as coming from a

14. Donne's and Marston's satires are in all the editions of their work; Hall's are in Dr. Grosart's *Occasional Issues,* as is *Skialetheia*; the *Transformed Metamorphosis* is in Mr. Churton Collins's edition of Tourneur.

[*Fifth Edition.* The study of the sonneteers has been immensely facilitated by Mr. Sidney Lee's rearrangement and amplification of Mr. Arber's *English Garner* issues in two vols. of *Elizabethan Sonnets* (London, 1904). This contains an *Introduction* of great length, learning, and value. But it may be permitted to suggest that Mr. Lee lays rather too much stress on the borrowed character of the Elizabethan sonnet. The facts are perhaps not quite so much in favour of borrowing (still less of stealing) as of a certain "community of goods" among sonneteers ever since Petrarch, and indeed before him.)

Eighth Edition. Mr. (now Sir Sidney) Lee has continued the same line of investigation and arrangement on a larger scale, and in regard to lyric and other things, in *The French Renaissance in England* (London, 1910). The caution just advanced applies increasingly to this; but the assistance given by it to the study of Elizabethan literature is great.

corrupt imitation of Persius. The satire, like satire generally, has some value for its picture of manners, especially in Hall and Donne; but even this is vitiated by an obvious and rather tedious exaggeration both of tone and detail, which reaches its acme in Marston, as obscurity of thought and phrase does in Tourneur and roughness of versification in Donne.

5

THE UNIVERSITY WITS

The general drama of 1570-90—The University Wits—Lyly—His plays—Peele—Greene—Marlowe—Kyd—Lodge—Nash—Their work—Its kind in drama—Its vehicle in blank verse—Peele's plays—Those of Greene, Lodge, Nash, and Kyd—The lyrics of the group—Marlowe's plays.

The general drama of 1570-90.

THE history of the English drama during the particular stage of evolution which preceded its fullest development is, except in one well-defined and interestingly-peopled section, not so much difficult as impossible to trace. We have seen how the dramatic work even of a person who stands out from the common herd so much as Stephen Gosson is (though it would have been to the interest of the actors and poets whom he deserted to publish it) entirely lost. We know that the "Marprelate" controversy (*vide* next chapter) was actually brought on the stage in the Armada year or thereabouts, and the fact that, as we should expect, the play was instantly stopped, does not entirely account for, still less reconcile us to, the loss of the piece. Above all, it must have been at this time, that is to say in the years between 1570 and 1590, that the early chronicle-plays and others which Shakespeare honoured by selecting them as the canvases or palimpsest parchments for his own work first saw the light and the boards. But such remnants as we have of these plays are almost invariably of later date in their existing forms.

For the disappearance of this transition work more than one cause, probable *a priori* if not certain historically, is usually and reasonably assigned. Not only were the plays wanted for acting, not reading; but it was in the first place the clear interest of the rival companies, strolling or fixed, to keep their *répertoires* as much as possible to themselves. Further, the constant demand for novelty by audiences, and perhaps also the operation, in a different form, of the just-mentioned wish to keep a monopoly, seem to have led to the working up from time to time of old favourite pieces with new material, either by members of the company or poets specially retained. The variations which (to take examples both from the beginning and end of the seventeenth century) we find between the quarto and folio editions of Shakespeare's *Hamlet,* between the quarto and the folio of Dryden's and Davenant's adaptation of the *Tempest,* show in the case of known men, who had an interest in keeping their work in some form, what must have happened in the case of unknown men, who were usually botching up, for a few shillings, matter which had not come to be regarded with even the smallest literary interest.

The University Wits.

Towards the close of this twilight period, however, we come to a group of dramatic work produced by known or at least named persons (for our positive knowledge of most of them is extremely small), distinguished from the doggerel of the interludes and the starched sterility of the early blank verse plays by the presence in almost all cases of considerable, and in one or two of all but the nights, gifts, and exhibiting a very interesting community of circumstance, equipment, and even definite literary aim. All these men were probably, and all but one or two were certainly, of University training, an advantage less uniformly possessed by their immediate successors. For once the centre and source of a great literary movement in England was what it ought to have been—the two Universities. Not indeed that in all cases the various sets which fostered, and the various schemes which carried out, the literary developments of the time were actually formed at Oxford or at Cambridge, though there is reason to believe that in most cases they were. But the vast majority of the distinguished writers of the time (Shakespeare, it may be remembered, is not early) were University men; their friendships, which in the eager discussion of literary novelties always play so great a part, were in many cases University friendships; and it is notorious that the mighty group of playwrights who founded the English drama were called, not quite amiably, by the players who employed and rivalled them, "University Wits."[1]

In this honourable function Cambridge had a little (though not so much as very pardonable partisanship has sometimes endeavoured to make out) the priority and the predominance. Thus Harvey, the "regent" (in scholastic and French sense at least) of the Areopagus or Sidneian coterie, was a Cambridge man, and so was Spenser; but Sidney himself was of Oxford. Of the great early dramatic group Marlowe, Greene, and Nash were Cambridge men, but Lyly, Peele, and Lodge were Oxonians, as Greene himself subsequently became by incorporation. But there is no need to urge this controversy. The important point is that both the Universities did now begin to play, and played as they never quite have done since, their proper part in the national literary life. The reasons for this are not difficult to find, but they are interesting. The conversion of monastic property, and the shutting up of chantries, monasteries, etc., as outlets for private benevolence and piety, had made the founding of colleges, and of grammar-schools, the feeders of colleges, more than ever popular. The climbing of the secular clergy on the ruins of the regular, the permission of marriage to them, and their close connection with the collegiate system, established perhaps the happiest combined scheme of education and professional subsistence that any country has ever had—a scheme existing nearly untouched till our own day, when it was rashly upset. The various forms of new learning made the Universities interesting, not least owing to their contests with the old; the gradual opening of professional careers to laymen gave outlet and promotion from them; and if the demand in this way for clever graduates was not so great as now, it was increased in a way not now open by the institution, bad or good, of great men's households, about which young men of education and promise were wont to hang in a fashion, vague

1. The *locus classicus* for all this is *The Return from Parnassus,* an extremely interesting set of three plays, first completely printed by W.D. Macray (Oxford, 1886).

and now not quite intelligible, but certain as a matter of historic fact.

The oldest of the University Wits, though an outsider of the principal group, was probably John Lyly, and he deserves first mention not merely for this double fact, but because his chief literary performance (to be mentioned in the next chapter) was, though not in drama, considerably anterior to most of their work. Although we do not know very much about him even in his earlier dates, while his later are quite obscure, our knowledge is full and clear when compared to the "blanket of the dark" which surrounds such names as those of Kyd and, later, Dekker. Lyly was a man of Kent, and must have been born somewhere about 1553. He went to Oxford, his college being Magdalen (where he was probably a demy), took his degree in 1573, and tried a year later to obtain a fellowship through Cecil's interest. In the spring of 1579 he took his place once for all, though with an interval of obscuration, in English literature by *Euphues* (*vide infra*), and in the same year was incorporated at Cambridge. He furnished Thomas Watson (*vide supra*) with a letter commendatory in 1582, and between 1584 and 1594 (in the first year at least he was still battling at Magdalen) furnished the Revels with nine plays, acted by the choristers either of the Chapel Royal or St. Paul's. These are *Campaspe, Sappho and Phao, Endymion, Galatea, Midas, Mother Bombie,* the *Woman in the Moon,* the *Maid's Metamorphosis* (?), and *Love's Metamorphosis.* A dismal petition to the Queen in 1593 sums itself up in one of its clauses: "Thirteen years your Highness's servant and yet nothing." After this we know nothing of him positively, and even the entry which is supposed to be that of his death in 1606 is only connected with him by guesswork, for "Lyly" (Lilly, Lillie, etc.) has always been a common enough name, and there is little identification in "John."

Lyly.

Lyly's plays,[2] like his person, stand quite apart from those of the rest of the group, with which they have nothing in common except the strong classicism, the presence of

2. Ed. Fairholt, 2 vols., London, 1858. *Works,* ed. Bond, 3 vols., Oxford, 1902.

"University Wit," the striking breach with the old tradition of horseplay interlude or wooden tragedy, the exquisite lyric which sometimes diversifies them, and their influence on the greatest dramatist of the next or any age. Written not for the public stage but as court amusements (or "abridgments," as Theseus would say), they have a good deal in common with the Masque. The very marked, not to say conceited style, and the strong, almost bitter, satirical spirit which appear in *Euphues* are also visible. But their most interesting historical characteristic is the way in which, uncertainly and tentatively, they strike out the way of Romantic Comedy, the most arduous and least frequently trodden of all dramatic ways, but when trodden successfully the way to the rarest and choicest of dramatic paradises. We must not say that if there had been no *Endymion* and *Woman in the Moon* there would have been no *Midsummer Night's Dream* and no *As You Like It.* But we may say boldly that before *As You Like It* and *A Midsummer Night's Dream* it is vain to look for anything of their special quality elsewhere than in Lyly.

His plays.

At all events the difference between these plays and those of the other members of the group is most remarkable, and lies not merely in individual genius but in kind. The whole scheme and texture contrast with the vast majority of the work from Peele to Shirley. They come nearer to the antique form of the Interlude, though with little or none of the crudity of this. *Endymion* is a euphuistic allegory, where the loves of the hero, of Cynthia, and of Tellus, themselves but a shadowy centre or canvas, are fringed with humours more shadowy still. The accepted story of Campaspe and Apelles is treated in the same manner; while those of Sappho and Galatea form mere starting-points, from which the author diverges in directions not at all warranted by what may be called his authorities. It is much the same with *Midas,* while in the three last certain plays (the *Maid's Metamorphosis*[3] is not at all like Lyly) the writer trusts

3. This piece (which is not in Fairholt's edition, but will be found in the first volume of Mr. Bullen's *Old Plays,* London, 1882) is in couplets chiefly, whereas Lyly mostly affects blank verse or prose, and has

his fancy almost entirely, weaving, for instance, in the *Woman in the Moon,* out of the myth of Pandora a satire on woman, only suggested, and that in a most modern fashion, by the original. In short, the dramatic element in these plays is more than shadowy, it is phantasmagoric; and the form does hardly more than serve as vehicle for the author's glittering, if somewhat cold, fancy, his melancholy satire, and the *point-de-vice* spruceness of his tyrannically mannered style. He "sits a little apart," like Claverhouse in *Wandering Willie's Tale,* and there is nothing in him of the "dancing and defray" of the rest.

Peele.

Of these George Peele[4] was slightly the eldest. He seems to have been of a Devonshire family, but may have been born in London about 1558. He was at any rate a Blue Coat boy and a member of Broadgates Hall (later Pembroke College) at Oxford, where he took his degrees—B.A. in 1577, M.A. two years later. Peele remained even longer than the customary seven years at Oxford, and seems to have only left it on his marriage, when he went to London and at once fell among the literary set. But he did not break his connection with his University, and in 1583, having already distinguished himself as a playwright, superintended the production of Gager's Latin plays at Christ Church before Prince Casimir. In the same year he contributed commendatory verse to Watson's *Hecatompathia.* Next year appeared his *Arraignment of Paris,* a sort of masque which had been written for the children of the Chapel Royal to play before the Queen. In yet another year, 1585, he was charged by the City with the disposing of the Lord Mayor's pageant, then no vulgar thing.

These details are not otiose, because, though they cannot be said positively to disprove, they do not by any means fit in with, the tradition which makes of Peele a Bohemian reprobate, who died of debauchery and lived as a sort of vulgar Villon in London taverns. The former scandal is due to a gibe of Francis

been thought, with some probability, to be an early work of John Day.

4. Ed. Dyce, in 1 vol. with Greene (London, 1885); ed. Bullen, a vols. (London, 1888).

Meres, the egregious person who spoke of Anthony Munday[5] as our best plotter (though there was possibly a gibe in this too); the second depends almost wholly on an apocryphal farrago of stories, most of them centuries older than Peele's time, called the *Jests of George Peele* or George "Pyeboard" (a play on the name). There is absolutely no known fact in the case except a letter of Peele's to Burleigh in 1596 (two years before, according to Meres, he died), which letter pleads poverty and sickness. It is possible for a man to be poor and ill without debauchery being the cause of either inconvenience.

Indeed much of the stuff which has been talked about the loose lives of this group of men of letters may be brushed away here *in limine.* It has been most insufficiently remembered—first, that the Puritan party, then growing always stronger and more unscrupulous, stuck at no libels against everybody and everything connected with the stage; secondly, that quarrels and jealousies between men of letters, unfortunately, have not been unknown to any age; thirdly, that the appetite for scandal in readers and the quest for "copy" in writers were not checked or corrected by any exact and regular attestation of fact. "Crowner's quests" were known, but it may be suspected that they were very irregularly held; there was no regular system of police, still less any of medical inspection, registration of deaths, and the like. In short, though there is no evidence justifying us in regarding the life of the University Wits in town as a pattern of morality and self-restraint, the evidence to the contrary is of the flimsiest and most suspicious description. In any case, Peele suffered less from it than either Marlowe or Greene.

Of this famous pair Greene, the less gifted, was the older. His birth-year is not known, but he may have been as old as Peele and can hardly have been born later than 1560. At any

5. Munday (1553-1633) was one of the busiest literary hacks of the time, a playwright, a constant botcher-up of pamphlets about crimes and executions (he had brought about some of the latter as an ex-Jesuit seminarist and informer against Jesuits), and a voluminous, but according to Southey unfaithful, translator of the Spanish Romances of chivalry.

rate, he was admitted at St. John's College, Cambridge, in 1575, and took his degree four years later. He subsequently not only proceeded M.A. in his own University but was incorporated as such at Oxford. Meanwhile he had travelled in Italy and Spain, and on his return to England in 1580 had launched one of the so-called "Pamphlets," which will be dealt with in our next chapter, or rather he had obtained a license for it. For almost exactly a decade, from 1582 to 1592, he seems to have lived in London (for the attempts to identify him with a Robert Greene who during part of the time was in orders and held a living are quite gratuitous), and he certainly died in the year last named. For some time before his death he had been engaged in writing a series of pamphlets, some of which appeared posthumously, and one of which, the *Groat's-worth of Wit,* contains a famous passage about his friends and Shakespeare, or at least "Shakescene." These purport to be dying speeches of repentance from a man who was conscious of an evil life and wished to warn his friends. They were taken at more than the letter by others, and a legend, due mostly to Gabriel Harvey, grew up of Greene's having died of a surfeit of "pickled herrings and Rhenish," and of his having lived in disreputable associations for some time previously.

Greene.

The Greene legend is still less lurid than that of Greene's greatest companion. Christopher Marlowe was of rather lower social status than Peele and Greene, both of whom seem to have been sons of persons of some position. His father was a shoemaker at Canterbury, a clerk of St. Mary's Church there, and a freeman of the city. The poet was born in 1564, and at the age of seventeen, after earlier education at the King's School of his native place, entered Benet (Corpus Christi) College, Cambridge. Perhaps he was a *protégé* of the Chief Baron Manwood, a Sandwich and Canterbury magnate, on whom Marlowe perhaps wrote a Latin epitaph. But all these things are uncertain, and some of them share the uncomfortable doubts thrown on the trustworthiness of John Payne Collier. At any rate Marlowe (whose name occurs in the original documents in varieties—Marly, Marlen, Marlyn, and so forth—unusual even for that age of orthographic license) took his B.A. rather soon, in 1583, and his M.A. about

Marlowe.

the usual time from matriculation, in 1587. He must have gone immediately to London, for *Tamburlaine* was produced in the same year, or even in 1586, though it was not produced or published under his name. His career was extraordinarily short, and except from the legend we know nothing of it, while even the closing fact that he was stabbed in the eye by a certain Francis Archer in a tavern at Deptford on 16th June 1593, the blow being given by Archer in self-defence, is partly legendary, and the slayer's name is sometimes given as Ingram. Further, the occasion of the quarrel, if it has any evidence at all, rests on an allusion in a satire of Marston's, which has absolutely no verification. Further yet, some of the unlucky persons who have grubbed up every wretched document about our great men of letters of this time have unearthed an information by one Bame or Baines, a man who was afterwards hanged at Tyburn, charging Marlowe with disgusting vices, with loathsome blasphemy, and with the most offensive brag and chatter about both. It is not sentiment but a sound feeling which has led all true scholars to take refuge in the magnificent eulogy of Drayton, who must have had abundant knowledge, and who was no milksop, though we know that he held aloof from the Bohemianism of the gutter.

This nauseous form of gossip fortunately gathers less about the rest of our group. Of the birth, fortunes, and death of Kyd next to nothing was known till the very recent discoveries of Mr. Boas. He may have been born about 1568, and was somehow

Kyd.

involved in the charges against Marlowe. Of Lodge and Nash we know a little more, but of the first even legend has nothing grimy to say, and of the latter not much. Both were named Thomas. Lodge was the son of a Lord Mayor and went to Trinity College, Oxford; while that he took

Lodge.

to literature early is shown by his answering Gosson, *vide supra*, 1579. It is thought that he was probably then about man's estate. He for some years pursued the way of play, poem, and pamphlet. But by a fortunate chance, which may partly account for his escaping the snares of London, he went to sea with Cavendish in 1591, and on his return, though he at first settled down to the old literary round, he seems to have soon had enough of it. He turned to medicine, took degrees at Avignon and Oxford, became a Roman Catholic, and died in 1625.

Nash.

Nash, the last of the group, was also the youngest. He was born in 1567, the son of a minister at Lowestoft, and entered St. John's College, Cambridge, as a sizar in 1582, when Greene had already made, and Marlowe was just about to make, a reputation. He died in the year of the century, at the age of only thirty-three, having lived apparently rather a struggling than a jovial life, having stoutly defended his friends (he left Cambridge in 1589, and therefore had time to know Greene and Marlowe), having done much rather ephemeral but vigorous and interesting work, in prose chiefly, and having repented with a repentance not open to the suspicion which besets that of his master and model Greene. He had perhaps the least genius of all the set, but he had abundant talent, and was even more than any of them a type.

Their work.

But it is time to pass from the lives of these men, so little known, so idly chattered over, so unimportant except to themselves, to their perennially important and interesting work. The constituents of this have been summed up above—play, poem, pamphlet. From Marlowe and Kyd we have no pamphlets; from Lodge very little play; from Nash not very much more, and hardly any non-dramatic verse worth speaking of. But the three classes were in this or that way the work of all. The prose will be dealt with in the next chapter; the non-dramatic verse—save in the case of Marlowe's *Hero and Leander*, and the exquisite lyrics which most of the group with unpremeditated, certainly with unimitated, art could pour forth—is not of much importance. "The play's the thing" with the group as such.

The devotees of explanation have wearied themselves over attempts to get at the origin of this play. Perhaps it cannot be got at. Dickens, with all his genius, was not a very literary person, and yet he settled the riddle of literary history once for all in his account of the origin of *Pickwick* "I thought of Mr. Pickwick," he says; but how he thought of Mr. Pickwick he does not tell us; probably he could not have told. It will be enough for the wise that to some man or some group of men in England somewhere about 1580 the kind, blended as usual, of English play suggested itself. It is related to the older developments of the interlude; it is related to the classical play; it is still more closely related to the curious sub-variety of that play which was achieved in Nero's time by Seneca the tragedian, which affected all Renaissance Europe with so strange an influence, and which, as has been told above, had been already introduced into English. Kyd, one of the group, translated *Cornélie,* the most Senecan of the great Pléiade dramatist Garnier's imitations of Seneca. All his companions, it is clear, were students of Seneca. Fortunately, however, what ultimately attracted them most in this enigmatical writer was not the regular but the irregular side of him—not the stately iambic and the correct construction, but the lyric excursions of the chorus, the frequent tendency to the introduction of ghosts and supernatural agencies, the "blood and thunder," the bombast and the rant. It may seem a singular thing to give critical thanks for these last. Yet, so far as it is possible to decide upon such matters, it is practically certain that the period of violent fermentation for which these things served as yeast did actually give us, and to all appearance was needed to give us, the strong wine of the completed and perfected drama for some thirty or forty years after Marlowe's death. The earliest Elizabethan theatre had many faults, but the worst of them is its terrible flatness and woodenness. The drama of the Marlowe school may be called, if any one pleases, "a barbaric yawp"; but it is, at any rate when it is characteristic, never wooden and never flat.

Its kind in drama.

Nobody ever innovates all at once and all of a piece; and it would have been something like a miracle if all of this drama had been characteristic. On the contrary, a good deal of it approaches the older stamp, and this may be particularly said to be the case with the work of the two eldest of the group, Lyly and Peele, though both informed it with far greater literary gifts and accomplishments than any earlier dramatist except Sackville had had it in him to show. This may be due, not merely to their

Its vehicle in blank verse.

age, but to the fact that, as has been said, both catered rather for court and other similar pageants than for the rough appetite of the popular theatre. But both did work strikingly good, and Peele much more than Lyly exhibits proficiency in that strange new vehicle of dramatic blank verse which is the triumph and glory of the school, which practically gave us Shakespeare, and which in isolated examples was fashioned—by Marlowe especially, but also by more than one other member of the school—with a majesty and music never since surpassed.

Peele's plays.

This is one of the points in which Lyly stands apart. He has blank verse, but it is of a different quality, and by far the greater part of his plays is in prose,—the natural instrument, though he could disport himself charmingly in lyric, of the author of *Euphues*. Where blank verse appears, as in the *Woman in the Moon*, it is noticeable that the play is late, and that the fashion of the verse has nothing in it very individual. Peele, if *Sir Clyomon and Sir Clamydes* be really his, wrote at least one play in the old fourteener which had been so popular, and which, as Shakespeare's *Love's Labour's Lost*, to take no other example, shows, retained its hold upon writers and hearers pretty late. This play, which may be called a romantic interlude—it has a "vice" and two or three allegorical characters besides Alexander the Great, the two knights, queens, princesses, etc.—is of great interest, marking as it does an experiment in transition. The very early *Arraignment of Paris* is part in fourteeners and in heroics, part in blank verse. *Edward I*—a play which has been rather unnecessarily reviled, because it adopts a popular ballad-scandal against Eleanor of Castile—has prose, blank verse, and doggerel. The *Old Wives' Tale*, which, in more ways than one, comes close to Lyly, is in prose with blank-verse passages. The *Battle of Alcazar* and *David and Bethsabe* are in blank verse only. Taking these facts together, combining with them that of Peele's seniority to Marlowe, and then examining the texture and quality of his blank verse itself, we may probably assign to this writer the chief originating impulse in the great change which the group impressed upon the form. His own, though it never attains to Marlowe's "might," is much sweeter than

Marlowe's usual strain, and perhaps more equably good. He has not discarded all the tricks which we noticed in Gascoigne, being still fond (though not to the extent of the *Steel Glass*) of beginning batches or arrangements in verse with the same or nearly the same phrase. He has not quite emerged from the tyranny of the stopped line, though he seldom or never allows his feet to stump with the wooden tramp of *Gorboduc.* But he has learnt modulation, variety, cadence, and occasionally he can even *soar*—the best gift that this group discovered in the unrhymed decasyllable. It would be hard to find, in any author born earlier, such a "tower" of verse as in this speech of Tamar, which yet is not one of Peele's stock beauties—

> Cast, as was Eva, from that glorious soil,
> Where all delights sat bating, winged with thoughts
> Ready to nestle in her naked breasts,
> To bare and barren vales with floods made waste—
> To desert woods and hills with lightning scorched
> Where[6] death, where[6] shame, where[6] hell, where[6] horror sit.

And he is sometimes almost Miltonic (Milton was a student of Peele) in such "carryings over" as—

> My sister Thamar, when he feigned
> Sickness.

In fact, the blank verse of Peele would repay a far fuller study than it is possible to give it here.

The minor members of the group are less remarkable in this respect. Greene,[7] especially in his best play, *Friar Bacon and Friar Bungay,* succeeds occasionally in imitating both the

6. The original has "with," but "where" is clearly needed.

7. His dramatic works, *A Looking-Glass for London* (the history of Nineveh written with Lodge), *James the Fourth of Scotland* (quite unhistorical), *Alphonsus of Arragon,* etc., are with Peele in Dyce's ed., and by themselves in a Clarendon Press ed. (1905) by Professor Churton Collins. Prose complete only in Dr. Grosarts "Huth Library." Lodge's and Kyd's plays are in Hazlitt's *Dodsley,* and Kyd in a Clarendon Press ed. (1900) by Professor Boas. Nash has been re-edited by Mr. K. M'Kerrow (London, 1904 *sq.*).

soaring and the fluency of Peele; but, as a rule, he is still somewhat too much addicted to the stopped line. Lodge, an agreeable prose writer and a charming lyrist, suffers still more from this old fault in his only known unassisted play, the *Wounds of Civil War*. Nash, a great pamphleteer, has but two plays to his credit, of which *Dido* is known to be partly the work of Marlowe, while great part of *Will Summer's Testament* is in prose, and the blank verse not merely shows a constant tendency to drop into couplet, but has no very distinct quality even when it is pure. Kyd, the last of the group, is much more important than any of these as a playwright. But *Jeronimo,* if it be his, constantly lapses into couplets; the *Spanish Tragedy* shows something of the same tendency as well as much of the stopped line; while the enormous speeches of *Cornelia,* overmastered by the monotony of their French original, succumb with too much regularity to the same malign influence.

Those of Greene, Lodge, Nash, and Kyd.

But side by side with the faculty for blank verse, all the poets hitherto mentioned have a lyric gift which certainly ought to have suppled and inspirited their "blanks," and perhaps did so. The universally known "Cupid and Campaspe" of Lyly is only one of the most regular, by no means of the most charming, of the songs scattered about his plays; and here as in other respects Peele is even more than his compeer. Greene's lyrical work, which is fortunately obtainable[8] separately from his very inaccessible prose and not too common theatre, contains nothing so exquisite as the best of these two men's work or of Lodge's; but is more abundant, has a little less the character of the mere snatch, and seldom or never sinks below a level more than respectable. As for Lodge himself it is in pure poetry, not in drama or in prose, that he can make his safest claim to a high position in English literature. His famous madrigal, "Love in my bosom like a bee," nearly the most

The lyrics of the group.

8. *See* Dyce's and Collins's ed. of plays, and a volume of Bell's *Poets* (with Marlowe's). See also Bell's *Songs from the Dramatists* and Mr. Bullen's *Lyrics from Elizabethan Dramatists* and *Romances.*

charming specimen of a charming kind, then popular, is very closely approached by others of his achievements. Kyd and Nash seem to have had their lips less touched to song; and Marlowe's taste does not seem very frequently to have inclined him to the lyric, though another world-renowned example, "The Passionate Shepherd," shows what he could do when he chose. But his great contribution to poetry other than dramatic was the still more "passionate" narrative of *Hero and Leander,* which ranks with Shakespeare's Juvenilia, and, if it lacks the range and amplitude which, even at this early time, distinguish the work of Shakespeare, exceeds them in intensity and flame.

In Marlowe[9] himself the mighty line is so closely associated with the whole spirit and tendency of his drama that we cannot but take them together. We have from him, besides the work just mentioned, and some translations of Ovid and Lucan, seven plays—the two parts of *Tamburlaine, Doctor Faustus, The Jew of Malta, Edward the Second,* the *Massacre at Paris* and *Dido*. The two last are the weakest, and contain little which we can feel sure that others may not have written. Of the remaining five *Edward the Second* is a regular chronicle-play, aiming at some unity of construction; the other four romantic tragedies of the wildest kind. In the two parts of *Tamburlaine* the conqueror, invincible in fight, insatiable of bloodshed, and hardly human except by his love for his wife, "divine Zenocrate," sweeps slowly past, regardless of all power and life and majesty but his own, trampling on Bajazet, putting man, woman and child to the sword, "showing" the virgins of Antioch "death" at the point of his lances, and only worsted by Death himself, who carries off first Zenocrate and then the tyrant. There is here no central action, only a dissolving series of scenes of terror and blood; no character except the dim and gigantic one of Tamburlaine. If the poet's imagination were of a less grandiose magnificence, or if he were not able to interpret it to us by the unsurpassed splendour and majesty of his versification and phraseology, the thing would be simply dull. The scale is too vast, the personalities too vague even to excite lively and poignant

Marlowe's plays.

9. Ed. Dyce in one volume; ed. Bullen in three.

terror. It has not even "the fierce vexation of a dream," only the chaos of one.

This cannot quite be said of the *Jew of Malta.* Barabas, the hero, is very much more of a person than the huge and shadowy figure of Tamburlaine, and the action is concentrated, or at any rate confined, within a much more manageable area. But the illimitable, the *apeiron* of Marlowe's imagination, intimates itself, for good and for evil, here also. Although the procession of the Jew's crimes is almost as little artistic as that of Tamburlaine's triumphs and butcheries, the intensity of the poet's personification of hatred and avarice and quasi-religious jealousy makes it far more alive. Yet perhaps no play makes us feel so acutely and distinctly the difference between Marlowe and Shakespeare, even if we take for comparison such possibly doubtful and certainly early and immature work as *Titus Andronicus.* Aaron has not received the touches which make Iago and Richard, Shylock and Macbeth what they are. He has still much, and too much, about him of the mere horror-mongering which is characteristic of this middle stage of or drama, and he is, of course, much less magnificent than Barabas. But he is also much more of a human being.

Although it is among the most chaotic, there can be little doubt that *Doctor Faustus* is the best of Marlowe's plays. For the chaos here is not quite out of keeping with the wild theme; and that theme itself, in every other respect, is absolutely suited to Marlowe's genius. The whole spirit of the Faust story comports with—nay positively requires—not so much a regular dramatic action as a phantasmagoria; and its separate scenes are, most of them, well suited to stimulate the towering imagination, the passionate fancy, the tameless and restless energy of this wonderfully though partially endowed poet. That the Helen passage and the death scene contain, with the single exception—if with that—of the great purple patch of *Tamburlaine,* as to "the pens that poets held," the most exquisite outbursts of sheer poetry in Marlowe, is no more than we should expect from the coincidence of inspiring quality in the subject and formal competence in the worker.

Edward the Second falls short, for the complement of the reason which makes *Faustus* so eminent a success. The history-play is not extremely exigent of order or of unity; but to be good it must have something of both. Now order and unity were what Marlowe could never give. Nothing is more natural than that the foully-wronged Queen Isabel should transfer her affections to Mortimer. But Marlowe either cannot or will not take the little trouble necessary to bridge the interval which separates the loving and even forgiving wife from the rancorous adulteress. It might have been a little more difficult, but it was certainly feasible, to project the character of Edward himself so as to render the awkward facts credible and not disgusting. But here again Marlowe does not so much as attempt it. The petulant and unmanly fribble of the first acts might have passed into the tyrannical and arbitrary prince, the not unwarlike lord, of the middle, and he in turn into the almost majestic victim of the end. But "the flats are not joined," and the magnificent speech—

> Leicester, if gentle words might comfort me,

sounds utterly out of place in the mouth of the abject to whom we have been earlier introduced.

Yet in Marlowe two things never fail for long—the strange, not by any means impotent, reach after the infinite, and the command of magnificent verse. He may, as I have said, have learnt something of this latter from Peele, and he seldom approaches his master in sweetness, while he has some of the tricks of the whole school—the constant and sometimes very irritating habit of making the characters speak of themselves in the third person, the still too great tendency to stopped lines, and the like. But the weight and splendour which he impresses on his best passages made them famous at once, and have kept them so, except during the period when all these good things were forgot.

And what is true of Marlowe eminently, of Peele in a not much lower degree, is true of the whole group, save perhaps Nash, who is only a poet and dramatist by accident. They all intend greatly; choose great subjects; handle them, if sometimes with an almost childish want of common sense, yet with poetic imagination and creative force; make them the occasion of passages distinguished by verse of a splendour and momentum, if less often of a lightness and easy movement, never previously known in English. For anything that resembles the echoing thunder of the best decasyllables of these poets (not by any means of Marlowe only) we must go back to the hendecasyllable of Dante, to the hexameter of Lucretius, to the choric phrase of Aeschylus, and there is no fourth parallel in any language before them. Their contemporaries might sometimes gird at the "drumming decasyllabon." But the rub-a-dub of a drum is a curiously weak and inappreciative simile for the sound of the line of Marlowe, even for that of Peele and Kyd, of Greene and Lodge. It much better deserves one suggested by the words of that poet and critic of our own who has best appreciated it—

> The thunder of the trumpets of the night.

6

LYLY AND HOOKER—THE TRANSLATORS, PAMPHLETEERS, AND CRITICS

Ascham's prose—Defects of the type—The ebb and flow of style—Euphuism—*Euphues—Euphues, the Anatomy of Wit—Euphues and his England*—Their style—Its ancient instances—Its vernacularity—Its unnatural history—Hooker—Contemporaries of Lyly and Hooker—The translators—Their characteristics—The pamphleteers—Martin Marprelate—The critics.

THE prose of the great period of Queen Elizabeth's reign is one of the most interesting divisions, historically speaking, of all English prose. We left that medium of expression some years after the Queen's accession in a state which was best indicated by the work of Ascham, the principal prose-writer by far of the time, and one who embodied its dominant characteristics. The period of mere tentative, of experiments in stocking the vocabulary and arranging the syntax, had ceased, experiments in all directions had been made in point of subject, and at length a fairly normal style had been attained, suitable, as Ascham himself showed, for a good variety of literary purposes, if not for all.

Ascham's prose.

"Fairly," it has been said, but by no means finally. The style of Ascham was a pretty good style of all work; but it was not capable of distinction in more than one or two kinds. It was perfectly clear, very fairly advanced in balance and cadence, and possessing yet further capacities in that direction, well proportioned, logical, and sane. But like the later plain prose style of the eighteenth century, it had two drawbacks. It was very ill fitted

Defects of the type.

for fanciful, gorgeous, or passionate expression, and it was constantly liable, when not used with something more than ordinary scholarship and taste, to degenerate into tameness, commonness, insipidity. In its horror of "inkhorn" terms, it was in danger of becoming dull; in its adherence to Latin arrangement and to certain stereotyped, or likely to be stereotyped, tricks of parallelism and antithesis it was in danger of losing raciness and vernacular variety.

Attempts to variegate it were certain, and they have been traced with more or less probability, or fancifulness, in the transition writers between 1560 and 1580. But these tendencies were carried so much farther, and the ideas which lay behind them were so much more brilliantly and importantly expressed in the famous book called *Euphues,* that it is really unnecessary to look behind that, except in making a special study of the particular subject. And even such a study might perhaps wisely avoid cumbering itself too much on the question whether Lyly's original is to be found through Berners in Guevara, or elsewhere, or in many elsewheres, or nowhere. The law of *maxima* and *minima* is more certain and constant in prose style than almost anywhere else. When the elements of such a style have been once got together, florid or plain style (it does not much, or at all, matter which) appears, and is in its measure and degree perfected. As it approaches perfection, men get tired of it and try something new, plain or florid, as the case may be, which in its turn rises, flourishes, decays, and is superseded. At hardly any time (though there are a few apparent exceptions) does either flourish quite alone; in hardly any case can the innovation, whatever it is, be directly traced back to any single case or beginner. Flux rules all, and we can only note with any precision the greater turns of the tide.

The ebb and flow of style.

Euphuism was certainly one of these. Like most things, it has been exaggerated as well as depreciated in importance, and objections have been taken to this or that use of the word—especially to the habit of employing the term generally, as well as specifically. This seems hypercritical. *Euphues* was the first conspicuous example

Euphuism.

in English of the determination to achieve an ornate, variegated, and rather fantastic style; and it is quite reasonable to allow the employment of the abstract terms formed from it as denoting, first, the specific characteristics of the book itself; and, secondly, in the usual transferred fashion, those of the genus to which it belongs, and which renews itself so constantly in species, with only minor differences.

The life of Lyly has been already (p. 361) dealt with, but this book[1] preceded his plays. He was probably about six-and-seventy when its first part, *Euphues, the Anatomy of Wit,* appeared in the spring of 1579. He was certainly still resident at Oxford, and an address to the "Gentlemen Scholars" of that University appeared in the second edition, which followed within the year. The second part, *Euphues and his England,* appeared next year (1580), and both were rapidly and frequently reprinted. The influence of the book has been sometimes a little exaggerated, and sometimes more than a little pooh-poohed, while from a period tolerably early in the seventeenth century to the middle of the eighteenth it was forgotten, and from the middle of the eighteenth to the middle of the nineteenth misrepresented. But there is no doubt at all that for at least twenty years after its first appearance, if not for thirty or forty, Euphuism was a living, an active, and in the usual way and with the usual limitations, a triumphant force. Almost the whole of the more literary art of the curious pamphlet literature of the time followed it; it coloured, at least as much by direct imitation as by indirect revolt, Sidney's equally influential *Arcadia*; it had a very great influence on the dramatists, especially Shakespeare himself in his youth. This history guards most carefully against the undue interchange of *post* and *propter*; and we might have had, we should doubtless have had, Donne first and Browne later, with all the gorgeous language and quaint thought of which the two are the chief representatives in verse and prose, without Lyly. But in that case Donne and Browne, and all those about them, would have had to do for themselves something that, as it was, they found done to their hand.

Euphues.

1. Ed. Arber, London, 1868, and Bond, *u.s.*

It is necessary (and it has not always been done) to keep the matter and intention of Lyly's work separate from his manner. In the first point he was no innovator, and though it would not be correct to say that he was behind his time, he was not more than on a level with it, and was nearer obsolescence than innovation. His book is, in drift and thought, exclusively a Renaissance one; it is concentrated upon Education, and takes that view of Education itself which the Renaissance derived from Plato, and conditioned with its own thoughts in politics, religion, art, and what not. Nominally *Euphues* is a romance. Its first part, *Euphues, or the Anatomy of Wit,* opens at Naples, and treats of the courtship of the heroine Lucilla by the two friends, Euphues and Philautus—the Amadis and Galaor[2] *mutatis mutandis* of the story—and by a third suitor, vastly inferior to either, named Curio. In all Lyly's work (whether for reason or not, we have no evidence) there is a deep and heartfelt satire on woman, which quite transcends the mere stock railing of the Middle Ages; and Lucilla, of course, chooses the unfittest. But the bulk of the book is not story at all, and is made up of various letters of Euphues, the longest being one to Philautus after he has quarrelled with his friend for Lucilla, and she has jilted them both; an orthodox dialogue between Euphues and "Atheos," the latter a person rather rife at this time; and, above all, a very important tractate entitled "Euphues and his Ephebus," which is based on Plutarch's treatise of education, and contains a great part of the real gist of the book. This includes a rather sharp criticism of the condition of things at Oxford, to which Lyly plays "Terrae Filius" a hundred and fifty years before Nicholas Amhurst, though not from the political point of view.

Euphues, or the Anatomy of Wit.

Euphues and his England lands the hero and Philautus in the author's own country, and after a short time at court. In

2. These contrasted (serious and light-o'-love) wooers of the great Portuguese or Spanish romance, themselves slightly altered copies of Lancelot and Gawain, produced an immense effect on the Renaissance, and were reproduced by hundreds of authors in different forms of poem, romance, and play.

this part Philautus is the chief actor. He pays his addresses to a certain Lady Camilla, a court beauty, who is unkind, and is, by the favour of another Lady Flavia, permitted a platonic friendship with her niece Frances as "his violet," which at the close of the book seems to give promise of being turned into something warmer. Meanwhile Euphues, after another quarrel with Philautus, withdraws himself first to study generally, and then, after eulogies on the ladies of England, Cecil (Lyly's patron), and the Queen, to the mountain Silexedra ("Flint-seat," in party Greek-Latin), whence the subsequent pamphleteers occasionally evoked his forlorn and somewhat priggish *eidolon.*

Euphues and his England.

The really noble aims and the somewhat romantic, but by no means unsound, views of love and life and learning which the age of Elizabeth held would hardly have saved this curious book from the fate of many others not far its inferiors in such respects, if Lyly had not been a great mannerist in style, as well as an active practitioner in thought, and if his style had not looked forward instead of backward, or at least merely at the present. It is evident that he was utterly discontented with the plain classicalised style of the Cambridge school. He was as classical as any of them, and he borrowed from them (or more probably from their originals) the practice of balanced sentences, in which some critics have erroneously seen his chief title to mention in the history of English prose. Here he was simply in the direct succession: he started nothing new as compared with Ascham or even Fisher. The point in which he was a pioneer, by which he caught the ear of the rising generation, and by which he has earned his real place in the story, is quite different. It is his revolt against the plain style, and the special means which he took for arming and enforcing that revolt.

Their style.

These were two, or it may be three, which shall be mentioned in the order of their departure from the practices common before him.

The first and by far the least original was a peculiar fashion of bringing in classical examples as similes or illustrations. Such examples in themselves had been commonplaces of the whole Middle Ages, and had come thicker and faster in the fifteenth century and the early Renaissance. But Lyly used them with a difference. "Bucephalus lieth down when he is curried," says he, passing over as known already the ancestry and birth of Alexander, his campaigns, his death, and few particulars about his successors, which the genuine mediaeval taste would have thought excusable, nay, desirable, at this juncture, while even writers like Brandt and his translator Barclay would have thought it sinful to dismiss Bucephalus in less than a paragraph or stanza.

The second, in which he innovated a little more, though still he had numerous forerunners, was the introduction—by way of contrast, to enforce his meaning, or for other reasons—of distinctly vernacular phrases, "I am of the shoemaker's mind who careth not so the shoe hold the plucking on." Such phrases, as we noted, are not uncommon in Ascham himself; but they are much more frequent in Lyly, who in this respect is as Ascham and Latimer rolled into one. To which head may be added his practice in alliteration—a common one, as again we have seen, at the time—but in him far commoner, and far more of a deliberate artifice of style than with most.

Its unnatural history.

Yet here again we may say that had there been nothing else than this in *Euphues,* it had never attained the position it held, and after a long period of eclipse now again holds. Its real differentia, its real *quality,* lies elsewhere, and under a third head, that of the extraordinary similes drawn from all heaven and earth, but especially from the fanciful zoology of the Middle Ages, which it is hardly possible to open two pages of *Euphues* without discovering in greater or less abundance.

The usual efforts have been made to show that this curious and salient feature is not entirely original, and may be found before Lyly. No doubt it may; no doubt any feature of any writer, except the last and highest strokes of the individual genius, may so be found, while even these strokes are sometimes only the result of slight changes on precedent matter. It is quite legitimate, if not supremely important, to indicate, in this writer and in that of the third quarter of the century, the symptoms which are premonitory of every literary change, and therefore of this. But what entitles writers to a conspicuous place in the story of literature is their use for the first time on a large scale, and with striking effect, of certain means to attain certain ends. Lyly was undoubtedly the first to lavish this peculiar kind of simile and illustration, especially with the definite end of heightening and variegating his style, so as to produce on the reader a distinct rhetorical effect, to make the common uncommon, to produce style in and for itself, manner independent of matter. Before Lyly, as we have seen, there had hardly been any one of whom this could be said, except Fisher, and Fisher's means were as different from Lyly's as was his aim.

We do not know that Lyly deliberately and consciously set himself against the principles which Ascham and his set had enunciated thirty years earlier, and which they or others had faithfully carried out; but that the opposition was in effect diametrical is certain. "Inkhorn terms" were no longer tabooed; the ambition to say things in a manner different from that of other people was not only not discouraged, but was distinctly and definitely encouraged; conceit, quaintness, individuality, were reintroduced into literature. The whole bulk of the pamphlet prose to which we shall come presently, expressed the understanding of this, which Lyly's juniors at once manifested.

Meanwhile a contemporary of Lyly's was bringing the plainer style itself to a perfection which in this particular stage was the highest it ever reached, and which showed that in competent hands it need not lack a sober grace, almost beyond that which ornater orderings could attain. Richard Hooker was a native of Heavitree, a suburb of Exeter, and had been born in 1554 in poor conditions. He had, however, forebears and living relations better off, and his uncle, John Hooker, was an Oxford man, a continuator of Holinshed, and a person of consequence under the Elizabethan reconquest of Ireland. He is said to have recommended his

Hooker.

nephew to Bishop Jewel, and Jewel assisted Hooker to go to Corpus Christi College, Oxford, procured him private pupils, and though he himself died when Hooker had not nearly completed his Oxford course, was the cause of his becoming first Scholar and then Fellow of his college, and Reader in Hebrew in the University. He married very foolishly, and was henpecked; but his friends were stanch to him, and he obtained first the living of Drayton Beauchamp in Buckinghamshire, then the Mastership of the Temple in 1584, then the living of Boscombe in 1591, and lastly that of Bishopsbourne in Kent, where he died in 1600. At the Temple he had become involved in an equally unsought and unseemly controversy with his subordinate, the Lecturer, Travers, a bitter Puritan. Hooker's views, when he was transferred once more to the quiet of the country, took form in the great treatise called the *Laws of Ecclesiastical Polity*,[3] of which the first five books, as it now stands, are certainly genuine, while as to the last three it is as certain that they do not appear as he wrote them, but not quite certain how far there was intentional garbling in the arrangement of their present form.

We are here concerned with only one side of this great Apologia for the Anglican Church, which, written while the spirit and intentions of those who presided over its transformation were well-known, has an authority that no later work could claim, and which in the most charitable spirit, and with absolutely no bitterness of feeling, utterly ruined, from the logical and historical side, the position of the English Puritans. Long after Hooker's death they achieved a brief victory by calling in the secular arm, but Hooker's argument, and his history, remained unanswered and triumphant. We are not here further concerned with it than as a masterly piece of English prose, and in this capacity it can hardly be too highly praised. No one, speaking otherwise than at random, would give this praise unmixed. Hooker's style has the faults of its class—a classicism now timid, now unduly audacious; an unnecessary fear of vivid and vernacular expressions. But its author handles the methods and means which he has received

3. Ed. Keble.

with original genius, attaining to a really exquisite balance of sentence, to a harmony sometimes quite ineffable, adjusting his longer and shorter constructions with almost infallible art, and affording a specimen never surpassed, and hardly ever equalled since, of argument maintained on abstract and scholastic points without the slightest dulness, of ornament which is never daubed or stuck on, but arises from the proportion of the phrase, and the careful selection of the vocabulary. Had it been possible to have all prose written by Hookers, nobody need have wished to seek much further experiment. But this was clearly impossible, and the constantly broadening and varying demands of the different subjects to which prose was applied helped the tendency in the air, the mere wish for change, to bring that change about. The *Ecclesiastical Polity* is at least ten years the junior of *Euphues*, but it is its elder by as much or more in the order of style.

Contemporaries of Lyly and Hooker.

Accordingly, in the general work of the time, it is the influence of Lyly, not the influence of Hooker, that we find prevailing. The idea that Sidney intended the *Arcadia* as a protest against Euphuism has been dealt with above, and is almost beyond doubt erroneous. Sir Philip is as great a Euphuist as Euphues himself. So, though his taste was much purer and he came nearer to the stately mannerisms of the Jacobean and Caroline time than to the fantastic coxcombry of purely Elizabethan prose of the ornate kind, was Raleigh; so was the difficult and sententious, but often striking, Fulke Greville. All these were almost exact contemporaries of Hooker and Lyly (Raleigh was born in 1552), and they present, as no others could do, the union of courtly practice, gentle blood, great talents, and a competent education. If Spenser, another contemporary, shows a plainer style, we must remember first that Spenser was a poet, and had the fuller harmony in which to express himself when he listed; secondly, that we have but one piece of prose of his of any length; and thirdly, that this piece is a sober State paper, though a very admirably written one. Historians like Camden (who, indeed, wrote chiefly in Latin) and Knolles and Daniel had also little temptation to indulge in ornateness, not to mention that Daniel, even in verse, prefers neutral tints to brilliant ones, and that Knolles (*c.* 1544-1610) belongs to a somewhat elder generation than that which we are now discussing, and, though he has a stately enough style of his own when he pleases, follows chiefly classical models. We should not expect much Euphuism, though there is some, in Philip Stubbes, the Puritan whose *Anatomy of Abuses,* a characteristic but childish work, appeared in 1583; or in an enthusiast for practical education like Richard Mulcaster. Yet this latter's *Treatise of Right Writing of the English Tongue,* 1582, is quite to our purpose in subject if not in style. Mulcaster, an Eton boy, a member both of King's College, Cambridge, and of Christ Church at Oxford, Master of Merchant Taylors' School in 1561, High Master of St. Paul's from 1596 to within three years of his death in 1611, and Prebendary of Salisbury, is an interesting person, and was an admirable schoolmaster for the time, holding as he did a firm belief in the virtues of the classics for study, and in those of English for practice. But he was not himself a great man of letters, and he had not reached the promised land of English prose style to which he cheered others on.[4]

Still, it is not an exaggeration to say that when a man of this period and generation does endeavour at style, it is much more probable that his attempt will take the form of ornateness, whether in the smaller or in the larger sense of Euphuism, than that it will aim at the simpler graces of strict proportion and cadence. And this is specially to be observed in some groups of prose writers, who may be best noticed here, postponing to the next Book some further comment on some of the works glanced at in the last paragraph, which belong to

4. Raleigh and others will have further notice. The chief pieces of Greville's prose (see Grosart's edition of his works, 4 vols., 1870) are his *Life* (which is not a life) *of Sidney,* for matter, and his *Letter to a Lady,* for thought and style. The late Mr. R.H. Quick, an enthusiast for education, printed (London, 1888) Mulcaster's *Positions,* dealing with that subject, but not the other treatise, entitled also, with a pleasant quaintness, *The First Part of the Elementary.* Richard Knolles's *History of the Turks* appeared in 1603, with subsequent editions in 1610 and 1621, which are not difficult to obtain.

the very latest years of the Queen, or to years later still. These are the translators and the pamphleteers, to whom the critics, as closely connected with both, may be usefully appended.

The translators.

The importance of the Elizabethan translators had never been wholly neglected, owing to their connection with Shakespeare; but it is only recently that it has been fully recognised and the texts themselves brought anew to general knowledge.[5] We have seen that from almost the earliest mediaeval times to some extent, and more fully as the centuries passed by, each generation endeavoured to familiarise itself with at least some of the great writers of antiquity, as well as with those modern books, chiefly in French but latterly in other tongues also, which supplied important literature. During the time, however, while English was simply in the making, it had more to receive than to give, and Caxton's naïve and delightful admiration of the "fair language of French" is only an instance of what was going on. But now an original sap was mounting through the trunk of English prose, and the results were nowhere more apparent, were perhaps nowhere more influential, than here. For a century to come North's[6] *Plutarch* and Florio's[7] *Montaigne* at least were read and re-read with an attention which few other English books (except the translation of the Bible) could command. The former, as all know, furnished Shakespeare with no small proportion of his subjects, and Shakespeare's

5. In the very handsome series of *Tudor Translations* published by Mr. Nutt and edited generally by Mr. W.E. Henley, with introductions by various hands. Florio has also been given by Mr. Waller in a very pretty little edition (6 vols., London, 1897).

6. Sir Thomas North was of the family which became so notable later, and was second son of the first Lord North. Very little is known about him. His *Plutarch* first appeared in 1579, and he did other translations.

7. Of Italian extraction, but born in London about 1553. He was a member of Magdalen College, Oxford, and began as early as 1578 a series of handbooks in the modern languages, of which he was a teacher. The chief is his *World of Words*, an Italian-English dictionary. He was much patronised by Elizabeth's nobility, and held places in the household of her successor. His *Montaigne* (licensed in 1599) first appeared in 1603, and he died in 1625.

generation, as well as at least that which followed it and another still, with their most familiar topics and instances of human conversation and political ethics. The latter helped to create the English Essay, determined to a large extent the course of English philosophy for a time, helped (not quite so fortunately) a certain ebb of the national character from romantic to sordid schemes of life, and by a cross of the French *politique* begat the English "trimmer." Nor were the minor translators in their own day and way less influential. Among these Philemon Holland, born at Chelmsford in 1552, a Fellow of Trinity College, Cambridge, a doctor of medicine and a schoolmaster at Coventry, where he died in 1637, executed rather late in his life versions of Livy, Pliny, Plutarch (the *Morals*), Suetonius, and Xenophon; Thomas Underdowne did Heliodorus and Ovid; Nicolls ventured on Thucydides, but Thucydides was beyond him; William Adlington, of University College, Oxford, took Apuleius; "R.B." Englished some Herodotus; Sir Henry Savile, the learned Provost of Eton, did Tacitus; and Angel Day wrought Longus through Amyot into the vernacular.

Their characteristics.

It will readily be understood that whatever interest these translations possess arises to hardly the smallest extent from faithful representation of the originals. Savile certainly, Holland to some degree, one or two others more or less, were scholars; but the most famous and popular of the versions were usually taken, not direct from the original, but from previous French or Italian translations, and it was hardly the object of a single one of these writers to give their author, their whole author, and nothing but their author, in rigidly classical English. Had it been so, they had been of far less interest and value to posterity. On the contrary, such community of design as is to be seen in them (and it is rather remarkable) consists in the effort to be at once as vernacular and as variegated as may be. They compress, expand, omit, or sometimes even insert, as no modem translator would dare to do; they exhibit to the very fullest the double tendency of Euphuism to the finest and the most familiar expressions; and following in this respect Lord Berners, if not earlier translators, they put English dresses on foreign words and terms in a way infinitely delightful and full of refreshment to the tongue, but such as would make our modern purists stare and gasp. To this day these translations are a repertory of slang that still exists, of racy but obsolete expressions which would else be lost, of Latinisms, Gallicisms—isms of every kind. No class of work is fuller of that most English of all idioms, the turning of any noun, adjective or substantive, into a verb. They had, no doubt, little idea of proportion, choice, grace; but these were not the things the language needed at the time. It wanted to be thoroughly suppled, thoroughly vernacularised, and at the same time to be charged with store of good words, native and foreign, classical and modern, from which a standard vocabulary could be, as it was, riddled out afterwards. The late fourteenth and the fifteenth century writers had done their part in teaching English prose "to go"; Fisher and the Ascham school had given it a thorough grammar-school education. But these writers and others of Elizabeth's time were putting it to the university, practising it in all sports and arts at once, allowing it, it may be, rather a full allowance of wild oats, but enriching it, exercising it, giving it possessions, memories, experience; preparing it for its future business in a fashion as necessary as the more orderly and sedate processes of training which it had previously undergone.

The pamphleteers.

Exactly the same drift and tendency, though in more original matter, is shown by the curious and interesting range of pamphlet literature which, connected very directly in point of authorship with the group of University Wits, fills the last twenty years if Elizabeth, and extends into those of James and even Charles. This touches all, or almost all, varieties of subject with a universality which comes not so very far short of the modern newspaper; while in some of its developments may be found a stage—a far-off and rudimentary one, it is true—of the great change which converted the romance into the modern novel. These pamphlets[8]—a form of publication which could hardly

8. Until recently most of them were inaccessible except in large libraries, and even now they are best found in the privately printed issues of

have come into being without the printing press, and which the printing press was almost certain to bring about—had been in their earliest shape either devoted to the controversies of the Reformation, or else shortened chap-book versions of mediaeval literature, romances in verse and in prose, jests, books of saws and instances. The sharp discipline of the Tudor Queen made the religious pamphlet a probable, and the political one an almost certain, short way to the gallows, or at least the whipping-post and chopping-block, so it was little cultivated. Yet one famous outbreak, that of the Martin Marprelate controversy, defied, though only for a time, these preventive checks. It concerned (as indeed the pseudonym of the various writers on the aggressive side confesses) the anti-prelatical movement in England, but was from the first strongly coloured by, and at last became almost wholly merged in, the flood of personal reviling which, to the great discredit of the Reformers, they had been the first to let loose. The defenders of orthodoxy and authority included some grave churchmen and more irresponsible men of letters, whom a not erring instinct told that Puritanism was as much the foe of literature as of loyalty and order in religion and politics. Lyly, Nash, and the Harveys almost or quite to a certainty took part in it, and their lampoons, as well as some at least of those of their antagonists, display the revel and riot of words which has been indicated above at its very wildest.

Martin Marprelate.

This, however, was only an episode in the pamphlet history; and it was quickly stopped.[9] The pamphlet itself persevered in

Dr. Grosart. His "Huth Library" contains Greene, Nash, Dekker, Harvey, and his "Chertsey Worthies" the enormous work of Nicholas Breton. The Marprelate tracts were printed half a century ago by the bookseller Petheram, and some more recently, with an invaluable account of the whole controversy, by Mr. Arber, whose *English Garner* contains a great number of scattered pamphlets. Lodge has been given by the Hunterian Club.

9. I may be permitted to refer the reader who wishes for more on "Martin" and the pamphlets generally to my separate history of *Elizabethan Literature,* pp. 223-52. These byways of history are almost closed to the general historian; at least he strays if he pursues them too far.

less dangerous forms—novels, generally of a strongly Euphuist tinge; personal reminiscences, true or feigned; disquisitions serious or comic, not very different, allowing for the time, from those of the Addisonian Essay; a very curious batch of sketches of the manners, especially the lower and looser manners, of the capital; and lastly, literary criticism. In all these respects except the last, Robert Greene (see last chapter) was the most prolific, and on the whole the most gifted. His short Euphuist stories, often diversified by scraps of verse, not merely furnished subjects to Shakespeare and others, but undoubtedly helped to foster in readers a taste for imaginative fiction. His personal sketches are among the earliest of literary autobiographies, though they have to be taken with rather numerous grains of salt. Above all, his series on "coney-catching" ("rooking," card-sharping, etc.), though again not to be taken too literally, is a most amusing and, with caution, instructive collection, and continued as it was by Dekker in the next generation, gives us a panorama of the shady side of London life for nearly half a century. Nash, with less romantic gift than Greene, and with no poetical power, yet achieved in *Jack Wilton, or the Unfortunate Traveller,* a novel of merit, which "coney-catched" many generations as to the loves of Surrey and "Geraldine," and besides his "Marprelate" contributions, perhaps in consequence of them, engaged in a furious paper war, the other party to which was Gabriel Harvey. Later, Nash, like others, wrote repentant and pious pamphlets. Perhaps, except in bulk, Lodge is even the superior of Greene, in respect of the romantic tone of his prose and the exquisite lyric touch of the verse with which it is strewn; while the enormous pamphlet work of Nicholas Breton, a step-son of Gascoigne and a voluminous writer in prose and verse, belongs, as does that of Dekker, rather to the next period than to this.[10]

10. The titles of these pamphlets play a great part in them—those of the "Marprelate" set having a Rabelaisian extravagance, and often a wonderful length; others abounding in favourite Elizabethan catchwords and word-plays, like that on "Will" and "Wit"; and the more romantic pieces attaining great prettiness, as in Lodge's *A Margarite of America.*

Lodge, however, will bring us conveniently to the critics of whom he was one, and who were very often the same persons just mentioned, engaged for the moment in literary controversies. The most important of these controversies were the Puritan attack on plays and poetry generally, which was opened by the *School of Abuse* of Stephen Gosson (*vide supra*), and the other, longer, and more important controversy, first between metrical forms exactly corresponding to those of the classics, and then between rhymeless rhythms adjusted more intelligently to the genius of English. The earlier stage of this is best represented by the *Four Letters* of Spenser and Harvey, the later by Campion and Daniel.

The critics.

The little book of William Webbe, and the much larger one attributed to George Puttenham, both,[11] especially the former, show the influence of the first part of this craze. The almost unknown William Webbe, who is thought to have been a member of St. John's College, Cambridge, and who appears to have been tutor to the sons of an Essex squire named Sulyard, published his *Discourse of English Poetrie* in 1586. It contains enthusiastic praise of Spenser, "the new poet," "our late famous English poet who wrote the *Shepherd's Calendar*" refers a good deal to the ancients, and rather superficially to the English poets, "scorns and spews out the ragged rout of our rakehelly rhymers—for so themselves use to hunt the letter," as "E.K.," for self or partner, had done before it, gives us some very comical hexameters for the two first eclogues of Virgil, and with more zeal than discretion turns Spenser's "Ye dainty nymphs" into a slipshod sort of slovenly Sapphics. But Webbe's enthusiasm is pleasing, and his style typical. Puttenham, if he was the author of the *Art of English Poesie* which appeared in 1589, was more cautious about the new mania. His volume, which is of some length, is a rather orderly treatise on Poetics and Rhetoric mixed as commonly, divided into three books, the first of Poets and Poesie, the second of Proportion, and the

11. Both in Mr. Arber's *Reprints*. But the documents of the whole subject have now been made accessible in a standard edition by Mr. Gregory Smith's *Elizabethan Critical Essays* (2 vols., Oxford, 1904).

third of Ornament—this last being almost entirely devoted to a very full list of the Figures of Speech. In dealing with proportion he does not disdain the fancy shapes—pyramids, etc.—which aroused the anger of Addison. As may be guessed from this, Puttenham, who quotes his own verse freely and seems to have written it fairly in the stiffer manner of the first half of the reign, is rather a formalist, but his judgment, when he can get it out of stays, is not contemptible. The book is very full, learned, and careful, the work of a scholar and a gentleman, and far exceeding in detail and scope anything of the kind that was written for ages afterwards.

INTERCHAPTER 5

ATTENTION has often been drawn to the ambiguity of the title Elizabethan Literature, as commonly used. "Is it not," they say, "absurd to include under such a head the work of men who, like Milton and Browne, were not born till after the Queen's death, and did not die till the last quarter of the seventeenth century had arrived or was at the door?" "Is it not even the fact that most of the masterpieces of this literature were not produced at all till the reign of James?" It is desirable to remember these facts; but it is still more desirable to remember the others, first that all the seed of the whole period called Elizabethan was sown, and that not a little of it had come up, before the Queen's death; and secondly, that the quality of the period 1580-1660 is essentially one and indivisible. There are differences between Milton and Spenser, but they are differences rather of degree than of kind. The differences between Milton and Dryden are differences at least of species, almost of genus.

Our present arrangement has the advantage of keeping both sets of facts in view, and in especial of directing attention to the characteristics of the first generation of the period, the generation which, as typified by Spenser, ended a little before the last evil days of Elizabeth's own life closed. It is perfectly true that among the completed work of this time we find but one name, that of Spenser himself, which represents, undoubtedly and unquestionably, a star of the first magnitude and the widest orbit, and that perhaps two others, Marlowe and Hooker, are the only companions that can be assigned to him by a criticism which unites exactness with liberality. But it is not at all necessary to take refuge from this fact in another, the fact that, in the last date at least of the time, we have the wonderful beginnings of Shakespeare in drama, of Bacon in prose, of Donne and others in pure poetry. There is a third aspect under which the period requires no allowance, no compensation of any kind, and which enables it to stand on the credit of its own capital and revenue. It is this aspect too, which makes it peculiarly desirable to mark it off distinctly, though not too sharply, from its successor. It was the period of the remaking, in different degrees for the different departments, but in all of the remaking, and in one practically of the making, of English Literature.

This process is most definitely and clearly mapped out in regard to Poetry. If the facts of the foregoing Hooks and the concentrated lessons of their Interchapters have been followed, the necessity for the remaking will here need little enforcement. Chaucer had gathered up all the stuff and all the methods of mediaeval work in English verse, had added much of his own, and had left poetry in a stage of relative perfection. But the succession failed. Even men who were of more than man's estate at the time of his death, like Lydgate and Occleve, could not manage what he left them; and changes, obscure in process but obvious in kind and in result, increased the difficulty for their successors. Nor were Wyatt and Surrey in a position to undertake the reshaping with a view to the future not the past. Both had genius, but it was genius rather fine than strong: both were short-lived; and both came a little too early for their task. Nor did they for a long time find any seconds, and perhaps it was just as well. The obscure alterations of constitution, the changes of life, had to complete themselves before the new poetry could come. Then "the new poet" brought it.

On the whole, what Spenser did has been rather under- than overvalued, and his greatness only depends in part, and hardly the largest part, on the personal opinion which this or that reader may form of the poetical merit even of the *Faërie Queene*. It may be, as some think, a venerable and in parts beautiful but tedious and out-of-date allegory, or it may be, as others think, by far the greatest long poem in English. It may be anything between these two estimates. But the aesthetic variation has no place in the clear verdict of history. It is indisputable (which is not the same thing as being undisputed) that Spenser practically created the diction and prosody of English poetry as both have subsisted in the main to the present day. He did not, of course, finish the creation. Shakespeare had to come, and Milton, at least, before that was done; but he did a great deal more than begin it. His versification had to receive not a little extension, and an infinite process—a process not yet ended—of permutations and combinations, but it has not to the present day undergone any fundamental change. His diction—correctly But short-sightedly condemned by Ben as "no language"—was in fact a bold recognition of the fact that merely the current language of the day or any common day can never be the diction of poetry, that poetry needs a diction cunningly and carefully, but always to a greater or less extent, alienated, refined, *distinguished* from the diction of prose. The enormous dead-lift which he gave to poetry, and the results of which were apparent in the ten last years of his life, and the fifty or more following it, was only in very small part due to direct imitation of his own work as such. It was due, even in the hands of Shakespeare, even in the hands of Milton, to the fact that Shakespeare first and Milton afterwards had in their hands the stock of language, the plant of prosody, which Spenser had first founded and set going. The kinds of sonnet and of satire, of history-poem and poem-philosophical which sprang up so abundantly in his footsteps are interesting, but they are not really so interesting to history as this complete reorganisation of the poet's material and of his means, as this remaking of English verse.

The position of the age in prose is hardly less important, though its achievement is much less decided. No single prose-writer of the time, not even Hooker, holds the same rank in prose that Spenser holds in poetry; perhaps, indeed, no single writer, not even Dryden, ever has held that rank. For prose, the lower and less intense harmony, is the more varied and indefinitely adjustable instrument. And while it is conceivable that one man—indeed Shakespeare has very nearly done so—should catch up and utter in hint and intimation at least, the whole sum of poetry, no one could do the like in prose. Here, too, the comparative newness of the form had its inevitable effect; even the period of sheer experiment and exploration was not over when the sixteenth century ended.

Very great advances had been made in both, and, above all, the *antinomy* of prose, the opposition of the plain and ornate styles which was to dominate the rest of its history, was for the first time clearly posed and definitely worked out on either side. This could not have happened in the earlier period of mere or main translation as regards subject, of tentative accumulation of vocabulary and experimental adaptation of arrangement. Vestiges, or rather rudiments, of the antinomy would, of course, appear encouraged by nature of subject or temperament of writer. A Chaucer translating the metres of Boethius about the motion of the heavens was not likely to write like a Cap-grave in his chronicle. But the opposition was accidental and rudimentary first of all. Not till the weariness of the "aureate" diction of the fifteenth century—itself shown chiefly in verse—led the Cambridge school to denounce ink-horn terms, and combined with their worship of the classics to devise a plain classical style, could the inevitable revolt and rebound array itself definitely with a purpose, a programme, a creed, and become, first in the hands of Lyly and his followers, a striking grotesque, and then in those of Bacon and the great seventeenth-century writers, a magnificent resurrection of rhetoric in a far more glorious form than she had ever known. But at any rate the quarrel was at last fairly put, the "dependency" distinctly established. Henceforward the ebb and flow of prose style has reigned with only superficial change for three centuries, alternately seeking the correct and simple or the out-of-the-way and gorgeous as ideals, and falling into the tame or vulgar, the extravagant or gaudy, as excesses.

In Drama, the third division, which deserves to be kept apart from poetry and prose, not only localise it indifferently applies the form of both, but because by its importation of speech and action it introduces elements not strictly appropriate to either, the importance of the time has commonly seemed greatest of all. It is certainly somewhat different in nature. Here we have neither a reconstruction and recovery in greater and more promising form of a state formerly reached and then lost, as in poetry; nor a comparatively orderly extension of a campaign not yet crowned with complete victory, as in prose. But we most certainly have the sudden shaking together into their right places of elements which hitherto have been loosely whirling like the Lucretian atoms; and it is at least arguable that we have the attainment of a final form. At any rate three entire centuries have failed to produce any new really fertile cross, or to import, in conditions suitable to the climate, any foreign form capable of standing comparison with that Elizabethan play, which shook itself into shape, a hundred minor hands besides those of Marlowe and Shakespeare aiding, by the date of the production of *Every Man in his Humour*.

Much as has been written about this play, it has perhaps been insufficiently recognised that its idea, whether the matter be tragical or comical, whether it keep these kinds apart or mix them as ingeniously as in the famous classification of *Hamlet,* is essentially the same—to wit, that the play shall be a piece of life, rendered as faithfully and separately as possible, with all its divagations, its interludes, its inconsistencies, its interruptions. This is, of course, diametrically opposed to the classical theory, and to the theory of almost every modern drama except the Spanish, even to a certain extent of that. Aristotle's at first sight odd, but, whether right or wrong, all-important comparison of a play to an animal[1] helps us, perhaps better than anything, to understand the difference. Nothing that is not vitally connected with the animal—with the central notion of the play itself—must appear; the Unities (not in their absurd seventeenth-century caricature, but in their actual Greek limitation) follow naturally; second plots are impossible, for two-natured is no nature. We may have intensity and accomplishment; but, above all, we must have limit.

1. I am aware that some of the latest authorities take *ζῷον* in the sense of "picture," but I cannot agree with them, at least for an exclusive explanation.

The Elizabethan idea is far more ambitious and grand, even if doomed to fail in all but the strongest hands. The poet does not attempt to isolate action or situation merely; his play is but a piece of the life of the actors—their life is but a piece of larger and ever larger lives. Nothing is superfluous, irrelevant, common, unclean; everything may and shall go in. The intenser nature of the interests of tragedy may give to the working of tragic plays a closer unity than that of comic; the majesty or the pathos of some particular character may dwarf in presentation as in attention the episodes and the interludes. But the principle is always the same. The touch with the actual is never loosed, the farrago of the play is the farrago of life.

It is the just and abiding glory of Marlowe that, so far as one man could, he really seems to have hit, consciously or not, on this vast conception, and that he certainly perfected, or went far to perfect, the only instrument of verse that could possibly serve as a medium of execution for it. But his own plays as plays are after all only the most magnificent of failures, and without a Shakespeare the possibility of the thing could never have been shown. Whether the possibility of it has ever been fully shown except by Shakespeare is a point on which it would be partly irrelevant and wholly anticipatory to dwell here.

That the mere form of play which was strong enough and elastic enough to give shape to this mighty attempt developed itself out of the beggarly elements of the mystery and interlude, with the undoubted but only partial help and crossing of the classical drama, has been, I hope, shown, with less violence to fact and probability than other theories require. But it can never be denied that the transformation is astonishing. It was not so rapid, nor does it display such individual power of genius, as that which in a single man's hands evolved the relatively perfect poetical work of Chaucer from the interesting but in no single case perfect experiments of the hundred and fifty years before him. More than a generation had to pass, a vast company of men, unknown, half-known, and known, had to be continuously at work, before the childish puppet-plays—comparatively speaking—of Udall and Sackville and Still passed into the completed work of Shakespeare. But as the process was slower, so the result was more sure. Chaucer's work, as we have seen, found no following except in a half-foreign country, and from men who were themselves unable to hand on the art in living condition. The thirty years of experiment in drama, from 1560 to 1590, were succeeded by fifty more of the most abundant, varied, vigorous, and, for the best of the time, brilliant production that any literary form has ever enjoyed.

Book VI

Later Elizabethan and Jacobean Literature

1

SHAKESPEARE

The luck of Jacobean literature—Concentration of the great drama in it—Shakespearian chronology—The life—The work—The poems—The *Sonnets*—Their formal and spiritual supremacy—Probable divisions of plays: the earlier—Their verse and phrase—Their construction—Their characters—The middle division: the *Merry Wives*—The Romantic comedies—The great tragedies, Roman and Romantic—Last plays—Doubtful plays.

The luck of Jacobean literature.

IT will have been seen already with what large cautions and provisos the familiar term Elizabethan Literature has to be taken. The phenomenon to which we apply it took its rise within the reign of the Queen, or—if we take that rise to be manifested by the publication and appreciation of the *Songs and Sonnets*—on the latest eve of that reign. But it grew very slowly. More than twenty years passed before anything really striking and decisive either in prose or poetry appeared; nearly thirty before really characteristic and original drama emerged, and then not by any means completely, from the condition of experiment. Even after *Euphues* and the *Shepherd's Calendar* had distinctly foretold great things in the two ordinary harmonies, another ten or fifteen years' schooling had to be undergone before the general time of production was reached. And the greatest work of all, putting Spenser, Hooker, and Marlowe aside, was mostly borne, though as *non sua poma,* by the reign of James.

Despite the extreme uncertainty of Shakespearian chronology, we do know that a considerable part of Shakespeare's work was done before 1603. But certainly the best part was not. Very little of Jonson antedates the Queen's death; the meagre bundles of notes, interesting and pregnant as they are, which constitute the first edition of Bacon's *Essays,* would, had they never been augmented, have given us no idea whatever of his real literary powers; the best work of men like Daniel and Drayton was to come. What is perhaps not more really surprising, but more startling at first sight than the slowness of the rise of this great literature, is the rapidity, in the case of its most notable and characteristic constituent, of the decline. Omitting the work of Marlowe, which was prematurely brought to a close, the early work of Shakespeare, and a little more on the farther side, with a much smaller part of that of Ford, Massinger, and others on the hither—the whole bulk of the English drama was written between 1600 and 1625. Almost the whole bulk of it that has really commanding merit was written between 1590 and 1640—periods of exactly a quarter of a century in the first case, of exactly half a century in the second. Fletcher died less than ten years after Shakespeare, and in the work of all the men who survived Fletcher decadence is apparent. There are, of course, those who would say that it is apparent in Fletcher himself, even in those works of his which, being certainly, or almost certainly, in part due to Beaumont (who died *before* Shakespeare), are contemporary with the masterpieces of the class. But this is perhaps an extravagantly rigid and arbitrary scheme of classification. It is enough to say that between 1600 and 1625 all the best of our dramatists except Marlowe were working more or less simultaneously; and that within this period all the known kinds of the great drama itself, had been discovered and practised. What is more is that within this same time the great metrical effect of drama upon English poetry had been, for good, entirely accomplished, and was already beginning to turn to evil—an evil which was not limited to its own immediate form.

Concentration of the great drama in it.

Reference has already been made to the fact that an attack, on the score of plagiarism and other misdemeanours, had been made by Greene, before his death in 1592, upon a certain Shakescene, who has been naturally identified with William Shakespeare. But we do not know with any certain or satisfactory knowledge upon what work of Shakespeare's this attack was directed. All the more careful and reasonable accounts of his life and work mark the earliest play-dates, where they give them, with a tell-tale *circa.* It is only by guesses that anything is dated before the *Comedy of Errors,* at the extreme end of 1594; and the *Comedy of Errors,* unmistakably Shakespearian as it is here and there in character and versification, is so exceedingly crude both in these points and in composition generally, that the conjectural antedating of plays like *Richard III,* and still more *A Midsummer Night's Dream,* becomes from the literary point of view almost utterly incredible. And it may not be improper to add a very earnest protest against the attempt to group plays and classes of plays according to successive supposed states of the poet's mind and temper. Where there is crudity of character, artlessness of verse, or very flagrantly chaotic composition (it must be remembered that Shakespeare's composition is not to be judged by the rules of any ancient *abbé* or modern journalist) then we may with a clear literary conscience ticket this as "probably early." Otherwise, in default of positive documentary evidence, there would not be much reason for putting *The Tempest* later than *A Midsummer Night's Dream,* or *A Winter's Tale* than *Romeo and Juliet.* A poet, especially a poet like Shakespeare, is not a vegetable; you cannot count the years of his work by any real or fancied number of rings in his heart. Bad verse, inhuman character, clumsy composition—become after a time impossible to him; in temper and choice of subject he abides supreme and free.

Shakespearian chronology.

The results of the almost ferocious industry spent upon unearthing and analysing every date and detail of Shakespeare's life are on the whole very meagre, and for literary purposes almost entirely unimportant, while with guesswork we have nothing to do. The certainties may be summarised very briefly. William Shakespeare was traditionally born on the 23rd of April, and certainly baptized on the 26th

The life.

of April 1564, at Stratford-on-Avon. His grandfather's name was Richard, that of his father, a dealer in hides, gloves, corn, wood, etc., was John, and the poet's mother was Mary Arden. He had two sisters and three brothers. The family, which through Mary Arden had some small landed property, was at one time prosperous, at others not. Shakespeare himself married early; the date of the actual ceremony is not known, but a bond of marriage passed between him and his wife Anne Hathaway on November 1582, when he was little more than eighteen, and his wife, a yeoman's daughter, eight years older. They had three children, Susanna, Hamnet, and Judith, and there is absolutely no documentary evidence of the slightest value as to the terms on which they lived together. Tradition there is—though of no great age, and of exceedingly slight authority—as to his leaving Stratford for London, perhaps in 1585, 1586, or 1587, and perhaps in consequence of a deer-stealing prank in the neighbouring park of Sir Thomas Lucy of Charlecote. He perhaps began his connection with the theatre as a horse-holder; and was pretty certainly an actor before long. In 1593 appeared his first work, the remarkable *Venus and Adonis,* and next year the rather less remarkable *Lucrece.* He was connected soon after the middle of the last decade of the century with divers theatres, became a shareholder in them, and by 1597 could buy a good house, New Place, at Stratford, where he afterwards enlarged his property. It is to be noted that his constant residence at London during these ten years, his desertion of his wife, etc., are all matters of guesswork founded on barely negative evidence. It is not in the slightest degree impossible that Anne Shakespeare was with her husband for the whole time, or that he made frequent visits home. But there are fair grounds for supposing that London was his headquarters during the decade from 1586 to 1596, his partial residence during the next, and only occasionally visited by him during the third—at the close of which, in 1616 on 23rd April, he died. The best-known detail about him perhaps, and a sample of the trivial things on which structures of gossip have been based, is his bequest of his second-best bed to his wife. Personal references to him are not numerous and rather vague, though except in the case of Greene's splenetic outburst (if it be meant for Shakespeare) always complimentary. His reputation, though it has steadily grown, has always been great; there has never from the day of his death to this day been wanting testimony to his position from the greatest living names of the time in English literature.

The work.

Shakespeare's works, in the generally accepted canon, consist of a comparatively small body of non-dramatic poems, the two pieces above mentioned, a body of 154 sonnets, and a very few shorter pieces somewhat more doubtfully genuine, on the one hand; on the other, of about twenty times as much dramatic work divided into thirty-seven plays, which in the original edition, published seven years after the owner's death by his friends Heminge and Condell (this does not contain *Pericles*), are classed as "tragedies, comedies, and histories." Before this edition, and during Shakespeare's lifetime, only a few of the plays had been printed in quartos of doubtful authenticity; the *Venus,* the *Lucrece,* and the *Sonnets* appeared with his name and pretty certainly under his superintendence. The spelling of the name varies from Shaxper to Shakespeare. But if Greene's gibe at it is good for anything, it settles the pronunciation as nearest the latter form, and this is the spelling on the title-page of the *Sonnets,* the only book of his published in his lifetime, after he was famous, and obviously with his leave if not by him.

In view of the extreme uncertainty of date of most of the plays before 1600, the certain attribution of the two larger poems to 1593-94, and of the *Sonnets* (though they were not printed till 1609) to 1598 or earlier, when they are mentioned in Meres's *Palladis Tamia,*[1] is very important and solid. These early dates, and the fact that all the three larger pieces or groups are concerned with love, show us in a more personal fashion than the scheme of the drama (always more or less impersonal, and in Shakespeare's hands extraordinarily so)

1. Meres's extremely interesting though singularly uncritical sketch of contemporary and other English literature will be found in Mr. Arber's *English Garner,* ii. 94; and in Mr. Gregory Smith's *Elizabethan Critical Essays,* as cited above.

what manner of man and poet Shakespeare was in his youth. The dominant tone in all three is passion, combined in the *Sonnets* with an intense and wide-sweeping thought. In some more general and obvious characteristics *Venus and Adonis* and *The Rape of Lucrece* differ little from other members of a large class of Elizabethan poems referred to above (p. 341). They select, on the pattern of many writers of the French and Italian Renaissance, subjects at once luscious and tragical, and they apply the new melodious verse, of which Spenser had taught the secret, to the discussion of them in a manner which appeals at once to the sensual and the sentimental emotions.

But if the class was the same, the individuals are very different. There were already many tuneful singers in 1593; but none of them except the master himself could raise such a pageant of voluptuous imagery, or accompany it with such a symphony of harmonious sound, as we find in *Venus and Adonis.* No one except Spenser and Sackville had evoked the rhyme-clangour of the stanza[2] with such delicate art; no one except these two had portrayed such vivid pictures as the arrest of Adonis by Venus, the captivity of Mars, the portrait of herself by the goddess, the escape of the courser, the description of the boar and of the hare-hunt, the solitary night, the discovery of the foolish youth who has fled from Love's arms to those of Death. But while none, save these, of men living had done, or could have done, such work, there was much here which—whether either could have done it or not—neither had done.

The poems.

In the first place there is, almost for the first time in English poetry since Chaucer, a directness of observation in the sketches from nature. Sackville, so far as his brief space and peculiar subjects allowed him, Spenser far more, are great painters and describers. But even the later and greater poet rather displays a magnificently decorative convention in painting than a direct re-creative or reproductive touch. Shakespeare, even in these earliest days, has this latter—the horse and the hare, though the most

2. *Venus and Adonis* is in the six-, *Lucrece* in the seven-lined stave.

famous and elaborate, are only two out of many instances of it in the *Venus.* In the second place, the slow movement, which is of the essence of the poetry of Sackville and of Spenser, and which is certainly invited by the six-lined stanza in which the *Venus* is written almost as much as by the rhyme-royal and the Spenserian, cannot adjust itself to the infinite variety and the directly lyrical flow of Shakespeare's versification. It is not a mere accident which has made composers choose "Bid me discourse" and "Lo, here the gentle lark" for setting to song measures of the lightest quality; and throughout the poet shows himself—even more than Spenser, how much more then than any one else!—the absolute master of his metre, the *tregetour,* to whom all conditions of phrase and rhythm are merely *materia prima* out of which he can make whatsoever he will. And lastly, though of necessity in less measure and degree, that gift of indicating character, of opening up whole unending vistas of thought by a single phrase, which is Shakespeare's as it is hardly any one else's, is here. Of Adonis, the story forbade him to make much. But it would have been so easy to make Venus contemptible or disgusting or simply tedious; and she escapes all three fates so completely! The escape, no doubt, is effected partly, if not mainly, by the unfailing intensity of passion which the poet suffuses, but we are concerned chiefly with the means of suffusion. They are, I take it, mainly, if not wholly, comprised in that magic of the single phrase in which Shakespeare (for this is not Spenser's gift) reminds us of no predecessor but Chaucer, and in which he outdoes Chaucer more than Chaucer outdoes others.

> Ten kisses short as one, one long as twenty—
> Leading him prisoner in a red-rose chain—
> Love is a spirit all compact of fire—
> He sees her coming and begins to glow
> Even as a dying coal revives with wind—
> Her two blue windows faintly she upheaveth—
> Was melted like a vapour from her sight—

are mere specimens selected half at random from the things of this kind with which the piece swarms. "Conceited," "over-luscious," "unoriginal"—half a dozen other epithets the merely stop-watch critic may heap upon *Venus and Adonis.* One epithet, sometimes used in disparagement, it does deserve—it is young, but with the youth of Shakespeare.

Much of what has been said will apply to *Lucrece,* which chiefly differs from its predecessor in having a seven-line stanza, and in dealing with criminal, and not merely unhappy and tragic, passion. It is, however, on the whole, inferior; being not merely longer (and the style is not improved by length), but written with something more of an approach to the old fifteenth-century manner of allegoric and other padding. We should be sorry not to have it as well as the *Venus,* but it could not supply its companion's place.

The *Sonnets* do not reveal to us a more exquisite or richly gifted poet than does the *Venus*; but they take us to a higher range of subject, where sensuous imagery is indeed not absent, but where the poet's absorption in it has given way to a more direct domination of the ideal, to meditation upon passion rather than realisation of it. The endless discussions on the personages probably or possibly concerned must be sought elsewhere. The famous dedication[3] is, almost to a certainty, enigmatic of malice prepense; but there is no reason to question the fact suggested by the text throughout, and explicitly asserted once in it, that "a man right fair" and "a woman coloured ill" were the objects, either successive or simultaneous, of the poet's passionate attachment. That these two persons were live individual beings; that the passion was actually felt, but for one, two, five, or fifty other persons quite different from those adumbrated; or that the poems have no necessary connection with any particular person,

The *Sonnets.*

3. "To the only begetter of these ensuing sonnets Mr. W.H. all happiness and that eternity promised by our ever-living poet wisheth the well-wishing adventurer in setting forth. T.T." "T.T." is admitted to be Thomas Thorpe the publisher; the "ever-living poet" is open to no doubt, as the title-page has Shakespeare's Sonnets. "But who Mr. W.H." was, that is the question. It matters extremely little, but general opinion and fair probability incline to William Herbert, Earl of Pembroke, Sidney's nephew.

will never be exclusively asserted or denied by any one acquainted with human nature.

All these theories and others are possible; none is proved; and, for the literary purpose, none is really important. What is important is that Shakespeare has here caught up the sum of love and uttered it as no poet has before or since, and that in so doing he carried poetry—that is to say, the passionate expression in verse of the sensual and intellectual facts of life—to a pitch which it had never previously reached in English, and which it has never outstepped since. The coast-line of humanity must be wholly altered, the sea must change its nature, the moon must draw it in different ways, before that tide-mark is passed.

Their formal and spiritual supremacy.

These *Sonnets* are written in the English form, which is sometimes called from them the Shakespearian, and which, as already explained, is quite entitled to claim equality with the chief Italian or Petrarchian. Three quatrains, not connected by any necessary or usual community of rhyme, are tipped with a couplet; and, generally speaking, though not invariably, the opposition or balance of octave and sestet which the Petrarchian form naturally invites is replaced here by a steady building up of the thought through the douzain, and then either a climax or a quick anti-strophe in the final couplet. The form is extraordinarily suitable to the subjects, and may be said to be, for the sonnet meditative, actually preferable to the octave-and-sestet, though the latter may have advantages for the sonnet descriptive. No such samples of the peculiar phrase beauty of the *Sonnets* can be given as those which were possible in the case of the *Venus*, simply because of their bewildering abundance. Every sonnet, and perhaps a majority of the two thousand lines or thereabouts, contains them; and among them are numbered no small proportion of the highest, the intensest, the most exquisite jewels of English poetry. But their general characteristic as verse is a steady soaring music, now lower, now higher, never exactly glad but always passionate and full, which can be found nowhere else—a harmonic of mighty heart-throbs and brain-pulsings which, once caught, never deserts the mind's ear. Like all the greatest poetry, this is almost independent of meaning though so full of it; you can attend to the sense or disregard it as you please, certain in each case of satisfaction. The thoughts are not so far-fetched, the music not quite so unearthly, as in some poems of the next generation, but they are more universal, more commanding, more human. The mastery which had been partially attained in *Venus and Adonis* is complete here. There is nothing that the poet wishes to say that he cannot say, and there is hardly a district of thought and feeling into which he does not at least cast glances of unerring vision.

Probable divisions of plays: the earlier.

The faculty, which in this direction attained such early command, seems in the more complex and various departments of dramatic exercise to have developed itself, as might be expected, more slowly in proportion to the bulk and variety of its accomplishment. What really is Shakespeare's earliest dramatic work is, as has been said, in the highest degree uncertain; and of the pieces which are with more or less probability ascribed to his earliest period it is not definitely known how much is his own, how much supplied by or borrowed from others. From the beginning of the play, as distinguished from the interlude, the habit seems to have established itself, in England as in other countries, of constantly reworking old pieces by new hands; and it is probably to some exceptional popularity of Shakespeare as a refashioned in this way that Greene's outburst refers. His early pieces, then, may be divided into anticipations, more or less original, of his special masterpiece, the romantic comedy, attempts in the blood-and-thunder melodrama of the time, and probably, in most cases, refashioned chronicle-plays or "histories," a kind, as we have seen, as old as Bale. To the first division belong *Love's Labour's Lost,* the *Two Gentlemen of Verona,* the *Comedy of Errors* (this touching the translated classical play), *Measure for Measure* (?), the series culminating in *A Midsummer Night's Dream;* to the second *Titus Andronicus;* to the last the majority of the great series of the English histories, while *Romeo and Juliet* stands apart as what we may call a romantic tragedy corresponding to the romantic comedy, and promising almost greater things to come.

In all this work, guessing as little as we can, and proceeding as gingerly as possible, we can see the poet's genius growing and settling itself in every possible way. In metre he begins with the lumbering fourteeners, not as yet quite spirited up even by him, the stiff blank verse which even from the first becomes pliant in his hand, the richer but almost stiffer Marlovian hectoring style, the quaint fantasies and euphuistic devices of Lyly, all frequently lapsing into rhymed couplet and even stanza. But almost from the very first there are glimpses, and very soon there are much more than glimpses, of something that we have never seen before. Such a phrase, for instance, to take but the first that occurs, as the

Their verse and phrase.

> And shake the yoke of inauspicious stars
> From this world-wearied flesh,

of *Romeo and Juliet* takes us a long way beyond Marlowe, a longer way beyond Peele. In both these masters there is a deficiency of vibration in the verse, and a certain poverty, or at least simplicity, of verbal music. "Native wood-notes wild" is rather truer of Peele than of Shakespeare. Even Shakespeare could not often outdo Marlowe in a sort of economy of majesty, the grandeur of a huge blank cliff-face, or of the empty welkin itself. But as his meaning is more complex, farther-ranging, more intricately developed than theirs, so are his versification and his form. The incomparable skill that was to achieve such things as

> Peace, peace!
> Dost thou not see my baby at my breast
> That sucks the nurse asleep?

or the famous *Tempest* passage about "such stuff as dreams are made on," confronts us in the making (and a very rapid making) quite early. We find it in the quaint euphuisms of *Love's Labour's Lost,* in the unequal speeches of the *Two Gentlemen,* even in such a partly farcical medley as the *Comedy of Errors,* and such an ill-mingled mass of farce and tragedy as *Measure for Measure.* The real Shakespeare cannot help showing himself, if only by a flash of verse here and there; and then we are in presence of something new—of a kind of English poetry that no one has hit upon before, and which, as we cannot but feel, is revolutionising the whole structure and character of English verse. He may rhyme, or he may not rhyme, or he may turn to prose; but always there is the new phrase, the new language, conceited to the despair of pedants, playing on words in a fashion maddening to dullards, not always impeccable from the stricter standpoints of taste, but always instinct with creative genius.

In respect of construction and dramatic conception these early works, as we might expect, are less advanced. The chronicle-play of its nature defies construction of the ordinary kind, though sometimes, as in Marlowe's *Edward II* and Shakespeare's two *Richards,* the actual story may be short and central enough to give something like definite plot. It is, however, remarkable how Shakespeare contrives to infuse into these chronicles, or, as they may be not inaccurately termed, these dramatic romances, something of the unity of the regular play or dramatic epic. He will do it by the most various means—sometimes as in *King John,* by the contrasted attraction of the tragedy of Constance and Arthur and the comedy of the Bastard Falconbridge; sometimes, as in *Henry IV,* by the inclusion of a non-historical character, like Falstaff, of the very first interest and importance, with the subsidiaries necessary to set it off; sometimes, as in *Henry V,* by projecting an idea (in this case the patriotic idea of England) in such a fashion that the whole of the play, humours and all, imposes it on the spectator. But in the miscellaneous plays there is much less unity of construction, and, as yet, the romantic attraction of character is not quite secured. The defeat of the project of seclusion from womankind in *Love's Labour's Lost* might hardly, in any case, have been sufficient by itself, and is certainly not made sufficient; the play, agreeable as it is, loses itself in humours, and episodes, and single combats of wit and love. The central story of the *Two Gentlemen* is not more than enough for an ordinary *nouvelle,* and it may be questioned whether that of *Romeo and Juliet* is in itself much more. But this latter is quintessenced,

Their construction.

and exalted to the heavens, by the pure and intense poetic quality of its verse, by the pity of it in the case of the hero and still more the heroine, and by the contrasted flashes of wit and gallantry in Mercutio and Tybalt and the rest. So in the other and lighter masterpiece, *A Midsummer Night's Dream,* which probably belongs to this period, the subtle fidelity to the dream-nature perhaps makes it unnecessary to give, but certainly as a matter of fact excludes, any elaborate character-drawing. Indeed, always and everywhere at this period, Shakespeare's character is far ahead of his plot. Some indeed, to whom critical adhesion can here by no means be given, would maintain that this was always the case, and that to the very last the dazzling and transcendent truth and mastery of the great personages help to blind the reader to the want of that "clockwork" excellence of construction which Jonson could perhaps already give, and was certainly to give before Shakespeare's death. Let it rather be said that Shakespeare at this time had not quite acquired the art of constructing up to his character-level; that later, when he had learnt it, he never cared to give more construction than was necessary for his characters; and that in this he was right. It may be questioned—heresy as the statement will seem to some—whether construction, pitched to the perfection of *The Silent Woman* or of *Tom Jones,* is not something of a *tour de force,* and whether it does not deserve Bacon's pleasant sneer in another matter, "you may see as good sights in tarts." Life does not consider or contrive so curiously. However this may be, Shakespeare at this time was certainly not "our best plotter"; he was already at times an almost perfect artist in character, as he was a quite perfect poet. Even in such "more rawer" work as the *Two Gentlemen,* "Who is Silvia?" does not more show us the master of lyric than Julia and Lance show us the master of the graver and the lighter, the more passionate and the more frivolous, psychology and ethnology. Even in that unequal medley, *Measure for Measure,* the great scene between Isabel and Claudio so far transcends anything that English, anything that European drama had had to show for nearly two thousand years, that in this special point of view it remains perhaps the most wonderful in

Their characters.

Shakespeare. Marlowe has nothing like it; his greatest passages, psychologically speaking, are always monologues; he cannot even attempt the clash and play of soul with soul that is so miraculously given here. Yet, though the play (which some call a comedy!) is not known to have been acted till 1604, its general characteristics put it far earlier.

The middle division: the *Merry Wives.*

The second or middle division of plays may be said to be connected with the first by the link between *Henry IV* and *Henry V*,[4] the latest and most matured of the early batch, and the *Merry Wives of Windsor,* probably the first of the second. The *Merry Wives* itself is a curious study. It has failed to find favour with some, owing to a not ignoble dislike at seeing the degradation or discomfiture of Falstaff, but it must be remembered that Shakespeare, though never cruel with the morbid cruelty of the modern pessimist, is always perfectly awake to the facts of life. And, as a matter of fact, the bowls that Falstaff played involve the rubbers that are here depicted. It has also been a common saying that the play is little better than a farce. If so, it can only be said that Shakespeare very happily took or made the opportunity of showing how a farce also can pass under the species of eternity. How infinitely do the most farcical of the characters, such as Sir Hugh and Dr. Caius, excel the mere "Vices" of earlier playwrights! Who but Shakespeare had—we may almost say who but Shakespeare has—made an immortal thing of a mere ass, a mere puff-ball of foolish froth like Slender? If Chaucer had had the dramatic as he had the narrative faculty and atmosphere he might have done Mrs. Quickly, who is a very near relative, in somewhat lower life, of the Wife of Bath, and rapidly ripening for her future experiences in Eastcheap. But Shallow is above even Chaucer, as are also the subtle differentiation between Mrs. Page and Mrs. Ford, and the half-dozen strokes which her creator judged sufficient for sweet Anne Page. As for Falstaff, it is

4. It is well to say nothing about *Henry VI,* because, though I have no doubt that this trilogy is, as we have it, in the main Shakespeare's, it is also beyond all doubt, and beyond all others, a refashioning of earlier plays.

mistaken affection which thinks him degraded, or "translated" Bottom-fashion. He is even as elsewhere, though under an unluckier star.

This completeness exhibits itself, not perhaps in more masterly fashion, but in a somewhat higher and more varied material, in the great trio of Romantic comedies which is supposed to represent the work of the last year or two of the sixteenth century—*Twelfth Night, Much Ado about Nothing,* and *As You Like It.* Whether this order represents the actual composition or not, it certainly represents an intellectual and literary progression of interest and value, though the steps between the three are not wide. *Twelfth Night,* like the *Merry Wives* though not quite to the same extent, is pure comedy with a leaning to farce. The exquisite delicacy of the character of Viola suffuses it with a more, romantic tone; but the disasters of Malvolio are even less serious than Falstaff's, and the great appeal of the play lies wholly on the comical side, in the immortal characters of Sir Toby and Sir Andrew, in Feste, the first distinctly and peculiarly Shakespearian clown, in Maria the "youngest wren of nine," in the glorious fooling of the plot against the steward, and the minor Comedy of Errors put upon Viola and Sebastian. There is no touch of sadness, though the clown's final song of "The rain it raineth every day" gives a sort of warning note; the whole is sunny, and if less romantically imaginative than *A Midsummer Night's Dream,* it is almost as romantically fanciful.

The Romantic comedies.

Much Ado about Nothing changes us from pure comedy to the tragi-comic—indeed, to what threatens at one time to be tragedy undiluted. Perhaps here only, or here and in the *Winter's Tale,* Shakespeare has used tragedy to heighten his comedy, just as he habitually does the opposite; and the effect is good. But it is for the lighter side—for the peerless farce of Dogberry, the almost peerless comedy proper of Benedick and Beatrice—that we love the play. And the attraction of this couple, anticipated very early in Rosaline and Biron, is used yet again and with absolutely supreme success in *As You Like It,* one of the topmost things in Shakespeare, the masterpiece of romantic comedy, one of the great type-dramas of the world. Here, as in so many other places, Shakespeare borrowed his theme, and even no small part of his minor situations; but this matters nothing. The *Tale of Gamelyn* is pleasant and vigorous; Lodge's *Rosalynde* is ingenious and fantastically artistic. But *As You Like It* is part of the little "library of La Quinte"—of the few books exhibiting imagination and expression equally married. Rosalind and Touchstone stand, each in his or her own way, alone.

The great tragedies, Roman and Romantic.

The apparent change in the subject and temper of Shakespeare's work at the beginning of the seventeenth century has been the subject of much idle talk. There is no more reason to believe that he was specially and personally merry when he wrote this group of comedies, than there is to believe that he was sad or embittered during the period which produced *Julius Caesar, Hamlet, Othello, Lear, Macbeth, Antony and Cleopatra*—to which some would add *Troilus and Cressida, Timon,* and even *Measure for Measure,* as well as *Coriolanus.* To the present writer it is pretty certain that *Measure for Measure, Timon,* and *Troilus and Cressida* represent much earlier work, whether or no they had been actually produced. The three Roman plays, *Julius Caesar, Coriolanus,* and *Antony and Cleopatra,* make an interesting section to themselves, which in *Antony and Cleopatra* almost passes into that of romantic tragedy, and so joins the supreme quartette, *Hamlet, Macbeth, Othello,* and *Lear*. In all the Roman plays Shakespeare applied his English-chronicle method pretty exactly to the material that he found in North's *Plutarch,* and, since his faculties both of stage-management and of versification were now in complete maturity, with the noblest effect. But in character he does not create much, he only interprets—till we come to the "Serpent of Old Nile" and her lover, who are neither the crowned wanton and besotted debauchee of uninspired history, nor the anti-Roman sorceress and victim of Horace's craven-crowing ode, but a real hero and heroine of romance, luckless though not blameless, sympathetic though not ill served.

Much, however, even of *Antony and Cleopatra* is only chronicle, and like the other two, great as they are, falls beneath the magnificent creation of the four great romantic tragedies. In each of these, of course, Shakespeare had again his authorities, and, as his wont, he sometimes followed them closely. But the interest of the four does not depend in the very least upon Cinthio or Saxo, upon Geoffrey or Holinshed. Here, as in the great companion comedies, the dramatist breaks quite free; his real themes are human passion and human action at large, caught and embodied for the nonce in individual character and fate. Nowhere else does even Shakespeare lavish his resources as he does in these four plays, and certainly in none does he manifest such a power of displaying the irony of life and fate. Viewed from one standpoint, all four are as well entitled to the motto "Vanity of vanities" as Ecclesiastes itself. The love, the heroism, and the great leading qualities of *Othello* and *Macbeth,* the filial duty and intellectual subtlety of Hamlet, the generous if reckless and passionate *bonhomie* of Lear, all make shipwreck against the rocks thrown in their way by inauspicious stars, and sought out too often by their own mistakes and crimes. With that supreme genius which distinguishes him from the common playwright, Shakespeare has never made his heroes or heroines types; and this has puzzled many, and driven not a few to despairing efforts to make them out types after all. It is exactly what they are not. Shakespeare was no duped or duping preacher of the ruling passion like his second editor. *Othello* is indeed the simplest of the four; but even here the character of Iago, which is almost as complex as that of Hamlet, invites a great, from some the greater, part of the interest.

Those who would make Hamlet a mere irresolute, a mere Waverley, not only do not supply a full explanation of him even in their terms, but forget that irresolution, at least such as his, is the most complex of qualities. The inability of the will to "let itself go" is partly caused by, much more complicated with, the inability of the intellect to decide. To compare *Lear* with the wretched other play[5] on the subject, which is beyond

5. To be found, with other similar apparatus, in Hazlitt's *Shakespeare's Library*.

all doubt anterior, or with Holinshed, or with Geoffrey's original, is perhaps the very best single means of appreciating the infinite variety and intricacy of Shakespeare's knowledge and expression of humanity. Although the hapless king is always in the Latin sense impotent—incapable of resisting the impulse of the moment—this fault of his is conditioned, coloured, transformed at every instant by circumstances, many of them Shakespeare's own invention, and all rearranged with new effects by him. The gifting, the unexpected fractiousness of Cordelia (and let it be remembered that Cordelia is not a perfect character, that she is as hyper-frank as her sisters are hypocritical), the petty insults at Goneril's, the bolder outrage at Gloster's under the orders of Regan and Cornwall, the terrors of the storm, and the talk (dangerous to already tottering wits) of the sham madman, the rescue even as it is too late, the second fall into the hands of his enemies, and the final blow in the murder of Cordelia—all these engines, all these reagents, the dramatist applies to Lear's headstrong petulance with the most unvarying precision of science, the most unfailing variety of art. We have the ungovernable king and ex-king in twenty different "states," in twenty different relations and presentments, all connected by the central inexorable story. And so in *Macbeth* the hero—ambitious, uxorious, intensely under the influence of nerves and of imagination, as different from the mere "butcher" of Malcolm's insult as his greater but not less complex-souled wife is from a "fiendlike queen"—passes before us whole and real, terrible but exact, before, at the crisis of, and in his criminal stage, at once with the fluttering and phantasmagoric variety of a dream, and with an utterly solid and continuous story-interest. The Macbeth who is excited by the prophecy of the witches is exactly the same Macbeth as he who shrinks from the visioned dagger, as he who is struck to a kind of numb philosophising by the cry of women that announces his wife's death.

Of the numberless and magnificent passages of our poetry which these four plays contain it were vain to attempt to speak. It must be sufficient to say that in them the Shakespearian line, which, with its absolute freedom of shifting the pause from the first syllable to the last, its almost absolute freedom of syllabic equivalence, and the infinite variety of cadence which the use of these two main means (and no doubt some magic besides) allowed it to attain, is the central fact of English poetry—this line came to its very farthest. We only observe in the plays of the last six or seven years of his life one change, and that not a quite certain one, the inclination to greater indulgence in the redundant syllable which is so exceedingly noticeable in his successors in romantic drama, Beaumont and Fletcher. It is pretty certain that this license, which he had always used to some extent, would never in his hands have reached the excess which we find in them, and which in their followers simply disbands the line into loose ungirt prose, with some reminiscences of verse here and there. But it cannot be considered on the whole an improvement.

Last plays.

The plays of, or probably belonging to, the last period of Shakespeare's life are fewer in proportion than those of either of the preceding periods, but those of them that are certain present interesting characteristics. These are *Cymbeline*, the *Winter's Tale*, and *The Tempest*, the others being *Henry VIII.* and *Pericles.* This last play, which was not included in the first folio of 1623 by Shakespeare's friends and colleagues, Heminge and Condell, presents curious difficulties. Great part of it *must* be Shakespeare's; there is perhaps no part that *might* not be; and the general characteristics of story-management and versification are a very odd mixture of his earliest and his latest manner—a *Love's Labour's Lost* blended with a *Winter's Tale.* Nor do I at least see reason for refusing any part of *Henry VIII* to Shakespeare, though the prominence of the redundant syllable has made many ascribe it in large part to Fletcher. But about the other three there is no doubt, and certainly there is more excuse than usual for those who read in them a special index of the author's temper in these his last days—of the "calmed and calming *mens adepta*" whereof Fulke Greville speaks. *Cymbeline* partakes somewhat of the same character as the earlier *Much Ado about Nothing.* It is very nearly a tragedy—indeed, unlike *Much Ado about Nothing,* it contains accomplished tragic incidents in the deaths of the Queen and Cloten. But as far as the interesting personages—Imogen, Iachimo, Posthumus—are concerned, the tragedy is averted, and the whole deserves the name of romantic *drame* in the French sense.

This word, indeed, exactly describes these last three plays, and with ever-increasing appropriateness. Pedants of the bookish theoric of playwright craftsmanship have found fault with the construction of *Cymbeline,* which is admittedly loose, like its fellows—a chronicle or romance rather than an epic, but perfectly sufficient for its own object and purposes. The backbone of *A Winter's Tale* is a little more carefully and distinctly vertebrated, though no doubt the action is rather improbably prolonged, and the statue-scene, in which Hermione is restored to Leontes, does not entirely atone by its extreme beauty for its equally extreme improbability. But here, as always, Shakespeare has done what he meant to do; and here, as always, it is the extremity of critical impertinence to demand from an author not what he meant to do but something that the critic thinks he might, could, should, or ought to have meant. The vivid truth of the Queen's frank courtesy, Leontes' jealous rage (so different from Othello's, yet equally lifelike), the fine lurid presentment of the "coast" of Bohemia, the exquisitely idyllic (a word much abused, yet here applicable) figure of Perdita, the inimitable *brio* of Autolycus, the pendant to Touchstone—to give all these and other things in a pleasing series was what the dramatist intended to do, and he did it.

The splendour of sunset in *The Tempest* can escape no one, and the sternest opponent of guesswork must admit the probable presence of a designed allegory in the figure of Prospero and the burying of the book, the breaking of the staff, at the close. Even if this be thought too fanciful, nowhere has Shakespeare been more prodigal of every species of his enchantment. The exquisite but contrasted grace of Miranda and Ariel, the wonderful creation of Caliban, the varied human criticism in Gonzalo and the bad brothers, the farce-comedy of Stephano and Trinculo, do not more show the illimitable fancy and creative power of the master in scene and character than the passages, not so much scattered as showered over the whole play, show his absolute supremacy in poetry. Both in the blank verse and the lyrics, in the dialogue and the set *tirades,* in long contexts and short phrases alike, he shows himself absolute, with nothing out of reach of his faculty of expression and suggestion, with every resource of verbal music and intellectual demonstration at his command.

The so-called doubtful plays[6] of Shakespeare form an interesting subject, but one which can be dealt with but briefly here. As attributed by older tradition and assertion or by modern guesswork, they amount to "some dozen or sixteen," of which only three, the *Two Noble Kinsmen,* usually printed as Beaumont and Fletcher's, *Edward III,* and *Arden of Feversham,* have any serious claims, though some have seen such in the *Yorkshire Tragedy,* a curious little horror-piece which, however, a dozen other men might have written. Others again, *Fair Em, Locrine, Sir John Oldcastle,* have absolutely nothing but unauthoritative though pretty ancient assertion to recommend them. As for the excepted three, the *Two Noble Kinsmen,* a dramatisation of Chaucer's *Knight's Tale,* has no suggestion of Shakespeare as a whole, but in parts shows extraordinary similarity to his versification. This has tempted some to think that Shakespeare may by chance have found his younger contemporaries (Beaumont, be it remembered, died in the same year with him) working at the play, have looked at it, and have mended or patched here and there for amusement or out of good-nature. *Edward III* has the same similarities of versification, and in part, though a small part, of handling, but it is more suggestive of an extraordinarily clever piece of imitation or inspiration than of actual Shakespearian authorship. *Arden of Feversham,* on the other hand, has no similarities of versification, and does not, in its dealing with the murder of a husband by his wife and her baseborn paramour, suggest Shakespeare's choice of subject, but is closer in some ways than any other play to his handling in character and psychological analysis.

Doubtful plays.

6. It was not till 1908 that a Shakespearian *Apocrypha,* containing 14 plays, was supplied by the Clarendon Press (Oxford, ed. C.F. Tucker-Brooke). Before this they were scattered in Hazlitt's *Dodsley,* Simpson's *School of Shakespeare,* and elsewhere; though there was a German edition (Halle, 1878-81) and a single vol. reprint (London, *n.d.*) of the plays added in the later folios.

2

SHAKESPEARE'S CONTEMPORARIES IN DRAMA

Disposition of the subject—Chronological and biographical cautions—Ben Jonson—His and other "humour"—His plays—His verse—The three master-pieces—Later plays—The *Masques*—Beaumont and Fletcher—Their lives—Their characteristics—And merits—Specimen plays—Shadowy personality of other dramatists—Sufficiency of their work—Chapman—Marston—Dekker—Middleton—Heywood—Webster—His two great plays—Day—Tourneur—Rowley.

Disposition of the subject.

FROM more than one thing which has been said already, it will be seen that the arrangement of the great period of the English drama for treatment in a literary history is beset by various difficulties. The phases come so quick and overlap each other so intricately, that separate treatment is apt to create an entirely wrong general idea chronologically, while collective treatment is in danger of confusing the successive stages. For our present purpose the best way will probably be to take here all or almost all the men who during Shakespeare's lifetime produced something more than the mere beginning of their work, leaving even Massinger (though it is almost certain that he wrote before 1616), much more Ford, Shirley, etc., for the next Book; but to preface the individual dealings with some warning remarks which may keep the general procession clear.

Let it then be always remembered that the formative period of the University Wits was a very short one, and was contained roughly speaking, in the decade from 1585 to 1596; that Shakespeare overlapped them at the one end, and the first ten years of Fletcher—the whole collaboration of Beaumont and

Fletcher—on the other; that Ben Jonson, beginning before the Queen's reign ended, by some years, was the dramatist more especially of the reign of James, though he survived till near the outbreak of the civil dissensions; that Fletcher's death coincided nearly enough with the accession of Charles, so that he represents one side of the purely Jacobean drama as Ben does the other; and that most of the minor but still great men, Chapman, Dekker, Middleton, Heywood, Tourneur, Day, Marston, Webster, while often anticipating the end of Elizabeth's reign, and sometimes prolonging themselves into the beginning of Charles's, are still in the main ornaments more especially of that of the British Solomon, who, for all his *Reulis and Cautilis* (*vide infra*), certainly reaped where he had not sown. From what has been said already of this curiously tangled character of the subject, it will be understood that a strictly chronological arrangement of the writers enumerated, and others, is practically impossible. But it so happens that, without violating chronology in any important degree, we can arrange them in an order corresponding quite closely enough to their literary importance.

Chronological and biographical cautions.

Ben Jonson[1] (whose non-dramatic poetry is in bulk, and still more in influence, so important that it must be treated separately in the next chapter, while his prose will also come in for handling in a third) was nearly ten years younger than Shakespeare, and was born in London in the year 1573, some time after the death of his father, who was in orders. There seems to be no reason for doubting that the family was a branch of the Annandale Johnstones. He was educated at Westminster, but probably at neither University, though he afterwards received honorary degrees from both. His mother married a master bricklayer or builder, and Ben appears to have tried the business, but naturally did not like it. He enlisted and served for some time in the Netherlands, but seems to have come home while still a boy and to have married very early. The famous conversations

Ben Jonson.

1. *Works*, ed. Gifford and Cunningham (3 vols. London, *n.d.*).

with Drummond (see below), which, though not the very best of evidence, are about the best we have, do not represent this marriage as a very happy one, though Ben gives his wife a somewhat ungracious testimonial on the most important point. He was certainly one of the most solidly read men of an erudite time. We do not know how he gravitated to the stage, but Meres's mention of him is so early (1598) that *Every Man in his Humour,* Jonson's earliest known play, is sometimes put before this date. But we do not know that it was acted till then, and Meres's commendation is for tragedy. The wild life of the actors and playwrights of the time had nearly made Jonson's own end tragically premature, for he fought a duel with an actor of Henslowe's, Gabriel Spencer, in this same year, killed him, was tried for murder, but escaped by pleading "clergy" and being burnt in the hand, with loss of goods and chattels, which were probably not extensive. During the early years of James we know little of him except from the *Conversations* and a few traditional stories, mostly of literary quarrels. But in the second decade of the seventeenth century he became a sort of regular dictator of literature, the head of successive groups of young men of letters whom he called his "sons," the furnisher, conjointly with Inigo Jones as designer and mechanician till they quarrelled, of many court masques, which contain exquisite poetry, and Poet Laureate, or something like it. The journey to Scotland, in which he visited Drummond at Hawthornden, took place in 1619. His last years were not wholly happy, for his health, partly owing to his conviviality, was impaired, and he was often in straits for money from the fickleness of the court and stage favour on which alone he depended. But when he died in 1637 there was probably no competent opinion which did not regard him as the head of English literature, a position which he practically-held till Dryden was served heir to it.

Jonson's first play, *Every Man in his Humour* (which after having been acted at the Rose in a form not now extant, about 1596, was transferred in its present shape to the Globe and acted in by Shakespeare two years later), expresses in more than its title the kind of drama in which he specially excelled. The successive or contemporary senses of the much-discussed word "humour" in English can be put shortly without too much assumption on debatable points. Taking its original meaning in the modern languages from the medico-philosophical sense of "humour" as a constituent of the bodily frame influencing health or disease, it passes into the connotation of "temper," "disposition," which it still retains. From this, and by a slight reaction and variation upon its first meaning, it comes to signify a particular idiosyncrasy—a whim or caprice distinguishing the individual—and it is in this sense that Jonson constantly uses it and illustrates it in his plays. Only much later, and by degrees very difficult to mark with any accuracy, did it acquire that sense of distinction from, though not opposition to, wit in which it has become the designation of a quality so frequently found in English literature and elsewhere—a feeling and presentation of the ludicrous which does not stop there but includes something more, a sympathetic, or at least meditative, transcendency. In this last sense Shakespeare is the greatest of all humorists, and Jonson has not much claim to be one, for his temper was unsympathetic and his intellect, though strong, was a little coarse. But in the delineation, never absolutely caricatured, of "humours" in the plural form and lesser sense he has had few rivals.

His and other "humour."

In *Every Man in his Humour* the freshness of the writer's vein prevents the tendency to "cut-and-driedness" to which his scheme is exposed, and the result is delightful, especially in the boasting coward Bobadil and the gull Master Stephen, who wants "a stool to be melancholy upon," while the sketches of manners, always the strong point of the humour-play, show us, almost for the first time, a variety of interest and of excellence which was one of the chief features of the Elizabethan drama out of Shakespeare. For there is nothing more distinctive of Shakespeare than the way in which, despite his intensely English patriotism and his intensely English spirit, his painting of manners always transcends the merely graphic and local. He has enough of this last for his purpose, but only enough, and it was no part of his purpose to indicate for us accurately the flat cap and shining

His plays.

shoes of the citizen, or to make us acquainted with Pickthatch and Hogsden.

Every Man out of his Humour, which followed in 1599, is undoubtedly open to some of those strictures on sequels which, though often applied with undiscriminating woodenness, have some basis of experience. The elaborate characterisings of the persons which the author thought it necessary to prefix betray a certain suspicion that they do not sufficiently explain themselves; the mostly Italian index-names, Deliro, Fallace, Asper, and the rest, are teasing to the reader, and slight his memory and his judgment by suggesting that the one is too short and the other too feeble to identify the specimen without the label. Yet there is both fine verse and fine prose in the play, and the satire on the word "humour" itself, which is constantly put into the mouths of the characters, shows that Jonson was never his own dupe, though he might sometimes be his own mimic. And his realism has the advantages of its defects. We might have gone all over the London of 1599 without meeting Falstaff (who indeed had long been in Arthur's bosom), but we should have had, in all probability, no difficulty in finding twenty Fastidious Brisks between St. Paul's and Westminster.

The third play, *Cynthia's Revels* (1600), is an attempt to follow Lyly, but with direct satire on Euphuism itself, and in a harsher, harder style than that of the author of *Midas.* Indeed, Jonson's tendency to rough personal attack, and to a self-assertion undoubtedly arrogant, though too well justified by his gifts to be absolutely ludicrous, was growing on him very fast. And his next play, *The Poetaster* (1601-1602), in which the ostensible characters are those of Augustus and his court, was recognised as a direct assault on his own rivals, especially Marston and Dekker, while Tucca, the principal comic character, was seen at once to be drawn from an actual parasite of the time, one Captain Hannam. Yet there is stuff in it, and fine stuff, while Jonson's progress in his own style of versification

His verse.

is very marked. This, while it never attains to anything like the universal adaptability of Shakespeare's and is seldom distinguished by the ease and grace of Fletcher's, has great dignity and rhetorical force not really injured by any compensating stiffness. And it served him well in the fine Roman play of *Sejanus* which followed (1603), which was acted in, and at first, perhaps, originally contributed to by Shakespeare, which, except some of the masques, contains Jonson's best dramatic verse as verse, and which exhibits extraordinary familiarity with the classic originals a familiarity not resulting, as is too often the case, in any overloading with erudition.

It was, however, in his three next pieces, *Volpone, or the Fox, Epicene, or the Silent Woman,* and *The Alchemist,* that Jonson's genius as a dramatist found the fullest scope. To the present writer's judgment they seem to present a gradual crescendo of excellence. Strong as is *Volpone* (in which the devices of a rich, wicked, and misanthropic Italian to bring shame and disaster on his flatterers and legacy-hunters result in his own utter ruin) it is still marred a little by a too great separation in the characters (the result of the humour-theory), by the unmitigated rascality or folly of almost everybody in it, and by the improbability of Volpone's playing a game as dangerous as it was detestable. *The Silent Woman* was unsparingly admired by its own and the following generation for the cunning of its plot, the satisfactory adjustment of the contributory humours, and the admirable character of Morose, the best of all the misanthropes of the modern stage. But both plays fall short of *The Alchemist.* Here is Sir Epicure Mammon, the one character of the dramatist who requires no allowances and exceptions in the description of him as absolutely of the first class, no longer the mere vehicle of a "humour," but the incarnation of a human temperament—that in which voluptuous and avaricious concupiscence is sublimed and idealised into something immortal. Even this great central figure is thoroughly supported by the group of his three deluders, and deluders of each other, Subtle, Dol, and Face, while all the minor characters, especially Abel Drugger (later Garrick's best character), are good, and the story of the play moves with a combination of exactness and alacrity rare in any writer, and particularly rare

The three masterpieces.

in Jonson. There is perhaps no old play which inspires even those who are not fanatically devoted to the theatre with such a desire to see it performed as this does, owing to the excellence of the stage-situations, though there is hardly any which, from the sensuous enthusiasm of Sir Epicure and the brazen yet not vulgar audacity of Dol, his "princess," to the fatuity of Drugger and the petulance of the Angry Boy, would require so powerful a cast.

As the great trio was led up to by one of Jonson's Roman plays, *Sejanus,* so the descent from it—for his later plays, though even at the worst not what Dryden in his rare moment of unkindness called "dotages," *are* a descent—was begun by the other, *Catiline,* a piece which is critically on a level with its pendant in force, learning, and a certain stiffness. There is no stiffness in *Bartholomew Fair,* which followed *Catiline,* but it is rather an immense and audacious farce, dealing with the Puritans and the general humours of holiday London in a fashion excellently vigorous though undeniably coarse, than a comedy. *The Devil is an Ass* soars higher in scheme and kind. It is a comedy with a purpose, and a rather ambitious and hazardous one, being in effect a satire, as Gifford says, on monopolists and projectors on the one hand, on witch-finders and sham demoniacs on the other. After this there appears to have been a very long gap in Jonson's productions for the regular stage, though he was fertile in masques. When he reappeared on the boards in 1625, with *The Staple of News,* there was no great if any perceptible falling off either in wit, in satire, or in the vivid portrayal of the "humours." But of his last three plays, *The New Inn, The Magnetic Lady,* and the *Tale of a Tub,* the first was definitely damned, with the result of an indignant protest from the poet and divers replies, consolatory or otherwise, from other writers. The second had a mixed reception, and it is not known whether the third was ever acted publicly, though it certainly did not please when performed at court. Nor in any of the cases, despite passages and characters of merit, can they be said to do full justice to the author's powers. That these powers were, however, by no means gone is shown by his last and unfinished work, *The Sad Shepherd,* a pastoral

Later plays.

drama fancifully blended of the story of Robin Hood and a fairy tale, which is one of the most exquisite things of the Elizabethan age—the "satire, wit, and strength" which, far more than to Wycherley, may be attributed to its author being here accompanied by a sweetness and poetical charm, discoverable indeed in his minor poetical productions, but seldom to be observed even in his greatest plays.

Between the poems and the plays, but connected with the latter by the *Sad Shepherd* itself, come the *Masques*,[2] the most considerable body of that kind, both as to bulk and as to excellence, to be found in English. Much has been written on the probably Italian origin of the masque, a performance specially meant for amateurs to act. But the thing is so natural a growth in the conditions which made dramatic entertainments the particular amusement of courts, that it requires no elaborate or precise pedigree. It may be described as a dramatic entertainment in which plot, character, and even to a great extent dialogue, are subordinated on the one hand to spectacular illustration, and on the other to musical accompaniment. It was thus a sort of precursor of the opera, and disappeared when the opera became popular. Till seventeenth century, and especially the first half thereof, was the palmy time of the masque in England. Of these pieces Ben Jonson has left us nearly forty. Most of them, as mentioned, were written in conjunction with Inigo Jones, who supplied the decorations, going far beyond mere scenery and dresses, and such as must often have taxed the utmost ingenuity even of a consummate architect and engineer. Special dancing-masters (a profession of importance at the time) arranged the choregraphy, and the best composers, such as Ferrabosco and Lanier, gave the music for these entertainments, on which sums representing scores of thousands of pounds in our money were lavished. But no expense could be more than worthy of the inexhaustible supplies of wit, learning, and real poetry on which Jonson drew unsparingly for the libretti. If Milton, as he undoubtedly did, bettered Jonson's instruction

The *Masques*.

2. Mr. H.A. Evans's *English Masques* (London, 1897) contains a good selection of others besides Jonson's.

in *Camus* and the *Arcades,* yet it was Jonson's instruction that he bettered, and by far less than is commonly thought. For hardly any one now reads these charming pieces, couched in an obsolete form and burdened with the rubbish, as it now is, of stage directions and stage business, but displaying in the dialogue constant felicity, and in the abundant lyrics that very sober grace and half demure elegance of craftmanship by which Milton has won not the worst or least genuine part of his own fame.[3]

Beaumont and Fletcher.

The work of Beaumont and Fletcher[4] is even more voluminous than that of Jonson; it is indeed the most voluminous of any that we have from the greater figures of our drama, so that to go through it here on the same scale as that which has been allowed to Ben would be impossible. It would also be unnecessary, for their plays are much more homogeneous than his in general conception. They are, with hardly an exception, romantic comedies or romantic tragedies, differing remarkably from Shakespeare's in their ethics, and usually in their versification, but distantly belonging to the same general group in scheme, and subordinating all their subjects, classical, modern, fantastic, or historical, to this general scheme. The lives of the pair are not much known, and the distribution of the dramatic work which commonly goes under their joint names is extremely uncertain, though from Beaumont's very short life he ran hardly have had much of a hand in the majority of it. The traditional allotment of the part of creator to Fletcher and of critic to Beaumont rests on

3. *The Case is Altered,* a crude but not uncharacteristic piece, was probably produced in 1598 or 1599, and was published in 1609, but not by Jonson himself.

4. The twin dramatists had not been re-edited as wholes since the editions of Darley (2 vols.) and Dyce (11 vols.) in 1840-50. The former is the cheapest, the latter the most authoritative. *Two* new editions by Mr. Bullen and Mr. Waller have recently made their appearance. A fairly full selection of complete plays will be found in 2 vols. of the "Mermaid Series." The old edition of 1750 (10 vols.), by various editors, though not very critical, is useful.

no solid authority, and is a sort of commonplace in reference to such collaborations.

Their lives.

John Fletcher, the elder, the longer-lived, and undoubtedly the more prolific of the two, though perhaps not the greater genius, belonged to a remarkable literary family, though the power was not so much shown in his father (who, as Dean of Peterborough, made himself unpleasantly notorious at the execution of Queen Mary, and died Bishop of London) as in his uncle, Giles Fletcher, the author of *Licia,* and his cousins, Giles and Phineas, the not too unequal followers of Spenser (*vide infra*). The bishop died poor, and his son, who had entered Benet or Corpus College at Cambridge early, was left to shift for himself at seventeen. We know nothing of him personally; but the anecdote in Shadwell's *Bury Fair,* which presents him as living in lodgings with one maid-servant, who, when he entertained friends, "had her sack in a beer-glass," is quite likely to be an actual tradition, for the forte of "Og" was not inventiveness. For some time, we are told, he and his partner in the dramas lived together. He died of the plague in August 1625. Francis Beaumont was the son of a Justice of the Common Pleas, and belonged to a good family in Leicestershire, in which county he was born at Gracedieu in 1584. He became a member of Broadgates Hall (afterwards Pembroke College), Oxford, in 1597, and entered the Inner Temple in 1600. Beaumont was an intimate friend not merely of Fletcher but of Jonson, to whom he wrote a very remarkable ode. He married in 1613, and died three years later. Except *Salmacis and Hermaphroditus,* an Ovidian paraphrase in the luscious school of which Shakespeare's two great poems and Marlowe's *Hero and Leander* are the chief, and the anonymous *Britain's Ida* the next best, Beaumont's poetical work is very uncertain, and the collections which go under his name (reproduced in Chalmers) are a mere medley of work, sometimes certainly, often probably, belonging to others. But the contemporary estimate of his poetical genius was very high, and he traditionally has the credit of most, if not all, of the exquisite songs which are scattered about the plays, while Fletcher in the same tradition contents himself with drama only.

As guesswork is kept out of this book as much as possible, no space will be given to the attempts which have been made (in hardly any case upon documentary evidence) to assign the authorship of the great total of fifty-two plays to Fletcher, Beaumont and Fletcher, Beaumont and Fletcher and Shakespeare, Fletcher and Massinger, Fletcher and Shirley, Fletcher and Rowley. It is sufficient to say that in the whole there is a sufficient similarity, and in almost every individual play there is sufficient elasticity and variety of manner, to make such distributions extremely hazardous, if not utterly idle. About *Philaster, The Maid's Tragedy,* and *A King and no King,* there can be no reasonable dispute; because the ascription of joint authorship to them is older than Fletcher's death. And it so happens that these three plays furnish a sufficient range both of comic and tragic handling and expression to enable us to separate the special joint quality of the collaboration. Nor is this wanting in any one of the others.[5]

Their characteristics.

In verse these plays tend to a looser style, and admit more redundant syllables than those of Ben or even of Shakespeare; and we have spoken of their general scheme as dramas. There is room for somewhat more discussion as to their temper and morality. This has been as a rule rather unfavourably spoken of, and it is true that the authors neither observe the bare poetical justice which is one of the notes of Jonson, nor that higher, more impartial ethic—admitting the actual conditions of life and fate, but always making for righteousness—which is one of the greatest glories of Shakespeare. Their sentiment, though frequently exquisite, as in *Philaster, The Maid's Tragedy, Thierry and Theodoret,* and elsewhere, is often if not always slightly strained and morbid, the pathos is, so to speak, "loaded," and the situations which bring it about are not always natural. Towards what is commonly and widely called "vice" they hold an attitude which, while it never even approaches the prurient and deliberate provocation of the Restoration drama, comes nearer to sympathy than the Olympian acknowledgment of

5. A brief reasoned catalogue of the whole will be found in my *Elizabethan Literature,* pp. 258-66.

Shakespeare, or the humorous tolerance of Fielding. In mere language they are no coarser than their fellows; and Dryden committed the proverbial blunder of self-excusers when he tried to shelter himself, and his fellow-sinners at the other end of the century, under even the exceedingly broad shield of the *Custom of the Country*. But it may be that the moral standard, to adopt the favourite phrase, is a little lowered in them, the moral currency a little debased. Indeed, this is almost implied in the fact that they were, and long continued to be, the most popular of all English dramatists, their plays not merely surviving the Restoration and its change of taste, but even the reaction from that change itself, and holding the stage all through the eighteenth century, and well into the nineteenth. This, while a testimony to their stage-craft on one side, and on another to a certain kind of nature, is on another also evidence of a certain vulgarity—though not in the worst sense of the word.

And merits.

At the same time, their merits are exceedingly great. The wonderful copiousness, variety, and, with inevitable inequality, freedom from failure, of this vast collection of plays must strike every reader. In one point—a delightful feature common, though not universal, at the time—the songs which they contain, they not seldom come near Shakespeare in quality, while in this particular respect they exceed him in quantity and variety. Indeed, it is not quite certain whether one of the most exquisite[6] of this entire section of literature is Shakespeare's or theirs. They brought on the stage a crew of harum-scarum, but not ungenerous young men; of lively, merry, but not unmaidenly or unladylike girls; who are very natural and agreeable people to keep stage company with. As distinguished from the merely chaotic construction of the earlier drama, and the correct but slightly ponderous and elaborately geared machinery of Jonson, their arrangement of plot and incident is at once workmanlike and easy. Nor, though it would be impossible to go through all their plays, must we omit more particular notice of some.

6. "Roses, their sharp spines being gone."

Specimen plays.

Perhaps the most general favourite of all, certainly that which has the prettiest passages, and which gives the best example of the authors' peculiar variety of romantic play, is *Philaster,* a tragi-comedy which turns on the causeless jealousy of the hero and the faithfulness of his love, who, in the disguise of the page Bellario, follows him. The situation, which was, of course, much favoured by the practice, universal before the closing of the theatres, of committing women's parts to boys, took the public fancy, and was much imitated; but the charm of the play is quite independent of it, and though far more unreal and merely *literary* than that of not wholly dissimilar things in Shakespeare, is perhaps, in its special and lower kind, unique in English literature. This same taint or *haut-goût,* whichever it be preferred to call it, of unreality, and morbid or hectic sentiment, appears with a more tragic cast, but with not less, or little less, of its own peculiar success, in another of the undoubted joint works, *The Maid's Tragedy,* The authors have here appealed to some of the most affecting, though not the most simply or naturally affecting, motives that the playwright can bring into action—the conflict of friendship between Melantius and Amintor, the strain on the courtier's loyalty when his sovereign's mistress (not even a cast mistress) Evadne is put off on him, and the anguished innocence of Aspatia. The pathos, and even in a sense the power, of the working out of these is assisted by very many passages of really exquisite poetry. In neither of these plays is there much pure comedy, but in *A King and no King* there is a serious part and a comic one, both *good,* and the latter containing the famous braggart Bessus, who makes up the great trinity of the English stage in this kind of part with Parolles and Bobadil. *The Scornful Lady,* which is usually attributed to Fletcher alone, is comic merely, and not only supplies comedy of a very high order, but had an immense influence on following generations down to, and perhaps even later than, Sheridan. The best pair with this is the equally famous *Humorous Lieutenant,* which inclines a little more in the direction of farce. Of plays approaching and sometimes reaching the first class there must be mentioned among the comedies *Rule a Wife and Have a Wife,* with its famous character of the "Copper Captain"; *The Little French Lawyer, Monsieur Thomas, The Chances, The Wild Goose Chase,* and that most agreeable burlesque *The Knight of the Burning Pestle;* among the tragedies *The False One, Valentinian, Thierry and Theodoret,* and *Bonduca,* each of which has one or more characters, and many more than one or two passages, of astonishing merit. The *Two Noble Kinsmen* would hardly rank very high, if it were not for the regular echo of Shakespearian verse which here and there meets us; but *The Faithful Shepherdess,* of which again Fletcher has the sole credit, is a most charming production, less pathetic, perhaps, than Jonson's companion fragment above noted, but more complete and not less sweet. And it may almost be said that in the whole half-century and more of plays there is hardly one, even of the weakest, where examples may not be found not merely of that strange "joint-stock poetry," as Scott, I think, once well described it, which is common to almost the whole Elizabethan drama from the highest to the lowest, but of special and peculiar music. Again, in a favourite catchword of their own day, they had "wit at will." On the merely humorous side it was almost as verbally felicitous as that of Congreve, and far more abundant, succulent, and various in its application; on the critical side it comes short of the very greatest only by an indefinite quantity. For the greater part of the nineteenth century, until very lately, they have paid by a certain slighting for their immense and enduring vogue during two centuries earlier. But with all their drawbacks, all the slight tokens of "decadence" in them, they must be ranked so high that none except *der Einzige* can be put above them.

Shadowy personality of other dramatists.

Of the personal history of those writers who will occupy the rest of this chapter almost incredibly little is known, the amount in some cases extending not much beyond the bare name, without any certain dates, and with not much certainty of authorship, while in hardly any case does it extend beyond the barest outline of a life. George Chapman was probably born at or near Hitchin in or about 1558, became a member of the University of Oxford in

1574, was known as a dramatist soon after the beginning of the last decade of the century, was a good friend of Jonson's, with personality whom and Marston he got into trouble in 1613 for a supposed insult to the Scotch in *Eastward Ho,* was patronised by Prince Henry and by James's favourite Carr, wrote plays, poems, and translations for many years, and died in or about 1634. John Marston (birth-date unknown, but of a good family in the Midlands) was educated at Coventry School and at Brasenose College, wrote poems and satires before the beginning of the seventeenth century, and plays after it, was beaten by Jonson, and had his pistol taken from him (Ben *teste*), took orders late, became vicar of Christchurch, and died in the same year with Chapman. Of Thomas Dekker we know no date, no fact, no anecdote, nothing at all, except that by his own statement in 1637 he was threescore or thereabouts. John Webster is in similar case, it being merely a guess that he was, as some one of his name certainly was, parish clerk of St. Andrew's, Holborn. Of Thomas Middleton we know a little more, which, however, includes neither the certain date nor the place of his birth (London and 1570 appear probable) nor his education. He began to write paraphrases and satires before 1600, passed like others into play writing, was chronographer to the City of London in 1620, and in 1623 imprisoned for the attack on Gondomar in his *Game of Chess.* He died at Newington Butts, in 1627, and left a widow named Magdalen. Of Heywood, another Thomas, we know little or nothing, save that he came from Lincolnshire and was a fellow of Peterhouse, Cambridge. Of John Day, little save that he was a member of Gonville and Caius College, in the same University. Of Cyril Tourneur a few facts of military service.

Sufficiency of their work.

Fortunately, however, if we know little about the men, which is a matter of slight consequence, or none at all, to literature, we know a good deal about the works, which are of the highest consequence. Much is no doubt lost, very few MS. dramas having escaped the rough usage in the original stage, the carelessness of the fifty years or more when such things were regarded as rubbish, and the positive destruction which occurred in at least one notorious case (that of the herald Warburton, whose cook used up old plays for household purposes), and beyond all question in scores of unrecorded ones. Even of those which got into print there has been loss. But nevertheless there is no author of Elizabethan drama whom there is any reason to believe to have been really remarkable, and of whom we have not more or less ample remains. The actual amount varies from the two dramas of Tourneur to the two or three dozen—remnants of between two and three hundred—of Heywood. And while we have thus sufficient material for discerning the idiosyncrasies of individuals, the total mass of matter is so great and so varied that we are very unlikely indeed to miss specimens of any general kind.

Chapman.

The dramatic work of Chapman,[7] almost first made and almost latest left of all the knights of this Round Table, includes no single play of very commanding excellence, and is distinguished, even in this period, for want of finish. But in individual passages it shows the same great though insufficiently co-ordinated and organised power which animates his poems and translations, and it includes one of those interesting series of mainly chronicle plays which form one of the most remarkable features of the whole subject. *Bussy d'Ambois, The Revenge of Bussy d'Ambois, Byron's Conspiracy, The Tragedy of Charles, Duke of Byron,* and *The Tragedy of Philip Chabot, Admiral of France,* all dealing with the nearly contemporary history of a neighbouring country, show, when regarded from one point of view, how the drama was striving to do the part of the uninvented newspaper and the still rudimentary novel. They even give the latest instances of the early "Titanic" style of Elizabethan drama. Chapman was connected in more than one literary way with Marlowe, whose *Hero and Leander* he finished; and while his best tragic passages preserve not a little of the "thunder-smoke" of his great predecessor, it is noteworthy that, by the confession of the greatest writer of the next age, they had considerable

7. *Works,* ed. R.H. Shepherd, with Essay by Mr. Swinburne, 3 vols. London, 1875. The *D'Ambois Plays,* by F.S. Boas (London and Boston, U.S.A., 1905).

influence on what we unkindly call the rant of Dryden's own heroic drama. Good examples of Chapman's tragic power are almost confined to these plays, the later tragedies of *Caesar and Pompey, Alphonsus Emperor of Germany,* and *Revenge for Honour* being unworthy of their author, if indeed the two last be his at all. Hut in the *Blind Beggar of Alexandria, An Humorous Day's Mirth, The Gentleman Usher, Monsieur d'Olive* (a kind of farcical offshoot of the French history series), *The Widow's Tears,* and, above all, *All Fools* and *May Day,* Chapman shows very satisfactory comic power. These plays, with *Eastward Ho,* in which, it must be remembered, he collaborated, place him high in the exposition of a kind of comedy less compact of mere humours than Jonson's, and if less airily gay than Fletcher's, and less saturated with poetry than Shakespeare's, yet exceeding in these various qualities the work of most other men.

Marston.

There is little gaiety—less than in Jonson himself—in the third shareholder in *Eastward Ho* and its misfortunes. Marston[8] began as a satirist; and both the deliberate misanthropy of thought and the not always well-carried-off extravagance of expression which mark his satires distinguish his plays pretty nearly throughout. The two parts of *Antonio and Mellida* might, for the sanguinary inconsequence of the plot and the high-strung and hectoring tone of the language, have been written some dozen or sixteen years earlier than they actually were. There is good poetry in the play, but hardly good drama. The subject of *Sophonisba,* which was particularly tempting to the more melodramatic dramatists of the seventeenth century in several countries, naturally did not tame Marston's disposition to horrors in incident and rant in language; but it kept him more to the point, and permitted fewer alarums and excursions. His masterpiece, however, must be sought either in *What You Will,* a comedy which could not be a more complete contrast to Shakespeare's play of the name, but which had distinct merits, or else in *The Malcontent,* a satirical play of the same stamp as Jonson's, Molière's, and Wycherley's, representing

8. Ed. Halliwell, 3 vols. London, 1856; ed. Bullen, 3 vols. London, 1887.

an honest misanthrope. *Parasitaster* and *The Dutch Courtesan* are inferior; while if *The Insatiate Countess* be his, it most certainly does not do him much credit. It was Marston's great misfortune that to a decided want of range he joined an intensity which is not itself entirely free from suspicions of affectation. His readers not only, like Lamb with Hazlitt, "wish he would not quarrel with the world at the rate he does," but sometimes doubt whether Marston really thought so badly of human nature as he seems to do. Nevertheless, he is by no means destitute of the towering strain of his predecessors and earlier contemporaries, and his gloomy rhetoric not very seldom becomes real eloquence.

Dekker.

No greater contrast of tone and temper could be imagined than that which is actually presented in the works of Marston and in those of his colleague in the unknown proceedings, which drew down on both the wrath of Ben Jonson. Nor, looking at Dekker[9] from another point of view, does any writer of the time illustrate more strikingly that other contrast which has been referred to, the contrast between the abundant literary and the almost nonexistent biographical documents about these men. Of Dekker the man, we know, as has been said, as nearly as possible nothing; from Dekker the writer, we have not only an abundant body of prose work which will be noticed below, but a plentiful collection of plays, sometimes written in conjunction with other men, but often enough independent. Moreover, it so happens, and luckily, that by putting together this last work, his work in collaboration, and the work either alone or with others of his collaborators, we can obtain an idea of his own literary temper and genius which is almost logically demonstrable. There is no evidence that he had any connection with the Universities, with the Inns of Court, or with any learned profession, or, as commonly reputed, respectable means of livelihood. He seems to have been simply a working dramatist and man of letters, an inhabitant of the earlier and more romantic, but not more fortunate, Grub Street. For some forty years he appears to

9. *Plays* (ed. R.H. Shepherd?), 4 vols. London, 1873; *Prose,* ed. Grosart, 5 vols. privately printed, 1884.

have written plays and pamphlets, the direct ancestors and representatives of the novels and the newspapers by which his kind live, sometimes in splendour, often in decent comfort, today. It is certain that Dekker did not live in splendour, and probable that he did not often live in comfort. But he displays in his prose works great talent for observation and descriptive narration, and in his plays a most charming dramatic genius, a little, as is the wont of the time, chaotic and irregular, but sweet and pathetic, as is no contemporary save the master of all, especially in the delineation of women's characters, while he has both blank verse and lyric touches and flashes, not seldom well sustained, of divinest poetry. In the plays that are attributed to him in part or ascribed to him by guess, such as the *Virgin Martyr,* which appears in Massinger's works, and the *Witch of Edmonton,* these characteristics are seen; but they are more eminently visible in his own undoubted plays, *The Shoemaker's Holiday, Patient Grissil, Satiromastix, Old Fortunatus,* and *The Honest Whore.* It is sufficient proof of Dekker's power in this way that in *The Shoemaker's Holiday* and *Satiromastix* neither the clumsy composite device then in favour, of blending or rather strapping together (for there is practically no blend) a serious and a comic plot, in both, nor in the latter, the desire to hit back at Jonson for his attack in *The Poetaster,* prevents the display of it. *Old Fortunatus,* the well-known story of the wishing-cap and other gifts, is his chief exploit in purely romantic and fanciful drama; and though chaotic beyond even his wont, has wonderful force and fancy. *Patient Grissil* and *The Honest Whore*—the former based, of course, on Boccaccio, the latter taking for heroine a woman who has lost her reputation, but retrieves it by her patience, constancy, and inviolable purity after marriage—are the great texts for Dekker's dealing with the characters of women, and the latter shows a felicity of conception and power of execution of which the very greatest dramatists might be proud. Nor does Dekker rank much below Shakespeare or Fletcher for his lyrics, the best of which, "Cold's the wind and wet's the rain," "Fortune's smiles, cry Holiday!" "Art thou poor, yet hast thou golden slumbers," "Cast away care," and others, are better known than the plays containing them.

Middleton, confining himself, or nearly so, to drama, was even a more voluminous playwright than Dekker, at least so far as extant pieces are concerned, his works extending in the best edition to eight volumes.[10] About half a score of these are examples of those dramas of manners of which, as has been said, the Elizabethan dramatists other than Shakespeare have left us so many. No one of these[11] is very much above or very much below the others; indeed, Middleton, while rather rarely reaching or approaching the highest rank, seldom drops so low as most of his fellows occasionally do. Yet he was capable of much better work than this journalist drama, as it may be called, and he showed it in nearly as many more plays written chiefly in collaboration with Dekker or Rowley, but distinguished very remarkably from their independent work. At the head of these stands the great play of *The Changeling,* where, as indeed usually in these mixed plays, the comic part is nearly worthless, while the tragic contains, in the characters of the heroine, Beatrice-Joanna and her—he can hardly be called lover—but first tool and then tyrant, the bravo De Flores, some of the greatest things out of Shakespeare. So, too, *The Mayor of Queenborough,* comically despicable, or at least commonplace, takes for the tragic subject Vortiger's passion for Rowena, and determination to get rid of his wife Castiza, and treats it with the same intensity and nearly the same wonderful projection of character. *Women beware Women,* sometimes spoken of as his masterpiece, is a tragedy more domestic in type than those, and less lurid, but almost equally, though more quietly, intense; and *The Witch* has interest besides the remarkable problem of its relation to *Macbeth. A Fair Quarrel* has received very high praise from some, but seems to others distinctly below these. But the political attractions of *A Game of Chess* are not its only ones; and *The Spanish Gipsy* is a romantic comedy which deserves to stand not too far below *As You Like It,* Middleton

Middleton.

10. Ed. Bullen, 8 vols. London, 1885.

11. *Blurt Master Constable, Michaelmas Term, A Trick to Catch the Old One, The Family of Love, A Mad World, My Masters, A Chaste Maid in Cheapside, Anything for a Quiet Life,* etc.

having for once transcended mere manners and humours, shaken off the atmosphere of Fleet Street and Duke Humphrey's tomb, avoided the way of extravagant tragedy, and hit upon that—less trodden but almost certain to lead the due feet to success—of romance crossed with or expressed in drama.

Heywood.

In the voluminous work of Heywood, the "prose Shakespeare" of Lamb (a phrase which has been a good deal misunderstood), there are less definite and eminent qualities than in that of almost any man yet mentioned in this chapter. He wrote much else besides plays, but his non-dramatic work is almost entirely forgotten, and of his dramatic it can hardly be said that more than one piece, the famous *A Woman Killed with Kindness,* survives as much more than a name. This has for theme the difficult and dangerous subject of the self-restraint, and—though not tolerance—charity of the betrayed husband Frankford. And Heywood has plucked safety and success from danger by the extreme pathos and tenderness with which he treats a rather impossible situation. Elsewhere, though never quite contemptible, he is seldom great. His chronicle plays (*Edward IV* and *The Troubles of Queen Elizabeth,* each in two parts) exhibit the want of unity which is the drawback of their kind, without the panoramic and historical-novel effect which can be got out of them by those who know how. His dramatisations of the *Metamorphoses* and other such things show a continuance of the earlier confusion as to what is and what is not matter for drama, which is rare after the beginning of the seventeenth century; while his masques and pageants entirely lack the grace and fancy, mixed with learning, which save spectacles in the hands of Jonson. He is, however, fairly strong in the comedy of London manners and humours, and very strong in the domestic drama, of which his already-mentioned masterpiece may claim to be our chief instance. Nor has he small command of another, not the least agreeable of the sub-varieties of the plays of the time, the adventure-drama, of which he has left us some remarkable specimens.[12] He is not

12. *The Fair Maid of the Exchange, The Fair Maid of the West, The English Traveller, A Challenge for Beauty, Fortune by Land and Sea, A Royal King*

a great master of versification, and one is apt to be more convinced of the "prose" than of the "Shakespeare" in Lamb's dictum. Yet, as if to show in a single instance the truth well put in Scott's observation quoted above, some of the very finest things of the whole body are his.

Webster.

In all respects John Webster[13] is the direct opposite to Heywood. The work existing as his is fairly voluminous, and we know that some, perhaps much, is lost; but a good deal both of the extant and non-extant work attributed to him seems to have been done in collaboration, and very little of this, as we now have it, is worth much. But two very great plays, *Victoria Corombona, or the White Devil,* and the *Duchess of Malfy,* and two lesser ones, the *Devil's Law Case* and *Appius and Virginia,* are ascribed to him, without assertion or suggestion of any helper. *Appius and Virginia* is a classical tragedy, showing neither the learning and dignity of Jonson's nor the universal humanity of Shakespeare's attempts in this style; and the *Devil's Law Case,* though attractive in parts, has a treble portion of the chaotic defect of the time. But the first pair would suffice to put Webster in the very first rank. All the four, as well as most of the work which remains extant as his, and the titles of some that is lost, imply a remarkable tendency to gloom, and to supernatural as well as natural terror and horror. He has left us, in the "Address to the Reader" of the *White Devil,* a curious appreciation of the seven contemporary dramatists whom he seems to have ranked highest, and though the language (especially taken with his own caveat) must not be strained too far, yet it may be suspected that his classification of Shakespeare with Dekker and Heywood, and the particular phrase[14] he selects for them,

and Loyal Subject, may represent these two classes. Indeed, we have between twenty and thirty plays of Heywood's reprinted (6 vols. London, 1874), and his actual production (much of it, no doubt, adaptation only) was some ten times as large.

13. Ed. Dyce, 1 vol. London.

14. "Right happy and copious industry." He had assigned a "full and heightened style" to Chapman, "laboured and understanding work" to Jonson, and "no less worthy companions" to Beaumont and Fletcher.

may have something to do with the general, though not universal, cheerfulness which prevails in all three.

His two great plays.

Of cheerfulness Webster himself knows nothing; his comedy, wherever he attempts it, is a forced guffaw, his passion of love, though powerful, has nothing bright or ethereal about it, but shares the luridness of his other motives; and he is most at home in the horrors, almost unmitigated, of his two great plays. The *White Devil* (printed 1612) is founded with extreme closeness, and only a few dramatic and poetic embellishments, on the historical story of Vittoria Corombona (or rather Accoramboni), which may be found, told by the late Mr. T.A. Trollope, in an early number of Dickens's *All the Year Round.* The heroine is an Italian Helen, whose beauty and unscrupulousness bring murder and crime wherever she goes. She is well seconded or egged on in her evil deeds by her brother Flamineo, a ruffian who, though less human and natural than Iago, De Flores, or even Aaron, in *Titus Andronicus,* completes the quartette brilliantly, and so stands far above all others. The action is so extremely compressed as to have the appearance of confusion, but it is in reality clear enough; and many of the separate scenes and passages have a gloomy intensity of passion difficult to parallel elsewhere, except in the companion play. The mad scene of Cornelia, Vittoria's mother, with her dirge over her son Marcello, murdered by his brother Flamineo, has received deserved praise from all for its wonderful "eeriness"; but perhaps Vittoria's own words after she has been mortally stabbed—

> My soul, like to a ship in a dark storm,
> Is driven I know not whither,

rank even higher for their attainment of the greatest poetical effect with the simplest language and the least out-of-the-way imagery.

The Duchess of Malfy (printed 1623), the story of which was no doubt taken from that usual storehouse of the Elizabethan dramatist, Painter's *Palace of Pleasure,* is of less concentrated attraction. The heroine marries her steward, and is persecuted for it by her brothers. They employ an instrument named

Bosola, a second but weaker Flamineo, who plays the outspoken misanthrope. The real excellence of the play is almost confined to the fourth act, where the unhappy duchess is first imprisoned in a madhouse by her brothers, and then murdered. The fifth, at the end of which everybody kills off everybody else—the husband, the brothers, and Bosola—is no improvement, and shows Webster's lack of dramatic tact. But he had a great though confused imagination, and a wonderful power of phrase.

Day.

The work of John Day[15] is a good example of the "intricate impeach" of these plays and playwrights generally. His life would appear to have extended practically over the whole of the dramatic period (1580-1640), and from record it would seem that in five of these years only (1598-1603) he collaborated in twenty-one plays, of which only the odd one, the *Blind Beggar of Bethnal Green,* survives in accessible form. Besides these he wrote with others and alone in later years, *Law Tricks,* the *Travels of Three Brothers* (the Shirleys), *The Isle of Gulls, Humour out of Breath,* and his most famous work, the *Parliament of Bees.* Most, if not all of these seem to have been produced in a space not longer than that taken by the earlier and mostly unknown batch. They display, however, or most of them do, a certain character which is distinct from that of most of the plays of the period, and comes nearest to Lyly's—that is so say, the presentation in dramatic form of a series of scenes or tableaux embodying a more or less fantastic satire of the ethical kind, rather than a definite play-story. This is especially noticeable in the *Parliament of Bees,* by which indeed, except to more or less thorough-going students, Day may be sufficiently known. For the last thirty years of his presumed life he appears to have written little or nothing; and indeed he would seem altogether to have been one of those men who were rather hatched and coaxed into production by the prevailing heat and inspiration of the time than driven to it by necessity of their own talent. A gay and graceful spirit of fantastic allegory is his chief note.

15. Ed. Bullen, privately printed, 1881.

Nothing that is gay and little that is graceful appears in the two grim plays of Cyril Tourneur,[16] though allegory had hold on him also, as is seen in his non-dramatic piece, the *Transformed Metamorphosis.* The *Atheist's Tragedy* and the *Revenger's Tragedy* are the extremes of the kind of extravagant horror-mongering in drama which Marlowe almost dragged to success in *The Jew of Malta,* and which Shakespeare tried and left in *Titus Andronicus.* The *Revenger's Tragedy* is by far the better of the two, having a glimmering of plot and some noble though austere sketches of character, with abundance of magnificent though gloomy poetry. The *Atheist's Tragedy* with glimpses of the pathetic, and the strange bronze-medallion stamps of line here and there which these horror-mongers not seldom contrive to impress, is mere chaos and nightmare, beside which the *Spanish Tragedy* is an orderly attempt in serious drama, and *The Insatiate Countess* a well arranged study of manners.

Tourneur.

From William Rowley, besides a very large amount of known or probable collaboration, we have two or three separate plays, such as *A New Wonder* and *A Match at Midnight,*[17] which are very far from contemptible, and help us to mark off and appreciate his work with others. His special gift would appear to have been the arrangement of that humours-and-manners comedy of contemporary London which, as has been said, played such a large part in the dramatic works of the first half of the seventeenth century. Of this he must have had no small command, for though his comedy is rather rough, and his construction seldom soars above a kind of rough-and-ready stage-craft, he has humour and power of direct presentation. If any one will take one of his plays and a specimen from even the more commended writers of the next century, Mrs. Centlivre, Cibber, Mrs. Cowley, down to Foote and O'Keeffe, he will begin to understand why the ordinary plays of the seventeenth century are ranked as literature, while those of the eighteenth are not.

Rowley.

16. Ed. Churton Collins, 2 vols. London, 1878.

17. This will be found in Hazlitt's *Dodsley,* a separate edition of Rowley has long been expected from Mr. Bullen.

3

THE SCHOOLS OF JACOBEAN POETRY

Drayton—The *Polyolbion*—Other poems—Daniel—Sylvester—Sir John Davies—Minor poets—Chapman—Fairfax—Campion—The Spenserians: minor poets—The Fletchers —Giles—Phineas—W. Browne—Wither—Basse—The lyrical impulse—Jonson's poems—Donne.

THE division which has been here adopted, striking a line at the death of Spenser, and starting afresh from it, enables us in most respects to make cleaner work than if the death of Gloriana had been taken instead of that of Colin. We have behind us, and still freshly behind us, the remarkable school of the sonneteers—occasionally overvalued, but more often and more likely to be under-estimated—the quaint batch of early satirists, a group artificial and transitory; and the beginnings of the historical style of poetry. We have before us three well-marked schools: those of Spenser, Jonson, and Donne; in two cases with the heads of them living and exercising personal influence, in the third with the leader dead but nonetheless living in his work.

We have, however, two remarkable writers in the strictly poetical way to deal with—one of them hardly a dramatist (so far as extant work goes) or prose-writer, though a very voluminous poet; the other the author both of prose and of plays, but a poet chiefly—who began to write some decade before Spenser's death. Of these, one lived till six years before the accession of Charles I, the other till six years after it. Both were sonneteers; both were historical poets; but both, with quite admirable touches of poetic genius now and then, and an almost too plentiful vein, lacked at once the initiative and the perfecting wit of Spenser. These were Michael Drayton and Samuel Daniel.

Drayton.

All former accounts of Drayton's life have been antiquated by Mr. Oliver Elton's capital monograph for the Spenser Society,[1] yet even now it cannot be said that we know very much about him. He came, like Shakespeare, from Warwickshire, and if not of gentle birth himself, was from the first attached in the honourable fashion of service to gentle houses, and seems to have had some employment at court. His life nearly covered the full seventy years, for he was born about 1563 and died in 1631. He seems to have had no permanent connection with the stage,[2] but he fell early into the custom of sonneteering, his *Idea* (1594) being very probably addressed to the daughter of the house which protected him. The notices that we have give the notion of a man of masterful and not very obliging temper, who perhaps did not reach the rank or position which he thought his due, and was unwilling to be hail-fellow-well-met with mere pot-companions. Yet he seems to have been widely known, and to have excited, if no vehement friendships, no sharp dislike.

The *Polyolbion*.

His poetical production is extremely voluminous; in fact, it is probably the largest that we have from any non-dramatic poet of real merit during the period. Its largest and most famous single item, the *Polyolbion* (1613-22) was not early—it could, indeed, hardly be so, for the idea of compiling a poetical gazetteer of the whole of England would be unlikely to occur to a very

1. Reprinted, with additions, London, 1905. There is no complete edition of Drayton, but one is promised, and Chalmers has nearly the whole.
2. It was, however, busy while it lasted, during, as it seems, the last five years of the Queen, when Drayton was one of Henslowe's hacks, botching up, generally in collaboration, nearly a score of plays, almost all lost. *William Longsword* (price £6, of which we have his receipt to Henslowe for forty shillings' advance) is the only one mentioned as his sole work. He had a fourth share in the pseudo-Shakespearian *Sir John Oldcastle,* the only certain play-work of his which survives. The attribution to him of the much better *Merry Devil of Edmonton* is only guess.

young poet, and could not possibly, in the dearth of books on the subject, have been carried out by any one who had not had many years to observe and amass materials. It has long been, and probably will ever hereafter be, little read; but those who read it doubt whether to reprobate the choice of poetic form (the Alexandrine with middle caesura) for such a subject, or to admire the extraordinary resolution, resource, and, on the whole, success with which the work is carried out. It leaves, moreover, a considerable balance of work to Drayton's credit, a little of which is actually familiar to the choicer memories, while much deserves to be so. The sonnets, with the famous one—

Since there's no help, come let us kiss and part,

which does not appear in all editions, and the authorship of which has been disputed; *The Shepherd's Garland* (1593), which was also addressed to "Idea," and in fact preceded the sonnets, as did the sacred poem of *The Harmony of the Chunk* (1591); *Mortimeriados,* which he issued in two forms and under two names, once in 1596 with the title just given, and once in 1603 as *The Barons' Wars;* and *England's Heroical Epistles* (1597), a batch of extremely vigorous historical pieces in miniature,—all came before the period at which, strictly speaking, we begin in this chapter. But Drayton did very much else besides these and the *Polyolbion,* being evidently much attracted to history. He wrote two poems on Agin-court, the one a slightly heavy narrative of length in ottava rima, the other the famous ballad beginning—

Other poems.

Fair stood the wind for France,

the excellence of which in itself, and its importance as a pattern, have long been recognised. *The Barons' Wars,* the expanded form of the *Mortimeriad,* extends to six books. The *Heroical Epistles* deal in couplets with passages of English story that give romantic persons such as Fair Rosamond, Matilda FitzWater, Queen Isabel and Mortimer, Queen Margaret and Suffolk, etc., together with Surrey and Geraldine (a proof how Nash's fiction had taken hold) in pairs of epistles on the Ovidian model. *The Miseries of Queen Margaret* is an independent poem in octaves, and in the same metre Drayton executed four other historical legends on Robert Curthose, the above-mentioned Matilda, Gaveston, and Thomas Cromwell. Of a different kind are *Nymphidia,* the most elaborate fairy poem in the language; *The Mooncalf,* an odd political and social satire in couplets; *The Owl,* a long bird-fable; and *The Man in the Moon,* a version of the Endymion story. Beside these Drayton has left a collection of odes in divers metres and some pastorals; *The Muses' Elysium* (this appeared in 1630, just before his death; he had collected many of the others in a volume three years before) in ten "Nymphals," and some odd versifyings of the stories of Noah, Moses, and David. He can be sometimes flat; but few English poets have grappled with a larger number of important poetic subjects more vigorously and with happier touches at times.

Daniel.

The shorter life of Samuel Daniel,[3] who was born near Taunton, in 1562, was mainly passed as tutor, "servant," or friend and inmate of divers noble families, the Cliffords, Wriothesleys, and Herberts. He received education at Oxford, and was Master of the Revels and Gentleman of the Chamber to James I, as well as groom thereof to his queen. His *Delia* and his Senecan plays have been already noticed. Besides them he wrote in prose the also-noticed *Defence of Rhyme,* and a considerable *History of England* (1612-17). In verse he produced the *History of the Civil Wars of York* and Lancaster (1595-1609), in seven books of octaves; a Funeral Poem in couplets on the Earl of Devonshire; a Panegyric Congratulation to James; verse-addresses to Lord Henry Howard, to the Countess of Cumberland, to the Countess of Bedford, to his pupil Lady Anne Clifford, afterwards a countess, to Lord Southampton; *Musophilus,* a verse-defence of learning; some minor poems; and *The Complaint of Rosamond,* in rhyme-royal, the best of his narrative work.[4] Daniel is less unequal than Drayton, less given to merely

3. Poems in Chalmers; complete works in a very handsome edition by Dr. Grosart (5 vols. privately printed, 1885-96).

4. He collected his poems repeatedly in his lifetime, and in 1623 the whole appeared.

prosaic statements of fact, and possessed of a command of high ethical reflection which inevitably reminds us of Wordsworth, and of hardly any one else. But he is apt to be dull; his lyrical power, though shown to great advantage in the choruses of his plays, in his masque *Hymen's Triumph,* and elsewhere, does not often pass into vivid or inspired verse in other kinds, and he almost entirely lacks Drayton's occasional fire, as well as his almost continuous *sinewiness*—the faculty which enables the author of the *Polyolbion* to grapple with and give a fair account of almost any subject. Daniel's meditativeness is apt to pass into languor, and except when he transports us, which is not very often, he is apt to send us to sleep.

Sylvester.

An almost exact contemporary of both Drayton and Daniel in point of birth, and of one of them in death-date, was Joshua Sylvester[5] (1563-1618). Sylvester, though not exactly a successful man (he seems to have been engaged in business, and died secretary of a Company of Merchants at Middleburgh, in Holland), was very popular in his own day. In the next generation or a little later he became a byword for "conceit" and extravagance, and later again was totally forgotten. It is improbable that he will ever re-acquire any considerable number of readers, for his genius was in no sense original; he had neither the sententious weight and occasional grace of expression of Daniel, nor the vigour and frequent force of Drayton; and his chief work, a version of the *Divine Semaine* of the great French Huguenot poet, Du Bartas, was unluckily not suited to correct eccentricities of taste and extravagance of diction. Besides this mighty task, which extends to some thirty thousand verses in couplets, he translated other pieces from the same and other writers in French and Latin, and has left many thousand lines of more profane and original work, usually in couplets or quatrains, but sometimes in lyrical metres. Of these last Sylvester has no effective control; he has neither "cry" nor song in him. But he is not destitute of a certain kind of poetical or at least verse-rhetoric, which, if it had been accompanied by a somewhat greater critical sense,

5. Ed. Grosart, 2 vols. privately printed, 1880.

might have ranked him higher among poets than he now stands. Such eminent oddities as the much-ridiculed one about snow "periwigging the woods" are not so fatal as the flatness which too often surrounds them.

Sir John Davies.

A very much better poet than Sylvester was Sir John Davies,[6] whose business as a lawyer caused him to abandon poetry in James's reign, but whose work, though all of it probably composed under, and some of it actually addressed to Elizabeth, is of the seventeenth rather than the sixteenth century in tone. Davies was of a good family in Wiltshire, and was born about 1569. He went first to Oxford and then to the Temple, lived for some considerable time in his University, and seems to have written most of his poems there. But he entered Parliament in the last years of Elizabeth, was much favoured by James, and became Attorney-General in Ireland, writing during his long residence there one of the most valuable books of the time on the country. Then he returned home, practised at the Bar, and did a good deal of work on the Bench, though he was never regularly made a judge, and died in 1626. We have from him in the way of verse *Nosce Teipsum* (1599), a poem on the Immortality of the Soul, in quatrains, which connects itself backwards with much of the poetry of Spenser, and forwards with the philosophic verse of More and Beaumont; a collection of acrostics in honour of Elizabeth, entitled *Astraea* (1599); and a poem of Dancing called *Orchestra* (1596). All three may, from their general description, sound uninteresting; all three, in fact, show both the extraordinarily diffused poetic power of the time and the large share of it which had fallen to this author. *Nosce Teipsum* is full of passages finely thought and expressed in a stately music; the hymns of *Astraea,* the initials of each making "Elizabetha Retina," and arranged in five-five-six-lined stanzas of octosyllables, full or catalectic rhymed, *aabab, aabab, aabaab,* have a grace which is beyond artifice, and manage their frequent double rhymes with singular skill.

6. Poems in Chalmers; with additions in Grosart, 3 vols. Capell's remarkable *Prolusions* (1760), the first attempt to edit old English poetry critically in the eighteenth century, contains *Nosce Teipsum.*

And lastly *Orchestra,* which is a whimsical praise of ordered movement of all kinds, with examples from history, cosmogony, anatomy, and everything else, is one of the crowning instances of Elizabethan power, by dint of sheer poetry, to transform fantastic conceit into matter of real value. Indeed, little known as Davies is, except to students, he is one of the most useful poets in English to show how very little the subject has to do with poetry.

Minor poets.

Another Sir John, Beaumont,[7] the elder brother of Fletcher's partner, died not long after Davies, but was a much younger man, as he was born in 1582. He was, like his brother, a member of Broadgates Hall and of the Inns of Court, but seems to have lived chiefly at home in Leicestershire. His title of baronet was given to him by Charles I only two years before his death in 1628. His principal work, *The Crown of Thorns,* a sacred piece well spoken of by contemporaries, seems to be strangely lost; his actual remains consist of *Bosworth Field,* a history poem, in couplets, and a few smaller poems on which his fame should rest. They are mainly of a sacred character, with some topographical pieces, complimentary addresses, and the like, with one remarkable exercise in, and apology for, the stopped couplet. We can but name here for the second time the voluminous pamphleteer in verse as well as in prose, Nicholas Breton;[8] for the first the writing-master John Davies of Hereford,[9] who sometimes has wit; Samuel Rowlands,[10] who very seldom has any; and the so-called "Water Poet," John Taylor,[11] 1580-1659, a waterman, publican, and pedestrian, who composed a vast quantity of doggerel, became in his own time and since a "curiosity of literature," and has had the very undeserved honour, denied to better men, of full reprint in our own times.

7. In Chalmers.

8. Ed. Grosart.

9. *Ibid.*

10. Partially printed for the Percy Society, more fully for the Hunterian Club.

11. By the Spenser Society.

Superior to Taylor by far in birth, education, and talents, yet, with one single exception in the whole of his voluminous work, like him merely a curiosity of literature, is Richard Braithwaite, who has shared the partiality of antiquarian students for the miscellanists of this age.[12] He was a Westmoreland man, born near Kendal about 1588, and seems to have died quite late in the latter half of the century (1665? 1673?) at his wife's house of Catterick, near the Yorkshire Richmond. He was a good Cavalier. In Braithwaite's voluminous work, which, if completely edited, would probably extend beyond Taylor's or even Breton's, there is no sense of criticism. The rare good, the frequent bad, and the usual indifferent, jostle each other without any apparent discrimination on the part of their author. He, like others of his time, was a member of both Universities, beginning at Oriel and moving thence to Cambridge. But he seems to have passed most of his life in his own north country. His journeys thither from sojourns in London form the subject of the odd and (from Southey downwards to all good persons) delightful *Barnabae Itinerarium,* or *Barnabee's Journal,* in bilingual doggerel, Latin and English, arranged in six-lined stanzas of the trochaic rhythm, which revive the true doggerel spirit of Skelton with a really marvellous felicity. The morals are rather doggerel, too, but they can be taken dramatically.

Chapman's work, as a poet and translator, seems to belong chiefly to the middle period of his life. He began to publish his *Homer* (seven books of the *Iliad*) in 1598, and issued the *Odyssey* in 1616. Before the first date he had published his earliest poems, the *Shadow of Night, Ovid's Banquet of Sense,* and the continuation of Marlowe's *Hero and Leander,* while the rest of them were scattered over his last thirty years.

The original poems of Chapman—the two first above mentioned, the *Tears of Peace* addressed to Prince Henry, *An*

12. As examples (they are not the only ones) of this may be mentioned the edition of *Barnabee's Journal,* given by Haslewood in 1820, and reissued by Mr. W.C. Hazlitt in 1876, with a very elaborate memoir and bibliography; and that of the *Strappado for the Devil,* and other poems by the Rev. J.W. Ebsworth in 1878.

Epicede on the death of that Prince, *Andromeda Liberata* (an either very awkward or very shameless adjustment of the story to the divorce of Frances Howard, the murderess of Overbury, from Essex, and her marriage to Somerset), *Eugenia* (an epicede on Lord Russell), and some others—are by common consent among the obscurest in English. His metre is by no means so harsh as that of some of his contemporaries; but his phrase is often extremely rugged, and his expression, especially in the *Shadow of Night* and *Andromeda,* is twisted, carried on, reinvolved, and subjected to every kind of unnatural manipulation, so that the sense is never easy to follow without extreme and constant effort, and sometimes escapes even this. Beauties are by no means lacking—on the contrary, it would not be easy to open a page of Chapman in search of a motto without finding some striking, though quaintly-put conceit, or even some distinctly poetical expression. But lucid and finished combination of thought and expression within reasonable limits is almost everywhere to seek.

Chapman.

In his translations, on the contrary, these objections hardly apply at all. Besides the *Iliad,* and *Odyssey,* he did the minor works attributed to Homer, Hesiod, and some Juvenal. But these latter pieces are not equal to the *Odyssey;* and the *Odyssey,* which is in couplets, is not nearly equal to the *Iliad,* done in a splendid swinging fourteener, better able than any other English metre to cope with the body as well as with the rhythm of the Greek hexameter, and managed with extraordinary skill and success by the writer. For nearly a century it has been usual to quote Keats's sonnet as a sponsor for Chapman. The connection is interesting, but Chapman does not in the least require it. His translation remains, in the first place, the only really good one of *Homer* into English verse; in the second place the best translation into English verse of any classic, ancient or modern, except FitzGerald's *Omar Khayyam.*

This position would by some be challenged for the work of Edward Fairfax, the translator of Tasso, whose birth-year is unknown, but who died in 1635. He was an offshoot of the great Yorkshire family of his name, and spent his whole life in that county, troubled by witchcraft (see Scott's *Demonology*), on which he wrote a *Discourse* (1621) deserving to be associated with the great demonological work of the period, Reginald Scot's *Discovery,* though on the other side. His version of the *Jerusalem* (1600) is in octavos with distinct final couplets. It was long popular, receiving praise in the most diverse quarters from Waller to Collins, while, from its subject and style, it was dear to students of romance, being credited with smoother versification than the Augustan ages would allow to most work of the "last age." It is a book[13] still to be read with pleasure, but, unless its praises be taken warily, with a little disappointment. Its style is rather flaccid; the very stamp of line which commended it to Waller impresses a touch of prose; and Fairfax seldom has either the mazy beauty of Spenser's music or the panoramic power of his painting.

Fairfax.

Thomas Campion,[14] whose name not so many years ago would have conveyed to but few readers any distinct idea of poetic quality, was born at an unknown date, and though he was certainly a member both of Cambridge and the Inns of Court, frequented both in unknown times and circumstances. Towards the end of Elizabeth's reign he was a popular physician in London, and connected in friendship and enmity with divers men of letters. He was buried at St. Dunstan's, Fleet Street, on 1st March 1620. He wrote, and wrote well, in Latin as well as in English, but his importance for English literature is of a double character, and the halves are curiously opposed to each other. We have from him, in the first place, besides some masques, certain collections of verses for music,[15] which contain much of the most exquisite rhymed poetry of the time; and, in the second place, a formal

Campion.

13. I use the edition of L'Estrange, London, 1682.

14. Complete works, ed. Bullen (London, 1889). Songs to be found in the same editor's *Lyrics from Elizabethan Song-books,* two series (London, 1887-88), and in Mr. Arber's *English Garner*.

15. *Book of Airs,* 1601; *Two Boots of Airs* (1612 ?); *Third and Fourth Books of Airs* (1617 ?).

treatise[16] intended to show, by precept and example, that English poetry ought to be unrhymed, and arranged on ancient quantitative models. It is not fair, though it has sometimes been done, to regard Campion as an thither from sojourns in London form the subject of the odd and (from Southey downwards to all good persons) delightful *Barnabae Itinerarium,* or *Barnabee's Journal,* in bilingual doggerel, Latin and English, arranged in six-lined stanzas of the trochaic rhythm, which revive the true doggerel spirit of Skelton with a really marvellous felicity. The morals are rather doggerel, too, but they can be taken dramatically.

Chapman's work, as a poet and translator, seems to belong chiefly to the middle period of his life. He began to publish his *Homer* (seven books of the *Iliad*) in 1598, and issued the *Odyssey* in 1616. Before the first date he had published his earliest poems, the *Shadow of Night, Ovid's Banquet of Sense,* and the continuation of Marlowe's *Hero and Leander,* while the rest of them were scattered over his last thirty years.

Chapman.

The original poems of Chapman—the two first above mentioned, the *Tears of Peace* addressed to Prince Henry, *An Epicede* on the death of that Prince, *Andromeda Liberata* (an either very awkward or very shameless adjustment of the story to the divorce of Frances Howard, the murderess of Overbury, from Essex, and her marriage to Somerset), *Eugenia* (an epicede on Lord Russell), and some others—are by common consent among the obscurest in English. His metre is by no means so harsh as that of some of his contemporaries; but his phrase is often extremely rugged, and his expression, especially in the *Shadow of Night* and *Andromeda,* is twisted, carried on, reinvolved, and subjected to every kind of unnatural manipulation, so that the sense is never easy to follow without extreme and constant effort, and sometimes escapes even this. Beauties are by no means lacking—on the contrary, it would not be easy to open a page of Chapman in search of a motto without finding some striking, though quaintly-put conceit, or even some distinctly poetical

16. *Observations on the Art of English Poesy,* 1602.

expression. But lucid and finished combination of thought and expression within reasonable limits is almost everywhere to seek.

In his translations, on the contrary, these objections hardly apply at all. Besides the *Iliad,* and *Odyssey,* he did the minor works attributed to Homer, Hesiod, and some Juvenal. But these latter pieces are not equal to the *Odyssey;* and the *Odyssey,* which is in couplets, is not nearly equal to the *Iliad,* done in a splendid swinging fourteener, better able than any other English metre to cope with the body as well as with the rhythm of the Greek hexameter, and managed with extraordinary skill and success by the writer. For nearly a century it has been usual to quote Keats's sonnet as a sponsor for Chapman. The connection is interesting, but Chapman does not in the least require it. His translation remains, in the first place, the only really good one of *Homer* into English verse; in the second place, the best translation into English verse of any classic, ancient or modern, except FitzGerald's *Omar Khayyam.*

This position would by some be challenged for the work of Edward Fairfax, the translator of Tasso, whose birth-year is unknown, but who died in 1635. He was an offshoot of the

Fairfax.

great Yorkshire family of his name, and spent his whole life in that county, troubled by witchcraft (see Scott's *Demonology*), on which he wrote a *Discourse* (1621) deserving to be associated with the great demonological work of the period, Reginald Scot's *Discovery,* though on the other side. His version of the *Jerusalem* (1600) is in octavos with distinct final couplets. It was long popular, receiving praise in the most diverse quarters from Waller to Collins, while, from its subject and style, it was dear to students of romance, being credited with smoother versification than the Augustan ages would allow to most work of the "last age." It is a book[17] still to be read with pleasure, but, unless its praises be taken warily, with a little disappointment. Its style is rather flaccid; the very stamp of line which commended it to Waller impresses a touch of prose; and Fairfax seldom has

17. I use the edition of L'Estrange, London, 1682.

either the mazy beauty of Spenser's music or the panoramic power of his painting.

Thomas Campion,[18] whose name not so many years ago would have conveyed to but few readers any distinct idea of poetic quality, was born at an unknown date, and though he was certainly a member both of Cambridge and the Inns of Court, frequented both in unknown times and circumstances. Towards the end of Elizabeth's reign he was a popular physician in London, and connected in friendship and enmity with divers men of letters. He was buried at St. Dunstan's, Fleet Street, on 1st March 1620. He wrote, and wrote well, in Latin as well as in English, but his importance for English literature is of a double character, and the halves are curiously opposed to each other. We have from him, in the first place, besides some masques, certain collections of verses for music,[19] which contain much of the most exquisite rhymed poetry of the time; and, in the second place, a formal treatise[20] intended to show, by precept and example, that English poetry ought to be unrhymed, and arranged on ancient quantitative models. It is not fair, though it has sometimes been done, to regard Campion as an apostle of the preposterous hexameters, etc., which deluded Harvey, and all but seduced Spenser. He had seen the unsuitableness of these to English (which as he acutely observed is rebel to dactyls); and though he made some Sapphics, his own attempts are chiefly in very cunningly balanced iambic and trochaic unrhymed measures, some of which—such as the most often quoted,

Campion.

Rose-cheeked Laura, come—

are at least the equals, if not the superiors, of Collins's "Ode to Evening" in this unnatural kind of abstinence from the greatest charm of English verse. In his "airs," on the other

18. Complete works, ed. Bullen (London, 1889). Songs to be found in the same editor's *Lyrics from Elizabethan Song-books,* two series (London, 1887-88), and in Mr. Arber's *English Garner*.

19. *Book of Airs,* 1601; *Two Books of Airs* (1612?); *Third and Fourth Books of Airs* (1617?).

20. *Observations on the Art of English Poesy,* 1602.

hand, he allows himself the full liberty of our poetical Sion, and with the very happiest results, literally dozens of his lyrics being among the most delightful of their kind. In fact, the difficulty is to find in the *Four Books of Airs* anything that is bad.

All these, however, with the exception of Sir John Davies, who might, with justice, be classed in tone, though not in language, with the Spenserians, lie outside the three schools which have been referred to above, and which make Jacobean poetry so extremely interesting both in itself and as a transition to Caroline. Of these we may take the Spenserian first, both as in origin the oldest and as lacking a living head and master.

The Spenserians: Minor poets.

The class contains some outsiders, anonymous and named, who come closest to Spenser on that side at which he himself touches the luxuriant style of such pieces as Shakespeare's first poems. "Sage and serious" as Spenser undoubtedly was, there is also no doubt that both his Italian originals and his own temper inclined him to the highly-coloured pictures of natural loveliness which are abundant in the *Faërie Queene.* One of the very best poems of this class, *Britain's Ida,* a piece describing the loves of Venus and Anchises ("Britain's," because the legendary Brutus was son of Aeneas), used to be printed among Spenser's own works,[21] though it did not appear till long after his death (1628), and is quite destitute of the allegorical and ethical purpose which always accompanied his most luscious imaginings. It has recently been assigned, without evidence, to Phineas Fletcher (*vide infra*), but is best taken as the work of a good uncertain poet. Beaumont's *Salmacis and Hermaphroditus* (p. 337) and Barkstead's *Myrrha* belong to the same school—to which I should myself assign, for reasons of style and metre, the *Mary Magdalene* referred to in the note on p. 330.

The general characteristics of Spenser, however, his allegorical fancy on the one hand, and his ethical-pastoral

21. It will be found in the useful one-volume Spenser, first published by Moxon and then by Routledge; also in the Aldine.

tendencies on the other, with a certain copious and fluent diction winch he introduced into poetry, are best represented by a group of Jacobean poets, two of them Cambridge men, two of the older university, who may be mentioned in the order in which they diverge from their pattern, Giles and Phineas Fletcher. William Browne of Tavistock, and George Wither.

The two first[22] belonged to the family already noticed, and were sons of the author of *Licia.* Giles, who, though he is said to have been slightly the younger, died first, was first known as a poet, and is usually mentioned before his brother, was probably born about 1585-88. But it is not certain that he was not older than Phineas, and even probable that he was, since he produced a poem on Elizabeth's death as early as 1603 at Cambridge, where he was a member of Trinity College. He took orders, and died vicar of Alderton, in Suffolk, in 1623. Phineas, who was educated at Eton, and proceeded thence to Kings College, Cambridge, is said to have been born in 1582. He followed his brother's and father's profession, and was for very many years parson of Hilgay, in Norfolk, where he died at an uncertain date, perhaps not much before the Restoration, perhaps even later (but some say 1650).

The Fletchers.

Giles takes his place in English poetry in virtue of a poem, not of the longest, entitled *Christ's Victory and Triumph,* in four books and some 250 stanzas of curious construction, and obviously modelled on the *Faërie Queene.* Fletcher has kept the Alexandrine termination, but left out one of the lines, so that the result is an octave of seven decasyllables and an Alexandrine, rhymed *ababbccc.* The device is not in itself very happy, and in particular the triplet at the end comes awkwardly. But Giles has written it with such a glow and fire of continuous inspiration, with such splendour of language and imagery, and occasionally (indeed very frequently) with single lines and passages of such force and

Giles.

22. Editions in Chalmers; by Grosart (privately printed) and by F.S. Boas (Cambridge, 2 vols). *Christ's Victory,* ed. Brooke, London, *n.d.*

beauty, that few poems of the kind by any but the very greatest masters can be read with equal pleasure. The picture and speech of Justice in the first canto with the contrasted portrait of Mercy; the description, in the warmest Spenserian style, and with a really exquisite insertion of octosyllables ("Love is the blossom where there blows"), of the temptress Pangloretta in the second; the overture of the third, which deals with the Crucifixion; and almost the whole of the fourth, with its glowing descant on Paradise, rank among the triumphs of the ornate and fanciful kind of poetry in English. The pre-Raphaelite effect of the poem is striking. It constantly reminds us, with allowance for the difference of centuries, of the work of the Rossettis, brother and sister, in its combination of vivid and elaborate pictorial effect with gorgeous word-music. Nor is the thought inferior to the expression.

Phineas.

The work of the longer-lived Phineas is very much more voluminous, and very much more various—qualities which perhaps inevitably comport greater inequality. It is not easy to say that this poet was actually less pervaded with poetic spirit than his brother. He was, however, certainly less well inspired in the choice of his principal subject, *The Purple Island*, which is neither more nor less than an excessively elaborate allegory—unwisely magnified from one or two, not in themselves happiest, sketches of Spenser's—of the physical body of man. As a vehicle for this he arranged a still further modified stanza, which retained his brother's final triplet with its concluding Alexandrine, but cut off the last line of the quintet, so as to make a septet of quatrain-and-triplet effect with three rhymes. Individually, the stanza is even less successful than Giles's, while the poem has the additional disadvantages of a very awkward subject, and of much greater length (there are twelve cantos). The first half is mere physiology; and of course, though sometimes extremely ingenious, constantly grotesque, sometimes nearly disgusting, and deserving, at the best, the praise of an ill-judged *tour de force*. The last six cantos, which shift to the moral and intellectual qualities, are much more Spenserian and much happier. But even in the earlier part an abundance of really fine passages may be discovered, and in overtures, episodes, and other ornaments of his song, the author shows, perhaps his sense that ornaments were sorely wanted, but certainly his skill in supplying them. Besides *The Purple Island,* Phineas wrote a masque, *Piscatory Eclogues,* in which the following of Spenser blends with that of Sannazar, a curious sacred poem called *The Apollyonists,* well-known, as indeed were all the poems of both the Fletchers, to Milton, and some miscellaneous pieces of divers kinds. Quarles called him the "Spenser of his age"; and though the compliment was rather commonplace and slightly ambiguous, there was truth in it.

W. Browne.

William Browne,[23] whose literary merits have been rather variously judged, was born at Tavistock, some time about 1591, and seems to have been of a very respectable family. He went to Exeter College, Oxford, but took no degree before passing to the Inns of Court (Clifford's Inn and the Temple) in 1611. He was twice married, his first wife dying when he was very young, and a considerable time (some fifteen years) passing before he married the second. Before the latter date he returned to Exeter as tutor to a young nobleman, and somewhat late took the degree of M.A. After his second marriage he lived in Surrey, where both he and his wife had relations. He was dead in November 1645, when probate was granted to his widow, who had the odd name of Timothy, short no doubt for Timothea. But some say that his age, like his youth, was passed in Devon, and he pretty certainly was buried at his birthplace.

The claim which has recently been made of the exquisite epitaph, "Sidney's Sister," for Browne seems without a sufficient external foundation, and is entirely refuted by internal evidence. But his reputation did not need it. His chief work is *Britannia's Pastorals,* a desultory book in three divisions, which appeared (its first part at least) in 1613; *The Shepherd's Pipe,* a pleasing collection of eclogues; and *The Inner Temple Masque,* on the story of Circe and Ulysses, which opens with some verses of

23. Poems not completely in Chalmers. Completely in two volumes of the "Muses' Library," ed. Goodwin, London, 1804.

quite extraordinary beauty, the well-known "Steer hither, steer," and includes others not far inferior to them. Besides these, he has a fair number of miscellaneous poems, thoroughly justifying the adjective—being serious, sacred, jocular, elegiac, and almost everything. Browne's extreme variety is conditioned by a corresponding inequality, and he is undoubtedly liable to a certain fluent prettiness, which lacks dignity, and sometimes approaches too near to the namby-pamby. This touch of mawkishness, as well as better things, helps to bring about the singular likeness between Browne and Keats which has been noticed by most good critics. And among the better things must be noted a great similarity in versification, the lines, whether couplets or other, being broken up and "enjambed," after the fashion which, after nearly two centuries, Leigh Hunt revived and taught to Keats; while the way of looking at nature, and the ornate presentation of it—a presentation less stately than that of the Fletchers, but almost equally pictorial—give another point of contact. Browne is not nearly so great or so good a poet as Keats; he had the disadvantage of coming after, not in the full tide of, the poetic energy of his time. But he has a large share of the special charm of this Spenserian group, its combination of habitual ornateness with occasional simplicity, its beauty of image and phrase, its love of nature, if of a nature "tricked and frounced" a little, its sensuous yet in no sense impure passion, and its occasional bursts of rare and elsewhere unheard music.

Wither.

The inequality, which is almost inseparable from the methods of this school of poetry, is again more perceptible in George Wither[24] than in Browne; while unfortunately Wither, unlike Browne, continued to write verse for many years after the faculty of writing had left him. He was born near Alresford, in Hampshire, in the year 1588,

24. Only to be found completely (if there) in the private reprints of the Spenser Society. His best things, *Philarete, The Shepherd's Hunting,* etc., are in Mr. Arber's *English Garner.* Not much of his *Hymns of the Church* and *Hallelujah,* reprinted by Mr. E. Farr in the "Library of Old Authors" (London, 1856 and 1857), is of his best; and most of his later verse and prose is rubbish.

and was educated (but did not take his degree) at Magdalen College, Oxford. Then he entered an Inn of Court, and hung about London. His first book, the satirical *Abuses Stript and Whipt* (1613), procured him, nobody has ever discovered why, imprisonment in the Marshalsea. His famous "Shall I, wasting in despair" is said to date from this sojourn, and from the next decade till 1623 come all, or almost all, his really good poems—*The Shepherd's Hunting* (1615), *Fidelia* (1615), *Motto* (1618), *Philarete* (1622), and the *Hymns and Songs of the Church.* At the time of the publication of the *Hymns* he was exactly thirty-five. He lived to be nearly eighty, dying in 1667; and he constantly tried to "recapture his first, fine, careless rapture," but entirely failed except perhaps in some of the passages of his *Hallelujah* (1641). As his writing became worse and worse, and as in his later life, and during the Parliamentary troubles, he became a Roundhead, his name (generally spelt Withers) was used as a sort of byword of contempt by the partisans of monarchy after the Restoration, from Dryden downwards, and the contempt was echoed from generation to generation afterwards by persons who probably had never read a line of his. Only when the work of the early seventeenth century was unearthed for serious reading, when nearly two hundred years had passed, was it discovered what an exquisite poet had been for some hundred and fifty years classed with Bavius and Codrus. Yet it must be admitted that in his very best work, which is to be found in *Philarete,* though *Fidelia* and *The Shepherd's Hunting* run this close, he is unequal. The easy, fluent, Keatsian note of verse and of nature-painting which is observable in Browne is even better found in him; indeed, if genuine pastoral sweetness—the sense of the country and of country joys—is anywhere in English poetry, it is in Wither, who has much besides. But the very word fluency suggests the dangers which this verse coasts, and into which it sometimes falls.

An addition to the poets of this school was made a few years ago by the printing for the first time of the works of William Basse,[25] who had been previously known, if at all, by

25. Ed. R.W. Bond, London, 1893.

some often-quoted lines about Shakespeare and Beaumont. Basse seems to have lived almost all his life in Oxfordshire as an honourable dependant of the families of Wenman of Thame and Norreys of Rycote. He may have been, though we do not know that he was, a member of the University, as well as an inhabitant of the shire. His initials, "W.B.," have led to some confusion with Browne, whose friend he was, to whose *Pastorals* he wrote commendatory verses, and whom he a good deal resembles in his own poems of the same kind, his *Urania,* his *Polyhymnia* (only surviving in fragments), and other pieces. But he is only a curiosity, and a very weak poet, though it may be a little stronger than another outsider of the Browne-Wither group, Christopher Brooke, whose poems have also been printed.

Basse.

The Spenserians, however, though their work was to be continued even later in the great, or at least large, philosophical poems of More and Joseph Beaumont, and though we shall find a more profane echo of them in the most interesting *Pharonnida* of Chamberlayne, were in fact behind their time, and did not represent anything like its characteristic tastes and impulses. These were to be found in two schools, or perhaps in one with two very different heads, who were Ben Jonson and John Donne. Both these men (we speak in this place, of course, of Jonson's non-dramatic work only) had an essentially lyric genius. It may seem strange that this should have co-existed with the rhetorical and declamatory tendencies of Jonson, and his bent to rough horseplay; with the satiric tastes, in singularly rough verse, of Donne, and his gift of grave, stately, and involved prose-writing. But we have already seen that the whole inspiration of the Elizabethan age proper tended towards the lyrical—especially if sonnets be included in lyric. And as the Euphuist tendency in phrasing, and the ever-growing thoughtfulness, inclining to melancholy in cast, of the later Elizabethan and Jacobean time disposed men ever more and more to conceit, lyric was also more and more the pet form in which they clothed their thoughts. Although the criticism of the time was not inclined openly to admit it, men of sense must have been more or less dimly conscious that a conceit in

The lyrical impulse.

twelve cantos like *The Purple Island,* even in several pages of enigmatic couplets like *The Shadow of Night,* was somehow overparted. In a few stanzas of exquisitely tuned lyrical verse it to this day wins favour from all but the sternest judges; it could not then fail to delight even the sternest.

Jonson's poems.

Ben Jonson's strictly poetical production was continued over the greater part of his literary life, and perhaps most of it dates from the time when he ruled as dictator over his band of "sons," the poets of his own latest day and the next age. He attempted, out of drama, nothing large; his plays at this time and his masques at that probably sufficed him, and, as has been pointed out in the last chapter, the masques, with *The Sad Shepherd,* are treasure-houses of poetry—dramatic only in a remote and unconnected fashion, and constantly delightful. But his actual poems are of sufficiently various kind. Few good words have been bestowed upon, and perhaps even fewer are deserved by, his epigrams, in which unluckily he set a fashion followed by others, especially Herrick, who did worse than their master. Martial's foulness without his wit, and too often without the least share of his "concinnity" of style; the extravagant tone and temper of a section of the playwrights and satirists of the last days of Elizabeth; and worst of all, an affected surliness and rude hectoring dogmatism which it pleased Jonson to assume, and for which posterity has too often justly punished him by taking it as genuine—these are the chief characteristics of the epigrams. The bad habit of ticket names—Lord Ignorant, Sir Voluptuous Beast, Doctor Empiric—which disfigures the plays, is even more obvious here. If we read any with satisfaction, it is those in which the author takes a wholly different tone, as in the excellent one to "Camden, most reverend head," in the charming epitaph on his first daughter, and the exquisite flattery of Lucy, Countess of Bedford, in the dirges on Salathiel Pavy and Elizabeth L.H. And these excepted poems at once show us in Jonson certain characteristics, which are much more generally noticeable in the far finer and more equal collections called *The Forest* and *Underwoods.* The piece with which *The Forest* opens[26] is perhaps as indicative as any other of the manner and the example which Jonson was to set to his contemporaries and followers. For centuries English had been striving, often blindly, to achieve the peculiar clearness, proportion, completeness of expression which are characteristic of the two classical languages. It had succeeded in other things as great as this, perhaps greater, but in this it had not succeeded. Now it did succeed. The thought in the verses quoted is only a conceit, and though a perennially natural one, yet for that reason not even new. But it is expressed perfectly, neither with the redundant ornament and imagery of the school we have just left, nor with the obscure, though precious flickers, the carbuncle-glimmer in darkness, of that to which we shall shortly come. The wording and phrasing are classical, rather of the late than of the early classics perhaps, but still classical, with nothing extravagant in their richness, nothing starched or prim in their grace.

The quality of grace has often been denied to Jonson, but of a surety wrongly. The pieces referred to above in the epigrams, this, the "Celia" songs, including the famous paraphrase from Philostratus, "Drink to me only," the magnificent epode "Not to know vice at all and keep true state," very much of the Charis collection, written when the poet was fully fifty, the song "Oh do not wanton with those eyes," the elegy in the *In Memoriam* stanza, and many others, display grace in the very strictest sense, and the list might be largely extended. Jonson is by no means the only poet who has thus united masculine and feminine characteristics—indeed, the union is rather the rule than the exception in poetry—but he is certainly an instance of it.

The influence of John Donne[27] was even more potent, though it is extremely difficult to understand the precise manner in which it was exercised. This very great and very puzzling

26. Entitled "Why I write not of Love," and beginning "Some act of Love bound to rehearse."

27. Poems in Chalmers, vol. v; ed. Grosart, 2 vols. privately printed, 1873; ed. Chambers, 2 vols. London, 1896. Ed. Grierson, 2 vols. Oxford, 1912 (the best).

poet was born in London about the year 1573, and was connected on his mother's side with the Heywoods and Sir Thomas More. He appears to have been a member of both Universities and of Lincoln's Inn. It is not certain whether he was actually a Roman Catholic at any time, but his family were of that faith. He travelled and served abroad, and perhaps spent his fortune in so doing. On returning to England he became a member of the household of the Chancellor, Sir Thomas Egerton, afterwards Lord Ellesmere, and having made a clandestine marriage with Anne More, a relation of the family, was sent to the Tower, but soon enlarged. He took up his abode with more than one other gentleman, and did some diplomatic work. At last, in 1615, when he must have been over forty, he took orders at the King's suggestion, but at first without any very lucrative result. His wife died in 1617. After some more diplomatic work, he was made Dean of St. Paul's in 1621, and died ten years later in 1631.

Donne.

It seems on the whole improbable that any part of Donne's poems,[28] except a very small one (*The Anatomy of the World,* a poem on Prince Henry, etc.), was ever printed before his death, and the earliest known edition of the larger part of them dates from 1633. On the other hand, it is perfectly certain that some of them must have been written nearly forty years earlier, and it is clear that many, if not most, were known to men of letters who cared about poetry during the whole of the last half of Donne's life and more. There is even probability, though not certainty, in the supposition that a fling of Drayton's (in a poem where he mentions almost every prominent poet among his contemporaries *except* Donne) at poems "which by transcription daintily must go Through private chambers," refers to Donne. At any rate, it is beyond controversy, from references in Jonson's *Conversations,* and from the poems written by Carew and others on Donne's death, as well as from internal evidence, that he was at least on a level with Spenser and Jonson himself as a master of Jacobean poetry, while in some ways his manner and matter are even more characteristic of that poetry and of its Caroline successors.

28. An alleged early edition of the *Satires* cannot be traced.

The Spenserians had made conceit in a manner their own; but as they had produced no poet who was at all equal in intellectual power to their master, they had mostly treated it from the outside, fantastically, though sometimes very happily, describing or dressing up no matter what subjects in a brocaded garb of gorgeous and (when they could manage it) harmonious phraseology. Jonson was setting beside this loose, florid romanticism a severer ideal of classical grace, and was perfecting lyric phrase; but Jonson's imagination rarely soared into strange or distant regions, and in particular his love-poems, though sometimes warm, are never metaphysically passionate. Donne, on the other hand, seems to have been born to combine all elements of the Renaissance spirit—the haunting meditation on death, the passionate attention to love, the blend of classical and romantic form. And he added a peculiar mystical charm, the result of the taste for conceit spiritualised, refined, and made to transcend. This it is which we observe eminently in his later prose contemporary, Sir Thomas Browne, and which communicates their distinguishing peculiarity, though not by any means always their distinguishing charm, to his sons, the so-called metaphysical poets, many indeed of whom owe something of a divided allegiance to Jonson and himself, but who are generally nearer to him in spirit, to Jonson in form.

The form of Donne is indeed the most puzzling thing about him. Some of its peculiarities are beyond all doubt due to the mere fact that he never printed most of his poems, and that of hardly any can we be sure that we have a definitive edition from his own hand. More perhaps should be charged to the certain fact that in his later life he repented much of the matter of his earlier poems, and the probability that he abstained with deliberation from publishing them. But this will not account for the whole phenomenon; and the roughness was undoubtedly to some extent deliberate. That Donne had any intention of attempting a new prosody there is not the least reason for believing. In his Satires, where the roughness is most perceptible, there can be no doubt that the imitation of Persius, which is so noticeable in all the Elizabethan and Jacobean satirists, accounts for a good deal. In his other poems, when they leave the satire, the mere metre is as a rule correct enough. It is only that the intensity and fulness of the thought does not lend itself to actually smooth expression, without more labour than the writer seems to have cared to expend upon it.

This intensity and this fulness appear with no very great, though with some, difference of degree in the various divisions of Donne's work—the Songs and Sonnets, the Elegies, the Epithalamia, the Divine Poems, the Verse Letters, the Epicedes and Obsequies, *The Progress of the Soul, The Anatomy of the World,* and the Satires. The last named are, in consequence of Pope's rather blundering patronage, the best known, but they are the least interesting part of Donne's work, displaying the conventionality and exaggerated indignation of the whole class to which they belong. The Elegies are most remarkable for the undisciplined exuberance of feeling to which Donne, outspoken as were many of the writers of his day, gave more unhesitating voice than almost any of them. The Verse Letters are full of autobiographic interest, and in some of the more elaborate pieces, the "Storm" and "Calm," which rejoiced Hen Jonson, very remarkable exercises in elaboration. The Epicedes, Obsequies, etc., are notable examples of the special ability of the time in these things. *The Progress of the Soul,* which seems early, is a singular poem, a cross between *The Purple Island* and *The Shadow of Night,* deeply shot with Donne's own peculiarities, but not exhibiting them in the most amiable and profitable form. We are thus left with the Songs and Sonnets, and *The Anatomy of the World,* which, though the latter, in its two "anniversaries," is certainly much later than most of the former, and serves to some extent as a pendant and palinode, yet complete each other in the most remarkable fashion. The Songs exhibit Donne's quintessenced, melancholy, passionate imagination as applied, chiefly in youth, to Love; the Anniversaries, the same imagination as applied later to Death, the ostensible text being the untimely death of Mistress Elizabeth Drury, but the real subject being the riddle of the painful earth as embodied in the death of the body. The Songs are, of course, in different lyrical forms, and the Anniversaries are in couplets. But both agree in the unique *clangour* of their poetic sound, and in the extraordinary character of the thoughts which find utterance in verse, now exquisitely melodious, now complicated and contorted almost beyond ready comprehension in rhyme or sense, but never really harsh, and always possessing, in actual presence or near suggestion, a poetical quality which no English poet has ever surpassed. It is from these poems that the famous epithet "metaphysical" (which Johnson not too happily, and with a great confusion between Donne and Cowley, applied to the whole school) is derived; and as applied to Donne it is not inappropriate. For, behind every image, every ostensible thought of his, there are vistas and backgrounds of other thoughts dimly vanishing, with glimmers in them here and there, into the depths of the final enigmas of life and soul. Passion and meditation, the two avenues into this region of doubt and dread, are tried by Donne in the two sections respectively, and of each he has the key. Nor, as he walks in them with eager or solemn tread, are light and music wanting, the light the most unearthly that ever played round a poet's head, the music not the least heavenly that he ever caught and transmitted to his readers. If this language seem more highflown than is generally used in this book or than is appropriate to it, the excuse must be that every reader of Donne is either an adept or an outsider born, and that it is impossible for the former to speak in words understanded of the latter.

4

JACOBEAN PROSE—SECULAR

Bacon—His life—His writings—His style—His use of figures—His rhetorical quality—Jonson's prose—The *Discoveries*—Their essay-nature—Protean appearances of essay—Overbury's *Characters*—The Character generally—Burton—The *Anatomy*—His "melancholy"—His style—Selden—The Authorised Version—Minors.

THE central figure in prose of the entire Jacobean period is undoubtedly Francis Bacon.[1] He holds this position a little in spite of himself; for it was his own opinion, apparently deliberate and persistent, that English was an untrustworthy makeshift, likely to play tricks to any book written in it, and that the only secure medium for posterity was Latin. And he also holds it in spite of the fact that he had more than reached middle life at the date of the King's accession, and that his one contribution of unquestioned importance to English literature, as distinguished from English science and philosophy, was first published long before that time. For the really characteristic editions of the *Essays*—those which are not shorthand bundles of aphorisms, but works of prose art—date much later, and the whole complexion of Bacon's mind and of his matured style has the cast of Jacobean thought and manner.

Bacon.

1. The editions of Bacon, both complete and partial, are extremely numerous, those of the *Essays*, the work which here chiefly concerns us, especially so. Of these latter may be singled out the "Harmony" of the various issues by Mr. Arber in his *Reprints*, and the excellent annotated library edition by the late Rev. S.H. Reynolds (Oxford, 1890).

He was born in January 1561, the son of Sir Nicholas Bacon, Lord Keeper under Elizabeth, and of Anne Cooke, whose sister married Lord Burleigh. His elder brother, Anthony, a man of weak health, who died in middle life, having talents and knowing Montaigne, has been thought not unlikely to have suggested the Essay to his junior. Francis was sent first, at the age of twelve, to Trinity College, Cambridge, then, when he was fifteen, to Gray's Inn, and spent three years, till 1579, at Paris in the suite of Sir Amyas Paulet. He was called to the Bar in 1582, and became a bencher of his Inn in 1586. Having his fortune to make, he had already entered Parliament as member for Melcombe Regis in 1584, sitting afterwards for Taunton and Middlesex. He had early been rather a favourite with the Queen, but he probably did not ingratiate himself further with her by elaborating arguments for toleration and comprehension in ecclesiastical matters, and in 1593 he actually took the Opposition side in the House. He had become the friend of Essex, but the favourite, owing either to Bacon's want of courtiership or to secret opposition from Burleigh, who seems (or at least was thought by his nephew) to have been jealous of him, could not do much, though he gave Bacon a very valuable present of land. After Essex's disgrace, Bacon acted as counsel against him in each of the trials, for misconduct in Ireland and for rebellion. But this baseness, which, after much dust of argument, is now practically aumitted, did him very little good, and it was not till after the accession of James that he received any solid proofs of royal favour. He was knighted, received a small pension, and in 1607 became Solicitor-General. This post he held six years, and became Attorney-General in 1613, a privy councillor some years later, and in 1617 Lord Keeper. Next year (all these latter preferments came to him from the favour of Buckingham) he obtained the still higher dignity of Chancellor and a peerage as Baron Verulam. He was afterwards created Viscount St. Albans, but was never, as he was once commonly, and still is sometimes, called, "Lord Bacon." He held the Chancellorship for more than three years, and then fell a victim to the jealousy of the Commons, the enmity of Sir Edward Coke, the desertion of Buckingham, and, it must be added, his own malpractices.

His life.

He was accused, and practically pleaded guilty to the charge, of taking gifts from suitors, or at least allowing his servants to take them, and the Peers sentenced him to a fine of £40,000, imprisonment, and exile from court. The fine was remitted and he was not long kept in prison, but his banishment was maintained, and he lived thenceforward chiefly at his seat of Gorhambury. He caught cold in March 1626 and died at Lord Arundel's house near Highgate. His character does not much concern us, but there is little doubt that, though personally good-natured, he had in a rather eminent degree all the bad qualities of Renaissance politicians except debauchery, and perhaps vindictiveness. He was profuse and greedy, ostentatious and mean, a born intriguer and tuft-hunter, and though it is probably a mistake to represent him as completely sympathising with the Machiavelian doctrine of the right of the brave, bold, and cunning man to attain his ends by any means, he had much too strong a tinge of this doctrine. Nor can it be said that, except scientific enthusiasm and a certain patriotism, he displays many of the nobler sentiments.

His writings.

The other vexed question of the precise nature and amount of his philosophical acquirements concerns us, if possible, even less, and we have to deal with him only as a great English prose-writer. In this capacity he published, in 1597, his first small batch of very succinct *Essays* (a work increased by successive instalments to fifty-eight of a much more elaborate character in 1625); the *Advancement of Learning* in 1605; and in the last years of his life, after his disgrace, the *History of Henry VII, The New Atlantis,* and some *Apophthegms,* besides some other chiefly minor works. His philosophical and scientific treatises were almost all written in Latin, in which language he even published an enlarged edition of the *Advancement* under the title of *De Augmentis Scientiarum.*

It is at once true of Bacon that no man has a more distinct style than he has, and that no man's style is more characteristic of its age than his. It has, indeed, been attempted to show that he had more than one style; but this does not come to much more than saying that he wrote on a considerable number of different subjects, and that, like a reasonable man, he varied his expression to suit them. Always when he is most himself—

His style.

in the *Essays* as well as in the *Advancement of Learning,* in the *Henry VII* as well as in any other English work—we come sooner or later on certain manners which are almost unmistakable, and which, though in part possessed in common with other men of the time, are in part quite idiosyncratic. All Jacobean authors, and Bacon among them, interlard their English with scraps of Latin, and constantly endeavour to play in their English context on the Latin uses of words. All aim first of all at what is called pregnancy, and attain that pregnancy by a free indulgence in conceit. Few, despite the stateliness which they affect, have any objection to those "jests and clinches" which even Jonson seems to have thought of as interfering with the "noble censoriousness" of Bacon himself. In all a certain desultoriness of detail, illustration, and the like—as if the writer had so full a mind and commonplace-book that he could not help emptying both almost at random—is combined with a pretty close faculty of argument, derived from the still prevailing familiarity with scholastic logic.

But Bacon, in addition to these characteristics, which he shares with others, has plenty of his own. His sentences, indeed, do not attain to that extraordinary music which is seen in some of Brooke and Donne, which is not wanting in Burton, which is the glory of Sir Thomas Browne, the saving grace of Milton's best prose, and the almost over-lavished and sometimes frittered-away charm of Jeremy Taylor. He had begun, as we see in the earliest form of the *Essays,* with a very curt, stenographic, sharply antithetic form; and though he suppled and relaxed this afterwards, he never quite attained the full, languorous grace of Donne or Browne. But he became gorgeous enough later, the glitter of his antithesis being saved from any tinsel or "snip-snap" effect by the fulness of his thought, and his main purport being by degrees set off with elaborate paraphernalia of ornament and imagery. In the successive versions of the *Essays* we see the almost skeleton forms of the earliest filling out, taking on trappings, acquiring flesh and colour and complexion in the later, while in some of the latest, the well-known ones on Building and on Gardens especially, the singular interest in all sorts of minute material facts which distinguishes him comes in with a curiously happy effect. Both the pieces just mentioned are much more like description of scenery in the most elaborate romance than like ideal suggestion, for practical carrying out, drawn up by a grave lawyer, statesman, and philosopher.

His use of figures.

No point in Bacon's literary manner is more characteristic, both of his age and of himself, than his tendency to figure. Such a sentence as this in the *Advancement,* "Nay, further, in general and in sum, certain it is that *Veritas* and *Bonitas* differ but as the seal and the print; for truth goodness; and they be but the clouds of error which descend in the storms of passions and perturbations,"—would show itself to any person of experience as almost certainly written between 1580 and 1660 in the first place, while in the second it would at least suggest itself to such a person as being most probably Bacon's. Although all the world in his day was searching for tropes and comparisons and conceits, the minds of few were so fertile as his; and it is not unworthy notice that even the apparently bold, even startling, change of metaphor from the "seal" to the "cloud" is in reality a much more legitimate change than it seems.

His rhetorical quality.

It will stand to reason that such a style is displayed to the best possible advantage by bold and richly-coloured surveys of science in general, like the *Advancement,* or by handlings of special points, like the *Essays.* Whether Bacon was really "deep," either in knolwedge or in thought, has been disputed; but he was certainly one of the greatest rhetoricians, in the full and varied sense of rhetoric, that ever lived. His knowledge, deep or not, was very wide, ever ready to his hand for purposes more often perhaps of divagation than of penetration. His command of phrase was extraordinary. No one knows better than he either how to leave a single word to produce all its effect by using it in some slightly uncommon sense, and setting the wits at work to discern and adjust this; or how to unfold all manner of applications and connotations, to open all inlets of side-view and perspective. That he dazzles, amuses, half-delusively suggests, stimulates, provokes, lures on, much more than he proves, edifies, instructs, satisfies, is indeed perfectly true. But the one class of performances is at least as suitable for literary exhibition as the other, and Bacon goes through the exhibition with a gusto and an effect which can hardly be too much admired. Fertile in debate as almost all his qualities have proved, there is at least one of them about which there can be little difference of opinion, and that is his intense literary faculty. It was entirely devoted to and displayed in prose—he wrote very little verse, and that little is nothing out of the way. But in prose rhetoric—in the use, that is to say, of language to dazzle and persuade, not to convince—he has few rivals and no superiors in English. His matter is sometimes not very great, and almost always seems better than it is, but this very fact is the greatest glory of his manner.

In those characters of style which, not to the utter exclusion of chronological order, but with a certain prerogative right over it, determine the arrangement of literary history, three writers hold with Bacon in Jacobean prose the place which we have assigned to Donne, to Jonson, and to Spenser after his death in Jacobean verse. Of these Donne and Jonson again appear, a duplication of itself sufficient to prove the high and too-long-ignored position of these writers in English literature; the fourth is Robert Burton. But Donne, for sufficient reasons, will be kept to the next chapter. We shall deal with Jonson and with Burton here.

Jonson's prose.

The independence and the importance of Ben's position are shown, among other things, by the fact that, while in the general history of English prose he makes a distinct advance, he appears among the writers of his own time as isolated, as, indeed, almost reactionary. The gorgeousness of Jacobean phrase, the involution of Jacobean thought, the tricks of both which almost approach the heraldic sin of "colour upon colour," do not appear in him; he is of his time chiefly, if not only, by his learning and by the compression and pregnancy of his style, in which latter points he approaches and sometimes almost excels Bacon in his most serried and least ornate moments. Unfortunately, the amount of Jonson's prose that we have is by no means large, some having certainly, and much probably, perished (with verse as well) in a fire which destroyed the contents of his study. Besides prefaces, dedications, and the like, we have only an *English Grammar,* valuable, but of course not for points of style, and the invaluable collection of notes, short essays, and *pensées* which, never having been published in his lifetime, goes by the alternative titles of *Sylva, Explorata, Timber,* or *Discoveries made upon Men and Matter*—the most usual, and perhaps the best, appellation being simply *Discoveries.*

The *Discoveries.*

These notes, 171 in number, each titled with a short Latin heading, and varying in length from three or four lines to the bulk of a good short essay, have much superficial and some real resemblance to the work of Bacon, whose intimate and, as far as it was in his nature, admiring friend Ben was. But a minuter examination shows that, except the compressed and pregnant tendency mentioned above, there are few points of real likeness, and that Ben belongs to an entirely different school from that of the Chancellor. The license of quip and jest is absent; the coruscating metaphors, more brilliant perhaps than luminous, but brilliant enough, are absent likewise; the volleying antithesis, though present, is more heavily shotted and less often blank cartridge; the unusual, and intentionally unusual, employment of Latin or Latinised terms is less for ornament and more for use. In short, Ben Jonson, allowing for his age and circumstances, belongs to the plain, not the ornate, section of prose-writers; he is at daggers drawn with Euphuism in the larger as well as in the smaller sense. Yet he does not revert to or imitate that kind of plainness which Ascham set in order, and which Hooker, by sheer genius for proportion and harmony, made more elegant than ornateness itself. He advances upon it; we find in him distinct shadows before, echoes in anticipation of, the plain style as it was to be reformed by Dryden, and to continue till the first quarter of the nineteenth century, with sentences of moderate length, symmetrically balanced, deriving little appeal from abundance of antithetic adjectives, but with the antithesis promoting, not obscuring, character and directness. Not, of course, that Jonson wholly escapes the figurative passion of the time. When he speaks of man "making a little winter love in a dark corner," we hear the contemporary and the friend of Shakespeare and Bacon. In such a sentence as "In being able to counsel others a man must be furnished with a universal store in himself to the knowledge of all Nature; that is the matter of seed-plot; there are the seats of all argument and invention," we have the mixed style; the first half might have been written by the other Johnson, or by any eighteenth-century writer of the higher class; the second brings us back to the fanciful and dreamy seventeenth. But often for whole sentences, and not very seldom for whole passages, the nervous, uncoloured, to some extent *sterilised,* fashion of the prose of 1660-1800 appears with hardly a touch of archaism about it. And we must remember that Jonson's influence continued mighty for at least two generations after his death; that it was very strong with Dryden himself, the literary prophet not merely of the second of these generations, but of the whole eighteenth century.

Their essay-nature.

Moreover, the matter of these *Discoveries,* as well as the aphoristic or axiomatic form of much of them, was such as was likely to impress their style on the more thoughtful readers, those who were actual or possible writers themselves. They indeed illustrate (though they do not bear the name and contain one direct gibe[2] at the form) the growing attraction and importance of the essay, which Bacon alone had as yet adopted by its own title, but which, as we shall see both in this chapter and in others, was, either under its own name or under others, gradually to absorb a greater and greater share of the attention of prose-writers and prose-readers. The farrago of the book is of the most miscellaneous character. Ethical remarks are, of course, numerous—the seventeenth century was nothing if not ethical—but they are found side by side with a body of discourses upon

2. "Such (*i.e.* desultory and ill-digested) are all the essayists, even their master Montaigne."

rhetoric, with valuable passages of criticism on individual writers—Spenser, Shakespeare, Bacon, Montaigne, and of course the ancients—with a remarkable tractate in little on education, and with notes on arts, politics, history. Indeed, Ben is the essayist whom he affects to slight, and his adoption of the plainer style may without too much fancifulness be taken as a sort of pointing of the vane in the direction almost of Addison, certainly of Dryden.

Protean appearances of essay.

The temptation of the essay, though under another name, shows itself as strongly, and with not less literary influence, though with far less literary accomplishment, in the famous *Characters* of Sir Thomas Overbury.[3] Their author was a man by no means specially estimable or specially amiable, but recommended in the first place by his performance in a kind which was of growing popularity, in the second by his miserable end. He was born of a respectable family in Warwickshire in 1581, went to Queen's College, Oxford, in 1595, took his Bachelor's degree, and passed to the Middle Temple. He travelled, and seems to have been a *protégé* of Robert Cecil, afterwards Lord Salisbury, but unluckily for himself became connected later with the favourite Carr, afterwards Earl of Somerset. He was knighted in 1608, and attained a very great reputation for ability. But he set himself against his patron's marriage with Lady Frances Howard, the divorced Countess of Essex, one of the worst women of whom history gives record; and having, as it seems, also contrived to offend Anne of Denmark, was sent in May 1613 to the Tower, nominally for refusing an ambassadorship. For about four months' attempts, equally bungling and remorseless, were made to poison him, and after suffering horrible tortures from them he is said to have been finished by vitriol. The matter came to light some three years afterwards, and though the chief criminals, Carr and his wife, escaped with imprisonment,

3. *Works,* ed. Rimbault (London, 1856). The late Mr. H. Morley published in the "Carisbrooke Library" a very interesting collection of *Character-Writers of the Seventeenth Century,* including Overbury, Earle, Butler, and much minor matter.

divers under-strappers, including the Lieutenant of the Tower and Mrs. Anne Turner, famous for her yellow starched ruffs, were executed, Bacon conducting the prosecution. But a great deal remained unexplained, and suspicion, which has never been quite removed or at all confirmed, attached to the King's physician, Dr. (afterwards Sir) Theodore Mayerne, and to the King himself.

This, however, is matter of history, not matter of literature, and it is only mentioned here because Overbury's singular promotion first, and his horrible and apparently mysterious fate afterwards, no doubt helped the reputation of his works. Yet intriguing, braggart, and insolent as he seems to have been, he must have had that art to divine the tendencies of the time which frequently belongs to men of the world. His *Observations on the Low Countries* (1609) is a fair ordinary State paper of the old-fashioned kind; his *Wife,* a poem in sixains, seems to have acquired interest from the probably false notion that it was written to discourage Carr from marrying Lady Frances; his *Crumbs fallen from King James's Table* purport to be, and probably are, mere reports of the utterances of the wisest fool in Christendom. They are chiefly interesting because they contain the crude matter of Rochester's saying on the King's grandson: "Some men never speak a wise word, yet do wisely; and some, on the other side, never do a wise deed and yet speak wisely." But he would now be entirely forgotten if it were not for his *Characters.*

They were not—indeed, none of his works seem to have been—printed during his lifetime, and from the first they bear ascription to "Sir Thomas Overbury *and his friends,*" while in successive impressions from 1614 they were increased in number from twenty-one to a hundred, including divers specimens of the old "News from this or that place" which had been common in the Elizabethan pamphlet. The most famous pieces that are at least probably Overbury's own are the "Milk Maid," constantly quoted in anthologies, the "Affectate Traveller," and the "Mere Fellow of a College." With the limitations to be observed of the Character generally, they are very closely connected with the pamphlet already noticed, and were continued throughout this reign and later. But they have some characteristics which, when we compare them with Earle and other followers (see next Book), seem likely to be Overbury's own—a sharp observation expressed with antithetical conceit, a hard, presumptuous, unamiable wit, and a general superciliousness which accounts in part for Overbury's fate.

The introduction of the Character, however, is a very important thing. It came, of course, from Theophrastus, and during the whole of the seventeenth century, in France as well as in England, indeed all over Europe, continued to be an exceedingly favourite form of the essay, which was in so many ways overrunning literature. "Humours" in prose *belles lettres* as well as in drama, were the fashion of the time, and the very staple and substance of the Character is a "humour" in the seventeenth-century sense. The advantage of the style was that it at least invited, and, as we shall see in Earle's case, successfully, to accurate study and artistic reproduction of its subject; the disadvantage that it lent itself to hardening of types—An Amorist, A Braggadochio, A Pedant, and hundreds more—to dressing them up simply out of the writer's own head, without any real induction from individuals, and also to certain conventionalities of expression. In Overbury particularly the forcing of Euphuist imagery to enliven the phrase, and the abuse of antithesis to give it point and "snap," are unmistakable, and to readers not of the time excessively tedious. The only thing to be said is that these excesses in one direction or another are peculiar to no time, and that from each, bad as it is in itself, ingredients of universal style have been picked up. The antithetic and pointed character helped to *crisp* style, to save it from languor and complexity, as well as constantly to invite the writer to study from the life.

More generally recognised than these, and perhaps equally significant of the general tendencies of the time, but with less direct influence on the form, though he had enormous influence on the matter, of English prose, is Robert Burton. We do not he was not of the elusive race of London Bohemians, but resident in a great University during almost the whole of his life, and that his work was at once, and with men of letters enduringly, popular. He was born in Leicestershire of a good family in 1577, and after education at the grammar schools of Nuneaton and Sutton Coldfield, went to Brasenose College, Oxford, in 1593. After six years he was elected to a studentship at Christ Church, which he held till his death in 1641, as well as the livings of St. Thomas in the University town, and of Segrave in Leicestershire. He appears never to have resided out of Oxford after his entrance at Brasenose, so that he had something like fifty years of uninterrupted study to provide him with the extraordinary learning that appears everywhere in his great and only work, *The Anatomy of Melancholy*,[4] first published in 1621, and much altered and increased in successive editions during the last twenty years of his life. His death has sometimes been attributed to suicide, but on merely fanciful grounds, and without any direct evidence to that effect.

Burton.

The Anatomy of Melancholy has sometimes been thought to have been suggested by a book called *The Anatomy of Humours*,[5] written by one Simeon Grahame, and published at Edinburgh in 1609. Examination of this, however, shows absolutely no similarity of style, thought, or treatment, Grahame's book being in most respects similar to the Elizabethan pamphlet in a sort of rambling railing at actual or supposed vice and folly, with free quotation in verse and prose. The title may to a careless observer seem more suggestive, but the fact is that the term "anatomy" (as it needs no more than two such well-known examples as Lyly's *Anatomy of Wit* and Stubbes's *Anatomy of Abuses* to show) had been a bookmaker's catchword for more than a generation before Burton wrote. Indeed, there are very few books in literature more original than his, in that best sort

The *Anatomy*.

4. Constantly reprinted, but never thoroughly edited. There is no handsomer or better form than that of Shilleto and Bullen (3 vols. London, 1893).

5. Reprinted for the Bannatyne Club (Edinburgh, 1830).

of originality which, exhibiting certain general features of time and race, stamps these with an individual and unmistakable expression.

The two features which are in a sense common to Burton and to all the men of his time are his learning and his melancholy. The former, in prose and verse, in matter ostensibly serious and matter ostensibly light, has been already sufficiently shown to be *the* Jacobean characteristic. It may be doubted whether any age since, and it is certain that no modern age before, has had so much solid reading; for the range of mediaeval possibilities in this respect was very much narrower, and if modern reading has still further widened, the widening is, it may be suspected, more than made up by scrappiness and want of depth. "Democritus Junior," the *nom de guerre* which Burton chose, has, in the enormous and most carefully arranged treatise which he has devoted nominally to Melancholy and its cure, but really to the life and thought of man, amassed such an extraordinary amount of reading that probably no follower of his has ever tracked him completely through the maze of canonists, physicians, historians of the Middle Age and Early Renaissance, not to mention almost the whole of the classics and a very considerable number of his own contemporaries. He shows his learning, not by mere references, though of these, both looser and exacter, he is singularly profuse, but by a unique tissue of actual citation, or paraphrase, or both combined, which he does not lay upon his own canvas in the ordinary fashion of quoting, but weaves and infuses into it in the strangest and subtlest manner.

His "melancholy."

Nor is his "melancholy" itself much less a characteristic. There is no reason to believe that it was, despite Ben Jonson's excellent anticipatory raillery in *Every Man in his Humour*, affected, and even that raillery itself shows that it was a popular symptom, thought worthy of affectation by fools, in the wise men of the time. It is by no means wanting in Ben himself; it is the special mark of Donne, perhaps the most gifted man of letters next to Shakespeare whom we notice in this Book, and of Browne, the equal of the most gifted that we shall have to notice in the next.

Even in Bacon, though kept back by his sanguine philosophical hopes, his personal ambitions, and his touch of Philistinism, it is not far behind the foreground, and it is evident in his master, and the master of many others at this time—Montaigne. It was, in fact, the natural reaction following upon the high and fantastic hopes of the earlier Renaissance, and ushering in the prosaic and slightly vulgar limitation to low aims of the late seventeenth and most of the eighteenth century. In Burton it shows itself not so much in the sense of the unattainable infinity of passion which we find in Donne, of the high feeling of mystery and *altitudo* that we find in Browne, as in a sort of quiet but intense *taedium vitae*—a wandering of the soul from Dan to Beersheba through all employments, desires, pleasures, and a finding them barren except for study, of which in turn the *taedium* is not altogether obscurely hinted. And it is almost unnecessary to add that in Burton, as in all the greatest men, except Milton, of the entire period from 1580 to 1660, there is a very strong dash of humour—humour of a peculiar meditative sort, remote alike from grinning and from gnashing of teeth, though very slightly sardonic in its extreme quietness and apparent calm.

With writers of this kind, and it may be added pretty generally of this time, it is difficult to keep strictly to those considerations of form and expression which the history of literature proper demands, so subtle is the connection between their temper and its utterance.

His style.

But if it were possible to abstract Burton's merely formal characteristics, they would still be of the most interesting character. To accommodate the wide purpose, indicate the voluminous citation and allusion, and infuse the subtle spirit already described might seem almost impossible, yet it is done with wonderful success and with such charm that those who have once acquired, or who naturally possess, the taste for Burton's style find enjoyment in it almost greater than that given by any other writer except Sir Thomas Browne himself. Its sentences are frequently of a length daring even for that age; and the clauses, largely consisting of the illustrative quotations or paraphrases above referred to, are strung together with a still more audacious looseness, the effect being not unfrequently that of a man thinking aloud without taking the trouble to insert the ordinary copulas and syntactical mortar. Yet Burton is never obscure, and when he has no need of a long sentence he can write a short one as nervous, as terse, as distinctly articulated as anything of Jonson's own.

Like Burton, and even more than Burton, John Selden outlived the reign of James; but his characteristics are rather Jacobean than Caroline, and his most noteworthy work was written well before the accession of Charles. He was born in 1584, the son of a Sussex yeoman, was educated at Chichester and Oxford, and became a famous "black-letter lawyer" in the Temple. His political life did not begin till the next reign, and does not greatly concern us; it is enough to say that he was one of those respectable but not very statesmanlike persons who undermined the royal authority till they saw it begin to totter, and then were aghast at the tottering and tried in vain to prop it up. In 1614 he had published his famous treatise on *Titles of Honour*, and in 1618 his *History of Tithes*—two works of extraordinary learning but somewhat cumbrous in style. He is now, except as a writer for reference, not reading, remembered almost entirely by his *Table Talk*,[6] collected by his secretary and published (1689) long after his death in 1654. This book not merely contains a great deal of practical though slightly Philistine wisdom, and a certain amount of sharp aphoristic wit, but also exhibits the same difference, when compared with Selden's published work, as that existing between the writings and the sayings of Johnson, to whom, indeed, though on the other side in political and ecclesiastical beliefs, Selden bore much resemblance. It is curious too to compare the book with Ben Jonson's *Discoveries* and to see how in each the Essay-tendency displays itself, many of the sections in the *Table Talk* being, in fact, essays in little.

Selden.

Selden was no literary critic, and his remarks on the Authorised Version of the Bible (1611) show an extraordinary

6. Ed. S.H. Reynolds, Oxford, 1892.

insensibility to the merits of that mighty book. That it is the greatest monument by far of Jacobean prose there can be very little doubt, and the objection which Selden himself made, and which has been rather unwisely echoed since—that it does not directly represent the speech of its own or any time—is entirely fallacious. No good prose style ever does represent, except in such forms as letter-writing and the dialogue in plays and novels, the spoken language of its time, but only a certain general literary form, coloured and shaped not too much by contemporary practice. The extraordinary merits of the Authorised Version are probably due to the fact that its authors, with almost more than merely human good sense of purpose and felicity of result, allowed the literary excellences of the texts from which they worked—Hebrew, Creek, and Latin—and those of the earlier versions into English from that called Wyclif's to the Bishops' Bible, to filter through their own sieve and acquire a moderate, but only a moderate, tincture of the filter itself in passing. No doubt the constant repetition, universal till recently and pretty general fortunately still, of the text in the ears of each generation has had much to do with its prerogative authority, and still more with the fact that it still hardly seems archaic. But the unanimous opinion of the best critics from generation to generation, and still more the utter shipwreck of the elaborately foolish attempt to revise it some years ago, are evidences of intrinsic goodness which will certainly be confirmed by every one who, with large knowledge of English at different periods, examines it impartially now. There is no better English anywhere than the English of the Bible, and one of its great merits as English is its retention of the "blend" character of all the truest English products.

The Authorised Version.

Certain minor writers of James's reign have at this time or that acquired admission to literary history, nor is it perhaps necessary to oust them. The chief historian of the reign, next to Knolles, was Sir John Hayward, a lawyer, who was born in 1564 at Felixstowe, went to Pembroke College, Cambridge, died two years after the accession of Charles, and wrote a *History of the First Year of Henry IV,* a *History of Edward VI,* and other historical and some theological

Minors.

work. Samuel Purchas (1577-1626) continued the work of Richard Hakluyt (1533-1616), the great collector and redactor of Elizabethan voyage and travel, as editor and populariser of geography with less, but still considerable, charm of writing; and Sir Henry Wotton, the author of some famous and charming poems, was a good letter-writer and produced rather numerous but seldom singly important prose tractates on a wide variety of subjects.

5

THE GOLDEN AGE OF THE ENGLISH PULPIT—I

Great pulpit oratory necessarily late—Function of sermons, 1600-1800—Andrewes—Ussher—Hall—Donne

Great pulpit oratory necessarily late.

THAT the title of this chapter belongs of right to the seventeenth century nobody but a paradoxer is ever likely to dispute. Even the eighteenth, which exaggerated the tendency of almost every century to look down on its immediate predecessor, had not much doubt about this. Nor will those who have followed the history here given of English literature, and especially of English prose, be surprised either that the particular development was so late or that it came when it did. In the first place, it is impossible that any, and especially that pulpit, oratory should be early, because it requires the previous development of a varied prose style. Moreover, the tradition of the Mediaeval and early Renaissance Church, which made vernacular preaching distinctly a *concio ad vulgus,* and encouraged the preacher to descend even to horseplay to make himself intelligible and popular, was not very favourable to the creation of a pulpit style at once flexible and dignified. The Reformation brought little improvement at first, for if the audience were learned it encouraged a mere tissue of scholastic and erudite citation and argument, if it were unlearned there was an inducement to the rude and often blasphemous railing which disgraced both sides. Before Hooker there is hardly an English preacher whose work is of the first class as literature. We must go back to Latimer, and earlier still to Fisher, before we find any with such pretensions; and Latimer is too homely, Fisher too formal, and both too archaic to have them admitted except by allowance.

Hooker, however, who did so much for English, was too much occupied in writing, and during the greater part of his priesthood had too uneducated audiences, to leave many sermons; and the great tradition of the English pulpit and of controversial and other English divinity of the best literary kind begins later. The amount of really noteworthy work of this kind composed for more than a century is enormous. During this century, and even during much of the next, sermons were extremely popular, and indeed discharged one part of the function of the modern newspaper, as the playhouse did others. They were also as a rule much longer than modern discourses in England, and they were far more used for reading than they have been for nearly a century. In fact, it may almost be said that the printed sermon, for some two hundred years, represented the whole modern furnishings of the circulating library to most women who had either education or character, and a large part of it to many men, even men of the world.

Function of sermons, 1600-1800.

We must therefore, from the beginning, proceed by selection; and it so happens that in this particular department selection is less injurious than in any other, at any time save the Middle Ages. The subject-matter of sermons, though admitting the widest individuality of particular handling, must always be within certain limits the same; and in hardly any kind of writing do famous and popular models tend to reproduce themselves so faithfully. From Hooker and Andrewes to Newman, the reader or hearer who knows the styles of the leaders knows those attempted, though no doubt often clumsily, by hundreds of followers, and except for special purposes he may therefore neglect these latter. On the present chapter we shall take as representatives Andrewes, Ussher, Hall, and Donne. The second division of the subject, to be taken up in the next Book, will be more populous.

Lancelot Andrewes[1] was born at Barking in Essex in 1555, and was educated at Merchant Taylors' School and Pembroke College, Cambridge, of which he became Master.

Andrewes.

He was from the first much patronised, and successively became Prebendary of St. Paul's and Westminster, Dean of the last-named cathedral under Elizabeth, and Bishop of Chichester, Ely, and Winchester under James. He was very prominent at the Hampton Court Conference and in the translation of the Bible, and though, like most prelates of the time, he perhaps dabbled more in court intrigues (specially in that *bolgia* of crime, the divorce and remarriage of Lady Frances Howard) than might be desired, he has never been justly judged a sycophant. He died in 1626. Of his learning and of the strange fervency and intense eloquence of his Private Devotions there have never been two opinions; his Sermons have excited more dispute. The charge against him is said to have been put early by "a Scotch nobleman," when the bishop preached in Holyrood Chapel. "He rather plays with his subject than preaches on it." The criticism was by no means unfounded, though it would apply to nearly the whole of the preachers of Andrewes's time, except Hooker himself, in England. Perhaps it may be put better by saying that the sometimes far-fetched and romantic symbolism and imagery which in Donne among the earlier, in Taylor among the later, preachers of the school produce such miraculous effects, are in Andrewes crude and not finally transformed by art. No doubt his immense learning, in which he excelled almost every one of that learned time except Ussher, aggravated the evil.

James Usher (or rather Ussher) himself was more a writer than a preacher, the most erudite of an erudite time, and one

Ussher.

of the most voluminous authors of a time when most authors were voluminous. But he cannot be omitted here, and he escapes the blame not quite unjustly

1. The standard edition of Andrewes is that in the Library of Anglo-Catholic Theology, Oxford, 1841-54. The Greek and Latin *Devotions* have been frequently translated and given separately, most recently by Dr. A. Whyte (Edinburgh, 1896).

passed upon Andrewes by never attempting flights or rhetoric at all. He did not wish his sermons to be published, though they were; his great chronological and historical works, which gained him a practically enduring fame, are mainly in Latin. In English he wrote chiefly on Celtic Antiquities, especially those of an ecclesiastical complexion, as well as on the burning questions of the time—the Protestant-Papist controversy, divine right, and the like. His style, like that of so many men of his day, is largely conditioned by his method of argument, which consists, though by no means wholly yet very mainly, in appeals to authority and citations from the inexhaustible store of his vast reading. Only the idiosyncrasy of a Burton can infuse writing of this kind with any particular tincture of style. But Ussher is always plain and clear. Neither his temper nor his immediate purpose inclined him to any superfluity of ornament, and when he gets free from citation and has a paragraph or two to write, as the common phrase is, "out of his own head," he rather exemplifies the Ascham-Hooker tradition than the more conceited manner of his own day. He was born in Dublin in 1581, and was nephew of Stanyhurst, the eccentric translator of Virgil. He was one of the first alumni of Trinity College, Dublin, became Fellow, and gave himself up to study, becoming Professor of Divinity in his University in 1607, Bishop of Meath in 1620, and Archbishop of Armagh in 1625. When Ireland became convulsed by the Rebellion, he went to England, and was for some time preacher at Lincoln's Inn. Though a steady Royalist, he was not molested by the Parliament or by Cromwell, and died quietly at Reigate in 1656.

Hall.

With Bishop Hall[2] we get into a higher sphere of literary accomplishment. His verse was entirely of the previous or strictly Elizabethan period, while his prose was entirely of this or the next. This early verse was purely secular; but the succeeding prose was by no means purely theological, though its most noteworthy division of the secular kind, the *Characters of Virtues and Vices,* seems to have been

2. *Works,* ed. Wynter, 10 vols. Oxford, 1863.

composed (1608) with a view to use in sermons. These Characters precede Overbury's in point of time, and though they never became so popular, excel them in simplicity, being often quite as pointed, and as a rule not nearly so contorted and fantastic. Hall's subsequent writings during his long, busy, and (till the evil days of rebellion) prosperous life, were extremely multifarious—sermons, meditations, autobiographical pieces, controversial tracts (such as those, for instance, which brought upon him Milton's clumsy invective), expository matter. In his sermons and casuistical work he particularly affects a plain but energetic style of attack on the consciences and hearts of his hearers; and this element of directness is also generally prominent in his politico-ecclesiastical polemic. In his meditations he is more flowery and figurative, as is reasonable enough. But at no time can he be said to share to the full the tendencies of his age in this particular direction, being too much of a fighter when he is not a mere meditative moralist. Perhaps also he may exemplify the rule to which his enemy Milton is one of the not many exceptions, and the great writer whom we are shortly to mention another, that those who write both poetry and prose usually write the latter with some restraint, while the very ornate or fantastic prose writers are chiefly those who cannot express themselves in verse.

This, however, as has just been hinted, is by no means the case with our last and greatest exemplar. Few are more of a piece in poetry and prose than Donne,[3] and much of what has been said of his verse will apply equally to his prose. This consists of a large body—some two hundred—of Sermons, a considerable number of Letters, a short and curious tractate to prove that in certain circumstances suicide may not be a sin, some Essays in Divinity, some Devotions, and a few miscellaneous treatises. All his work, however, even in prose, whatsoever it be called, essay, sermon,

Donne.

3. Ed. Alford, 6 vols. 1859 (not good and incomplete). Dr. Jessopp's little edition of the *Essays* can sometimes be picked up. Since this History appeared Mr. Gosse has given the *Letters* and a much needed *Life* (2 vols. 1899).

letter, or what not, is again strikingly like itself and strikingly unlike anything else, being, like the verse, saturated and pervaded by Donne's peculiar melancholy. The expression of this seems to be as easy for him in prose as in verse, or, to speak more justly and accurately, he succeeds in elaborating a prose style just as suitable for it as is his style in verse. He is clearer in prose than in verse except (curiously enough) in his Letters, which often display almost as much metaphysical conceit as the most recondite passages of his poetry. But he has the three great characteristics of Jacobean writing—the learning, the profundity, and the fantastic imagination. And the profundity is here not merely real, but of a depth rarely surpassed in English, while the fantastic imagination becomes something more than merely fantastic. The "kingship" which Carew ascribed to Donne is at least as noticeable in his prose as in his verse, and though the realm over which he rules is rather a Kingdom of Night than of Day, a place of strangely-lit gloom rather than of mere sunlight, it is a kingdom of wonderful richness and variety. It may be questioned whether Donne's very best passages are exceeded, even whether they are equaled, by any English prose-writer in the combination of fulness and rarity of meaning with exquisite perfection of sound and charm of style. In these latter points he is at least the equal of Jeremy Taylor at his best, and though Jeremy Taylor is no shallow thinker, his thought is a mere pool to the oceanic depth and breadth of Donne's. There is a certain quality of magnificence, too, in Donne beside which the best things of Taylor are apt to suggest the merely pretty. Unlike most of his contemporaries, Donne knew when to let a great thing alone; and few of them, for instance, would have been content to let such a phrase as the likening of the coming of God to the soul "as the sun at noon to illustrate all shadows, as the sheaves in harvest to fill all penuries," without frittering away its massive and complete effect into subdivisions and added epithets, into appendices and fringes of thought and expression.

Moreover he, as Hooker in his very different style had had before him, but as hardly any one else, had the sense of the paragraph—of the crescendo and diminuendo of cadence required to wind it safely and melodiously from start to finish. His sentences are sometimes too long, they are too often made to do the work of the paragraph itself; but this is often more a matter of punctuation than of real structural arrangement. And whether they be called sentences or be called paragraphs, there linger round each of them the glimmer of an unearthly light and the notes of a more than earthly music.

INTERCHAPTER 6

IT has been frequently pointed out that the connection of the present Book with the last and next is of a kind which will not be repeated, and which has not been earlier found between the successive divisions of this work. All three are wholly busied with what is usually and rightly, from one point of view, called Elizabethan Literature. All three are mainly busied with the productions of a not extraordinarily long lifetime—1580 to 1660; while such a lifetime as that of Fontenelle would have taken a man from Wyatt's days almost to the publication of the *Hesperides,* from that of *Euphues* to the death of Milton, or from the birth of Shakespeare to the Restoration. Yet the separation into three, besides avoiding cumbrousness and confusion of arrangement in other ways, enables us to bring out the three divisions of rise, of culmination, and if not exactly of decadence, yet of a long and gorgeous sunset, in a very satisfactory fashion.

There can be no real difficulty in according to our present stage the title of culmination. We have indeed lost two or three, but only two or three, of the very greatest names of the whole period. To the reign of James (though no thanks to James himself) belong the greatest work of Shakespeare, almost the whole work of Bacon, the great bulk of the more accomplished work of the minor dramatists, a volume of exquisite non-dramatic poetry, and a body of most interesting, if still partly inorganic, prose.

It is no doubt in the department of pure poetry that the period, partly by accident, partly not, contrasts least favourably both with its predecessor and its successor. That Spenser is dead at its beginning, and Milton a boy at its close, is itself not wholly accidental. For Spenser, though he could have added to the volume of our delight, would probably have given us nothing new in kind, had the Irish rebels allowed him to reach his seventy years in peace; and Milton would not have been quite Milton without the Jacobean period itself behind him. We have seen what the character of that period was in poetry, and how Spenser's own influence, with Donne's and Jonson's, was at work in it, shaping and preparing the forces. Accumulating the matter, which were to result on the one side in the massive structure of Milton, and on the other in the exquisite filigree of the Caroline lyrists. But we can here better perceive in the work of the three themselves, as in that of their followers, the special Jacobean profundity, its weight of thought, and its slight consequent weariness. The "bloomy flush" of the Elizabethan period proper has fled; the conceit remains, but it is graver, less childlike; the play of words continues, but it is changing into the play of thought, sometimes hardly to be called play, so laborious and Cyclopean is it.

It follows that the actual poetry of the reign, that which exclusively or especially belongs to it, is somewhat less charming than that of the poets who owe more direct allegiance to Elizabeth or to Charles. Yet the best of the songs of the dramatists date from this time; the masques of Ben Jonson and others contain, in the good old phrase, "poetry enough for anything"; we cannot find out of Spenser and Rossetti more gorgeous things than the best passages of the Fletchers; anywhere perhaps sweeter things than the best trifles of Ben, of John Fletcher, of Wither, of Browne; anywhere at all such mysterious melody as that of Donne. Yet, since we find most of those who are thus gifted dating back from Elizabeth or persevering to Charles, we may be justified in reserving for the middle stage, here as elsewhere, the special qualities of weight and thought.

There can be no doubt at all that this place is the proper one for its prose. As we have seen, Euphuism in the large sense, ornateness, gorgeousness, horror of the obvious, has altogether the upper hand as compared with succinctness, directness, appeal only to power of matter and proportion of arrangement. Yet Ben Jonson relies very mainly on these last, and no one, not even Bacon, succeeds in manipulating the dictionary like an organ after the fashion of the great Caroline writers, unless indeed it be Donne, to whom here as elsewhere the universal monarchy of wit is subject. But the prose of James's reign, putting aside the half-accidental magnificence of the Authorised Version, must rest its claims on the fantastic and splendid, but not fully-organised, form of Bacon and Burton, on the weighty and sterling matter of both these and of Jonson.

In neither case had a perfection of style been reached. The author of the *Essays* and the author of the *Anatomy* have discarded the more childish things of Euphuism; but they have not quite attained the full perfecting of its best things that Browne and Taylor were to show. Ben Jonson has recoiled from this same Euphuism (always using the term as a sign and symbol rather than as a limited designation), and has sometimes achieved a plain style almost perfect in its way. But he had been busied with other things, and was perhaps not equipped with sufficient versatility to make a prose writer absolutely of the first class. The others, except Donne, who did but trans-prose his verse and trans-hallow his profanities, are minors.

Yet in both directions the period, especially for so brief a one, did more than its fair share in the mere furthering of style, in doing its stage on that circular but always interesting journey. And in point of kind as distinguished from style that establishment of the Essay, in more forms than one, which we have seen was a matter of the very greatest importance, that development of the sermon which we have also seen, a thing of importance hardly lesser. The *opuscle* as opposed to the *opus magnum* was thus, in matters sacred and in matters profane, promoted to distinct literary rank; and in each case literature was carried from the study into other apartments of the house, if not even into the street.

But undoubtedly the very greatest accomplishment of the time was its accomplishment in drama. After making every reasonable allowance for the obscurity which rests on so many of the exact dates of the Elizabethan theatre, we can be fairly certain that the larger number of its consummate examples date from the first quarter of the seventeenth century—most of the best work of Shikespeare, all, with one exception at each end, of the best work of Jonson, all the work of Beaumont, of Fletcher, and probably most of the best work of all the rest save Shirley, belong to it. Moreover, in what follows there is little or nothing *new*. The effects which have been achieved with such gigantic expenditure of genius, if not exactly of criticism, first by the University Wits and Shakespeare in his initial period, then by Shakespeare and his great contemporaries in this special time, are merely repeated, weakened, and at last frittered away. It would hardly be rash to say that of the really great plays included in the general list of the Elizabethan drama, not merely four out of five or nine out of ten, but nineteen out of twenty belong to this time. Yet we need, in this special place of summary, say less of it than we have said of the Elizabethans proper, and still less than we must say when, after the next Book, we sum up the whole great epoch of which it forms a part. For the centre of any period partakes necessarily more of the characters of the two ends than they do of it. In so far as the Jacobean age deserves a description of qualities to itself, that description must be what has been more than once given. Depth and weight appear in it as they appear in none other; yet does it not lack finish and grace.